Praise for
The Hidden Roots of White Supremacy

"Robert P. Jones is an extraordinary moral force in this country. *The Hidden Roots of White Supremacy* is his latest effort to help the nation imagine itself apart from the distorting effects of racism and the violent genocide of Indigenous people at its root. This book is the latest in his own personal journey as a white southerner from Mississippi, and I am thankful that he has shared it with all of us."

—Eddie S. Glaude Jr., James S. McDonnell Distinguished University
Professor, Princeton University, and author of *Begin Again:
James Baldwin's America and Its Urgent Lessons for Our Own*

"*The Hidden Roots of White Supremacy* is timely, if not timeless. Robert P. Jones invites us to journey with him to Mississippi, Minnesota, and Oklahoma, daring to listen, learn, and be transformed by the communities he encounters. *Hidden Roots* is about the hidden stories of Black and Indigenous peoples who, in navigating the violent legacy of the Doctrine of Discovery, have charted a course toward a more just future. In this book we discover that the very stories we hide from are the ones that can bring America closer to becoming the democracy it claims to be."

—The Very Rev. Dr. Kelly Brown Douglas, interim president of Episcopal
Divinity School, winner of the 2023 Grawemeyer Award in Religion

"In *The Hidden Roots of White Supremacy*, Robert P. Jones weaves together the unsettling stories of early Americans that are often missing from our national storytelling: Indigenous, Black, and colonizer. In doing so, Jones explains who we are and how we came to be, truths that help illuminate where we might go from here."

—Simran Jeet Singh, executive director of the Religion
and Society Program, the Aspen Institute, and author of
The Light We Give: How Sikh Wisdom Can Transform Your Life

"No white author seems to understand how America got itself into its racial mess more than Robert P. Jones. This breathtakingly broad and painfully specific retelling of the American story is filled with hope. It's the vision of an America I want to live in and bequeath to my grandchildren. I cannot imagine a more timely or helpful contribution to the project of our common future."

—Gene Robinson, former bishop in the Episcopal Church

"Jones exposes the role of white Christian supremacy that originated in fifteenth-century Vatican documents called the Doctrine of Discovery justifying slavery and land theft—the hidden roots of white supremacy. His message is deep and profound. If a multi-religious, ethnic, and racial democracy is to be realized, a combined healing needs to address the foundations of the problem."

—Philip P. Arnold, associate professor, Syracuse University; president, Indigenous Values Initiative; and author of *The Urgency of Indigenous Values*

"*The Hidden Roots of White Supremacy* will be nothing less than transformative in the thoughts, attitudes, and hopefully, actions of many people. It's an essential read in this time of historical re-evaluation. With detailed historical and statistical research, Robert P. Jones relates narratives of the harm caused by white supremacy, but he also reveals how communities are trying to repair the damage through truth-telling. If, as the saying goes, we are the stories we tell ourselves, then this book reminds us of two equally salient truths: stories can misshape us, but better stories can also heal us."

—Jemar Tisby, Professor of History, Simmons College of Kentucky, and author of *The Color of Compromise* and *How to Fight Racism*

"Through its linking of narratives typically considered separately, the book provides a revelatory view of US history and its guiding assumptions. . . . A searing, stirring outline of the historical and contemporary significance of white Christian nationalism."

—*Kirkus Reviews* (starred review)

Also by Robert P. Jones

White Too Long: The Legacy of White Supremacy in American Christianity

The End of White Christian America

Progressive and Religious: How Christian, Jewish, Muslim, and Buddhist Leaders Are Moving Beyond the Culture Wars and Transforming American Public Life

Liberalism's Troubled Search for Equality: Religion and Cultural Bias in the Oregon Physician-Assisted Suicide Debates

THE HIDDEN ROOTS *of* WHITE SUPREMACY

and the PATH *to a* SHARED AMERICAN FUTURE

Robert P. Jones

SIMON & SCHUSTER

New York   London   Toronto   Sydney   New Delhi

Simon & Schuster
1230 Avenue of the Americas
New York, NY 10020

First Simon & Schuster hardcover edition September 2023

SIMON & SCHUSTER and colophon are registered trademarks of Simon & Schuster, Inc.

For information about special discounts for bulk purchases, please contact Simon & Schuster Special Sales at 1-866-506-1949 or business@simonandschuster.com.

The Simon & Schuster Speakers Bureau can bring authors to your live event. For more information or to book an event, contact the Simon & Schuster Speakers Bureau at 1-866-248-3049 or visit our website at www.simonspeakers.com.

Interior design by Wendy Blum

Manufactured in the United States of America

10   9   8   7   6   5   4   3   2   1

Library of Congress Cataloging-in-Publication Data

Names: Jones, Robert P. (Robert Patrick), author.
Title: The hidden roots of white supremacy : and the path to a shared
    American future / Robert P. Jones.
Other titles: Path to a shared American future
Identifiers: LCCN 2023021032 | ISBN 9781668009512 | ISBN 9781668009529
    (trade paperback) | ISBN 9781668009536 (ebook)
Subjects: LCSH: United States—Race relations—History. | Racism—United
    States—History. | Reconciliation—United States—Case studies. |
    Reparations for historical injustices—United States—Case studies.
Classification: LCC E185.615 .J635 2023 | DDC 305.800973--dc23/eng/20230601
LC record available at https://lccn.loc.gov/2023021032

ISBN 978-1-6680-0951-2
ISBN 978-1-6680-0953-6 (ebook)

To Chris Scharen and Ted Smith,
who have long helped me navigate the waters

CONTENTS

BEFORE AMERICA

On May 4, 1863, the steamboat *Northerner* pushed up the Mississippi River from St. Louis, bound for Fort Snelling, a military outpost north of St. Paul, Minnesota. Just a few miles into the journey, Captain Alfred J. Woods encountered a large handmade raft adrift in the strong currents. Aboard were seventy-six African Americans: forty men, ten women, and twenty-six children.

The leader of this determined group was Robert Hickman, who was attempting to free himself, along with his family and neighbors, from enslavement on a plantation in Boone County, Missouri. Hickman, a preacher who could both read and write, had seen newspaper accounts of President Abraham Lincoln's Emancipation Proclamation four months earlier. Although the proclamation did not apply to Missouri because it was under Union control, this news nonetheless inspired him to begin making plans to escape north. The Hickman party aimed to reach free soil by way of the river, which was by then safely patrolled by the Union army. They embarked under cover of darkness on the moonless night of May 3, but because their makeshift craft was not equipped with sails or oars, they drifted for a day in the wrong direction before encountering the *Northerner*.[1]

Seeing the floundering party with so many children aboard, Captain Woods asked if they needed assistance. Sympathetic to their plight and knowing that the strains of the Civil War had left Minnesota with a labor shortage, Woods ordered the raft to be securely tied to the steamboat and offered to take them as far as his final destination.

Neither Woods nor Hickman anticipated the vitriol that awaited them. On May 5, the *Northerner* approached the levee in Lowertown, on the outskirts of St. Paul. As local dock workers, mostly Irish, caught sight of the self-emancipated African Americans (commonly referred to as "contraband" by whites) on the trailing raft, they became increasingly agitated, seeing them as competition for jobs. As word spread, a threatening crowd gathered on the levee. The commotion was so great that St. Paul police arrived on the scene. But after assessing the situation, they sided with the mob and threatened to arrest not the Irish rabble-rousers but the Black asylum seekers, should they disembark.

Captain Woods ordered the boat with its trailing raft to steam on to Fort Snelling. There, Hickman and his party came ashore without incident on May 5, but they were met with an unexpected sight: hundreds of disheveled Native Americans were huddled together, forcibly assembled near the docks.

The desperate and anxious crowd they encountered were part of an original group numbering more than 1,600, mostly women, children, and elderly Dakota people who had been held under armed guard all winter, following the Dakota War of the year before, in a miserable encampment in a lowland area below Fort Snelling. Unbeknownst to them, Minnesota government officials and military leaders were awaiting the spring thaw that would allow for their mass deportation downriver from their ancestral homelands to a bleak reservation in the Nebraska Territory. By the time the ice finally melted and river levels rose, hundreds had died. A group of 770 Dakota people had been shipped off the day before on another steamer, the *Davenport*.

Having set the Hickman party safely ashore and unloaded the wagons and supplies for the military fort, Captain Woods ordered preparations to receive his next "cargo": 547 Dakota people, whom he was transporting for the fee of $25 per head plus 10 cents a day for sustenance. Soldiers from Fort Snelling herded the ragtag remnant aboard the *Northerner* "like so many cattle," as one observer put it. As they pulled away, a local minister's wife remarked, "May God have mercy on them, for they can expect none from man."[2]

Neither Hickman and his companions, nor the Dakota people, would have had the perspective to realize they were witnessing the momentous final chapter of both chattel slavery in the US and "Indian removal" in Minnesota. They would not have grasped the paradox the two groups represented that afternoon on the banks of the Mississippi River: that the end of bondage for Hickman's band also marked the last vestige of sovereignty for the Dakota people. And they would certainly have been unaware that, in the closing weeks of 1862, just five months earlier, President Lincoln was simultaneously considering two documents that would dramatically change the fates of each group: a warrant for the mass execution of thirty-eight Dakota men and the Emancipation Proclamation.

This encounter on May 5, 1863, contains multiple narrative streams, each of which tells a different story about America. The question is, which do we follow? Do we tell the story of Fort Snelling, the military outpost established to protect the westward expansion of settler colonialism? Do we embark back down the Mississippi River to Missouri and the story of enslaved Africans in the South? Do we push upriver from St. Paul to its headwaters and stories of Indigenous peoples populating this land for millennia? Or do we portage east and cross the larger waters connected to the homelands of Europeans who first set foot on these shores just a few hundred years ago? Each narrative pushes back to a different beginning.

AMERICA'S IDENTITY CRISIS

Across the last few decades in the US, we have experienced widespread debates and even violent conflicts over American history. Battles like these typically erupt during times of social change, when cultural convulsions shake the foundations of old ways of knowing and living. In these unsettling times, closely held stories, long-established institutions, and taken-for-granted features of the landscape itself are questioned. We fight over heroes and monuments and scream at school board meetings. Teachers and librarians are surveilled; writers and artists are suspect; books are banned and burned. We move with increasing hesitation in uncharted cultural territory, like explorers venturing into those voids on ancient maps marked only with the ominous words "Here be dragons."

Identity, rather than policy, drives divisions. History becomes the new front line in the culture wars, as claims about who we are as a people inevitably turn on competing narratives about when and how we arrived at this place. These contests are not mere verbal abstractions. Each narrative arc, each "in the beginning," privileges one set of interests over others and ultimately validates the accumulation of power and wealth and land in the hands of some and not others.

We are living in such a time of uncertainty and transition. As I documented in *The End of White Christian America*, over the last two decades the country has, for the first time in our history, moved from being a majority-white Christian nation, demographically speaking, to one in which there is no ethno-religious cultural majority. When Barack Obama, our first African American president, was elected in

2008, a solid majority of Americans (54 percent) still identified as white and Christian. But by the end of his second term, as Donald Trump entered the national political scene and was elected president, that number had fallen to 47 percent.[3] According to PRRI's American Values Atlas, by 2022 that number had dipped further to 42 percent.[4] Even if everyday Americans weren't familiar with the statistics, they could sense the tectonic plates moving via the shifting demographic composition of their neighborhoods, the variety of food on their grocery store shelves, the appearance of Spanish-language local radio and roadside billboards, and the class photos on the walls of their public schools.

The juxtaposition of our forty-fourth and forty-fifth presidents—and the new identity politics of white Christian nationalism that has emerged across these last dozen years—exposes the heart of the conflict. Obama's election in 2008, and his reelection in 2012, were unmistakable signs that the old cultural foundations were failing. Trump's narrow election win in 2016—fueled by a wave of anger and resentment among conservative white Christians who were increasingly feeling displaced from the center of a new American story—was the desperate attempt to shore them up.

The 2016 presidential election provides unambiguous evidence of America's identity crisis. One of the public opinion survey questions most predictive of the 2016 vote was this one: "Do you think that American culture and way of life has changed for the better or changed for the worse since the 1950s?" The country was, remarkably, evenly divided in its evaluation of American culture today, compared to an era prior to school desegregation, the civil rights movement, the banning of Christian prayer by teachers on public school grounds, the widespread availability of the pill and other forms of contraception, legalized abortion, and marriage equality.

Attitudes among partisans were striking mirror opposites. Two-thirds of Democrats said things have changed for the better, but two-thirds of Republicans said things had changed for the worse since the 1950s. White Christians also stood out from other Americans. Majorities of white evangelicals (74 percent), white mainline Protestants (59 percent), and white Catholics (57 percent) believed things had changed for the worse since the 1950s.[5]

In my most recent book, *White Too Long*, I found similar patterns in the prevalence of racist attitudes among white Christian subgroups.[6] There I developed a Racism Index, a composite statistical measure based on fifteen survey questions about Confederate monuments, the effect of past discrimination on the present, the treatment of African Americans in the criminal justice system, and the existence of racial discrimination—where a score of 1 represented holding the least racist attitudes and a score of 10 represented holding the most racist attitudes. White evangelicals scored 8 out of 10 on the Racism Index, while white mainline Protestants and white Catholics each scored 7. By contrast, white Americans who claimed no religious affiliation scored 4.

Among white Christians, these fears about cultural change and attitudes about race were strongly correlated with electoral choices. While it is well known that approximately eight in ten white evangelical Protestants voted for Trump in 2016 and 2020, it is less frequently noted that six in ten white mainline Protestants and white Catholics cast their lot with Trump in both elections as well.[7]

Particularly in the wake of Trump's "Make America Great Again" (MAGA) takeover of the Republican Party, our two political parties are increasingly animated by two starkly different visions of the nation's past and future. Is America a divinely ordained promised land for European Christians, or is America a pluralistic democracy where all stand on equal footing before the law? Most Americans embrace the latter. But a desperate, defensive, mostly white Christian minority cling to the former.

THE 1619 PROJECT AND THE BATTLE OVER
AMERICA'S BEGINNINGS

While this contest played out on the national political stage, the battle over American history was also roiling journalism and the academy. The most powerful manifestation of this conflict was "The 1619 Project," an ongoing long-form journalism project conceived of and led by Nikole Hannah-Jones, which was first published in the *New York Times Magazine* on August 18, 2019.

On the home page dedicated to the project, the following words appear in white letters against Dannielle Bowman's monochromatic photograph of a dark, empty ocean meeting a gray, cloudless sky:

> In August of 1619, a ship appeared on this horizon, near Point Comfort, a coastal port in the British colony of Virginia. It carried more than 20 enslaved Africans, who were sold to the colonists. America was not yet America, but this was the moment it began. No aspect of the country that would be formed here has been untouched by the years of slavery that followed. On the 400th anniversary of this fateful moment, it is finally time to tell our story truthfully.[8]

The power of the 1619 Project was its endeavor "to reframe the country's history by placing the consequences of slavery and the contributions of black Americans at the very center of our national narrative."[9] Its principal tool for accomplishing this goal was to give America a new genesis: not 1776, when British colonies and slavery were well established, but 1619, the year a group of Africans were brought against their will to the British territories. The introduction to the 1619 Project boldly declared that "the country's true birth date, the moment that its defining contradictions first came into the world, was in late August of 1619" and that this moment represented not just "the country's original sin" but rather "the country's very origin."[10]

It was a provocative move, particularly in the volatile climate created by the Trump presidency. The project was immediately controversial, in both foreseeable and unpredictable ways. On the one hand, there was the denouncement from an all-white group of historians; they argued that the 1619 Project had drastically overstated the extent to which the American colonists were motivated to revolt against Great Britain by a desire to preserve slavery, a point the *New York Times Magazine* essentially conceded in a correction issued in March 2020.[11] But some critics then seemed intent on using this objection or other quibbles about specific facts to discredit the entire project.[12]

On the other hand, there was also criticism from the widely respected scholar Nell Irvin Painter, emeritus professor of history at Princeton University. Painter, who is African American, endorsed the goals of the project but pointed to a problem with the project's core narrative: the Africans brought to the colonies in 1619 were not enslaved. Painter explained the importance of the distinction in an op-ed published in the *Guardian* the same week the 1619 Project launched:

> People were not enslaved in Virginia in 1619, they were indentured. The 20 or so Africans were sold and bought as "servants" for a term of years, and they joined a population consisting largely of European indentured servants, mainly poor people from the British Isles whom the Virginia Company of London had transported and sold into servitude. Enslavement was a process that took place step by step, after the mid-seventeenth century. This process of turning "servants" from Africa into racialized workers enslaved for life occurred in the 1660s to 1680s through a succession of Virginia laws that decreed that a child's status followed that of its mother and that baptism did not automatically

confer emancipation. By the end of the seventeenth century, Africans had indeed been marked off by race in law as chattel to be bought, sold, traded, inherited and serve as collateral for business and debt services. This was not already the case in 1619.[13]

Moreover, while 1619 marked the first forced arrival of Africans in the British colonies, historians generally agreed that enslaved Africans arrived nearly a century before as part of the first European colony in what would become the United States. In 1526, Spanish conquistadors founded San Miguel de Gualdape, located on the Atlantic coast near the Georgia/South Carolina border, as an outpost that would help establish Spain's new-world claims. Before the end of the year, however, the enslaved Africans launched a rebellion— the first slave revolt north of the Rio Grande—that resulted in the colony's demise. Though precise records do not exist, it is probable that some of the Africans who survived the ordeal escaped and lived with the local Guale tribe. If this is true, these courageous and defiant Africans were the first transatlantic permanent residents of what is now the United States since the Vikings.[14]

Despite these controversies, the 1619 Project became a cultural juggernaut. Jake Silverstein, the editor in chief of the *New York Times Magazine*, noted that its initial publication "was greeted with an enthusiastic response unlike any we had seen before."[15] Copies of the magazine, including an additional print run of tens of thousands, sold out immediately. Issues were posted for sale on eBay at eye-popping prices. The opening essay by Hannah-Jones was cited on the floor of Congress, and Democratic nominees for president referred to it in stump speeches. A school curriculum, created in partnership with the Pulitzer Center, was soon disseminated to more than 4,500 classrooms.[16] The 1619 Project grew from its original home in the *New York Times Magazine* to an expanded website, a podcast, a bestselling book, *The 1619 Project: A New Origin Story*, and a six-part docuseries on Hulu.[17] It won Hannah-Jones a 2020 Pulitzer Prize for Commentary.[18]

The project also produced significant political pushback. By 2021, Republicans in five states introduced legislation to withhold funding from public schools that used the 1619 Project curriculum. The biggest grandstanding, not surprisingly, came from President Trump. Just over a year after the 1619 Project launched, Trump organized a White House Conference on American History to counter it. At a press conference on September 17, 2020, following the event, he declared:

> By viewing every issue through the lens of race, they want to impose a new segregation, and we must not allow that to happen. Critical race theory, the 1619 Project and the crusade against American history is toxic propaganda, ideological poison, that, if not removed, will dissolve the civic bonds that tie us together, will destroy our country.[19]

As in many of his speeches, Trump's usage of the pronouns *they* and *we* are nakedly racist. He treats "American history" like a piece of amber, where white founding fathers are forever captured in their colonial finery at the dawn of the Revolutionary War, and he casts any attempt to redirect attention away from that scene as "toxic" and "poison."

Taking aim at the 1619 Project's claims to establish "a new origin story," Trump announced his own project, "the 1776 Commission," an advisory group that would focus on "patriotic education" and produce resources that glorified "the legacy of 1776." It was short-lived. The commission, which lacked a single professional historian among its members, released a report on January 18, 2021, less than two weeks after the failed insurrection, attempted in Trump's name and with his encouragement, at the US Capitol.[20] The materials were widely panned by historians, and one of President Joe Biden's first orders after taking office just two days later was to disband the commission and take down the website.[21]

THE IMPORTANCE AND INADEQUACY OF 1619 AS AMERICA'S "NEW ORIGIN STORY"

Nearly six decades ago, in *The Fire Next Time*, James Baldwin vividly described the gift that a Black perspective holds for white Americans who are invested in a truer understanding of our shared history and our own heritage:

> The American Negro has the great advantage of having never believed the collection of myths to which white Americans cling: that their ancestors were all freedom-loving heroes, that they were born in the greatest country the world has ever seen, or that Americans are invincible in battle and wise in peace, that Americans have always dealt honorably with Mexicans and Indians and all other neighbors or inferiors, that American men are the world's most direct and virile, that American women are pure.[22]

The most important contribution of the 1619 Project is the decentering of an American history of untenable innocence and impossible virtue. Whatever its shortcomings, the 1619 Project has helped make that vision of history indefensible. It has disrupted the old master narrative, creating an opportunity for Americans to mature, to embrace a more complex and truthful understanding of our heritage. And that is a remarkable achievement.

Again, Baldwin:

> Negroes know far more about white Americans than that; it can almost be said, in fact, that they know about white Ameri-

cans what parents—or, anyway, mothers—know about their children, and that they very often regard white Americans that way. And perhaps this attitude, held in spite of what they know and have endured, helps to explain why Negroes, on the whole, and until lately, have allowed themselves to feel so little hatred. The tendency has really been, insofar as this was possible, to dismiss white people as the slightly mad victims of their own brainwashing.[23]

The 1619 Project's purchase on the American imagination has been a long time coming, built on the public historical witness of a chorus of Native American and African American writers, artists, and leaders: William Apess, James Baldwin, Frederick Douglass, W. E. B. Du Bois, Vine Deloria Jr., Lorraine Hansberry, Chief Joseph (Hinmatóowyalahtǫit), Martin Luther King Jr., Malcolm X, Luther Standing Bear (Matȟó Nážiŋ), Wilma Pearl Mankiller, Tecumseh, and Ida B. Wells, to name just a few. Nell Painter's calibrated characterization of the importance of the 1619 Project, featured in an interview with *The Atlantic*'s Adam Serwer, is apt. While she stood by her criticism of the project and conceded that it was not history "as I would write it," she nonetheless declared, "I support the 1619 Project as kind of a cultural event."[24]

Even so, the 1619 Project overreaches with its goal "to reframe American history by regarding 1619 as our nation's birth year."[25] In its claim to be *the* new American origin story, the 1619 Project risks trading one exclusion for another. The original 1619 Project published in the *New York Times Magazine* mentions Native Americans only five times, mostly in passing. Hannah-Jones's much-heralded twenty-two-page opening essay makes no mention of Native Americans.[26] Throughout, Native Americans appear because of their connections to African American history in the context of European settler colonialism, not on their own terms. By starting with the oppression of Africans in British colonial America, the 1619 Project cloaks from historical view at least sixteen thousand years of Indigenous history prior to European contact.[27] And by pushing more than a century of Europeans' prior violent interactions with the continent's Indigenous peoples into the shadows, it obscures the headwaters from which the brutal colonial impulse—and more importantly, its moral justification—flows.[28]

While many Native Americans applauded the 1619 Project's de-centering of a Eurocentric history, there were some sharp responses to the myopia produced by the focus on the year 1619. For example, writing in Norfolk's *Virginia-Pilot* in late 2020, Dawn Custalow, a member of the Mattaponi tribe and a descendant of Pocahontas (born Amonute and later known as Matoaka), strongly objected to the 1619 Project's dominance in educational circles. "How can any group of people reframe another's history when the descendants of the original people are still alive and can testify to the validity of their history?" she asked incredulously. "If the idea that U.S. history began in 1619 is accepted, then my people's collective memory is blotted out forever."[29] Custalow's denouncement gained little public traction.

FROM 1619 TO 1493: THE CHRISTIAN DOCTRINE OF DISCOVERY

Indeed, by 1619, the Indigenous bodies that were subject to the initial acts of invasion, domination, and colonization by Europeans in North America were, by more than a century, cold. Viewed in this light, the transportation of twenty indentured Africans to this continent in 1619 was one of many outcomes of a collusion between European monarchies and the western Christian Church that began nearly 130 years earlier.

One candidate for a more promising point of departure for America's origin story is 1493—not the year Christopher Columbus "sailed the ocean blue," but the year in which he returned to a hero's welcome in Spain, bringing with him gold, brightly colored parrots, and nearly a dozen captive Indigenous people.[30] It was also the year he was commissioned to return to the Americas with a much larger fleet of seventeen ships, nearly 1,500 men, and more than a dozen priests to speed the conversion of Indigenous people who inhabited what he, along with King Ferdinand and Queen Isabella, still believed were Asian shores. That trip resulted in the founding of La Isabela, in present-day Dominican Republic, the first permanent European occupation attempted in the Americas. While the colony would not last, the ripple effects of the journey would soon be felt in all spheres of human interaction and relationships. As Charles C. Mann, author of *1493: Uncovering the World Columbus Created*, notes, Columbus's actions "began the era of *globalization*—the single, turbulent exchange of goods and services that today engulfs the entire habitable world."[31]

The return of Columbus in 1493 also precipitated the culmination of one of the most fateful but unacknowledged theological developments in the history of the western Christian Church: the Doctrine of Discovery.[32] Established in a series of fifteenth-century papal bulls (official edicts that carry the full weight of church and papal authority), the Doctrine claims that European civilization and western Christianity are superior to all other cultures, races, and religions. From this premise, it follows that domination and colonial conquest were merely the means of improving, if not the temporal, then the eternal lot of Indigenous peoples. So conceived, no atrocities could possibly tilt the scales of justice against these immeasurable goods. With its fiction of previously "undiscovered" lands and peoples, the Doctrine fulfilled European rulers' request for an unequivocal theological and moral justification for their new global political and economic exploits.

Robert J. Miller, professor of law at the Sandra Day O'Connor College of Law at Arizona State University and an enrolled citizen of the Eastern Shawnee Tribe, summarized the Doctrine's purpose as follows:

> In essence, the Doctrine provided that newly arrived Europeans immediately and automatically acquired legally recognized property rights over the inhabitants without knowledge or consent of the Indigenous peoples. When English explorers and other Europeans planted their national flags and religious symbols in "newly discovered" lands, as many paintings depict, they were not just thanking God for a safe voyage. Instead they were undertaking a well-recognized legal procedure and ritual mandated by international law and designed to create their country's legal claim over the "newly discovered" lands and peoples.[33]

The Doctrine of Discovery, in short, merged the interests of European imperialism, including the African slave trade, with Christian missionary zeal.[34] *Dum Diversas*, the initial edict that laid the theological and political foundations for the Doctrine, was issued by Pope Nicholas V on June 18, 1452. It explicitly granted Portuguese king Alfonso V the following rights:

> To invade, search out, capture, vanquish, and subdue all Saracens [Muslims] and pagans whatsoever, and other enemies of Christ wheresoever placed, and the kingdoms, dukedoms, principalities, dominions, possessions, and all movable and immovable goods whatsoever held and possessed by them and to reduce their persons to perpetual slavery.[35]

The papal bull elevated what had been accepted practice into official church doctrine and international law. It marshaled theological categories, targeting Muslims and all other non-Christian peoples, who are described as "enemies of Christ," as the primary metric for determining who deserved political or human rights. Most notably, it explicitly gave European leaders permission not only to subdue such peoples initially but to "reduce their persons to perpetual slavery." This decree, promulgated by the person western Christians considered the Vicar of Christ on earth, provided the blueprint for an unfettered European colonial race for "undiscovered lands" and fertilized the blossoming African slave trade.

The most relevant papal edict for the American context was the bull *Inter Caetera*, issued by Pope Alexander VI in May 1493 with the express purpose of validating Spain's ownership rights of previously "undiscovered" lands in the Americas following the voyages of Columbus the year before. It praised Columbus, "who for a long time had intended to seek out and discover certain islands and mainlands remote and unknown and not hitherto discovered by others." It again affirmed the church's blessing of and interest in political conquest, "that in our times especially the Catholic faith and the Christian religion be exalted and be everywhere increased and spread, that the health of souls be cared for and that barbarous nations be overthrown and brought to the faith itself."[36]

Given the competition between European powers, *Inter Caetera* also had an important additional purpose: to help provide rules of engagement that would minimize the blood and treasure Europeans would expend fighting each other. To this end, Pope Alexander VI included two caveats. First, he drew a vertical demarcation line extending from one pole to the other, "one hundred leagues to the west and south of any of the islands that are usually called the Azores and Cape Verde," to allocate land claims between Spain and Portugal. Second, he added a provision that lands could be claimed only if they were "not previously possessed by any Christian owner."[37] Robert J. Miller and his colleagues note the convergence of powerful shared motives: "The Church's interest in expanding Christendom and adding to its wealth, and Spain's and Portugal's economic and political interests in acquiring new territories, assets, and colonies had solidified by 1493 under the canon and international law of the Doctrine of Discovery."[38]

Not to be left out of the international contest among the leading European powers to carve up the "new world" among themselves, in 1496 King Henry VII also drew upon the logic of the emerging Doctrine of Discovery to commission John Cabot and his sons to represent England with the following mission:

> To find, discover and investigate whatsoever islands, countries, regions or provinces of heathens and infidels, in whatsoever part of the world placed, which before this time were unknown to all Christians. We have also ... given licence [*sic*] to set up our aforesaid banners and ensigns in any town, city, castle, island or mainland whatsoever, newly found by them. And that the before-mentioned John and his sons or their heirs and deputies may conquer, occupy and possess whatsoever such towns, castles, cities and islands by them thus discovered.[39]

I concede that, on its face, the claim that edicts issued by European popes and kings in the fifteenth century are vital for understanding our current divides may seem strained. Indeed, to my knowledge, no mainstream American history textbooks have focused on the Doctrine of Discovery as critical for American self-understanding. Across my decade of graduate education in the 1990s, completing a seminary graduate degree and a PhD in religion, I never encountered the Doctrine of Discovery. But its absence from the historical canon of predominantly white academic institutions is testimony to its continued cultural power. While the Doctrine of Discovery has escaped scrutiny by most white scholars and theologians, Indigenous people and African Americans have long been testifying to these Christian roots of white supremacy, while dying from and living with their damaging effects.

Indigenous scholars such as Vine Deloria Jr. (Lakota, Standing Rock Sioux) have been highlighting, for over fifty years now, the centrality of this fateful theological and political turn, in well-documented books with provocative titles such as *Custer Died for Your Sins: An Indian Manifesto* and *God Is Red*.[40] Deloria summarized the dehumanizing logic of the Doctrine of Discovery and the devastating consequences it brought for Indigenous people globally and for those within the vicinity of the fledgling United States:

> The natives had rights to occupy the lands on which they had traditionally lived until such time as those lands were needed by the invading Europeans. At that time, the European nation could extinguish the natives' title by purchase or conquest. With respect to each other, the European nations accepted the claims of the nation that first explored new lands and had sufficient military power to protect its claim. With respect to the natives who happened to occupy the lands, they were completely at the mercy of the acquisitive Christian nation. . . . Almost the first claim put forth by the new nation after the successful break with England was that the colonies had succeeded to the claims made by the mother country under the Doctrine of Discovery. The United States was therefore under no obligation to deal justly with the continent's tribes.[41]

As I've continued my reeducation journey over the last ten years, I have come to consider the Doctrine of Discovery as a kind of Rosetta Stone for understanding the deep structure of the European political and religious worldviews we have inherited in this country. The Doctrine of Discovery furnished the foundational lie that America was "discovered" and enshrined the noble innocence of "pioneers" in the story we white Christian Americans have told about ourselves. It animated the religious and cultural worldview that delivered Europeans to these shores far before 1619. Ideas such as Manifest Destiny, America as a city on a hill, or America as a new Zion all sprouted from the seed that was planted in 1493. This sense of divine entitlement, of European Christian chosenness, has shaped the worldview of most white Americans and thereby influenced key events, policies, and laws throughout American history.[42]

The white male leaders of the thirteen British colonies began their 1776 Declaration of Independence from the British Crown with these inspirational words: "We hold these truths to be self-evident, that all men are created equal, that they are endowed by their Creator with certain unalienable Rights." But just thirty lines down—in this document marking the year Trump and many conservatives want to hold up as exemplary of the nation's character at its origin—the Doctrine of Discovery rears its head. The British colonists complain that King George III has encouraged slave rebellions ("domestic insurrections amongst us") and speak of Native Americans as "merciless Indian Savages, whose known rule of warfare, is an undistinguished destruction of all ages, sexes and condition."[43] As for self-evident truths, and the rights following from them, these principles were compatible at the time not only with such views of Indigenous people but also with the continued enslavement of African Americans and the exclusion of women from democratic participation.

Similarly, the 1789 US Constitution, which opens with the inclusive words "We the people," is, rightly, understood as a watershed moment in the history of democracy and self-government. But its first article—just four sentences into the document—runs aground on the legacy of the Doctrine of Discovery. Article I, Section 2 clarifies that the real "we" constituting "the people" are European men. The apportionment of state representatives is "determined by adding to the whole Number of free Persons, including those bound to Service for a Term of Years, and excluding Indians not taxed, three fifths of all other Persons." Despite being "free persons" on their own land, Indigenous people are explicitly excluded from the constitutional "we." Enslaved Black people are counted as only three-fifths of a person, and then only for the purpose of buttressing the political power of white enslavers. White women, though counted for the purpose of allotting representatives, are excluded from voting, never mind holding elected office themselves.

or much longer else

The Doctrine of Discovery also guided Thomas Jefferson—a lawyer trained in the legal tradition built on its logic—in his approach to the 1803 Louisiana Purchase. He knew that the agreement was technically an acquisition of France's discovery rights (the right to pre-emptive title to this vast tract of land against other European claims), rather than a purchase of the land itself, which remained occupied by Indigenous people. And he understood that this logic justified any subsequent violence toward and displacement of Native Americans in that territory as the US sought to convert its discovery rights into a claim of complete title through occupancy.[44]

The Doctrine of Discovery was formally incorporated into US law in 1823 in *Johnson v. M'Intosh*, which held, by unanimous decision, that "discovery gave [the US government] an exclusive right to extinguish the Indian title of occupancy, either by purchase or conquest." In a sprawling thirty-three-page opinion penned by Chief Justice John Marshall, the court grounded its argument explicitly in the narrative of the Doctrine of Discovery:

> The character and religion of [the new world's] inhabitants afforded an apology for considering them as a people over whom the superior genius of Europe might claim an ascendency. The potentates of the old world found no difficulty in convincing themselves that they made ample compensation to the inhabi-

tants of the new, by bestowing on them civilization and Christianity, in exchange for unlimited independence. . . .

The Indians were admitted to be the rightful occupants of the soil, with a legal as well as just claim to retain possession of it, and to use it according to their own discretion; but their rights to complete sovereignty, as independent nations, were necessarily diminished, and their power to dispose of the soil at their own will, to whomsoever they pleased, was denied by the original fundamental principle, that discovery gave exclusive title to those who made it.

While the different nations of Europe respected the right of the natives, as occupants, they asserted the ultimate dominion to be in themselves; and claimed and exercised, as a consequence of this ultimate dominion, a power to grant the soil, while yet in possession of the natives.[45]

Chief Justice Marshall's conscience was evidently troubled enough that he felt the need to address the prima facie injustice and arrogance of these discovery claims. But he argued that moral concerns or "abstract principles" were irrelevant beside the power of historical precedent and inertia: "However extravagant the pretension of converting the discovery of inhabited country into conquest may appear, if the principle has been asserted in the first instance, and afterwards sustained; if a country has acquired and held under it; if the property of the great mass of the community originates in it, it becomes the law of the land, and cannot be questioned."[46]

Johnson v. M'Intosh, rooted deeply in the Doctrine of Discovery, set the legal standard for how the US would deal with the Native American population, and actively shapes both US and international law today.[47] It provided the legal basis for Georgia's aggressive imposition of state laws on Native Americans within its borders in violation of federal treaties and the pursuit of its claim of a legal right to coerce the removal of the Cherokee in the late 1820s and 1830s.

Johnson v. M'Intosh provided the basis for Federal Indian Law and set the stage for the creation of the Office of Indian Affairs, which was notably first located within the Department of War, becoming later the Bureau of Indian Affairs within the Department of the Interior.

Via the *Johnson v. M'Intosh* decision, the Doctrine of Discovery was also exported into international law and remains today "the original and controlling precedent for Indigenous rights and affairs" in four countries whose legal systems derive from British law: Australia, Canada, New Zealand, and the United States.[48] Our continued reliance on that legal precedent was the key reason that these countries were the only four, out of 147, to vote against the adoption of the Declaration on the Rights of Indigenous Peoples at the 2007 United Nations General Assembly (although each later changed their votes to approval after public pressure and outcry).[49]

Against this historical backdrop, the shortcomings of reifying 1619 as the birth year of the nation become glaringly apparent. From that vantage point, Indigenous peoples and their history are barely visible, and the American story is seen primarily in terms of white oppression of Black enslaved people. But if we go back to 1493, the protracted sweep of European contact with Native peoples is fully visible—as is the religious, cultural, and political worldview that motivated European conquest and colonization of "newly discovered" lands. This longer view also importantly reveals the connected historical streams of the US and the Americas, and of Native Americans, African Americans, and European Americans. Moreover, it brings us closer to the root of the problem: the disastrous cultural influence of the Christian Doctrine of Discovery, which continues to threaten the promise of a pluralistic American democracy.

Of course, there is nothing magical about any particular date. The concept of a year, after all, is an artificial human attempt to demarcate the fluidity of events using an arbitrary measure, the time our planet takes to make its way around the sun. I do not want to commit my own act of overreach by claiming that 1493 should be considered the nation's birth year. Even the critical events of that fateful year were not born ex nihilo but emerged out of the long flow of history, with roots in the Crusades between 1096 and 1271, and going back at least to the fifth century as popes began to assert authority over territory and to bind the spread of the gospel to the advance of empire.[50] But we can point to that year as a culturally significant one, marking the beginning of sustained European contact with people in the Americas; and as a morally significant one, when the logic of the Doctrine of Discovery crystallized into early international law, shaping more than five centuries of Christian moral imagination and Western European treatment of Indigenous peoples around the globe.

A MAP FOR THE JOURNEY

At its heart, this book sets out to expose the deep, hidden roots of America's current identity crisis. This moment of reckoning with our fraught and contested heritage is spawning new practices of remembering: reckoning with mistakes made, commemorating victims forgotten, and imagining paths not taken. It is also generating a visceral, and sometimes violent, resistance. As historian Scott Ellsworth, a scholar of the 1921 Tulsa Race Massacre and a Tulsa, Oklahoma, native, recently observed, the US is currently in a great "Age of Reevaluation":

> Longstanding institutions are coming under brand-new scrutiny, histories are being challenged and reexamined, statues are toppling. Moreover, those whose voices have long been kept from being heard are claiming their rightful place at the table, while others are waiting in the wings.[51]

As a southerner, I've always been intrigued by the power of place. While the national struggles grab the headlines, local efforts are reshaping the stories we tell about our communities. This book tells the story of how contemporary residents of three places—Tallahatchie County, Mississippi; Duluth, Minnesota; and Tulsa, Oklahoma—have worked across racial lines to tell a truer story about their past. These three communities represent unique points in our history and disparate geographic and cultural environments. Like facets of a prism, each community refracts the historical light differently. And each is at a different point on the path toward reckoning with this legacy, repairing its downstream damage, and building a shared future.

In my home state of Mississippi, the Delta is the site of the 1955 murder of fourteen-year-old Emmett Till, and the courthouse where his killers were quickly acquitted by an all-white jury sits in Sumner, a county seat of Tallahatchie County. Although these events made international headlines and helped spark the modern civil rights movement, the local community has only recently begun working to commemorate these events. Over the last two decades, a group of citizens, working across racial lines, formed the Emmett Till Memorial Commission, which organized a public apology to the Till family for the injustice, raised funds for the renovation of the courthouse to restore it to its 1955 appearance, founded the Emmett Till Interpretive Center, and transformed the local landscape with historical markers and a civil rights driving tour.

In the far north, Duluth, Minnesota, witnessed a horrific—and much less well known—lynching of three Black itinerant circus workers in 1920 by an estimated mob of nearly ten thousand people, approximately one-tenth of the town's heavily white Christian population. In 2003, Duluth also became one of the first major cities in the post–Jim Crow era to officially memorialize the victims of a lynching, creating a large plaza on a city corner that has for the last two decades served as a gathering place for marches and demonstrations for civil rights.

Tulsa, still a rough-and-tumble city on the Oklahoma oil frontier in the early twentieth century, was the site of one of the worst events of white mass racial violence in American history. Over the course of two days in 1921, bands of roving white residents murdered as many as three hundred of their fellow Black citizens and burned the entire African American Greenwood neighborhood to the ground. In 2021, a century after this horrific event, the 1921 Tulsa Race Massacre Centennial Commission raised millions of dollars to create a museum dedicated to the memory of Greenwood and the victims, along with scholarships and community development funds for North Tulsa residents. In his speech at the centennial memorial event, Joe Biden became the first sitting president to acknowledge these horrific events and to name white supremacy as the cause of the violence.

This book began with my interest in the ways the Black Lives Matter movement, which erupted into virtually all areas of American public consciousness in the wake of the police killing of George Floyd in 2020, was strengthening the work of historical truth-telling, healing, and justice at the local level. But as I spent time in Mississippi, Minnesota, and Oklahoma, I came to realize that a full understanding of the contemporary currents could only come from a clearer knowledge of the tributaries that have fed them. Upstream from the stories of violence toward African Americans, in all three communities, were the legacies of genocide and removal of the land's Indigenous peoples. Each of these communities—one in the heart of the South, one in the North, and one in the West—has a history of brutal exploitation of and violence toward the Indigenous people who were the original inhabitants of their region.

The murder of fourteen-year-old Emmett Till in Tallahatchie County flows from the killing and expulsion of Choctaws forced to walk the Trail of Tears from Mississippi. The lynching of three Black circus workers in Duluth is downstream from the mass executions of thirty-eight Dakota men and the exile of the Dakota people from Minnesota. The massacre of African American residents and the conflagration in Tulsa emanates from the murder and exploitation of both the Indigenous people of Oklahoma and the systematic oppression of the more than eighty thousand Native American refugees arriving from the Southeast during the "Indian removal" policies of the early 1800s.

This longer, interconnected perspective presents a better understanding of who and where we are. It eschews the naïve innocence of 1776. And it avoids the myopic Black/white binary of 1619. Most importantly, by illuminating the different ways our communities have been fractured by the logic of the Doctrine of Discovery, it inverts the gaze. Rather than focusing on the oppression of African Americans or Native Americans, whose siloed histories in our telling rarely intersect, the focus turns to white Americans, a people whose story, at least in this part of the world, begins with an audacious claim: that God intended America to be a new Euro-Christian promised land; and its corollary: that the systemic violence we have wielded to seize it is justified.

In the concluding chapters, I reflect on what the country can learn from these three communities' efforts at truth-telling, commemoration, and repair. Each has provided a different model for retelling their community's story. Each has struggled, with varying degrees of success, to express their commitment to a different future. These community actors teach us that remembering and truth-telling are not ends in themselves, nor are they acts of self-flagellation or avenues of cheap absolution for the guilty consciences of white Americans. Rather, confession and memorialization are powerful rituals that rehabilitate and kindle our moral and religious imaginations. These acts dispel the confounding mist, helping us see where we are and how we arrived at our current circumstances. They also reorient us toward the work of repair that is vital for charting a new path forward at this critical time of reckoning in our country.

PART ONE

THE DELTA

Chapter One

BEFORE MISSISSIPPI

I have no more land. I am driven away from home, driven up the red waters, let us all go, let us all die together and somewhere upon the banks we will be there.

—A song of Sin-e-cha, member of the Creek nation, who drowned
when the Trail of Tears steamboat *Monmouth* sank in the
Mississippi River in 1837[1]

THE DELTA

The place we know today as Mississippi remains a land of contradictions. Religion, culture, history—even the land itself—are full of paradox. Nowhere is this truer than in "the Delta," the broad, diamond-shaped alluvial floodplain between what are known today as the Mississippi and Yazoo Rivers, running two hundred miles south from Memphis, Tennessee, to Vicksburg, Mississippi, and extending east, at its broadest point, seventy miles. The opening deposits of its famously rich soil were first made more than fifteen thousand years ago as the waters rose from melting glaciers at the end of the last ice age. Year over year, they have been enriched by

annual floodwaters delivering installments of stolen upstream nu-
trients.

When you travel today along one of the man-made ribbons that
slice through the Delta such as Highway 49 or 61, there are stretches
where the shimmering heat transforms them into long asphalt
streams that plummet over the edge of the horizon. As the locals like
to joke, flat-earthers never made much headway among religious
fundamentalists here because the land is so level you can see the curvature of the earth.

If it's between planting and harvest time, and if you keep your
driving speed steady and your gaze oblique, the rich brown spaces
between the verdant rows flicker by like frames on old film stock. The
even topography and the tidy crop lines conjure a false sense of order,
security, and permanence. Cruising along in air-conditioned comfort,
it's easy to forget how recently white settler colonists arrived, killing
and driving Indigenous people from their homes while importing enslaved Africans whose labor created the contemporary landscape.

Archeological evidence indicates human presence in what is now
Mississippi as far back as 10,000 BCE. These early people were
largely nomadic hunters of large animals like mastodon and bison.
As the area began to warm over the next few millennia, Indigenous
people adopted a more sedentary farming lifestyle and established
villages throughout the area connected by trade routes. By 1000 CE,
Native Americans were living in complex societies, which included
extensive settlements and the building of large ceremonial temple
mounds.[2]

For centuries prior to the mass arrival of European settler colonists, the Delta and north Mississippi were part of the vast domain of
the Choctaw confederation. According to Choctaw legend, the people originated from "Nanih Waya," a sacred mound in what is now
Winston County in east central Mississippi. Archeological evidence
suggests that the platform mound was constructed between 300 CE

and 600 CE.[3] Historians trace modern Choctaw lineage to a coalescing of several clans in the late seventeenth century, including tribes descending from the mound builders.[4] Because of the density of the vegetation and regular flooding, the Delta served as a site of hunting forays rather than settlement for the Choctaw.

Even as late as the end of the Civil War, most of the Delta was not yet farmland but a verdant lowland forest of old-growth hardwood trees, cypress-studded swamps, canebrakes, and mats of thorny vines. But with the arrival of white settler colonists in the early 1800s, the Delta began to be transformed, first by the backbreaking labor of enslaved Africans and then after the Civil War by the freedmen and their sharecropper descendants, along with smaller numbers of Italian and other immigrants, who braved ravenous mosquitoes, venomous snakes, and lurking alligators. Fueled by the prospects of wealth generated by "king cotton" in the second half of the nineteenth century, they cleared underbrush, cut timber, burned stumps, and drained swamps to unlock access to some of the most fertile agricultural soil in the world. Over the last century, massive modern flood control projects have taken the place of hand-dug mud levees; rail lines and black asphalt laid by Caterpillar pavers have replaced bayous and dirt roads; and GPS-enabled John Deere tractors have supplanted manual laborers and mule teams, opening even the most stubborn tracks.

But the water still refuses to yield.

As recently as 2021, the Mississippi Levee Board and local representatives were seeking approval from the US Environmental Protection Agency for a $400 million scheme to pump water out of the lower Delta area known as the Yazoo Backwater, because it had been flooded nearly every year over the last decade.[5] In contrast to the neatly laid out rectangular farms of the Midwest, the Delta remains ornately carved by minor rivers such as the Tallahatchie and Big Sunflower, ancient oxbow lakes, and hundreds of tributaries feeling their way to the Mississippi and Yazoo Rivers on its boundaries.

Highways pull off the illusion of mastery by leaping the waters on small bridges. Razor-straight crop rows are compelled to contract and extend their reach, their terminus dictated by the meandering waters. From above, the land appears more swirled than sectioned, the waters less tamed than accommodated.

FOUR HUNDRED YEARS BEFORE EMMETT TILL

Emmett Till was born on July 25, 1941. But his story begins four hundred years earlier, on May 8, 1541.

On that date, Hernando de Soto became the first documented European to reach the Mississippi River. Likely landing south of Memphis, near the Mississippi county that bears his name today, de Soto claimed a massive area, including the Mississippi-Yazoo River basin, as the domain of Spain. De Soto was an ambitious man on the rise. He had recently been named governor of Cuba by Holy Roman Emperor Charles V. Just two years earlier, he had led a six-hundred-person-strong incursion into the continent that set out in 1539 from near Tampa Bay, claiming Florida and vast tracts of other "undiscovered" lands that he encountered for Spain.

De Soto's conquest—particularly his arrival at the Mississippi River—was considered central enough to America's founding myth that it was commemorated in 1855 as the final installment of eight large historical paintings commissioned by Congress that are still displayed in the Rotunda of the US Capitol building today. Painted by William H. Powell, the eighteen-by-twelve-foot *Discovery of the Mississippi by De Soto* depicts a white fantasy of American origins, a romanticized Euro-Christian vision of divinely ordained conquest. While the significance of the details is lost on most contemporary observers, Powell carefully captured the performance of the specific ritual acts that were required to secure the legal claim to Indigenous land under the Doctrine of Discovery.

The large canvas has two distinct visual fields. In the well-lit background, the painting depicts de Soto astride a white horse, adorned in Renaissance-era finery, entering a Native American village that is perched on a bluff overlooking the river. He is surrounded by a dense phalanx of mounted armed soldiers. The Native Americans, both men and women, are all shirtless. Native women warily cling to each other, with some hiding behind a large teepee. Three male Native leaders stand over a few crude weapons spread on a blanket on the ground, one in a majestic headdress, one extending a peace pipe, and another guardedly crossing his arms.

In the foreground, cast in shadow, is the remarkable juxtaposition of European implements of war and the symbols of Christianity. On the bottom left, there are allusions to the fighting that had taken place the day before between de Soto's men and Native Americans. One man is tending a wounded leg; another, part of a cohort pushing a large cannon, has his head bandaged. In the center, directly below de Soto's horse, is a cache of muskets, ammunition, armor, and a battle axe. Occupying the entire lower right corner of the painting is a massive crucifix—consisting of rough-hewn timber tied with rope and adorned with a white crucified Jesus—being raised amid the village. A Catholic monk blesses it with his right hand while reading a proclamation from a manuscript held with his left.[6]

These acts were not spontaneous expressions of thanks to God for a safe journey, nor were they simply routine religious ceremonies. Rather, they were performances of a specific set of rituals designed to secure legal claims through the invocation of the moral and religious framework of the Doctrine of Discovery. If Powell's painting were animated with audio, you would hear the monk reading these words aloud to the assembled throng:

> God our Lord gave charge to one man, called St. Peter, that he
> should be Lord and Superior of all the men in the world, that all

should obey him, and that he should be the head of the whole human race, wherever men should live, and under whatever law, sect, or belief they should be; and he gave him the world for his kingdom and jurisdiction. . . . One of these Pontiffs, who succeeded St. Peter as Lord of the world, in the dignity and seat which I have before mentioned, made donation of these isles and *Tierra-firme* to the aforesaid King and Queen and to their successors, our lords, with all that there are in these territories, as is contained in certain writings which passed upon the subject as aforesaid, which you can see if you wish.[7]

This truly remarkable text, which became known as the *Requerimiento*, was developed for use by Spanish conquistadors by jurist Palacios Rubios of the Council of Castile in 1514. It was written in Latin, the language of the European Catholic Church, spoken neither by most of the Spanish soldiers nor the Native Americans. Nonetheless, it was created to proclaim to Indigenous people their new status—effective upon their "discovery"—as subjects of the Spanish monarchy by order of the pope. It was a carefully developed part of the Euro-Christian choreography of conquest, designed to legitimate European claims to dominion over specific people and territory under the Doctrine of Discovery.

After asserting the divine authority invested in the pope and delegated to the Spanish monarchs, the *Requerimiento* claims that other Indigenous peoples everywhere have gladly accepted this news and have voluntarily submitted to be Spanish subjects. It also alleges that "all these, of their own free will, without any reward or condition, have become Christians" and declares, "You too are held and obliged to do the same."[8] The *Requerimiento* goes on to reassure the Indigenous people of the benefits of becoming Christian Spanish subjects: "You will do well . . . and we in their name shall receive you in all love and charity."[9]

But the document also concludes with this ominous description of the consequences of not "freely" accepting these terms:

> But, if you do not do this, and maliciously make delay in it, I certify to you that, with the help of God, we shall powerfully enter into your country, and shall make war against you in all ways and manners that we can, and shall subject you to the yoke and obedience of the Church and of their Highnesses, we shall take you and your wives and your children, and shall make slaves of them, and as such shall sell and dispose of them as their Highnesses may command; and we shall take away your goods, and shall do you all the mischief and damage that we can, as to vassals who do not obey, and refuse to receive their lord and resist and contradict him; and we protest that the deaths and losses which shall accrue from this are your fault, and not that of their Highnesses, or ours, not of these cavaliers who come with us. And that we have said this to you and made this Requisition, we request the notary here present to give us his testimony in writing, and we ask the rest who are present that they should be witnesses of the Requisition.[10]

De Soto did not find the gold or riches he was seeking, and the unforgiving wilderness claimed the lives of nearly half his expeditionary force. De Soto himself succumbed to a severe fever and was secretly buried at night in the Mississippi River so that Native Americans, some of whom thought he had godlike powers, would not know of his mortality. Despite these losses, de Soto's violent campaign accomplished its purpose back home. It left a string of crosses in their wake, putting any other Europeans on notice of their claim. The survivors returned to Spain in possession of a few valuables such as a clutch of pearls, enslaved Native Americans as examples of the conquered people, maps, and properly notarized records that the rites of the Doctrine of Discovery had been correctly performed.

These ritual acts accomplished two things in the eyes of the western Christian Church and other European powers. They succeeded in claiming for Spain the rights to an immense tract of land, including the present areas of Florida, Georgia, the Carolinas, Tennessee, Arkansas, Alabama, and Mississippi.[11] And they morally absolved Spain for the killing, enslaving, and other violent mistreatment of Indigenous peoples in these areas. Having "rejected" an offer they could not understand, Indigenous demise would be, in the eyes of the church and the Christian state, the deserved consequence of their own intransigence.

THE "INDIAN PROBLEM" AND THE TRAIL OF TEARS

Traced from the European perspective, the preemptive right to control the land and people of this region was claimed alternatively by France, Great Britain, and Spain. The US finally secured its own right to preemption in 1795, when Spain relinquished its claim in the Treaty of San Lorenzo. White occupation did not pick up until the Mississippi Territory was organized in 1798 and extended to include the Delta region in 1804. Even at the recognition of Mississippi statehood in 1817, the fertile Delta land remained undisturbed, sheltered by an impenetrable tangle of vegetation. In his 1948 memoir, *Where I Was Born and Raised*, David Cohn described the Delta's early history (from the European perspective) this way:

> The Spaniard came and Hernando De Soto was buried in the Delta's river, but the land did not stir in its sleep. More than a century later, when Cornwallis surrendered at Yorktown, it was still primeval wilderness. It sent no soldiers to the War of 1812 because there were no men to send. It was not until 1825,

scarcely more than thirty years before the Civil War, that the first settlers came.[12]

The passing of territory rights among European powers proceeded without consideration for the Choctaw, Chickasaw, and Creek nations, who continued to live on their ancestral lands, even as they were being surveyed and captured on paper by European and then American cartographers. As white colonizers poured into the area in the early 1800s, resulting in sometimes violent clashes, Choctaw leaders looked for ways to coexist with the newcomers. But the settlers' ravenous appetite for land—a phenomenon dubbed "Mississippi Fever"—meant that agreements were continually abrogated and both the individual and communal land rights of the Choctaw were regularly violated.

Under duress, the Choctaw Nation relinquished rights to the southwestern third of their lands (about five million acres), which included the southern portion of the Delta, in the 1820 Treaty of Doak's Stand. In exchange, the Choctaw were assured that their remaining lands "shall remain without alteration" and that "the peace and harmony subsisting between the Choctaw Nation of Indians and the United States, are hereby renewed, continued, and declared to be perpetual."[13]

This treaty was underwritten by the same moral and religious logic, rooted in the Doctrine of Discovery, that drove de Soto to the Mississippi nearly three centuries earlier: divinely ordained political domination, justified by the provision of "civilization and Christianity" to those depicted as backward savages. The treaty also embodied what was fast becoming a tenet of US Indian policy in the early nineteenth century: a genocidal goal of destroying Choctaw cultural and religious life as a condition of physical survival in that place.[14]

The treaty stipulated that any Choctaw who insisted on continuing a traditional hunting lifestyle (who "refused to work," in the language of the treaty) would be forcibly moved west across the river. Those who wanted to stay could do so only by abandoning their culture and religion, including sending their children to Choctaw boarding schools run by missionaries or the government that mandated the teaching of English and Christianity while banning Native languages and religious practices. If they agreed, they were given one-mile-square plots of land for subsistence family farms and promised the right to become US citizens in the future.[15]

For those willing to move, the treaty offered as compensation one year of supplies and title to other lands beyond the Mississippi River in what is today Arkansas, Oklahoma, and Texas (failing to consider that there were both other Indigenous people and white settlers already in these areas). To the disappointment of white officials, few emigrated after the ratification of the 1820 treaty, choosing either to attempt to assimilate in place or to move to unceded land to the north.

By 1830, the strong preference of whites for "Indian removal" over assimilation and sharing of resources became clear. After personally overseeing brutal military campaigns against Native Americans as a general in the US Army, Andrew Jackson was elected president in 1828. Leveraging the incorporation of the Doctrine of Discovery into US law in the 1823 *Johnson v. M'Intosh* case, Andrew Jackson made "Indian removal" the center of his presidency and the official policy of the United States. His speech to the US Senate celebrating the passage of the 1830 Indian Removal Act is revealing:

> [The removal of the Indians beyond the white settlements] will relieve the whole State of Mississippi and the western part of Alabama of Indian occupancy, and enable those States to advance rapidly in population, wealth, and power. It will separate the Indians from immediate contact with settlements of whites; free them from the power of the states; enable them to pursue happi-

ness in their own way and under their own rude institutions; will retard the progress of decay, which is lessening their numbers, and perhaps cause them gradually, under the protection of the Government and through the influence of good counsels, to cast off their savage habits and become an interesting, civilized, and Christian community.[16]

In Mississippi, the state increased the pressure on the Native American nations by abolishing their tribal governments and extending the jurisdiction of state laws over their people. Just four months after the passage of the Indian Removal Act, federal officials forced the Choctaw to cede the remainder of their lands east of the Mississippi River in the Treaty of Dancing Rabbit Creek, also called the Choctaw Removal Treaty, which was signed on September 27, 1830. The execution of this treaty made the Choctaw Nation the first of the major Native American nations to be completely driven from their homelands. Having lived with years of duplicity and coercion from federal and state officials, most Choctaw understood the dire situation. One leader summarized the terms of the treaty deal this way: "Let me give you money to allow me to kill you."[17] Rev. William Winans, a proslavery minister and secretary of the Mississippi Conference of the Methodist Church, described the treatment of the Choctaw as "a wanton disregard of the claims of humanity and a display of ingratitude rarely equaled in the annals of human depravity."[18]

Frustrated with the pace of legal dispossession, impatient white settler colonists took matters into their own hands. Speculators of all kinds swarmed into Choctaw lands, wielding violence and concocting every conceivable type of fraudulent scheme. Choctaw residents reported hundreds of these incidents to federal commissioners, to no avail. Elderly and infirm Indigenous people were particularly vulnerable.

In *Unworthy Republic: The Dispossession of Native Americans and the Road to Indian Territory*, historian Claudio Saunt vividly describes the violence and theft many Choctaw experienced at the hands of white settler colonists during this period:

> Immaka, a sixty-five-year-old woman, lived with her three grown children until a white man built a house near her and plowed a field right up to her front door. After he pried the boards off her house while she was living in it, she fled to "an old waste house" and survived on a small crop of corn. Oakalarcheehubbee, described as "an old grey headed man having but one eye," stayed at home until Hiram Walker drove him out with a whip. Walker then put his fifteen slaves to work on the land. . . . Okshowenah, said to be "an old and infirm" woman, was a widow at the time of the treaty. All but one of her children had moved west, but she remained in the Choctaw Nation until a man plowed around her house and fenced her in. She fled, and in 1838 was preparing to move west. "I hardly expect she will get there," said one relative, who commented, "She is remarkably old."[19]

Alexis de Tocqueville, the young Frenchman traveling in America to observe what he understood as the vibrancy of American democratic institutions and culture, witnessed one of the early waves of forced Choctaw migration as he crossed the Mississippi River just south of Memphis—not far from de Soto's landing nearly three centuries earlier—in the winter of 1831. He began his account of this event: "It is impossible to conceive the frightful sufferings that attend these forced migrations. They are undertaken by a people already exhausted and reduced; and the countries to which the newcomers betake themselves are inhabited by other tribes, which receive them with jealous hostility. Hunger is in the rear, war awaits them, and misery besets them on all sides."[20]

Tocqueville then gave this vivid description of "sufferings that I have not the power to portray":

> These savages had left their country and were endeavoring to gain the right bank of the Mississippi, where they hoped to find asylum that had been promised them by the American government. It was then the middle of winter, and the cold was unusually severe; the snow had frozen hard upon the ground, and the river was drifting huge masses of ice. The Indians had their families with them, and they brought in their train the wounded and the sick, with children newly born and old men upon the verge of death. They possessed neither tents nor wagons, but only their arms and some provisions. I saw them embark to pass the mighty river, and never will that solemn spectacle fade from my remembrance. No cry, no sob, was heard among the assembled crowd; all were silent. Their calamities were of an ancient date, and they knew them to be irremediable. The Indians had all stepped into the bark that was to carry them across, but their dogs remained upon the bank. As soon as these animals perceived that their masters were finally leaving the shore, they set up of a dismal howl and, plunging all together into the icy waters of the Mississippi, swam after the boat.[21]

Between 1831 and 1834, massive, forced removal of approximately 18,000 of the 23,000 Choctaw residents to Oklahoma resulted in the deaths of over 2,500—predominantly children, the sick, pregnant women, and the elderly—due to starvation and exposure on what a Choctaw chief described as "the trail of tears and death."[22] The Choctaw Removal Treaty also contained yet another empty US promise about the security of their new homes west of the Mississippi

River: that "no part of the land granted them shall ever be embraced in any Territory or State."[23]

WHITE COLONIZATION AND CHATTEL SLAVERY

With "the Indian problem"—as President Jackson and other white leaders commonly referred to it—solved by violence in the name of Christian virtue, the northern part of Mississippi, including the Delta, was opened for the benefit of white settler colonists. Given the inhospitable jungle that guarded the rich earth, the early Delta farmers who attempted to unleash its potential tended to be wealthy planters from Georgia and South Carolina. Because of poor farming techniques, many of these planters had depleted the soil on their southeastern plantations. But they had sufficient capital, in cash and enslaved people, to undertake the arduous work of clearing and draining these new lands for farming.

Because land had to be continually cleared to enlarge the productive proportion of the plantation, the normal agrarian harvest rhythms were replaced with a year-round work schedule. On Doro, the Charles Clark plantation, enslaved workers were only given six or seven Saturday afternoons off per year. A British travel writer for the *Daily News* reported in 1857 that most Delta slaves spent their lives "from the moment they are able to go afield in the picking season till they drop worn out in the grave in incessant labor, in all sorts of weather, at all seasons of the year without any other change or relaxation than is furnished by sickness . . . indebted solely to the forbearance of the good temper of the overseer for exemption from terrible physical suffering."[24]

This cruel system, however, paid handsome dividends. Emigration and the importation of enslaved people ballooned in the thirty years preceding the Civil War. In the Delta's Washington County, the total population in 1830 was 1,976, of whom 1,184 were slaves. A decade later, the slave population had increased by a factor of six, with a ratio of ten enslaved Africans to every white citizen. By 1850, this ratio would increase to 14.5 to 1, with the average white family in Washington County enslaving 81.7 people.[25]

In 1860, just a year before the outbreak of the Civil War, the US Census revealed that four Delta counties (Bolivar, Coahoma, Issaquena, and Tunica) were among the thirty-six wealthiest counties in the United States—wealth accounted for less by landholdings or production than by holdings of enslaved people.[26] Even this remarkable wealth only hinted at what seemed to be the limitless profit possibilities of the region. As historian James C. Cobb notes in his landmark book, *The Most Southern Place on Earth*, "with only 10 percent of its land cleared in 1860, the Yazoo Delta was little more than a sparsely inhabited plantation frontier as the antebellum era drew to a close."[27]

The abduction and enslavement of millions of Africans was, like the killing and deportation of Indigenous people, rooted in the vision of European and Christian superiority captured in the Doctrine of Discovery. The brutal treatment of the two groups supported the same ends: the securing of land and the exploitation of its resources exclusively for people of European descent. Genocide and exile of Indigenous people were key to the former, and enslavement of Africans secured the latter.

The leaders of the Confederacy saw their project as the culmination of the divine promise of Euro-Christian domination contained in the Doctrine of Discovery. At the opening of the Alabama Secession Convention in 1861, Basil Manly Sr., a prominent Southern Baptist minister who became known as the chaplain to the Confederacy, for example, praised God for reserving "this fair portion of the earth so long undiscovered, unpolluted with the wars and the crimes of the old world that Thou mightest here establish a free government and a pure religion."[28] He went on to author a provision in the

Constitution of the Confederacy that invoked "the favor of Almighty God" on their endeavors and, in a prayer opening the Provisional Congress of the Confederate States, called on God to preserve the Confederacy "as long as the sun and the moon" shone.[29]

But the Civil War brought destruction and disarray to this idealized vision and to the Delta planter world. Coahoma County saw widespread destruction of plantation houses, gins, and even the ramshackle cabins of the enslaved. Given the high value of cotton, the wealth of planters was threatened even by their own side, as Confederate soldiers were under orders to destroy any cotton that might fall into the hands of Union soldiers. As the chaos of the war continued, many enslaved people seized the opportunity to secure their freedom. On January 29, 1862, sixteen enslaved people on the Doro Plantation rebelled against the overseer and fled. By the end of that year, most plantations were losing enslaved people in large numbers, some fleeing to join Union forces.[30]

The biggest blow to the planter lifestyle and future fortunes was the final demise of the institution of slavery, the system of exploitable, free labor that carved farms out of swampy wilderness and transformed cotton fibers into white wealth. At the close of the Civil War, Delta planters not only had to wrestle with a still-untamed wilderness, but they also had to contend with the unpredictability of a newly freed Black labor force. In *The Negro in Mississippi*, historian Vernon L. Wharton summarized uneasy postbellum planter sentiment this way:

> For the first time in their lives, they found it necessary to deal and bargain with their laborers. Negroes who had worked for them for twenty years were simply walking off the place. How did one go about getting new workers under this abominable system? There was a strange and unhappy silence around the old slave auction blocks.[31]

POSTWAR RESISTANCE AND RECONSTRUCTION

Planter bewilderment at the demise of the Confederacy, however, soon gave way to an ironclad resolve to restore the power dynamics of the master-slave hierarchy by other means, using all tools at their disposal: political, religious, social, and economic. The words of one Yazoo Delta planter in 1866 capture this worldview: "I think God intended the niggers to be slaves. Now since man has deranged God's plan, I think the best we can do is keep 'em as near to a state of bondage as possible. . . . My theory is, feed 'em well, clothe 'em well, and then, if they don't work . . . whip 'em well."[32]

The infamous "Black Codes," passed by the Mississippi legislature in November 1865, contained a raft of onerous provisions designed to keep Black people dependent on their former masters, both socially and economically. Blacks were prevented from carrying weapons, consuming alcohol, and from having any standing in a court of law as a plaintiff or witness against whites. Anticipating the power of Black religious organizations, Black citizens were prohibited from "assembling themselves together, either in the day or night," and Black religious leaders could not preach without a license issued by white authorities.[33] The Black Codes also enshrined into law the countless daily deferences demanded by whites in the social caste system; Blacks accused by whites of "mischief" or "insulting gestures" were subject to arrest. The penalty for intermarriage was "confinement in the State penitentiary for life."[34]

In addition to these systems of social control, the Black Codes contained draconian economic provisions. Blacks were prohibited from leasing land outside cities, and all freedmen were required to sign an annual labor contract with a white landowner. Any who refused could be arrested for vagrancy and have their labor auctioned off to the highest bidder. The laws even extended white control over Black children. Orphans or children of freedmen under eighteen could be forcibly apprenticed to any "competent" white person, with the former white owner of the Black family given first priority.[35]

While the most egregious provisions of Mississippi's Black Codes were short-lived—they ran afoul of the federal Civil Rights Acts of 1866 and the Reconstruction Act of 1867—they nevertheless exposed the mindset of white Mississippians, who were determined to resurrect the vision of the Doctrine of Discovery, phoenix-like, from the smoldering ashes of the Confederacy. This unrepentant response cast the die that has shaped race relations in the Delta and the state to this day.

In addition to invalidating the Black Codes, the enforcement of the Reconstruction Act of 1867 brought sweeping changes to Mississippi. Federal officials registered more than 80,000 freedmen to vote, outnumbering the 60,000 white men on the voter rolls statewide and producing even larger Black majorities in the Delta. By 1870 there were Black elected officials—all representing the Republican Party of Lincoln—serving at all levels as sheriffs, mayors, and legislators. John R. Lynch became the first Black Speaker of the Mississippi House of Representatives. Blanche K. Bruce was elected sheriff, tax collector, and superintendent of education in Bolivar County and went on to be appointed to the United States Senate in 1874. For many angry whites, Hiram R. Revels became the symbol of their world turned upside down. In 1870, he became the first African American to serve in the US Senate, a position previously held by Jefferson Davis, who had resigned the office to become president of the Confederacy.[36]

REDEMPTION

White Mississippians retrenched and set out to regain with violence what they had lost at the ballot box. One of the bloodiest events occurred on September 4, 1875, in the Baptist college town of Clinton, home of my own alma mater, Mississippi College. An estimated crowd of two thousand Black Republicans and their families gathered on the grounds of the former Moss Hill plantation for a barbecue and political rally, just ahead of the 1875 elections. Approximately seventy-five white supporters also attended. During a speech, several young white men from the nearby Raymond Democratic Club began to heckle the speaker. When Alex Wilson, a Black deputy, confronted them and attempted to arrest one of the men, they shot him. Then a white man in the crowd let out a rebel yell, shouting, "Fall in, you Raymond crowd!" Representative Eugene Welborne, an African American state representative and one of the rally organizers, testified that the white group moved into a military-like formation, brandished pistols, and opened fire on those assembled. "The thing opened just like lightning," he recalled, "and the shot rained in there just like rain from heaven." When the mayhem ended, five African Americans, including two children and one of Mississippi's first Black state senators, and three white people were dead. Nearly thirty others were wounded.[37]

The violence then spilled over across Warren and Hinds counties. Over the next few days, organized white mobs broke into homes and indiscriminately shot and killed as many as fifty African Americans in the surrounding area, along with a white schoolteacher working in the African American community. Representative Welborne testified that whites "just hunted the whole country clean out, just every [Black] man they could see they were shooting at him just the same as birds."

The mass political violence by white supremacists emboldened whites and frightened Blacks. Over the next few weeks leading up to the 1875 elections, whites engaged in a broad effort to rig the elections, including vigilante violence, voter intimidation, bribery of election officials, and ballot tampering. Despite the mass violence and appeals for federal help by Republican leaders and Black officials,

President Ulysses S. Grant refused to intervene. Election Day found many Republican leaders "hiding out in the woods and swamps," and many Black voters stayed away from the polls in fear for their lives. In Yazoo County, for example, only seven Republican ballots were counted, compared to four thousand Democratic ballots. The result was a landslide Democratic victory statewide, with the party dedicated to restoring white rule securing a four-to-one majority in the state legislature and occupying five of six congressional seats.[38]

This Democratic supermajority moved quickly once seated in the state legislature. One of their first moves was to impeach and remove Lieutenant Governor Alexander K. Davis, who was Black. They then set their sights on Republican governor Adelbert Ames, demanding that he resign. This cleared the way for John M. Stone, the Democratic president pro tempore of the state senate, to become governor as next in the line of succession. With that final move, white supremacy restored its grasp on Mississippi. As Cobb described this watershed moment, "Reconstruction, whose promise of economic, political, and social advancement for Blacks had seemed so genuine only two years before, drew to an abrupt and disappointing close."[39] It was a disaster for African Americans. Drawing on their Christian faith, whites called the end of Reconstruction "Redemption."

BLACK DISENFRANCHISEMENT AND WHITE DOMESTIC TERRORISM

As the federal government allowed Mississippi and the other southern states to dismantle the short-lived achievements of Reconstruction, Delta planters created sharecropping as a new model to secure Black labor. This arrangement allowed Black workers to live and work a specific piece of land in return for giving the white landowner a percentage of the final crop. An 1870 US Department of Agriculture report described the arrangement as "an unwilling concession [by planters] to the freedman's desire to become a proprietor."[40]

The combination of potential independence through sharecropping and a doubling of acreage and production in the 1880s led to unprecedented Black population growth of 60 percent in the core Delta counties. This promise of exorbitant profits, along with renewed concerns that Blacks might outvote whites, led to renewed efforts at control, squeezing Blacks economically and disenfranchising them politically. As Mississippi senator Hernando De Soto Money—a Confederate veteran and planter named after the Spanish conquistador and after whom the future town of Money would be named—admitted in 1893, the goal of Redemption-era whites was "to maintain a civilization that is dependent very largely upon the [white] Democratic Party being in control."[41]

The most powerful tool for restoring white supremacy was the creation of the new Mississippi Constitution of 1890, which implemented a series of measures aimed at stemming the power of Black voters, such as the poll tax and the literacy test. The new constitution effectively shut the door to political power among Mississippi's Black citizens, who were already buffeted by violence and intimidation. In 1888, 71 percent of Black males did not vote in the presidential election, but this number rose to nearly 100 percent in 1895. In Bolivar County, nearly equal numbers of Black and white citizens had been summoned for jury duty in 1890, but no Black citizens were called by the early 1900s.[42] In *Lanterns on the Levee*, William Alexander Percy, a lawyer, planter, and poet who was born in Greenville in 1885, openly described his father's Redemption generation as the men who sought to "protect the country from overflow . . . bore the brunt of the Delta's fight against scalawaggery and Negro domination during reconstruction, . . . stole the ballot boxes which, honestly counted, would have made every county official a Negro . . . [and] helped to shape the Constitution of 1890, which, in effect and legally disen-franchised the Negro."[43]

On the economic front, although Congress had long outlawed the practice of requiring laborers to repay debt with work, the Delta continued to be the source of countless complaints of peonage. In the early 1900s, Mississippi passed laws reminiscent of the Black Codes, such as a vagrancy law that explicitly aimed at pushing "negro loafers to the fields" and stipulating criminal punishments for abandoning labor contracts with white planters. In addition to these racist poli-cies, there was the frequent dishonesty of landowners with often illit-erate Black sharecroppers. A Works Progress Administration (WPA) worker recorded many accounts such as this one: "I'se been cheated outen my rights, short weighted at de gin, short weighted at de store on de place and my account has been tampered wid. I can't read nor write but I made a mark every time I bought something but de man at de store on de place out marked me."[44]

Still, with the cotton economy booming, the opening of the twen-tieth century saw continued emigration of Blacks into the Delta, seeking opportunity amid the prosperity. The Black population in the Delta increased by nearly 50 percent between 1900 and 1930. But even as the Black population swelled, the percentage of Black farm-ers who owned their own land dropped from 7.3 percent in 1900 to 2.9 percent in 1925. As Cobb summarized developments during this period, "The first two decades of the twentieth century witnessed the final stages of the transformation of a labor-hungry frontier into a modern plantation region that afforded its rigorously supervised Black workers little reason to hope for a better, more satisfying to-morrow."[45]

To prevent African American organizing efforts to resist these unfair economic practices and political disenfranchisement, white Mississippi community and religious leaders participated in, sup-ported, or at the very least accepted as a necessary evil a steady campaign of domestic terrorism reminiscent of their treatment of Indigenous peoples a few decades before. Between 1888 and 1901 the Delta counties accounted for one-third of the nearly one hundred Mississippi lynchings recorded by the National Association for the Advancement of Colored People (NAACP). During the first few decades of the twentieth century, there were sixty-six confirmed lynchings, averaging a vigilante murder of a Black citizen every five and a half months.[46]

The violence was so frequent it became an accepted and tolerated part of the culture, often failing to cause even a ripple in placid white consciences. In June 1903, Greenville resident Harry Ball recorded in his diary the lynching of a local Black man accused of assaulting a white woman. Ball wrote that a mob, including many prominent white citizens, hung the man from a telephone pole and then invited friends to come view the grisly scene. He described the atmosphere this way: "Everything was very orderly. There was not a shot, but much laughing and hilarious excitement. . . . It was quite a gala occasion, and as soon as the corpse was cut down, all the crowd betook themselves to the park to see a game of baseball."[47] For far too many whites, lynching had become Mississippi's pastime.

With the US Supreme Court upholding the constitutionality of the state's disenfranchisement laws in 1898 and little appetite for intervention by the federal government, white Mississippians felt themselves vindicated from the devastating upheavals of Reconstruction just three decades earlier. They entered the twentieth century having laid the foundation for a new white supremacist regime enshrined in law, enforced with violence, and legitimized by a Christianity still animated by the Doctrine of Discovery. Most Native Americans had long been exiled or pushed to small reservations. Slavery was vanquished, but whites were replacing it with a new legal form of involuntary servitude. They sought nothing less than total control over the lives of African Americans, keeping them perpetually economically dependent, politically voiceless, and socially deferential. This "closed society," as historian James Silver aptly described it, was especially powerful in the Delta, where strict command of cheap Black labor was required to produce white wealth.[48]

THE GREAT MIGRATION

Even as Black laborers were drawn to the Delta from the nearby hill country and elsewhere in the South by the thriving cotton economy, masses were also leaving. More than one hundred thousand disillusioned African Americans left Mississippi between 1915 and 1920 alone, fleeing the state's white supremacist mechanisms of control and subjugation. As Black hopes for opportunity were dashed nearly upon arrival by the oppressive realities and limited possibilities of plantation life, the Delta became more like a temporary staging area for departures to the North than a permanent destination.[49] One exasperated sharecropper put it to a WPA interviewer this way: "My old 'oman and nine children worked and went naked all of de year . . . , an[d] I born to die, so I am lighting a shuck off of dis place."[50] In other words, "Life is too short to work for nothing, so I'm out of here."

One of the primary destinations for Blacks fleeing Mississippi's toxic environment was Chicago, which saw more than one hundred Black emigrants arriving each day at the height of the migration. Between 1910 and 1920, the percentage of African Americans in Chicago who had been born in Mississippi increased 500 percent, and the number of Mississippi-born African Americans in the state of Illinois increased by 400 percent. On the other end of the route, in 1917, more than two hundred abandoned houses were documented in the Black neighborhoods of the Greenville area alone.[51]

The rail lines, built by white capitalists to export cotton to northern industrial centers, played a paradoxical role in the Great Migration. Trains ferried away both cotton and the Delta's Black labor force. But the railroad company's Black train porters also carried Black newspapers such as the *Chicago Defender* south. With a circulation of more than two hundred thousand by the 1920s, the *Defender* became the most important Black newspaper in the country in the first half of the twentieth century. With calls for federal intervention against the South's vigilante violence falling on deaf ears, the paper came to embrace and promote Black migration from the South both as a means of improving the lives of African Americans and of breaking the stranglehold of white elite power in the South. A front-page story in the September 2, 1916, edition, for example, carried a photograph of a large crowd of well-dressed Black men and women waiting for a northbound train in Savannah, Georgia, under the bold headline "THE EXODUS."[52]

The *Defender* played an important role in piercing the veil of perpetual servitude that was sold as fate, or even Providence, in the South. "The newspaper carried with it messages, dreams, and hopes and plans," a Black migrant to Chicago from Alabama explained. "They weren't just selling a newspaper. They were informing the people of a better world."[53]

DESEGREGATION AND VIOLENCE

While many African Americans were leaving, others were fighting, with increasing success, to secure equality for themselves and their children at home. The US Supreme Court ruling in *Brown v. Board of Education*, handed down on May 17, 1954, was an unmistakable sign that the federal government was dismantling a major Jim Crow stronghold, one that was specifically designed to hand white supremacy down to the next generation: its segregated schools. Whites supporting segregation dubbed the day "Black Monday," and began forming White Citizens' Councils to oppose it, the first of which was organized just two months after the decision in Indianola, Mississippi, a small town in the heart of the Delta.

The *Brown* decision was a nuclear event that shattered whites' confidence in the security of the Jim Crow society they had built since the demise of Reconstruction. This new threat produced a wide range of responses in virtually every area of society: the creation of a new official state body, the Mississippi State Sovereignty Commission, essentially a domestic spy operation created to fight desegregation; the filing of legislation to abolish public schools altogether; a flurry of Confederate monument building in public spaces across the South; a revival of Christian theological defenses of white supremacy; and a rekindled willingness of whites to embrace violence to defend their "way of life." In an Associated Press article on September 9, 1954, one Delta-based state legislator declared that "a few killings" would be the best thing for the state because they would ensure passage of the legislation to protect segregation and "save a lot of bloodshed later on."[54]

On May 7, 1955, Rev. George Lee, a Black minister and successful local businessman in the small Delta town of Belzoni, was shot in the face with a shotgun from a passing car while driving home, as retaliation for his role in organizing Black citizens to vote; local authorities declared it a traffic accident and no charges were brought.[55] On August 13, 1955, Lamar Smith, a farmer and World War I veteran who had been working to register Black voters, was shot at close range in broad daylight on the Lincoln County Courthouse lawn in Brookhaven, in full view of dozens of witnesses including the sheriff. Three men were later arrested, but charges were dismissed because white witnesses refused to testify.[56]

African Americans knew that virtually any interactions with whites could put their lives at risk. Registering Black people to vote or organizing Black labor to bargain collectively for fair contracts was almost certain to be met with violence. Moreover, Black residents understood that even minor social infractions—such as a Black man declining to tip his hat to a white person; refusing to address whites as "sir" or "ma'am"; failing to step off the sidewalk to yield right of way to whites; or placing money directly in a white store clerk's hand rather than on the counter—could put one's life at risk.

Chapter Two

THE MURDER OF
EMMETT TILL

MAMIE AND EMMETT'S EARLY LIFE

Among the hundreds of thousands of African Americans whose lives were shaped by the Great Migration was Mamie Elizabeth Carthan, later the mother of Emmett Till. Mamie was born on November 23, 1921, near Webb, Mississippi, in the Delta's Tallahatchie County.[1] Soon after her birth, her father, John Carthan, decided to leave the limited opportunities of the cotton fields and secured a job at the Argo Corn Products Refining Company, on the outskirts of Chicago. When Mamie turned two, she and her mother, Alma Smith Carthan, moved to the suburb of Argo to join her father.[2]

Illinois was no racial utopia. In her autobiography, Mamie describes Argo as "a sleepy little town where whites called blacks by their first names and where blacks would never dare do the same thing." Even as an adult in the flagship Marshall Field's department store in downtown Chicago, Mamie surprisingly found herself directed by a security guard to shop in the basement (she refused). Still,

Argo had reliable manufacturing jobs with decent wages available to African Americans and the public schools were open to all.

Although Mamie had no memory of living in Mississippi, as a child she returned each summer to visit extended family and friends in Tallahatchie County. In her autobiography, written forty-seven years after the death of Emmett, she recalled one incident from her childhood that eerily foreshadowed her son's fateful interaction with a white grocery clerk. When she was twelve, she came down to visit her grandparents, who owned farmland near Webb. One day, her grandfather brought her into the modest downtown commercial area and let her wander for a bit while he went into a store. She had some money of her own and decided to pick up a roll of toilet paper as a help to her grandparents and get herself an ice cream cone as a reward. She confidently strode across the street and into the drugstore, unaware that it sat on the segregated "white side" of the street. The store owner immediately confronted and interrogated her: "What do *you* want?" When she asked for the toilet paper and the ice cream, the owner slowly replied, "Where y'all from?" Her reply of "Chicago" was met with open resentment. He replied, "You know what? I'm gonna give you that ice cream cone. But I'm not going to sell you no toilet paper. You go on home, use corncobs like everybody else."

Just then, her grandfather entered the store and quickly escorted her out. As they hurried back across the street, he gave her a stern lecture never to "cross over" by herself, warning her that she had just faced a great danger. "I would never forget that incident, and, my goodness, that talk with Papa Carr. The lessons of that moment would always stay with me," Mamie wrote. "In Mississippi, there were certain things that Black people were denied by white people. The freedom of movement. The luxury of choice. And a roll of toilet paper."[3]

Mamie became the first Black honor roll student and the fourth Black student to graduate from the mostly white Argo Community

High School. Over time, so many friends and relatives followed the family north that they came to call Argo "Little Mississippi." As Mamie described it, this tight-knit community was held together not only by their optimism and newfound freedoms but by a palpable common sense of "what people knew they had fled."[4]

After graduating from high school, Mamie married Louis Till, who initially seemed worldly and sophisticated. Within a year, on July 25, 1941, Mamie delivered a son, whom she named Emmett Louis Till after her husband. Louis, however, quickly turned out to be alternatively absentee and abusive. The first paragraph of Mamie's autobiography contains this line: "The fact that it was my mother and not my husband who took me to the hospital to have a baby probably tells you just about everything you need to know about Louis Till."[5] After Louis repeatedly violated a restraining order that Mamie had secured against him for attempting to strangle her, a judge gave him the choice of going to jail or joining the army. He chose the latter. But even there he ran into trouble, going AWOL before he was shipped out as part of America's entry into World War II. By July 13, 1945, two weeks before Emmett's fourth birthday, Mamie learned that Louis had been found guilty of "willful misconduct" while in Italy and that he was dead.[6] When the army shipped his personal effects to her, the only thing of value was a plain silver ring, purchased in Casablanca, Morocco, and engraved with his initials and the date "May 25, 1943." She saved it for Emmett.[7]

Emmett's entry into the world was difficult. He was in breech position, and doctors used forceps so aggressively that his head was badly misshapen; they warned Mamie that he might never speak. Emmett blossomed, however, into an energetic, confident boy who loved to talk, laugh, and be the center of attention. But at age six, he was struck with polio. While his large motor skills were not impacted, the disease left him with a stutter so severe that only his immediate family could understand him. After speech clinics and therapy, he managed to keep it under control for everyday speech, but the stutter returned when he was nervous or excited. He didn't outgrow his stutter, as some doctors had promised, but despite the intermittent halts, he relished jokes, enjoyed debates over matters big and small, and, as early teens do, tested his ability to talk his way out of nearly anything, particularly with his mother.[8]

Paralleling Mamie's own childhood experience, as a younger child Emmett also visited his relatives in Mississippi a couple of times with his grandmother. While the predominant movement of the Great Migration ran south to north, there were constant flows of African Americans visiting extended family in both directions. The train line running from Chicago to Cairo, Illinois (where Black passengers heading south had to move to the segregated Jim Crow car at the front of the train before entering Kentucky), to Memphis to Winona, Mississippi, was filled with those returning from their explorations of the big city and those anticipating visits "down South." Especially in the summer, the southbound trains ferried Black children and teenagers to visit grandparents and cousins. Mamie recalled, "For our kids, it was as close to summer camp as they were going to get."[9]

A month after Emmett's fourteenth birthday, an unexpected opportunity presented itself. Mamie's uncle, Moses Wright, known in the family as Papa Mose, had come to Chicago for a family funeral. Papa Mose was a well-known and respected man in the area near Money, Mississippi. He'd previously been a minister, and even though he hadn't delivered a sermon in over five years, people still called him "Preacher." During his visit, he invited Emmett and his cousins to come stay with him for two weeks. There would be cotton to pick, but there would also be fishing, swimming, and the joys of rural life in the Mississippi summer.

Emmett was immediately excited about this adventure. When he heard his cousin Wheeler Parker, who was like a brother to him, was going, Emmett was determined to convince Mamie to let him go.

Mamie initially rejected the plan out of hand, but Emmett persisted. Only after a long talk with Moses and her mother did she relent. But first she had to have a conversation about white supremacy and racism with Emmett, something she had intentionally avoided up to this point in his life.

Now, with his heart set on Mississippi, knowledge of those brutal racial realities became a matter of life and death. Mamie's account of the conversation—one that, for Black mothers, was just as vital and as common as packing a suitcase—is heartbreaking.

> Don't start up any conversations with white people. Only talk if you're spoken to. And how do you respond? "Yes, sir," "Yes, ma'am." "No, sir," "No, ma'am." Put a handle on those answers. Don't just say "yes" and "no" or "naw." Don't ever do that. If you're walking down the street and a white woman is walking toward you, step off the sidewalk, lower your head. Don't look her in the eye. Wait until she passes by, then get back on the sidewalk, keep going, don't look back.[10]

Mamie noted that, even with these stern instructions, she went further to impress the danger upon him. "If you have to humble yourself," she said, "then just do it. Get on your knees, if you have to." Emmett replied, "Oh, Mama, it can't be all that bad." Looking him in the eye and driving the point home by invoking his nickname, Mamie countered, "Bo, it's worse than that."[11]

A few days before the trip, Emmett asked his mother about his father and whether he could begin wearing the ring he'd seen over the years in the jewelry box. It was still too big, but with the addition of some masking tape, he was able to wear it securely. He arrived at Chicago's Englewood train station on August 20, 1955, just before the 8:01 a.m. departure of the *City of New Orleans*. He quickly doubled back from the platform to give Mamie a final kiss good-bye and handed her his watch, saying he wouldn't need it given the agrarian rhythms of Mississippi summers. She slipped off her own watch, replacing it with his. Then he was off, sporting a new set of clothes and his father's silver ring on the middle finger of his right hand; he was carrying a suitcase, a shoebox packed with his favorite dark meat chicken, and a round-trip ticket.[12]

EMMETT TILL'S MURDER

Emmett, along with his cousins, arrived without incident at the four-bedroom home of Papa Mose and Aunt Lizzy. The Wright place was one of the largest tenant homes on the 150-acre plantation owned by Grover Frederick. It sat three miles from the nearest town, Money, Mississippi—a tiny map dot named for Confederate veteran and former senator Hernando De Soto Money, mentioned above.[13] For the next two weeks, the house would be full. Emmett would share a bed with his twelve-year-old cousin Simeon. Wheeler Parker was in another bedroom with cousin Maurice. Another relative, Curtis, would join the following week and share a bedroom with cousin Robert.[14]

The Mississippi summer wasn't quite as leisurely as Emmett had dreamed. August is the early part of the picking season in the Delta, when the bolls begin to open to reveal the white fluffy treasure within. The Wrights were responsible for thirty acres, with another full acre set aside for their personal use, which they had cultivated with vegetable gardens and apple trees. So Emmett was pressed into service on day one to work alongside his cousins, picking cotton to fill nine-foot sacks that they dragged behind them, as well as tending the vegetable gardens. Unaccustomed to the heat, Emmett didn't last the full day and spent the rest of the week mostly helping his aunt with chores in the house. After the cotton was brought in, there was still plenty of time, as promised, for swimming or fishing in the lake across from the house or the Little Tallahatchie River, just a short hike through the woods.

This was the first time Emmett had been away on his own like this, and Mamie had been on pins and needles every day. Late in the first week, Mamie managed to connect with Aunt Lizzie and Emmett via a neighbor's phone. They both assured Mamie everything was fine. Emmett asked if she could send him some money, since he had been treating other kids to candy when they'd go to a local store in Money. Emmett also sent her a letter early in the trip, which she received on August 27, in which he reassured her, "I am having a fine time will be home next week."[15]

But on August 28, early on a Sunday morning, she received the call. It came from Willie Mae Jones, the mother of Curtis, who had just arrived to join the boys in Mississippi. "I don't know what to tell you. Bo. . . . Some men came and got him last night."[16] Mamie had difficulty taking this nightmarish news in and struggled to hold out hope against what she knew it meant. As the day went on, Mamie gathered with her Chicago relatives at her mother's house, trying to get more information and working every contact imaginable: friends, friends of friends, union contacts, and even Chicago reporters who might help. Mamie finally got word that the other boys were okay, but also the horrifying detail that Emmett had been accused of whistling at a white woman. Mamie described the church community rallying around them:

> At the Argo Temple Church of God in Christ, the church Emmett loved so much, the church his grandmother helped to found, the entire congregation stood and prayed. The members prayed for Emmett, they prayed for Mama and me. They prayed that their prayers had come in time.[17]

But Emmett was already gone.

Some of the details of the events leading to Emmett's death remain murky, but the broad contours are reasonably clear.[18] In the early evening of Wednesday, August 24, just four days into his trip, Emmett joined his three cousins and a neighbor for a short drive to Money to buy some treats at Bryant's Grocery and Meat Market, a white-owned store that serviced a mostly Black clientele of local sharecroppers. With her husband, Roy Bryant, out of town, twenty-one-year-old Carolyn Bryant was working the counter. Most of the kids stayed outside, watching a game of checkers being played on the porch. Wheeler went in and bought some sweets and came back out.

Then Emmett entered the store alone. Emmett had only been inside for about a minute when Maurice, the oldest, sent in his younger brother Simeon. In an interview nearly half a century later, Simeon recalled, "Maurice sent me in behind Emmett to make sure he didn't say anything that he shouldn't, because he just didn't know the ways of the South." When he entered, everything seemed normal; Bryant was calm and still behind the counter while Emmett paid for some bubble gum and left. The rest of the group, out on the porch, also recalled hearing nothing odd coming from inside the store.

But after Emmett left, Carolyn Bryant followed immediately outside and headed for her car, testifying later that she was going to retrieve a gun. Whatever the veracity of that claim, Emmett then indisputably ignored his mother's warnings and broke one of the most fiercely defended taboos in Mississippi: flirtation with a white female by a Black male. Both Simeon and Wheeler later confirmed that he let out a loud "wolf whistle"—"a big-city 'whee wheeeee!'" according to Simeon. Wheeler vividly remembered his response: "And we just could not believe . . . where did this come from? What's wrong with him, and even now we don't know what possessed him. He had no idea. He had no idea, didn't have any idea the danger."[19]

Everyone else immediately understood the transgression, and

they scrambled for the car. Maurice hastily threw the car in gear, and they sped toward home. En route, they became concerned that a car was following them. They panicked, pulled the car over, and bailed for the cover of the cotton fields. The car passed and they continued home, agreeing not to tell Papa Mose about the incident. As the days passed, they quickly put the event behind them, even returning to Money one more time before the weekend. By Saturday, no one was thinking any more about it.

At 2:00 a.m. early on Sunday, Papa Mose was abruptly awakened by aggressive pounding on his front door. "Preacher, Preacher . . . This is Mr. Bryant. I want to talk to you about that boy." When he opened the door, he found Roy Bryant and his half brother J. W. Milam, along with an unidentified Black man, with their truck still running behind them. Brandishing flashlights and with Milam holding a .45-caliber pistol, they pushed past Emmett's uncle Moses and began systematically going from bedroom to bedroom, finally locating Emmett in bed with Simeon. They shook him and demanded that he get up and get dressed. As he was being marched toward the door, Moses tried to intervene, even offering to whip Emmett if that would assuage them. His aunt Lizzy desperately offered to pay the men; they shrugged her off, replying that they hadn't come for money but for the boy. They brought Emmett outside to the vehicle, where Moses could make out what he described as a lighter female voice, almost certainly Carolyn Bryant, who said, "Yeah, that's the one."

Before they drove Emmett away with the truck lights off, Milam had a warning for Moses.

"Preacher . . . how old are you?"

"Sixty-four."

"Well, if you know any of us tomorrow, you won't live to be sixty-five."[20]

By Monday, Leflore County sheriff George Smith had arrested both Bryant and Milam on charges of kidnapping. They admitted taking the boy but claimed they had released him when they determined he was the wrong person. But on Wednesday morning, August 31, a local fisherman saw two legs jutting above the water in the Tallahatchie River and contacted authorities. Recognizing this could be the missing boy's body, deputies from Leflore County picked up Moses Wright and brought him to the river, where he positively identified Emmett. Emmett's fourteen-year-old frame was excessively bloated from being immersed in the river for three days, and a seventy-five-pound cotton gin fan was tied around his neck with barbed wire to weigh it down in the water. His head was grotesquely disfigured, with a major head wound, an eye dislodged, and a bullet hole in the back of the head. Moses could still recognize some features, but there was one undeniable sign that the body was Emmett's: a silver ring engraved with "LT" on his hand.

Because the body had floated a few hundred feet into Tallahatchie County, Sheriff Clarence Strider was also on the scene and assumed control of the investigation. Strider issued the death certificate with the following description: "Emmett Till, Negro, Male, homicide by gunshot or blow with an ax, body removed to Chicago Illinois for burial."[21] Contradicting this description, and without consulting the family, Strider instructed the Leflore sheriff's department to send the body to Greenwood and called an undertaker to bury the body as quickly as possible in a Black churchyard in Money.

As soon as the Till family learned of this activity, which would prevent any autopsy and collection of forensic evidence, Mamie's uncle, Crosby Smith, stepped up, vowing that Emmett's body would not be laid to rest in Mississippi. Just three hours after the body had been pulled from the river, Smith arrived in Money to find a shallow grave already being prepared. Mamie was finally able to secure her son's return, but only by agreeing to an exorbitant $3,300 transfer fee and pledging to bury him immediately upon arrival in Chicago.

On Friday, September 2, the body arrived in Chicago via train, and Mamie, along with a throng of friends, family, neighbors, and reporters, gathered on the platform to receive it. Workers unloaded a large crate. It was opened, releasing a terrible smell and revealing a smaller box, which was transferred to a hearse headed for the A. A. Rayner Funeral Home on Cottage Grove Avenue. Although everyone involved, including the funeral home, had promised Mississippi officials they would not open the casket, which had a large decal with an official Mississippi state seal securing the lid to the base, Mamie insisted. She had to see her son's broken body.

> I thought about what it must have been like for him that night. I studied every detail of what those monsters had done to destroy this beautiful young life. I thought about how afraid he must have been, how at some point that early Sunday morning he must have known he was going to die. I thought about how all alone he must have felt, and I found myself hoping only that he died quickly. . . . And I can never forget the complete devastation I experienced when I realized . . . [that] at some point during his ordeal, in the last moments of his precious little life, Emmett must have cried out. Two names. "God" and "Mama." And no one answered the call.[22]

As she stood over the body, she made a decision: "Let the people see what they did to my boy."

Mamie did allow the morticians at Rayner Funeral Home to do some cosmetic work, returning his eye to its socket, sewing his mouth shut, and closing the skin across the gash on the back of his skull. They dressed him in the suit Mamie had given him for Christmas the year before, and they placed a pane of glass over the casket's base. Mamie taped a few Christmas photos of her smiling son on the casket lid so everyone could see her boy as she knew him. She allowed David Jackson, staff photographer for *Jet* magazine, to take a photo.[23]

Rayner opened its doors for viewing late afternoon, and over the next two days an estimated fifty thousand people came to pay their respects. On Sunday, the body was moved to Roberts Temple of the Church of God in Christ for the funeral. Bishop Isaiah Roberts, founding pastor at Roberts Temple, presided over a service that ran an hour and a half with multiple speakers. Attendees were cautioned against taking revenge into their own hands, but they were also urged to contribute to an NAACP fund to pay legal expenses and end lynching in the South.

Bishop Louis Ford preached the funeral sermon, choosing two poignant texts from the book of Matthew in the New Testament: "For as much as ye have done unto these, my little ones, ye have also done unto me." And, "But whosoever shall offend one of these little ones which believe in me, it is better for him that a millstone was hung about his neck and that he be drowned in the depths of the sea."[24]

So many people came to the service that Mamie made the decision to delay the burial and allow Emmett's body to lie in state at the church for two additional days. Over that long Labor Day weekend, more than one hundred thousand people—many of whom themselves had made fraught trips down south to visit friends and relatives—came to stand in solidarity with the Till family. After brief prayers at the church, the family and close friends laid Emmett to rest in Burr Oak Cemetery on Tuesday, September 6.

SNAPSHOTS FROM THE EMMETT TILL TRIAL

The small town of Sumner, Mississippi, was founded in 1900 and named after Confederate veteran and its first mayor, J. B. Sumner. By the mid-1950s, the town had approximately five hundred residents and drew attention to its existence off Highway 49 with a Coca-Cola—subsidized roadside sign. The top panel contained an arrow pointing left to the turnoff with the word "Sumner" written in black on a white background. Just below, a second panel contained the town's tagline in bold block letters: "A GOOD PLACE TO RAISE A BOY."[25]

Sumner's original courthouse and a replacement each burned down in the town's early years, but the third building, built in 1909, stands today.[26] On June 3, 1913, the United Daughters of the Confederacy was permitted to erect a thirty-foot-high Confederate monument on the stately courthouse lawn, which was topped by a Confederate soldier standing at attention, saluting with his right hand and holding a rifle with his left. Below the words "OUR HEROES," a pyramid of three granite stairs spills out on all sides of the square pedestal. At eye level, there is a relief of a partially unfurled Confederate battle flag on the obverse side and a "lost cause" poetic inscription on the reverse: "For truth dies not, and by her light they raise the flag whose starry folds have never trailed. And by the low tents of this deathless dead, they lift the cause that never yet has failed."[27]

For five sweltering days, between September 19 and 23, 1955, the world's attention was focused on this place, where, for the first time in the state's history, a grand jury had handed down indictments for two white men for murdering a Black person, and African Americans were openly testifying against white defendants in a capital murder trial.[28] International press, along with reporters from the leading Black and white papers in the US, endured the lingering Mississippi heat to see if justice could be done in America's Deep South. For many, the trial became not just a referendum on the state but on whether—midway through the twentieth century—America would stand for justice or white supremacy.

Sheriff Clarence Strider was a larger-than-life figure in the county and at the trial. The middle-aged Strider was six foot two and 270 pounds, with a cigar perpetually in his mouth. He was not only the lead investigator of the murder, but he also owned one of the largest plantations in the county: 1,500 acres worked by thirty-five Black tenant families. On the roofs of each of seven side-by-side tenant shacks sitting near the main road he had painted in block letters S-T-R-I-D-E-R, a reminder of his power and influence to those dwelling within and those driving by.[29]

John Herbers, who covered the trial for United Press International, described Strider as "a big, fat, plain-talking, obscene-talking sheriff you would expect to find in the South," and described his conduct as less concerned with seeking justice than acting "to be sure that his courtroom was totally segregated."[30] In his trial testimony, Strider either contradicted or cast doubt on nearly everything he himself had written on the death certificate. He was no longer sure the body was that of Emmett Till; he now claimed it was so badly decomposed that it must have been in the water far longer than two or three days; he couldn't be sure whether the corpse was Black or white. When equivocation wasn't enough, he flatly lied, claiming not even to know whether the death certificate had Emmett Till's name on it. Instead of presenting clear evidence to support the prosecution, the county's leading law enforcement officer became the star witness for the defense.[31]

Even off the witness stand, Strider made no effort to hide his white supremacist beliefs. "We've kept the races separated for a long time, and we don't intend to change now," he declared to African Americans attending the trial. He required Black reporters, and even visiting congressman Charles Diggs from Detroit, to sit in the back of the courtroom at a table that was sometimes out of earshot of testimony and always held a partially obstructed view of witnesses. He made a point of starting each day of the trial with a stroll past that table, delivering the same cheerful greeting: "Good morning, Niggers."[32]

All of Sumner's five attorneys volunteered their services pro bono to help defend Bryant and Milam, a move that conveniently also prevented any of them from being assigned to help the prosecution. Leading the defense, from their offices directly across the street from the courthouse, were J. J. Breland, the sixty-three-year-old lead attorney, and his junior partner, John W. Whitten Jr., first cousin of the staunch segregationist congressman Jamie Whitten. Not to be outdone in expressing their solidarity with the white defendants, local businessmen raised over six thousand dollars in support of the defense.[33]

Despite the racist atmosphere, Mamie and Moses Wright were profiles in dignity and courage. Moses Wright had to endure not just intimidation and demeaning questions from the defense team, but even the prosecution's strategy of depicting him as a good southern Negro, by addressing him with the colloquial "Uncle Mose" instead of "Mr. Wright." Wright testified clearly about the unique silver ring with the initials "LT" that was removed from the body after it was pulled from the river, the key piece of evidence definitively identifying it as Emmett. One of the most iconic photographs from the trial depicts Moses Wright, standing tall for his small frame in a white shirt, blue tie, and suspenders and raising his arm to identify the defendants across the courtroom. The Associated Press reported, "Mose Wright pointed a knobby finger at J. W. Milam Wednesday and said, 'There he is'—identifying him as one of the men who abducted his nephew." When asked if he recognized the second kidnapper, he calmly repeated, "There he is," while pointing directly at Roy Bryant.[34]

The indignities for Mamie began even before the trial, when she arrived during jury selection. While Bryant and Milam sat in the front of the courtroom, accompanied by their wives and children (a strategy of the defense to portray them as good family men), Mamie was escorted by Sheriff Strider to the rear corner of the courtroom, where she was seated at the segregated table reserved for the Black press.

The defense hammered her from every angle. They hinted that she was motivated to lie about the body being Emmett's so she could collect on a life insurance policy; attempted to paint her as a disloyal and ungrateful "Chicago Negro" by asking about her family's decision to leave Mississippi and whether she subscribed to the *Chicago Defender*; and implied that her pre-trip cautionary instructions to Emmett (which had been printed in newspaper interviews) indicated either that Emmett was a troublemaker, or that she held disparaging views about the state, or both.

The only time Mamie's composure cracked was when she was shown a photograph of Emmett's body that was taken at the Century Funeral Home in Greenwood, before his body had been prepared for shipment to Chicago, an image she had never seen. "Oh, everything just washing over me again," she recalled years later. "The force of it rocked me in that old cane chair, back and forth. I bowed my head. I had to do that to collect myself. I mean, the tears were welling up and I wanted so much to hold them back. . . . I had to be strong for Emmett." But in the end, Mamie refused to be shaken, confirming that the ring belonged to Emmett and movingly describing the battered body of her lost son.[35]

Much has been made of the all-male, all-white jury seated for the trial. This monolithic composition, however, was not the result of nefarious selection methods by the attorneys but rather a reflection of underlying structural realities. In mid-1950s Mississippi, women were not considered for jury duty. And although all males who were registered to vote were eligible to serve on juries, in 1955—due to a long-standing combination of barriers and threats from whites— there was not a single African American registered to vote in all of Tallahatchie County. As a result, even the initial venire of 120 people from whom the twelve would be chosen was composed entirely of white men.[36]

The trial also contained an odd twist for the jury. Because neither the prosecution nor the defense called the two defendants to the stand, jurors never heard directly from them. And because the judge disagreed that the kidnapping was an action directly connected to whatever occurred at the grocery store days before, the jury never heard Carolyn Bryant's testimony.[37]

On the closing day of the trial, the nearly hour-long closing argument of Tallahatchie County district attorney Gerald Chatham was powerful, bringing tears to the eyes of many in the courtroom. Chatham appealed to the jury as a fellow southerner and made appeals both to principle and self-interest. "If your verdict is influenced by anything except the evidence," he told the jurors, "you will endanger every custom and tradition we hold dear." An article by reporter James Hicks, which was syndicated in several Black newspapers, characterized Chatham's closing remarks as "one of the most passionate pleas ever made by a white man in the South on behalf of a Negro." Mamie agreed, leaning over to the reporter after Chatham rested to say, "He couldn't have done any better."[38]

But the defense would win the day. The defense strategy presented the jury with two mutually incompatible but independently attractive story lines for any white juror wanting to acquit a white defendant. First, despite the clear evidence, the defense relentlessly attempted to cast doubt on whether the body was actually Emmett's. Second, and most powerfully, their aim was to depict Till as "the living embodiment of the white South's worst fear—a big, out of control, sexually rapacious black buck, a product of Chicago's 'black belt,' where African American appetites went unchained," as historian Elliott Gorn summarized it.[39] Emmett might not even be dead; but if he were, Bryant and Milam were merely fulfilling the demands of the well-recognized white male honor codes of the Jim Crow South.

Closing arguments for the defense relied heavily on straightforward appeals to white supremacy. J. W. Kellum cautioned the jury that if they convicted the defendants, "freedom was lost forever" and "your forefathers will turn over in their graves." John Whitten widened the frame beyond the trial to focus on an outside existential threat. "There are people in the United States who want to destroy the custom and way of life of southern white people and southern black people," Whitten thundered. These people could conceivably "go so far as to put a stinking body in the Tallahatchie River with the hope that it could be identified as Emmett Till." But even with such a wild accusation, Whitten wasn't finished. Looking each juror in the eye, he closed his remarks by imploring them to demonstrate "that every last Anglo-Saxon one of you has the courage to free these men in the face of that pressure."[40]

The judge gave the jurors their final charge, and they filed out. They returned just sixty-seven minutes later and delivered the verdict: "We, the jury, find the defendants: not guilty." A cheer went up among the mostly white crowd inside the courtroom, which rippled into a wave to the spillover crowd out on the lawn.

REACTIONS TO THE VERDICT

Not surprisingly, most southern newspaper editorials applauded the verdict, crowing that the case had proven that Mississippians could handle their own affairs without outside meddling. The unstated corollary was also clear: not only white vigilante terrorism but also the underlying tenets of southern culture and its "way of life"—that is to say, white supremacy—had been both vindicated and protected by the verdict. The editorial in the *Jackson Daily News*, run by the politically influential and staunchly segregationist Hederman family, concluded that "the cold hard fact concerning the acquittal in Tallahatchie County of the two alleged slayers of a black youth from Chicago is that the prosecution failed to prove its case." The

Greenwood Morning Star, which had referred to the trial in previous coverage as "the Till Rape Attempt Case," declared, "Mississippi people rose to the occasion and proved to the world that this is a place where justice in the courts is given to all races, religions and classes."[41]

The African American press was appalled but not surprised. "White Supremacy Wins Again," read the resigned headline of the *Kansas City Call*. Under the headline "Mississippi's Shame," the *Oklahoma Black Dispatch* argued that the South was "hiding behind white women's skirts while the real purpose is to terrorize and intimidate Negroes in the exercise of their constitutional rights." The *Chicago Defender* concluded that "every aspect of the trial was edged by flagrant racism."[42]

Outside the South, criticism of the verdict in the mainstream press was unrelenting. The *Chicago Sun-Times* described the defense team's explicit appeals to white supremacy as "nothing less than a lynching." The *New York Post* editorial, headlined "Mississippi Nightmare," declared that justice had been replaced with mob rule in the state. The *Christian Century*, a paper widely read by mainline Protestants, ran a column that was akin to an obituary for the rule of law in Mississippi, noting that "justice died with all its formalities in perfect order."[43]

The acquittal also generated scathing international coverage, with newspapers calling it "scandalous," "monstrous," and "abominable."[44] The verdict created serious problems for post–World War II US foreign policy, when the Cold War involved not just geopolitical competition but a public relations battle for moral superiority, with America casting itself as the virtuous and Christian capitalist West over against the godless communist East. Understanding the blatant contradictions between American principle and reality that the Till case exposed to the world, former first lady Eleanor Roosevelt published an op-ed noting that, with this verdict, the United States had "again played into the hands of the communists and strengthened their propaganda in Africa and Asia."[45]

Nationwide, protests erupted on an unprecedented scale. On September 25, 1955, just two days after the verdict, an estimated total of more than one hundred thousand people attended rallies not just in Chicago, but also in Baltimore, Buffalo, Cleveland, Detroit, New York, New Rochelle, Philadelphia, and many other cities.[46] In Paris, American-born singer and dancer Josephine Baker—the first African American woman to appear in a major motion picture—organized a protest and delivered a petition with a thousand signatures to the American ambassador, charging that the verdict "consecrates the legality of lynching in the United States and insults the conscience of the civilized world."[47]

Till's lynching is widely recognized as a spark that helped ignite the modern civil rights movement. Although David Jackson's photo of Till's mutilated body in the open casket was generally not circulated in the white press, it made its way into the hands and homes of many Black Americans. After its first publication in *Jet*, it was quickly picked up by the *Chicago Defender* and other Black media outlets, helping to galvanize young Black activists across the country.[48]

Mississippi native and Student Nonviolent Coordinating Committee (SNCC) activist Joyce Ladner was twelve when she saw that photograph and read about Till's murder. She and others of her generation thought of themselves as what she called "the Emmett Till generation." "He was our age . . . here's a boy, and the feeling was if they could do that to him they could kill my brothers," she recalled thinking. "That was the image for our generation, to galvanize our generation, and all of us saw it."[49] The late congressman John Lewis, who was fifteen in 1955, wrote in his memoir that he was "shaken to the core" by Till's lynching.[50] When Rosa Parks refused to sit in the designated Black section in the rear of the bus in Montgomery, Alabama, just one hundred days after Till's murder, she said that she had him on her mind.[51]

CONFESSIONS

Even Bryant and Milam's bombshell admission to Till's murder—just four months after pleading "not guilty" and being acquitted—failed to generate a massive outcry for justice in white-dominated Mississippi. William Bradford Huie, a self-serving reporter known for engaging in questionable "checkbook journalism," saw in the verdict a twisted golden opportunity. He would publish an account centering the voices of Bryant and Milam, which the jury never got to hear.

He devised a scheme that would pay handsome dividends to the two acquitted men, their lawyers Breland and Whitten, a publisher—and himself. Protected by double jeopardy, legal agreements drawn up by their lawyers, and jointly paid $3,150 (roughly the average national annual income for men in 1955), Bryant and Milam agreed to allow Huie to publish their version of events, which included their confession of murdering Emmett Till.[52]

On January 10, 1956—just four months after the trial—*Look* magazine published the article, revealing the men as Emmett's killers.[53] In it, Milam incredulously claimed the brothers had initially only wanted to punish and scare Emmett, only later deciding to kill him after he remained defiant, even as he was being beaten. Among the many direct quotes attributed to Milam is this one, which contains in microcosm the twisted worldview of white southern justice, with its unflinching defense of the place of whites at the top of the social hierarchy:

Well, what else could we do? He was hopeless. I'm no bully; I never hurt a nigger in my life. I like niggers—in their place—I know how to work 'em. But I just decided it was time a few people got put on notice. As long as I live and can do anything about it, niggers are gonna stay in their place. Niggers ain't gonna vote where I live. If they did, they'd control the government. They ain't gonna go to school with my kids. And when a nigger gets close to mentioning sex with a white woman, he's tired o' livin'. I'm likely to kill him. Me and my folks fought for this country, and we've got some rights. I stood there in that shed and listened to that nigger throw that poison at me, and I just made up my mind. "Chicago boy," I said. "I'm tired of 'em sending your kind down here to stir up trouble. Goddam you, I'm going to make an example of you—just so everybody can know how me and my folks stand."[54]

In light of these revelations, the NAACP and others at the federal and state levels pressured the state to pursue at least the open kidnapping charges against the two men. But in Mississippi, the story produced little traction. Devery Anderson summarized its impact this way: "In the end, Huie's 'Shocking Story' only confirmed the fact that the two men got away with murder. It would not serve as a springboard for justice, and Mississippi officials never tried to prosecute the men again."[55]

The white press in Mississippi predictably denounced the *Look* story as an attempt to defame the state and the South. And most white residents of the Delta attempted to bury the story, just as they had sought to hastily entomb Till's body. For example, Elizabeth Spencer, a white Mississippi novelist, discovered, when she returned from a trip to Rome in late 1955, that Till had been killed near her father's farm. When she attempted to talk to her father, whose views on race she considered progressive, he flatly refused to engage the topic, asserting that "we [white people] had to keep things in hand." This response created a permanent rift between Spencer and her father, causing her ultimately to leave the state for New York.[56]

In the white Mississippi community, a curtain of silence quickly descended.

Chapter Three

COMMEMORATION AND REPAIR IN MISSISSIPPI

A DELTA WELCOME

"Can I help you?"

The polished southern drawl floated over my left shoulder as I stood in the Sumner, Mississippi, town square. It was a sunny June day, the heat already rising off the pavement at 9:00 a.m. I was taking a photograph of the Tallahatchie County Second District Courthouse, recently brought back from years of neglect and restored to its former genteel stateliness, as it appeared in newspapers around the world as the site of the infamous Emmett Till murder trial in 1955.

As I turned, a white late-model SUV slowed to a stop behind me with the passenger-side window down. Inside was an elderly gray-haired white gentleman, dressed in khaki pants and a crisp button-down oxford shirt.

"Good morning," I replied, leaning down and trying to seem less like the outsider he knew I was. "I'm Robby Jones, up from Jackson, and I'm just taking some pictures of the courthouse here. I'm a little early for a meeting with Jackson Webb."

There was a long, uncomfortable pause. "He's our mayor."

"Yes," I said. "I'm hoping to talk with him about the courthouse restoration. And what's your name?"

"I'm Frank Mitchener."

"Oh, I know who you are. I've been reading about the Emmett Till Memorial Commission and your involvement with that work. Pleased to meet you."

A nod. A long silence. I wondered what he was thinking.

"You be careful now." Another long pause. Then a slow half smile. "He might get you into some trouble." Yet another pause.

I became vividly aware that I was quelling my discomfort by reminding myself that I was basically of his tribe (white, male, and from Mississippi). But before I could muster a clever response to dispel the awkwardness, Mitchener broke the silence.

"Take care now," he said with a half-raised hand. The window whirled up, and the car slowly rolled out of the square.

FORGETTING

In the aftermath of the trial, the *New York Post* had written, "Like other great episodes in the battle for equality and justice, this trial has rocked the world, and nothing can ever be quite the same again— even in Mississippi."[1] This statement, however, was only partially true.

Back in the Delta, the status quo appeared relatively unshaken. After the national press reporters filed their stories following the Friday verdict, most packed up and headed back home. A few, such as John Popham from the *New York Times*, stuck around Sumner to gauge the local reaction. He was surprised to observe nothing out of the ordinary, save the trampled grass on the courthouse lawn. Saturday brought the typical groups of locals shopping in the one-block downtown. "Negroes and whites formed their customary separate groupings on the Court House Square under the shady oak trees hard by the Confederate monument."[2]

Emmett's story now belonged to the world. But as the modern civil rights movement took off after Rev. Dr. Martin Luther King Jr. organized the Montgomery Bus Boycott, the stage was broadened, and Emmett Till's legacy became one of many touchstones. Mamie Till-Mobley, once one of the biggest draws at NAACP events, had a falling-out with the organizational leadership and no longer appeared at events after 1956. As other events unfolded, and other actors emerged, Till's name was no longer an obligatory reference in newspaper stories about the movement or in speeches by movement leaders.

The story of Emmett Till was both present and absent at the massive 1963 March on Washington. Organizers intentionally picked the eighth anniversary of Till's death, August 28, to hold the event because of its symbolic power. But Till's name was not heard in the most famous speech from that day. A previous version of King's "I Have a Dream" speech, which he delivered in Detroit on June 23, 1963, was anchored by a reference to two Mississippi civil rights martyrs: "I have a dream this afternoon that we will no longer face the atrocities that Emmett Till had to face or Medgar Evers had to face, that all men can live with Dignity." But when King delivered his iconic speech at the Lincoln Memorial, the one that would be preserved and revisited for generations, he cut the references to Till and Evers. As historian Dave Tell noted, "Till is written out of the speech at the very moment it became a civil rights primer for generations of American grade school students."[3]

Emmett had changed everything. But just as a match that lights the kindling fades as the fire takes hold, Till's story became less known in the next generation.

By the time the thirtieth anniversary of Till's murder rolled around, few whites knew much about the case, and the memory of Emmett Till was beginning to fade even among some African Americans. Rich Samuels, a white reporter who grew up on the north side of Chicago, had never heard about the case when he met Mamie Till-Mobley at the funeral of a local high school coach who had been murdered. Intrigued and then inspired, he created *The Murder and the Movement*, a half-hour documentary. This first-of-its-kind treatment of the Till story aired July 11, 1985, on Chicago's NBC affiliate, WMAQ Channel 5. In addition to interviewing several of the central figures in the case who were still living, he talked with younger people in the Delta and Chicago areas, interactions that confirmed he was not alone in his ignorance of Till's story. The Sumner town clerk, who had lived in the area for more than a decade at the time, told Samuels she'd never heard anything about the case. "Emmett Till?" said one Black interviewee from Chicago. "I've never heard of him."[4]

In all, the thirtieth anniversary of Till's trial generated only modest media coverage. In addition to the Samuels documentary that aired locally in Chicago in July, the *Jackson Clarion-Ledger* and *Jackson Daily News* ran a joint Sunday edition recalling Till's death and trial in Mississippi. The only national media coverage was a three-minute segment on NBC's *Today* show, which featured Mamie Till-Mobley and Bill Minor, a Mississippi reporter who had covered the trial for the *New Orleans Times-Picayune*.[5]

There was one exception to the anemic media attention in the 1980s. In 1987, a remarkable documentary with an accompanying book, *Eyes on the Prize: America's Civil Rights Years*, provided a foothold for a renewal of Till's memory in the American public imagination. The film, viewed by an estimated five million people in its premiere run on PBS, anchored its storytelling with an opening fifteen-minute segment titled "Awakenings," which focused on Emmett Till. *Eyes on the Prize* won four Emmy Awards, a Peabody Award, the International Documentary Award, and the Television Critics Award.[6]

REMEMBERING EMMETT TILL IN THE DELTA

It is telling that the earliest public memorials dedicated to Emmett Till were not erected in Mississippi. The first public memorial appeared in 1976, just over two decades after his death—located neither in Chicago nor the South but in Denver, Colorado. The initial idea came from Herman Hamilton, a Denver-area bowling alley owner who was part of "the Emmett Till generation." He was nine years old when Till was killed, and he remained deeply shaped by the event. With support from the Martin Luther King Jr. Foundation and the Colorado Centennial-Bicentennial Commission, the city erected a twenty-foot statue in a local park depicting Dr. King standing with his arm around Emmett. In addition to the stirring imagery, the memorial drew attention to the short arc of eight years between Till's death on August 28, 1955, and King's "I Have a Dream" speech, given the same day in 1963.[7]

Emmett was honored again in a major monument on the plaza of the Southern Poverty Law Center's headquarters in Montgomery, Alabama, on November 5, 1989. His name is the third engraved on a beautiful, polished granite table, which is designed so that water continuously flows over the names of forty martyrs of the modern civil rights movement. The monument sits just two blocks from the site where Mississippian Jefferson Davis took the oath of office to become the president of the Confederacy. In her remarks at the monument's unveiling, Mamie noted her ongoing struggle to reject the white South's attempt to shrug off the death of her son as just *and never proven or alleged more than once and never* [handwritten marginal note]

another incident of white racial violence. But this monument, at this place, she declared, was proof to the world "that Emmett's death was *not* just one of those things."[8]

Finally, one of the most meaningful public memorials Mamie lived to see was unveiled on July 25, 1991, when the city of Chicago renamed a seven-mile section of Seventy-First Street as Emmett Till Road. Chicago mayor Richard M. Daley spoke, explaining that the new name "is to commemorate a victim of racial hatred that exists in America, even today."[9]

Yet, if you had driven through the Mississippi Delta during the 1980s or 1990s, you would have encountered no signs, no markers, and no memorials to Till. You could have enjoyed eighteen miles on the Henry Clarence Strider Memorial Highway, a section of Highway 32 that runs east–west between Webb and Charleston.[10] In Sumner, the Confederate monument still stood tall, but the infamous yet beautiful courthouse was suffering from a regrettable "modern" facelift it received in 1973—one that many speculated was designed to distance it from its past association with Till—that destroyed its architectural charm.[11]

Till's story was also nowhere to be found in Mississippi's public school textbooks or history curriculum, as I can personally attest. The 1980s were my high school and college years, all of which I spent in and near Jackson. I was an honors student, learning everything put in front of me in a Mississippi history course, a civics course that included state history, and various American history courses. I graduated first (co-valedictorian) in my 1986 class from Forest Hill High School, affiliated with the Jackson Public School System, which was integrated while I was in elementary school, and summa cum laude four years later at Mississippi College, just twenty minutes down the road from Jackson in Clinton. My brother's college roommate for two years—someone I saw quite often since they were randomly assigned the room next to mine in the men's dorm—was from Sumner.

In 1990, I was launched into the world with my high school diploma and college degree, equipped with the core knowledge that the state of Mississippi and the Southern Baptist Convention thought was essential for living a well-rounded and successful life. I had never heard the name Emmett Till.

Fifty years after Till's death and trial, the wall of silence about Mississippi's white violent resistance to civil rights began to crack. In 2005, the Mississippi legislature passed a bill renaming a section of US Route 49E between Leflore and Tallahatchie counties as the Emmett Till Memorial Highway.[12] True to the ever-present contradictions in Mississippi, the section of Highway 49E honoring Till intersects with the portion of Highway 32 honoring Clarence Strider in Webb, the small town nearest to Mamie Till-Mobley's birthplace.[13]

Nevertheless, the two roadside signs, which read simply EMMETT TILL MEMORIAL HIGHWAY, are notable as the first public markers to memorialize Emmett Till in Mississippi. But they were an awkward first step in the wake of half a century of silence. The signs themselves provide no historical context, and there was no deliberate process for preparing the local community for their installation. They lacked buy-in, particularly from local white residents, many of whom were unprepared for and annoyed by their sudden appearance on July 1, 2005, on one of the main north–south transportation arteries in Tallahatchie County.

But events were already in motion that would soon disrupt the relative silence about Emmett Till in the Delta. Following the passage of the 1965 Voting Rights Act, Black voters—for the first time since Reconstruction—once again began to register to vote in significant numbers. They began to elect Black officials, particularly in the Delta counties where the Black population significantly outnumbers the white population. In 1994, Jerome Little, along with Bobby Banks, became the first African American members elected to the Tallahatchie County Board of Supervisors. By 2005, Little—who grew up in a sharecropping family on the nearby Frank Mitchener Sr. plantation—became the first Black president of the board.

Little had personally experienced the silence of the Delta about its violent racial past. Despite spending his entire childhood in the county, he did not hear Emmett Till's story until he joined the Marines as a young adult and was stationed overseas. He was dumbstruck. From that point forward, he described his efforts to tell Till's story as "a calling." "Something was just in me," he said, to "make sure that everybody in this county, everybody in this state, and everybody in this nation understands what happened, why it happened."[14]

In his new leadership position, Little prioritized tackling two problems: shoring up the county's sputtering economy, where the unemployment rate stood at 9 percent, and publicly acknowledging the county's role in the miscarriage of justice at the Emmett Till trial. While his motives in memorializing Till were heartfelt and genuine, Little was also a savvy politician (in the best sense of that word) and understood that yoking these two priorities together would enhance public support for the project, particularly among the reticent local white community. In early 2006, Little began the work of forming the Emmett Till Memorial Commission (ETMC), with the twin goals of telling the truth about Emmett Till and securing funds to renovate the courthouse to return it to its 1955 appearance at the time of the trial, which he hoped would attract cultural tourism to Sumner.[15]

Little enlisted the help of eighty-five-year-old Betty Bobo Pearson to build out the committee. Pearson was an ideal and energetic bridge builder. She hailed from a prominent seven-generation planter family with deep familial and social ties to other influential white families in the county. The old Clarksdale High School, which served as an all-white public high school from 1930 to 1970 and an integrated school from 1971 to 1999, sat on land donated by the Bobo family that featured views of the Sunflower River to the east and a Bobo family cemetery on the main lawn. Despite her family's investment in the regimes of slavery and sharecropping, Betty was known for being a fiercely independent thinker and an unflinching advocate for civil rights.[16] Like many in the planter elite, she attended the University of Mississippi, where, to the chagrin of her family, she helped organize a 1942 strike among the African American women who worked in the university laundry. Her college paper "Why Schools Should Be Integrated" won her a full graduate scholarship to Columbia University. When her father declared that "no daughter of mine is going to live in New York City . . . in Yankee land," she drove to Memphis and joined the Marines.[17]

After the war, she returned to Tallahatchie County and attended all five days of Emmett Till's trial, where she was deeply disturbed at the overt racism she witnessed. Although they ultimately remained friends, she was so appalled by attorney John Whitten's racist defense strategy and closing argument that she refused to speak to him for six months after the trial.[18] Sykes Sturdivant, a founding committee member and also part of a multigenerational plantation family, told me in an interview that Pearson was "a force." He agreed to join the ETMC before he knew much about its mission simply because Pearson asked him to do it. "Happy to do it, Betty, anything you want," he recalled saying. "I'm on your side."[19]

When the Emmett Till Memorial Commission finally convened on January 4, 2006, on the second floor of the dilapidated Sumner courthouse, it welcomed eighteen members, nine Black and nine white. Pearson and Tutwiler mayor Robert Grayson, an African American who grew up as a sharecropper on a Delta plantation and was himself fourteen when Emmett Till was killed, were elected co-chairs of the committee.[20] In the Delta, the creation of such a body was itself an achievement. But it soon became clear that keeping people in the room as the work evolved would be a challenge. Differing motivations and goals immediately surfaced. The Black members were mostly interested in projects such as historical markers or a museum to memorialize Emmett Till, while the white members were mostly interested in restoring the courthouse. These competing perspectives, clearly running along racial lines, threatened the work of the committee before it even got going.

Fortunately, Little had also secured the participation of Susan Glisson, the executive director of the William Winter Institute for Racial Reconciliation, as an advisor and facilitator for the group. Glisson was well versed in the challenges of racial reconciliation work in Mississippi, particularly from her experience advising a multiracial group in Neshoba County that was reckoning with its connection with the murders of three civil rights workers during the summer of 1964. Glisson advised the committee that they would need to deal directly with the Till case, and the differing perspectives on it, before they could make much headway on concrete projects. At a meeting on June 20, 2006, the committee came to the consensus that its first job was simply to "acknowledge what happened."[21]

Steadied by deeper discussions held over a nine-month period and spurred by an unsuccessful 2007 attempt by state senator David Jordan to get the state to apologize for Emmett Till's murder and trial, the committee decided to pen its own apology on behalf of Tallahatchie County residents. But when the draft document hit the committee's docket, the racial fault lines again appeared. Frank Mitchener, the man who had greeted me that morning in the town square, balked. He argued that an apology would be admitting guilt, and that no one on the committee had committed the crime. He was so angry that he walked out of the meeting and drove home. As one of the most influential members of the committee, particularly among the white community, this was a problem.

Pearson reached out with no results, but she did get him to agree to talk with Glisson. Glisson drove to his house and spent several hours with him, mostly listening. His objections were typical in the white community. The crime wasn't even committed in Tallahatchie County. Sumner was merely the accidental home of the trial. We didn't kill anyone. While those objections were technically true, Glisson reiterated the bottom line before leaving a copy of the statement with him: "What is unfortunate is that the jury that convened was the official body that spoke for your county. No one has ever spoken up and said that they were wrong." Mitchener showed up two weeks later to the regularly scheduled meeting on May 9, 2007, and presented the committee with a revision. He had replaced the words *apology* and *apologize* with the words *regret* and *sorry*. He moved that the proclamation be adopted, and the committee unanimously approved it.[22]

At 10:00 a.m. on Tuesday, October 2, 2007, commission cochairs Betty Pearson and Robert Grayson stood together on the beautifully decorated stand erected in front of the courthouse and took turns reading the resolution.[23] It reads in part:

> We the citizens of Tallahatchie County believe that racial reconciliation begins with telling the truth. We call on the state of Mississippi, all of its citizens in every county, to begin an honest investigation into our history. While it will be painful, it is necessary to nurture reconciliation and to ensure justice for all. By recognizing the potential for division and violence in our own towns, we pledge to each other, black and white, to move forward together in healing the wounds of the past and in ensuring equal justice for all of our citizens. . . .
>
> We the citizens of Tallahatchie County recognize that the Emmett Till case was a terrible miscarriage of justice. We state candidly and with deep regret the failure to effectively pursue justice.
>
> We wish to say to the family of Emmett Till that we are profoundly sorry for what was done in this community to your loved one.

> We the citizens of Tallahatchie County acknowledge the horrific nature of this crime. Its legacy has haunted our community. We need to understand the system that encouraged these events and others like them to occur so that we can ensure that it never happens again. Working together, we have the power now to fulfill the promise of "liberty and justice for all."[24]

After Pearson finished reading, she stepped back while Simeon Wright, who had shared the bed with Emmett Till on the night of his abduction, came to the stage. Pearson reached out her hand. As he took it, the hot microphone picked up these ad-libbed words from Pearson: "We apologize."[25]

Wright collected himself and went on to deliver his prepared remarks. "I accept your apology. . . . We want to thank you all today for what you are doing here. You are doing what you could. If you could do more, you would."[26] The event received national press, and despite Mitchener's word parsing, most headlines read like NPR's: "County Apologizes to Emmett Till Family."[27] Mitchener raised no public objections; when asked about it, he replied, "If that's the way they want to describe it, it's ok with me."[28]

The presence of state and county officials—including former governor William Winter, state senator David Jordan, County Commissioner Bobby Banks, and Tallahatchie County sheriff William Brewer, among others—showed how far Mississippi had come. Squad cars escorted Till family members Wheeler Parker, Simeon Wright, Deborah Watts, and their families into town ahead of the event. More than four hundred people turned out for it. But the composition of the crowd also signaled the work still to be done; few of them were whites from the local area.[29]

At the conclusion of the ceremony, Jerome Little unveiled a modest new historical marker on the courthouse lawn—on the opposite corner from the Confederate monument—the first of a planned eight markers related to Emmett Till in the county. It contained carefully calibrated language, negotiated with the Mississippi Department of Archives and History. It notes that after "a five day trial held in this courthouse, an all-white jury acquitted two white men, Roy Bryant and J. W. Milam, of the murder [of Emmett Till]." It continues, "Till's murder, coupled with the trial and acquittal of these two men, drew international attention and galvanized the Civil Rights Movement in Mississippi and the nation."[30]

Looking back on that event a decade later, Patrick Weems, executive director of the Emmett Till Interpretive Center, described it as "powerful," noting that "for so long, the community had tried to ignore this." Weems marked that day as a new beginning, where the community was finally saying, "We want to create a new story, a new narrative, and while this will be a somber day, a remorseful day, we know this is necessary to have a brighter future."[31]

EMMETT TILL'S LEGACY IN THE DELTA TODAY

By the time I visited the Mississippi Delta in the summer of 2022, there had been an explosion of cultural memory work around the legacy of Emmett Till. Across the sixteen years since Little formed the Emmett Till Memorial Commission, these efforts have attracted more than $5 million in investments—a staggering amount for an impoverished and remote rural area. Little met an untimely death from cancer at the age of fifty-nine in 2011, and tragically didn't get to see the fruition of the work. But by 2014, Tallahatchie County had restored the courthouse in Sumner, transformed a defunct grocery store across the street into the Emmett Till Interpretive Center, built an Emmett Till walking trail, and—patterned after successful Delta blues cultural tourism efforts—created a "Civil Rights Driving Tour" featuring eight roadside markers at sites related to Till's story.[32]

Beyond these external results, the ETMC was still meeting, still working toward what Betty Pearson had identified as one of its most important goals: "the opportunity it gives us to develop a new kind of bi-racial community here."[33]

The efforts to restore the courthouse were a resounding success. The ETMC enlisted the well-respected Belinda Stewart architectural firm from nearby Eupora, which also served as the lead grant-writing arm of the commission. In the end, federal earmarks secured by Representative Bennie Thompson and Senator Thad Cochran, along with a $250,000 grant from the USDA, were enough to both restore the courthouse and build out the Emmett Till Interpretive Center across the street, which serves as a museum space memorializing Till and a community center incubating conversations and projects about racial justice today.

During my visit on a hot Tuesday in late June 2022, the Emmett Till Interpretive Center was bustling with an interracial group (approximately 90 percent Black, 10 percent white) of thirty local high school kids who were engaged in a two-week summer documentary film class. When they weren't inside learning about the state-of-the-art camera equipment provided by the ETIC and the craft of filmmaking, their tripods commanded positions all around the town square. They fanned out on the courthouse lawn and set up inside the empty courtroom, capturing footage for their final projects.

I couldn't help but think what a dramatic contrast this scene was from a typical one in 1950s Sumner. This interracial group expressed an unmistakable ownership of and comfort in the town's public space. They weren't huddled in segregated spaces and conversations. They were working side by side on shared projects. At the lunch break, they enthusiastically poured into the Sumner Grill, with two young African American men spontaneously joining me at my table.

The ETIC itself is set up as a multiuse space, with offices for staff and an open floor plan design with multiple rooms for meetings or classes. On the walls throughout are narrated scenes from the life and death of Emmett Till, along with press photos from the trial. It was generally well appointed with modest but functional furniture, embodying the authentic ambience of controlled chaos familiar to anyone who has spent time inside a working local nonprofit that runs community programs.

The courthouse renovations are affecting and meticulous. To get to the second-floor courtroom entrance, you take the original outdoor curving stairs on the left or the right, which deposit you in a small foyer. Opening a set of dark wooden double doors reveals the stately courtroom, well lit by matching banks of tall arched windows on either side. Most of the furnishings from the 1955 courtroom have been reproduced, down to two brass spittoons on the floor flanking the rear door. There is one notable exception to the faithfulness of the restoration—Sheriff Strider's segregated "Black press" table is missing from the back corner.

I had one surprise encounter at the courthouse that was an uncomfortable reminder of complicated racial dynamics in the Delta, even today. I had been told by Patrick Weems that court was not in session and that I was free to see the courtroom for myself. As promised, I found the courtroom open and deserted. As I was exploring the space, a young Black man entered. "Don't mind me, sir," he said. "I'm just cleaning up a bit." At first glance, seeing his Windex bottle and cleaning cloth, I thought nothing of it. But then I noticed his attire, the unmistakable broad horizontal green and white stripes issued to prisoners. My discomfort wasn't from being in the presence of someone who was incarcerated but from knowing the history of the brutal and exploitative convict leasing program in the state.

When I asked Sumner mayor Jackson Webb about the arrangement, his explanation sounded like something out of a twisted version of *The Andy Griffith Show*. Because the courthouse isn't staffed when out of session, and even being the mayor is a part-time job, they've arranged an awkward makeshift system for facilitating off-hours visitation with the local jail, which houses inmates who are serving time for minor offenses. "The inmate at the jail has the key," Webb explained. "So, you go to the jail, . . . they go get the inmate and ask him to open the courthouse."[34] Looked at one way, this system communicates trust in an incarcerated person, and light cleaning of an air-conditioned building is far from the backbreaking labor for which places like nearby Parchman Farm are infamous. But from another angle, in 2022, even at a site of civil rights commemoration, the state is benefiting from the labor of an incarcerated African American man who is required to be the keeper and cleaner of the courtroom where the lynchers of Emmett Till were exonerated.

Before I knew anything about the courthouse renovations, I had heard about vandalism of a commemorative sign in Tallahatchie County that was part of the ETMC's "Civil Rights Driving Tour." The final sign on the eight-stop tour is titled simply "River Site," and marks the place the ETMC and many locals believe Emmett Till's body was pulled from the water.[35] The marker was unveiled on October 2, 2007, and members of the Till family gathered at the confluence of the Tallahatchie River and Black Bayou for the ceremony. The site is the most remote on the tour, located due east of Glendora as the crow flies but accessible only by crossing the river on Sharkey Road and then driving 2.6 miles down a narrow dirt road running between a cornfield and the river. You don't arrive there by accident.

Just six months after the sign was installed, it disappeared, with tire tracks indicating it had likely been tossed into the Tallahatchie River. For many, the unmistakable message was devastating. Jessie Jaynes-Diming, the public relations officer for the ETMC, said it felt like a deliberate "reenactment" of the murder. "It seems they threw this sign into the river, just like the body of Emmett Till was thrown into the river."[36] At the time, Little blamed local whites and was adamant in his response: "I want to make sure that whoever did this knows that this sign is going back up. Every time it's taken down, it's going back up."[37] The commission immediately replaced the sign. But by the spring of 2013, the sign had been riddled with bullet holes, and the commission was slow in putting up a third one.

In October 2016, New York University film student Kevin Wilson Jr. was visiting the Delta working on a film about Till when he came across the desecrated sign. He posted a photo on Facebook that went viral, and soon there were stories in the *New York Times*, the *Washington Post*, and scores of other outlets. In the wake of a national outcry to replace the sign, the Brooklyn-based Lite Brite Neon offered to manufacture and ship a replacement sign to the county free of charge, which would have a new feature: it would be bulletproof.

By the time I visited the site in 2022, the bullet-ridden sign had been placed on display in Washington, DC, at the recently opened National Museum of African American History and Culture. The new sign in Mississippi, with a highly reflective hardened background, stood tall and unblemished, like a sentinel guarding the path to the site. Importantly, though, the ETMC chose not to erase the evidence of its troubled past. A record is now preserved in the impenetrable sign itself: "Signs erected here have been stolen, thrown into the river, replaced, shot, removed, replaced, and shot again. The history of vandalism and activism centered on this site led ETMC founder Jerome Little to observe that Graball Landing was both a beacon of racial progress and a trenchant reminder of the progress yet to be made."[38]

Sixteen years after it was founded, the ETMC is still working to secure Emmett Till's memory as a foundation for thinking about the racial justice work that remains to be done today. On Thursday, June 23, 2022, I attended the noon meeting of the ETMC, held just outside Sumner at the Bayou Bend Country Club.[39] After a buffet lunch of fried chicken, potatoes, and green beans that was catered by the Sumner Grill (which itself opened after the renovation of the courthouse and opening of the ETIC brought more people into the town square), the ETMC meeting was called to order by Patrick Weems. Before getting to the official business, Susan Glisson, still facilitating and advising, led commission members in an exercise to ground their thoughts in the purpose of the work, asking everyone to write down what they hoped their grandchildren would say about their efforts. Belinda Stewart, head of the architectural firm that oversaw the Sumner courthouse restorations, also reminded commission members of three interconnected nodes of their work: confronting truth, promoting healing, and channeling emotion and energy in service to the community.

The first item of business was the consideration of plans to create an enhanced visitor experience at the remote and overgrown Graball Landing site. The site is indeed in need of attention. With the sign vandalism resolved, at least for the present, the site is one of the most moving but one of the most difficult to reach on the driving tour. On my visit, I felt fortunate that ETMC member Jessie Jaynes-Diming had agreed to guide me personally to the site. Even when I emerged from the car, assured by a large gleaming sign I had arrived, it took a moment to find the trail. After I had followed her over tire ruts and stepped over weeds for about thirty yards, the river finally appeared. We stood silently, taking it in. The remarkable quiet on this muggy afternoon was broken only by the periodic jumping of fish. The only evidence other visitors had found their way to this spot was a single red rose left near the roots of a cottonwood tree that reaches out from the bank over the flowing muddy water.

The commission rightly understood that even those determined to see the site might think they were lost or feel unsafe venturing down an unmarked trail, even during the day. They also understood that there was something powerful, sacred even, about this site, where young Emmett Till's battered body was recovered from the waters, starting its journey back to his mother. Stewart and her team presented several options for developing the small clearing into a more accessible place, including plans for a walking trail and platforms that would allow visitors to easily touch the water. After the presentation, Jaynes-Diming was visibly moved. Wiping away tears, she said, "It's beautiful, just to see it. Things have been so tumultuous there at that site. It will bring some healing."

The second agenda item for the meeting was the creation of a new Emmett and Mamie Till-Mobley National Historic Park, which the commission has come to see as the culmination of their work. In March 2021, the Emmett Till Interpretive Center, in partnership with the Till family, launched a campaign to support the creation of this national historic park, consisting of multiple sites across the Mississippi Delta and Chicago.[40] The effort has also received the support of the National Parks Conservation Association, a hundred-year-old national advocacy group that works to protect existing national parks and lobby for new ones. At the time of this writing in July 2022, the NPCA is actively working with the ETMC to "create a new park site that will ensure that the tragic death of Emmett Till and the strength and resolve of his mother, Mamie Till-Mobley, are never forgotten."[41]

In an interview with me, Alan Spears, senior director for cultural resources at NPCA, explained that they are particularly committed to helping the national park system tell the full American story, especially where we need to "relearn an appropriate American history" that is more inclusive and honest. The Till story is important, he explained, because we have to face the uncomfortable parts of our history "if we have any hope of moving forward together."[42] The creation of a national park would permanently secure both the economic and cultural goals that guided Jerome Little's initial vision: to tell the truth about Emmett Till in order to promote racial healing and justice and build a better economic future for the community.

As the ETMC meeting closed, Susan Glisson stood before the group with an offering. During our two hours together, Glisson had been carefully listening to the group conversation and taking notes, which she had spontaneously transformed into a poem. She described it as "a demos found poem by community leaders of Tallahatchie County"—"demos" denoting its origins in a civic body; "found poem" indicating a genre of poetry that is composed by using existing words or phrases from outside sources. It beautifully captures the spirit of this group that has been working, for nearly two decades, to tell the truth about Emmett Till and to promote racial justice and healing in their community. With Glisson's permission, I've included it below in full.

What We Can't Yet See but Still Believe

I.

The ground is liquid.
Impermanent. Precarious.
But my great-grandfather fought for us to have rights to the water.

They tried to hide Emmett in the river. They thought he'd never be found.
But the Tallahatchie keeps on moving.

My grandfather inspired Jerome Little to fight.
Is this enough?

II.

I want my grandchildren to say, "I can't believe people used to be so little. So little in empathy, so detached from reality, so unwilling to be humane and human."

It seemed like it couldn't change. But the ground is liquid. It changes.
The river couldn't hide Emmett.
It reflects a journey that needed to be taken.

I want my grandchildren to say, "They got tired of all the fighting and violence and meanness. They woke up one day and said, 'No more.'"

The current changed. The water moved.
They said, "We can be better."
They put a stake in the ground. They said, "We will go through this so our grandchildren don't have to."

III.
They went on a journey. They weren't superheroes.
In fact, they were just a few.

But they began to open a few eyes.
They changed a few perspectives.

Sometimes, you can only see the tops of things.
But radical imagination can show us what's not easy to see, can change the tide, can build a future in this place. Imagination lets us smell the flowers in the seeds we plant.

Even the white people in their white churches finally saw themselves as part of a movement.

What if we cross? What if we make a connection?

They told the stories. They listened.
The current changed. The water moved.

Though they were few, they represented many. And the many became a chain of hearts as long as the river.
And they formed a family across time and across hate and fear.
A healed community came from hard work.

What had been desecrated and a place of fear became a place of honor and love.

They will say, "My family did that." They will say, "We stood and endured." They will say, "The river changes but eventually it goes to the ocean." They will say, "The river can obscure but it can also cleanse."

They will say, "Hate seemed permanent. Fear seemed forever. But we learned the ground is liquid, and, together, we decide where we stand." And now, they will say, "We stand as one. We made the trail better than we found it.

And we will hold this ground."[43]

CONTRADICTIONS AND REACTIONS

The power of a beginning is especially important for how it influences stories about our national identity and the racial and ethnic conflicts that have marked it. To understand Emmett Till's story, do we begin—as the civil rights tourism trail does—in Money, Mississippi, where he allegedly whistled at a young white woman working at a small grocery store, a setting that foregrounds an act of teenage transgression of the South's rigid, hierarchical racial behavior codes? Do we begin the story in Chicago, with a nervous Mamie Till warning her son about the dangers of interacting with white people in the South? Do we start the story with the racially violent environment that spurred Emmett's grandparents, along with countless other Black Americans, to flee Mississippi to find safer and better fortunes in Chicago as part of the Great Migration? Or do we push upstream even farther, to the disenfranchisement and forced removal of Native

Americans from Mississippi to Oklahoma on the Trail of Tears, which allowed land to be seized by the US government and created the opportunity for whites to own the land and bring enslaved labor to clear and cultivate it?

Efforts to memorialize Emmett Till and to tell the truth in the Delta remain a work in progress. Such efforts have indeed cleared important ground and helped drain some of the festering backwaters of white supremacy. There is a sense of movement, but the path of racial healing and justice, like the Tallahatchie River, is meandering. The contradictions of the Delta, with its stark economic and racial divides, remain. In Tallahatchie County, the poverty rate of Blacks is nearly three times that of whites (35 percent versus 13 percent); eight of the county's nine remaining Native American residents live below the poverty line. Statewide, the poverty rate for Black residents (31 percent) and Native American residents (34 percent) is more than twice that of white residents (12 percent). Mississippi has the distinction of being the state with the second-highest poverty rate for both Black and Native Americans in the country.[44]

Even as the cultural work of telling the truth about Mississippi's white supremacist past has gained traction in such unlikely places as Neshoba and Tallahatchie counties, many of Mississippi's white Republican and Christian leaders have joined a reactionary backlash. On March 14, 2022, for example, Governor Tate Reeves—who paradoxically also signed the 2021 law expunging the Confederate battle flag from the state flag—signed into law a bill purporting to ban the teaching of "critical race theory."[45]

Given that there is no evidence that anything resembling critical race theory—a decades-old body of scholarship that appears mostly on law school syllabi—was being taught in state primary and secondary public schools, the law achieved nothing. But it allowed Reeves to grandstand on a Facebook video, where he described its real purpose with language that eerily echoes the rhetoric of Mississippi apologists following the Till trial:

> Across this great country we are seeing a full court press by a vocal minority of well-organized and well-funded activists who seek to tear down the unity that has helped make our country great. . . . Children are dragged to the front of the classroom and are coerced to declare themselves as oppressors, taught that they should feel guilty because of the color of their skin, or that they are inherently a victim because of their race. . . . Today, Mississippi is taking another step toward ensuring our kids receive the unbiased and impartial education they need to reach their full potential as individuals, not as liberal operatives. . . . This is a good day for educational truth in Mississippi.[46]

After pausing during the video to sign the bill into law, Reeves's demeanor shifts. His remarks take an aggressively defensive turn, as he positions himself as the protector of Mississippi and southern values against outside critics. He claims that the bill in no way limits the teaching of slavery or the civil rights movement. But he nonetheless predicts that "Mississippi will become subjected to an onslaught of insults; there will be false assertions that our state is racist." Reeves's final remarks are defiant: "We're not backing down. . . . So, to those looking to tear us down, you do what you gotta do. Because at the end of the day, Mississippi will do what's right."[47]

Despite the generic and vague language in these bills, they are, as Reeves's speech makes clear, driven by a desperate desire to shield white children and white parents from any sense of collective acknowledgment of centuries of oppression and disenfranchisement of Native peoples and African Americans, and the current consequences of these actions, by their ancestors. If we're not explicitly racist toward people in the present, the logic goes, then we're all good. The past is the past, never mind its obvious effects on the present. Nothing to see here. Neither those historical actions nor their present consequences are of moral concern to us today.

By contrast, attention to structural racism, not just to racist acts by individuals, has been one of the most important insights from the community work on the ground in Mississippi. Tallahatchie's 2007 public apology insisted on the need to understand the underlying systems that created the conditions for Till's death. Two years before that statement, a biracial coalition working in Neshoba County also specifically noted the problem of systemic racism—even casting it in the Christian vocabulary of "sin"—in a statement following the 2005 indictment of Edgar Ray Killen for the murder of three civil rights workers during Freedom Summer in 1964: "Today we have a cause for hope because our community came together to acknowledge its sin. . . . We must understand the system that encourages it to happen so we can dismantle it. We must never allow it to happen again. We have the power now to fulfill the promise of democracy."[48]

CHRISTIANITY AND DEMOCRACY IN MISSISSIPPI

Governor Reeves's defensive speech is a reminder that any lens that brings into focus the powerful flow of the past into the present is a fundamental threat to those southern whites who so desperately want and need to see themselves as good Christians and benevolent people while living amid the ruins of centuries-long oppression. As I demonstrated in *White Too Long*, white theology developed, by design, a strong sense of individualism that circumscribed the realm of moral responsibility to personal relationships and interactions. This willful myopia allowed many white Christians to believe themselves faithful disciples, while supporting slavery, Jim Crow, and segregation. Many supported these systems passively, but some were willing to respond aggressively, and others even violently, in their defense. In the Delta, this religious worldview fit hand in glove with planter culture. As historian Dave Tell noted, "At the heart of the 'river planter myth' is the ability to think of oneself as racially tolerant while remaining fully committed to white supremacy. . . . Because racial progress was coded as individual kindness it could coexist with widely documented systematic racism."[49]

Indeed, one of the most disturbing lessons I've taken away from this deep dive into the troubled history of my home state is how deeply committed white Christian Mississippians are to the principles embedded in the Doctrine of Discovery. Rather than generating sturdy moral principles that challenge white supremacy, in the hands of white Mississippians, Christianity has, more often than not, been deployed in its service.

Any honest reading of the history of the white population in Mississippi reveals that its commitment to democracy has been largely instrumental, a marriage of convenience that was easily annulled when it stopped serving white interests. White Mississippians have mostly loved democracy—or more accurately, the veneer of democracy—on those days when they could use it to ensure a self-serving outcome: the era prior to the Civil War and the nine decades between 1875 and 1965, the period they called "Redemption" (even the term betrays their allegiances here). It took the Voting Rights Act of 1965, passed a century after the end of the Civil War, and federal court oversight of its implementation to force white southerners to reluctantly accept the most basic principle of democracy, that every citizen's vote should be counted equally. Even now, we see renewed efforts among white Republicans across the South to cast aside democratic principles—using old tactics and new schemes so transparent as to have been unimaginable just a few years ago—to achieve their goal of reestablishing what today can only accurately be described as white minority rule.

Christianity, as practiced by white Mississippians, has also proven to be more pliant than principled. It has been too often anchored in a self-serving emotional experience that is untethered from morality and justice. A twenty-six-year-old Rev. Dr. Martin Luther King Jr. reflected on this grim reality in a sermon he delivered at Dexter Memorial Baptist Church in Montgomery, Alabama, on September 25, 1955, the Sunday after the Emmett Till trial:

> The white men who lynch Negroes worship Christ. That jury in Mississippi, which a few days ago in the Emmett Till case, freed two white men from what might be considered one of the most brutal and inhuman crimes of the twentieth century, worships Christ. The perpetrators of many of the greatest evils in our society worship Christ. This trouble is that all people, like the Pharisee, go to church regularly, they pay their tithes and offerings, and observe religiously the various ceremonial requirements. The trouble with these people, however, is that they worship Christ emotionally and not morally. They cast his ethical and moral insights behind the gushing smoke of emotional adoration and ceremonial piety.[50]

The religious attachments of many of the white men who either killed Till or defended those responsible by fanning the flames of bigotry validate King's indictment. In the infamous *Look* article, Huie summarizes Roy and Carolyn Bryant's social life as consisting chiefly of "visits to their families, to the Baptist church, and when they can afford it, to the drive-in."[51] At least four of the five defense attorneys who volunteered to represent Bryant and Milam were active members of local churches. John W. Whitten Jr. was an active member of Sumner Presbyterian Church. Sidney Carlton served as a member of the board of stewards at the Webb-Sumner Methodist Church. J. W. Kellum had two sons who became Baptist ministers and presided at his funeral, held at First Baptist Church in Tutwiler. Finally, Harvey Henderson was a Sunday school teacher and superintendent at Sumner's Episcopal Church of the Advent.[52] Till's killers saw no contradiction between their Christian values and the violence they unleashed on his fourteen-year-old body. And the Christian consciences of Bryant and Milam's defense team were untroubled, even as they knowingly appealed to the basest racial animus of the white jury, most of whom were also likely Christian.

But there are also religious connections and attachments among the founding white members of the ETMC. Most notably, Betty Pearson was deeply motivated by her religious views. At the time of Till's trial, she shared the pews with John Whitten at Sumner Presbyterian Church, and in 1958, she and her husband, Bill, were founding members of the Episcopal Church of the Advent, where Henderson oversaw the Sunday school program.[53] Pearson became very active in the Episcopal Church at the local, state, and national levels, and was a force for pushing the church to be more active on civil rights and integration, both outside and inside the church.

Sykes Sturdivant, another founding member of the ETMC, was also a longtime member and former president of the board of trustees of a local Methodist church. He ultimately left the church because of its unwillingness to fully accept LGBTQ people as members and clergy. "And how, how do you not love somebody?" he asked me rhetorically in an interview. "But in the Methodist Church, you can't, if you're gay, you can't preach. . . . So that's discrimination. I just don't believe in discrimination at all. So it's very difficult for me."[54] For Pearson, Sturdivant, and many other white members of the ETMC, Christianity demanded love for all people and the rejection of discrimination in all its forms.

In the shadow of the Trail of Tears and the murder of Emmett Till, what shall we make of the impotence of Christianity as a moral foundation of American democracy? I believe we have little choice but to acknowledge that, thus far, it has failed to defeat the forces of white supremacy. Worse, it has been pressed into its service.

Writing one year after the Emmett Till trial, with the Eisenhower administration remaining unwilling to take a clear stand on civil rights, the hard-hitting independent journalist I. F. Stone wrote these prescient lines: "The South must become either truly democratic or the base of a new racist and Fascist movement which could threaten the whole country and its institutions."[55] Ten years ago, I might have been lulled into believing we had made it past such desperate times. But recent events have revealed that we must reorient ourselves. To understand who and where we are, we need our "in the beginning" to start much earlier.

Telling Till's story has most often been understood as important because it establishes an honest place to stand and see something better on the horizon. That process of truth-telling is vital for healing and for any viable future we might yet have together as a multiracial, pluralistic democracy. But if we are to fully understand the significance of Till's life, we can't miss the other thing this hard-won ground also allows us to see: the lingering power of centuries-old settler colonial values that first brought Europeans to the Delta; that justified the murder and exile of Indigenous peoples; that attracted planters who enslaved Africans; that produced white men who felt justified extinguishing a fourteen-year-old boy's life. This Christian doctrine spawned the moral monsters, as James Baldwin so unnervingly put it, who would be capable of going on with their ordinary lives amid such barbarity and injustice.

Coda: Repatriation

The remains of 403 people from disturbed graves.
Eighty-three stolen items buried with them.

These were the findings made public on January 22, 2021, by the Mississippi Department of Archives and History (MDAH) after a three-year comprehensive inventory of the state agency's holdings. The full notice, in the bureaucratic language of federal reporting, reads:

> Notice is here given in accordance with the Native American Graves Protection and Repatriation Act (NAGPRA), 25 U.S.C. 3003, of the completion of an inventory of human remains and associated funerary objects under the control of the Mississippi Department of Archives and History, Jackson, MS. The human remains and associated funerary objects were removed from the region of Mississippi north of the Yazoo and Yalobusha Rivers including DeSoto, Clay, Lafayette, Monroe, Panola, Pontotoc, Quitman, Tate, Tunica, Union, and Webster counties.[56]

One couple was buried together with wolf's teeth and turtle shells. Other people were buried with everyday items such as bone awls and needles, stone-cutting tools, and ceramic vessels. Some bodies were adorned with jewelry made of clay and glass beads, or with a gorget, a decorative ceremonial item made of shells that covered the throat of the deceased. A few graves held two occupants together even in death: a mother with her baby, and a man with his faithful dog.[57] In a press release announcing the repatriation, MDAH director of archeology collections Meg Cook emphasized the necessity of re-covering the humanity of the objects: "It is important to remember that these are people, buried with items with strong cultural ties to their communities, the same way that people today might be laid to rest wearing a wedding band," she explained. "While these artifacts inform the archaeological record, it is our ethical and legal obligation to see that they are returned."

The largest single originating site of these disinterred human remains with their personal items were from Tunica County in northwest Mississippi, located along the Mississippi River due north of Tallahatchie County and adjacent to the southwest corner of DeSoto County. From that single county, beginning in 1966, MDAH received the remains of 216 people and more than fifty personal items. Most of the items were donated to MDAH by private individuals beginning in the 1960s, during a time when farms were expanding, particularly in the Mississippi Delta.

The treatment of the items as objects to be studied and displayed, rather than as human remains to be treated with dignity and respect, reflects the dominant attitudes of most white Mississippians up until the very recent past. Melanie O'Brien, national program manager for the Native American Graves Protection and Repatriation Act (NAGPRA), described the trauma many Indigenous people experienced because of the desecration of Native American burial sites: "There are stories of excavations that occurred in the 1960s or '70s where tribal communities would watch as archeologists would excavate their ancestors, their grandmothers and grandfathers." For most white archeologists, Native bones held no more sanctity than a shard of pottery.

But in 1990, after years of advocacy by Native American nations and the American Indian Movement, President George H. W. Bush signed NAGPRA. The new law required federally funded institutions like museums and schools to return human remains and other sacred items to their Native American, Alaska Native, and Native Hawaiian descendants. Suzan Shown Harjo (Cheyenne and Hodulgee Muscogee), who led the national campaign for the cultural and human rights repatriation laws and received the Presidential Medal of Freedom from President Barack Obama in 2014, told Native News Online that the 1990 repatriation laws have also done important cultural work, most notably by changing "the focus from collectors' property rights to Native American human rights."[58]

In March 2021, MDAH announced that it had turned over the remains of all 403 people, along with the eighty-three objects buried with them, to the Chickasaw Nation, since they were disinterred from areas that were historically part of their lands. The transfer was the first action of this type in Mississippi history.[59] Amber Hood, director of historic preservation and repatriation for the Chickasaw Nation, reminded Mississippians of their shared humanity in a press release issued by MDAH. "We see the repatriation process as an act of love," noted Hood. "These are our grandmothers, grandfathers, aunts, uncles and cousins from long ago."[60]

Extensive consultations with Chickasaw tribal leaders shaped the work by MDAH staff. Above the door leading to the room where the remains were stored at MDAH, the preparation team placed a sign that read, "This is a reverent space. Please respect the individuals that are resting here." When Chickasaw tribal leaders advised MDAH staff that they wished the remains and related personal objects to be returned in muslin bags, which would biodegrade when reburied, dozens of MDAH volunteers—in lockdown because of the COVID-19 pandemic—hand-sewed the bags at home.[61] These volunteers would never see the items themselves, but they understood their labor to be part of a sacred task not only to help lay these individuals to rest but also to facilitate healing between white Mississippians and the state's Indigenous people.

Because of security concerns, the reinterment ceremonies were not public. We know neither what the ceremonies looked like nor the precise location where the remains and objects were buried. But we do know that after six decades of desecration and disrespect, the ancestors of the Chickasaw Nation were embraced once more, in graves dug by their descendants, by the soil of their ancestral land.[62]

PART TWO

DULUTH

Chapter Four

BEFORE MINNESOTA

We were ready to defend the land
And the people against those
Who wanted what was not theirs to take.
We were called heathen
But who is heathen *here?*

—"Mama and Papa Have the Going Home Shiprock Blues,"
Joy Harjo, performer and writer of the Muscogee (Creek) Nation
and poet laureate of the United States[1]

THREE HUNDRED EIGHTY-SIX YEARS BEFORE THE
LYNCHINGS IN DULUTH

The headwaters of the Mississippi River are in Minnesota, approximately two thousand miles north of where the mighty river enriches the Mississippi Delta. Like Mississippi, Minnesotans have strong connections to the water. The state is known as the "Land of 10,000 Lakes." Lake Superior bites into its northeast boundary, and to the

117

south, the twin cities of St. Paul and Minneapolis sit at the confluence of the Minnesota and Mississippi Rivers.

According to archeological evidence, the first Indigenous people arrived in this area about twelve thousand years ago, hunting large game, including mastodons at the end of the last ice age. As the weather warmed around 7,000 BCE, Indigenous people enjoyed more plentiful foods and hunted a wide variety of game with weapons tipped both with stones and copper mined in the Great Lakes area. Approximately 2,500 years ago, the Woodland mound-building cultures emerged, which were characterized by established village sites, the creation of pottery, and agricultural production of corn, squash, and beans.[2]

Before European contact in the sixteenth century, the largest group of Indigenous people in the northern and central portion of what is now Minnesota were the Dakota. Western archeologists believe they are likely descended from the Psinomani people, who in turn descended from the Woodland people.[3] Dakota origin stories describe their continual presence on these lands after descending from the stars eons ago. During this period, northern Minnesota was also home to two smaller neighboring tribes, the Assiniboine and the Cree. In the seventeenth century, the Ojibwe arrived in the area, concluding a centuries-long gradual migration westward from what is now southeastern Ontario. The Dakota welcomed the Ojibwe and created an alliance in 1679 that lasted nearly six decades, until a conflict with the French in 1736 placed them on opposite sides. The groups remained in conflict up through the mass arrival of European immigrants in the mid-1800s, which united them in common cause for survival amid the incursion.[4]

European claims to the land that is now Minnesota (a Dakota term meaning "sky-tinted water") date back to 1534, when French explorer Jacques Cartier arrived on the upper east coast of North America, following the St. Lawrence River inland. He had been commissioned by King Francis I to search for new lands that might contain "a great quantity of gold and other precious things" and to search for the fabled Northwest Passage, which would provide an efficient trade route to the riches of China and the Far East. After anchoring in Gaspé Bay, Cartier and his crew encountered and traded goods with the local Huron-Iroquois people who were fishing along the river. In his journal, Cartier remarked multiple times on what he perceived as their nakedness, declaring that "these people may well be called savages, because they are the poorest folks they may be in the world." He concluded that "they are to a marvelous degree thieves of all that they can steal," but also that "these people would be easy to convert to our holy faith."[5]

On July 24, 1534, Cartier performed the ceremony that secured France's rights of preemption, under the authority of the Doctrine of Discovery, to what ultimately became Nouvelle-France, a vast tract of land stretching from the mouth of the St. Lawrence River to the Great Lakes and following the Mississippi River down to its terminus with the Gulf of Mexico at New Orleans. He recorded a detailed account of that discovery ritual, which both puzzled and angered the local people, in his journal:

> We caused a cross to be made thirty feet in height, which was made before a number of them on the point at the entrance of the said harbor, on the crossbar of which we put a shield embossed with three *fleurs-de-lis*, and above where it was an inscription graven in wood in letters of large form, "*VIVE LE ROY DE FRANCE.*" And this cross we planted on the said point before them, the which they beheld us make and plant; and after it was raised in the air we all fell on our knees, with hands joined, while adoring it before them, and made them signs, looking up and showing them the sky, that by it was our redemption, for which they showed much admiration, turning and beholding the cross.[6]

But Cartier also records, in the very next paragraph of the journal, that the local Indigenous leader, Chief Donnacona, and a group of four others, including his two sons Domagaya and Taignoagny, immediately paddled their canoes out to the French ship, complaining loudly about the erection of this unsanctioned icon. According to Cartier, Donnacona made "a long harangue, showing us the said cross and making the sign of the cross with two fingers, and then showed us the country all about us, as if he had wished to say that all the country was his, and that we should not plant the said cross without his leave."[7]

In response, Cartier held out a metal hatchet as if it were a gift, but when Donnacona pulled alongside the ship to receive it, the crew forced the entire party aboard. Cartier offered them a meal on the ship and gave the chief's sons fine European clothing, placing copper chains around their necks. By Cartier's account, he persuaded Donnacona to let his two sons remain on board and continue with him on the journey, promising to bring them back the following year with valuable wares. Before leaving, Cartier gave Chief Donnacona and the two others gifts of a hatchet and three knives each. On July 25, Cartier recorded that "the wind came right and we got under way from the harbor."[8]

Upon returning to France, along with other treasures from the newly "discovered" lands, Cartier presented Domagaya and Taignoagny to the king as representatives of the "Asian" people he had encountered on the journey.[9] Cartier kept his initial promise and returned in 1535 with Domagaya and Taignoagny, who had now learned French and become valuable interpreters. But in 1536, Cartier determined that they and their clan had become an obstacle to his power in the area. Acting with the impunity that often flowed from the conviction of Euro-Christian superiority, Cartier betrayed their trust. He abducted Chief Donnacona along with his sons and exiled them to France, where they died two years later.[10]

By the early 1600s, French fur traders and explorers had reached the Great Lakes area, with a hunger for valuable beaver pelts to feed the European hat trade and faint hopes that the "great river" might yet lead them to the Northwest Passage. In 1670, Daniel Greysolon, Sieur du Lhut (from which the city of Duluth derives its name), an ambitious French nobleman and commander of French troops in Montreal, traveled west with seven Frenchmen and three enslaved Native Americans. The party reached the far western tip of Lake Superior, where he encountered and traded with the Dakota people. Upon reaching their primary village, Greysolon raised the French standard, claiming the Dakota lands for King Louis XIV and France, an act that was largely lost on the Dakota but that secured their discovery rights, via the Doctrine of Discovery, vis-à-vis the British, who were also exploring the area. On June 17, 1673, Louis Joliet and Father Jacques Marquette, a French explorer and a Catholic priest and missionary, respectively, became the first documented Europeans to reach the upper Mississippi River.[11]

Over the next nine decades, European competition and conflict in North America erupted into a series of conflicts known in the US as the French and Indian War. In the 1763 Treaty of Paris, the French ceded their claims (relative to other European powers) east of the Mississippi River to England and most claims west of the river to Spain. The British territory was in turn relinquished just two decades later to the United States of America at the 1783 Treaty of Paris, which ended the Revolutionary War, giving the fledgling nation control of significant territory to their west, including the portion of Minnesota east of the Mississippi River. By 1800 Napoleon had regained control of the Louisiana Territory from Spain, and in 1803 President Thomas Jefferson agreed to acquire this land claim from France for $15 million. With the stroke of a pen, this agreement doubled the territorial claims of the United States, adding the portion of southwest Minnesota that lies west of the Mississippi River.

While the Louisiana Purchase is often taught in American history courses as one of the great real estate bargains in world history (the price worked out to less than four cents per acre), this conclusion relies on a critical misunderstanding about the nature of the transaction. The vast territory under consideration wasn't under the control of the French government or colonists. Rather, it remained—as it had been for thousands of years—the homeland of various Native American nations who were mostly oblivious to the transatlantic dealmaking. In short, the vaunted Louisiana Purchase didn't secure a legal title to a bounded section of earth. Rather, it codified a transfer, from France to the United States, of the right to assert dominion over Native peoples in that area without interference or competition from other European powers. What the United States purchased from France, in the language of the Doctrine of Discovery, was not property but the right to "preemption," the "exclusive authority to obtain Indian title by conquest or contract" within agreed-upon geographic boundaries.[12]

WHITE INCURSION AND DAKOTA DISENFRANCHISEMENT

Even after the area that became Minnesota was officially declared open for white occupation at the turn of the nineteenth century, the arrival of whites in the first few decades was more a trickle than a flood. When Minnesota was organized into an official territory by Congress in 1849, Alexander Ramsey, the newly appointed territorial governor and superintendent of Indian Affairs, found a military presence at Fort Snelling (founded 1819) but no capital city. Apart from a handful of fur traders and Christian missionaries, there were also virtually no European people to govern among the approximately ten thousand Native Americans and small groups of intermarried Anglo- and Franco-Indian families.

Ramsey did find one important ally in Henry Sibley, head of the American Fur Company and the most powerful and connected man in the new territory. Even though Sibley was a Democrat and Ramsey was a member of the newly formed Republican Party, the men found common ground on one shared priority: wresting control of the Dakota people's homeland from them, thereby preparing the way for the coming white incursion.[13]

With the decline of the fur trade due to decreased demand, diminishment of the local game population due to overhunting, and decimation by diseases introduced by Europeans, Native Americans in the Minnesota Territory were suffering. Sensing an opportunity, Ramsey and Sibley began laying the groundwork for a deal: land in exchange for immediate assistance and long-term monetary payments. They coordinated an agreement with Dakota leaders that was, on paper, one of the most generous terms ever offered by the US government for Native American land. In the Treaty of Traverse des Sioux and the Treaty of Mendota, both signed in 1851, Dakota leaders ceded approximately 24 million acres of their homeland to the US government. In return, they agreed to relocate to a strip of land ten miles wide on either side of the upper Minnesota River extending one hundred miles north and south, and to receive a combined compensation of $2,770,000, which was to be kept at 5 percent interest and paid out yearly for agricultural development and cash annuities. Additionally, there was $490,000 earmarked for relocation assistance and $65,000 allocated for immediate aid and education.[14]

But the promises in the treaties were immediately broken. The US Senate did ratify the Treaty of Traverse des Sioux, but not before eliminating the provisions for the reservations along the Minnesota River. This modification of a major provision of the treaty required that it be re-ratified by Dakota leaders. Some of the more desperate clans signed under duress, but the Mdewakanton people refused.

To help close the deal, President Millard Fillmore agreed to use his executive powers to grant "temporary occupancy" of the reservation lands for five years to the Dakota, from 1854 to 1859. The meaning of "temporary" was, however, not clearly explained to Mdewakanton leaders. Thinking the provision had been restored, they too signed the revised treaty.

Before the ink was dry, Ramsey and Sibley went to work designing schemes that would direct the massive treaty funds into white rather than Indian hands. The "Indian removal" account was treated as a bureaucratic slush fund that was nearly completely emptied along its journey from Washington, DC, to Minnesota. Seventy thousand dollars never left the capital, as it lined the pockets of senators in exchange for their votes approving the treaty. Ramsey arranged for a 15 percent cut for himself, and his co-commissioner of Indian Affairs pocketed $55,000 as a personal administrative fee for "handling" the rest of the money. Even when money was distributed—such as $20,000 to the Mdewakanton and Wahpekute chiefs—they were forced to sign a receipt verifying they had received $180,000. And the balance of the relocation fund was depleted—much of it simply unaccounted for—by payments large and small to various white people who Ramsey and Sibley thought needed to be appeased in both directions along the roads of ratification and distribution. As to the emergency subsistence money, Ramsey also forced the chiefs to sign a receipt for the $275,000 while giving him power of attorney to distribute it. They never received the money.

The thefts from the initial treaty funds were just the beginning. The most enduring of these fraudulent schemes was the demand that any Dakota "debts" be paid directly to their white trader creditors *before* any annual subsistence funds were distributed. For example, Sibley claimed the Mdewakantons and the Wahpekutes owed white traders back debts of $129,885. The total of the contrived debt to traders that Sibley attributed to the other two Dakota bands, the

Sisseton and Wahpeton—which he inflated by tallying up debts as much as three decades old and applying exorbitant markups—totaled $144,984.40.[15]

Historian Gary Clayton Anderson concluded, "The entire debt scenario was a massive fabrication."[16] Beginning in 1853, $250,000 annual annuity payments made their way from government coffers to Minnesota, funds that would have been adequate to support the Dakota people. But each year, a greedy swarm of white intermediaries descended to bleed them nearly dry.

Following the treaty ratifications, the Dakota witnessed an unprecedented mass invasion of white colonists in the 1850s, leading to ongoing conflicts between the Native inhabitants and newly arrived whites. The 1860 US Census, for example, recorded that 17,000 people had settled in the "Big Woods" in central Minnesota alone. Because the money designated to support "removal" of the Dakota to the reservations had been pilfered, there was no coordinated enforcement effort by the Minnesota government. As a result, most Dakota remained in place, many unaware of the terms of the treaties. Whites, on the other hand, arrived with an aggressive sense of entitlement. They essentially performed a local version of the Doctrine of Discovery, respecting existing white land rights but claiming "settler sovereignty" over whatever land wasn't already staked by another white person.

Bands of newly arrived and heavily armed whites regularly attacked unsuspecting Dakota villages in desirable locations, burning them to the ground and scattering the survivors—including the elderly, women, and children—into the woods with only the clothes on their backs.[17] The Dakota fought back at what they saw as an invasion of their homeland, particularly considering the broken treaty promises. One white farmer petitioned the government for help, complaining that Native Americans were "continually committing grievous depredations upon our crops, shooting our cattle, and greatly annoying and harassing us in the enjoyment of our rights."[18]

With designated funds for "Indian removal" tucked into white pockets, large-scale relocation never occurred. Moreover, living on the reservation lands was made even more unattractive by the often late and nearly nonexistent annuity payments and the systematic suppression of Dakota culture. On the reservation, Dakota people were pressured to exchange nomadic hunting for farming, Native dress for European, their own language for English, and their own religious practices for Christianity.

To add insult to injury, Dakota leaders were summoned in 1858 to Washington, where they were informed, to their surprise, that their rights to even their reservation lands would expire the following year. They were forced to sign a new treaty ceding half the reservation, the west bank of the Minnesota River that was coveted for its fertile river basin land. The four Dakota clans were promised $266,880 in compensation. After white trader debt claims were received and tallied via the corrupt practices that were now institutionalized, only $881 remained. The government never bothered to deliver this small balance.[19]

Pushed off their lands and with most of their promised annual compensation stolen each year before it ever arrived, the situation became desperate among the Dakota people in the winter and spring of 1861–62. Many were dying or living on the brink of starvation. There are records of Dakota women digging in fields for wild turnips, and even more desperate acts such as gathering mule dung to look for undigested oats that could be washed and ground into flour, or attempts to eat marsh grass, which, while edible, had little nutritional value and caused diarrhea when consumed without protein.

As conditions worsened on the ground, several thousand Dakota gathered in July 1862 at the Upper Sioux Agency, where food was distributed, demanding emergency food provisions and warning agency administrators that violence would likely break out if treaties were not honored. When the agency refused, several hundred young

Dakota men broke into the warehouse and stole twenty sacks of flour. Two companies of soldiers from nearby Camp Lexington responded and turned a howitzer menacingly at the desperate, emaciated crowd. They stood their ground, only dispersing temporarily when soldiers brought up a cannon and moved toward lighting the fuse. Word of the standoff spread quickly; more Dakota leaders and more soldiers arrived on the scene over the next three days.

Finally, the agency agreed to hold council with the Dakota leaders, including Little Crow (Taoyateduta) of the Mdewakanton clan, who had been one of the first leaders to voluntarily move to the reservation lands. Little Crow and the other Dakota leaders demanded that food be distributed, appealing to the immediate hunger crisis and also to the instability and possibility of violence that might erupt given the broken treaty provisions and the desperate situation. The agency administrators huddled. The first answer came from the agency spokesperson, Andrew Myrick. He rose and moved toward the door, then turned with this response: "As far as I am concerned, let them eat grass." As Myrick left the room, a collective cry rose from the Dakota leaders. The agency reluctantly opened the warehouse and distributed the small amount of food that remained. The Dakota departed without incident, but a spark had been ignited.[20]

THE DAKOTA WAR OF 1862

Over the following month, talk of revenge circulated through Dakota councils. While awaiting a delayed government annuity payment, a dozen Dakota men went hunting in the Big Woods near a white settlement called Acton. Along the way they encountered Robinson Jones, who often sold whiskey to Native Americans from his cabin. A dispute broke out over payment and extending credit, and the four Native Americans first shot Robinson and then killed four others on the premises, including two women. They then fled back to their village, confessing to leaders what they had done. There was serious debate about turning over the four men responsible for the violence to white authorities to avoid retribution. But by the morning of August 18, a consensus had arisen among the Dakota tribe that their only hope for securing their rights as delineated in government treaties, along with long-term survival, was to go to war.

Their first targets were the traders at the Lower Sioux Agency—which included an establishment owned and run by Myrick—who ran the debt system that had for years cheated them out of their government annuity payments. Once the violence began, Dakota warriors went from building to building, killing traders and their employees on sight. Myrick was shot twice but managed to escape to the attic of his building. When the warriors attempted to burn him out, he escaped through a window and headed for a field. He was killed before he reached the other side. Survivors later found his arrow-riddled body alongside his severed head, with his mouth stuffed with grass.[21] In just one hour, twenty-nine traders and employees lost their lives.

Over the last hot weeks of August and into early September, Dakota warriors fanned out across a 150-mile swath of the state, attacking forts, towns, and white homesteads in what would become the most violent ethnic conflict in American history. The battles resulted in the deaths of over five hundred Dakota people and over six hundred white colonists. The ensuing panic also precipitated a white refugee crisis, with more than thirty thousand white colonists abandoning their farms across twenty-six counties and pouring into unprepared towns and forts for protection.[22]

By mid-September, the US government—stretched to the limit by the demands of the Civil War—finally sent reinforcements to restore order. A chance encounter on September 23 at Lone Tree Lake proved to be the final battle of the conflict. Indian forces led by Little Crow attacked government forces led by Sibley (who had managed to receive a commission as a colonel despite having no military background) after Sibley's troops had wandered into a field to dig potatoes. Little Crow's forces were defeated, but he, along with the remainder of his warriors, managed to escape to the north. Increasingly, the Dakota were demoralized and divided. There were disagreements about tactics, particularly the killing of women and children, and about the ultimate goals of what had now escalated into an outright war that was clearly unwinnable.

After Little Crow's forces retreated, Sibley was promptly promoted to general. He sent word that any Dakota wishing to declare their loyalty to the US government could gather in a friendly camp, which was soon dubbed "Camp Release." Sibley promised those who gathered there that if they raised a white flag and had not killed white colonists, they would be treated fairly. Over the latter part of September and early October, Sibley allowed more Dakota families to enter, and the ranks of Camp Release grew substantially. White rags waved in the breeze atop tepee poles across the crowded fields, with some individuals going much further to display their peaceful commitments. One observer recorded that "one Indian who was boiling with loyalty threw a white blanket on his black horse and tied a bit of white cloth to its tail . . . and wrapped an American flag around his body."[23]

SIBLEY'S MILITARY TRIBUNALS

Sibley's promises of restraint and fair treatment were not sincere. Anderson concludes, "It was a devilish plot: he wholly intended to capture as many of these Indians as possible, believing most to be guilty of killing civilians."[24] In personal correspondence dated September 27, 1862, Sibley informed General John Pope of his plan to use a military commission to separate the innocent few from the guilty throng. Meanwhile, Governor Ramsey gave an address to the Minnesota legislature on September 9, 1862, that reflected the bitter taste of revenge in the mouths of many white Minnesotans. Revving up his listeners with sensationalized tales of infanticide and rape (for which he had little evidence), he declared, "Our course then is plain. The Sioux [Dakota] Indians of Minnesota must be exterminated or driven forever beyond the borders of Minnesota."[25]

In all, Sibley's ruse at Camp Release resulted in the imprisonment of more than 1,600 men, women, and children. On October 15, Sibley corralled 392 Dakota men accused of murdering white civilians, shackled them together in chains, and moved them to the site of the Lower Sioux Agency. There he had troops build a 30-by-150-foot log prison, quickly dubbed "Camp Sibley," to hold them while they awaited their fate before his military tribunals.[26]

Even during the Civil War, the use of military tribunals was controversial because of their lack of protections for the accused. Sibley's tribunals were a sham even by these diminished standards. Sibley had only briefly studied law and had never practiced it. Sibley's court consisted of five military officers (the bare minimum required), plus a single officer with legal training who acted as "recorder." The most egregious violation of military legal standards was the absence of a judge advocate, a person appointed to act in the interest of the defendants, informing them of their rights, cross-examining witnesses against them, and even holding the authority to seek the removal of a member of the court for prejudice. Besides all this, there was no reason—other than the hunger for quick revenge and Sibley's desire to enhance his reputation by personally bringing the Indians to justice—that these cases could not have been brought before the regular Minnesota state courts, which remained intact.[27]

Sibley's tribunal moved forward with breakneck speed, ignoring due process, to meet his stated goal of trying nearly four hundred men and executing those found guilty, all before winter, when the frozen ground would complicate the disposal of the bodies. Toward the end of October, the pace quickened to more than thirty hearings per day. On November 2 alone, forty-three Dakota men stood trial. In some cases, as many as eight defendants were brought before the tribunal at a time, making an authentic consideration of justice for any individual impossible.[28] When the last verdict was read, 303 names appeared on a list of the guilty who were condemned to be hung by the neck until dead.

The presumption of guilt was heavy. As Anderson notes, "In 90 percent of the trials, the entire event lasted only a minute or two; of the 392 trials, 352 contain one page or less of testimony, with often as little as two sentences."[29] Due to the speed of the trials, the absence of a judge advocate, and a lack of English proficiency among many Dakota defendants, most left the room not knowing that a death sentence had been rendered. Undeterred, Sibley remained firm in his belief not only in the legitimacy of the trials, but also, and perhaps more importantly, in the necessity of their results, assuring his wife in a letter that the number of executions "will be sufficiently great to satisfy the longings of the most bloodthirsty" white Minnesotans.[30] In correspondence with Episcopal bishop Henry Whipple, Sibley employed Christian religious terms to defend his position, arguing that a "great crime against our common humanity demands an equally great atonement."[31]

Word of the unauthorized mass execution plan, however, had gotten back to President Abraham Lincoln, who sent instructions to General Pope, Sibley's superior, clarifying that no executions would take place without his sanction. Hoping to secure a quick approval, Pope responded by telegraphing to Lincoln, at the exorbitant expense of four hundred dollars, the list of the men to be executed, while he and Sibley continued with preparations. They began moving the 303 convicted men south to Mankato on November 7, where they planned to hold the executions. On November 9, they ordered the large group of 1,658 mostly women, children, and the elderly to be moved to Fort Snelling, where they could be more easily deported down the river at a later date. Neither group was informed of their fate.

Along the journey, Sibley's forces had to defend the Dakota from white settler colonists who attacked them with sticks, stones, and other makeshift weapons. Several were killed before soldiers could defend them. One enraged white woman rushed a wagon, wrenched an infant away from a Dakota mother, and dashed it to the ground. The infant was retrieved and returned to its mother, but it died in her arms a few hours later. After a brief service, it was buried in the hollow of a tree before the caravan pushed on.[32]

Major newspapers followed Governor Ramsey's lead and joined the angry chorus of white colonists, many of whom were still living as refugees. The *St. Paul Press* ran a banner headline demanding "Nothing Short of Extermination." The *St. Croix Monitor* declared that the Indians' "refusal to be civilized forces upon us the hard alternative of exterminating him."[33] By the fall of 1862, with Ramsey and Sibley fanning the flames, many good white civilized and Christian Minnesotans had become outright advocates of genocide.[34]

THE LARGEST MASS EXECUTION IN US HISTORY

Pope's hopes that he would receive a quick authorization from Lincoln for the executions were dashed. When Lincoln finally replied, to Sibley's and Pope's dismay, he asked for the entire trial record to be sent to the White House. Knowing that this request alone would delay the executions for weeks, and that any impartial examination of the trial records would expose their shoddy nature, Ramsey and Pope lobbied the president for immediate action. Ramsey wrote to the president, emphasizing his hopes that "every Sioux Indian condemned by the military court will be at once executed." Pope took a different approach, arguing that the good white and largely Christian Minnesotans might take things into their own hands if the executions did not go forward; he wrote, "I think it nearly impossible to prevent the indiscriminate massacre of all the Indians, old men, women and children."[35]

There were also some prominent Minnesotans lobbying the president to stay the executions, at least for the few convicted Dakota men who were Christian converts. Rev. Thomas Williamson, a Presbyterian minister who had been working among the Dakota people for years, became particularly incensed with the convictions of two men who were members of his church. Williamson penned a letter to his friend John C. Smith, a lawyer and prominent Presbyterian who knew Lincoln and had close ties to the Bureau of Indian Affairs. Williamson had convinced Sibley to let him review the trial records and wrote to Smith that he had found the prisoners "ignorant of the specifications of the charges against them and of the testimony to support those charges as this testimony was given in a language they understood not."[36]

The level-headed Episcopal bishop Henry Whipple was perhaps the bluntest of those who had an audience with Lincoln. Whipple had long publicly complained that the Indian Affairs department was the most corrupt in the government. If the nation were to be fair, he argued, it must see the violence perpetrated against white Minnesotans in the larger context of the injustices toward the Dakota people. "At whose door is the blood of these innocent victims?" he asked. "I believe that God will hold the nation guilty."[37]

These dual lobbying efforts (along with cautions from Secretary of the Interior Caleb B. Smith that such a mass execution would be "a stain on our National character") hit Lincoln's desk at an enormously stressful time. The war effort against the Confederacy was not going well. As he considered how to handle the fate of the 303 Dakota men, he was also wrestling with the decision to free enslaved people in the rebellious southern states.

Lincoln asked two trusted attorney colleagues to return to the commission's initial guiding principle, to distinguish between those who had "participated in massacres as distinguished from participation in battles." After the examination, they presented Lincoln with a list of forty men they believed should be executed. Lincoln commuted the sentence of one additional man and then signed the execution papers on December 6, sealing the fate of thirty-nine Dakota men but sparing 264 lives.[38] He would issue the Emancipation Proclamation on January 1, 1863, less than one month later.

Lincoln's order set the execution date for December 19, but Sibley found himself forced to ask for an extension. Large crowds of angry whites were expected to converge on the small town of Mankato, and there were delays in gathering sufficient troops to ensure order. There was also a more mundane, practical reason he needed more time: there was not enough rope in Mankato to hang thirty-nine men simultaneously. Lincoln agreed to the extension and pushed the date back a week, to December 26. The day before Christmas Eve, the special order of rope arrived from St. Paul, completing the provisions.[39]

Relieved at Lincoln's decision to spare so many lives, Williamson began visiting and preaching to the Dakota men confined at the Mankato prison. During the first weeks of December, Williamson reported that 137 men expressed a desire to be baptized. While the legitimacy of the report is questionable under the circumstances, his work among the prisoners produced one verifiable result. Williamson discovered evidence that one of the thirty-nine condemned men had been misidentified by two young witnesses. Sibley reluctantly agreed to remove him from the list.

On December 22, the thirty-eight condemned men were separated from those who had received a reprieve, and Sibley allowed two clergy—Williamson, along with a Catholic monsignor, Augustin Ravoux—to offer those facing execution a final opportunity for Christian baptism. All but two reportedly accepted. Standing over the thirty-six recipients, who remained shackled together at the ankle, Ravoux and Williamson administered the sacrament of baptism the evening of Christmas Day.[40]

On December 26, despite the mass Christian baptism the evening before, all thirty-eight men prepared themselves for death in traditional Dakota fashion. They donned feathers, beads, and traditional Dakota clothing. Nearly all painted their hair and face bright red, a practice that, according to Dakota beliefs, would allow them to be recognized in the afterlife by a Dakota woman who stood in the middle of a mythical river and allowed only those she recognized to pass over into paradise.

At 7:30 a.m. on the day of the execution, the men's ankle shackles were removed, while their arms were restrained behind their backs at the elbow, leaving their hands free. They were then arrayed in a double line for the short, forced march to the massive gallows. When the doors swung open, they were confronted with what must have seemed like an overwhelming spectacle. In addition to approximately four thousand white spectators, over one thousand infantry soldiers, with bayonets fixed, stood at attention in concentric squares around the gallows, and five hundred cavalry, with swords drawn, patrolled the outside perimeter of the crowd.[41]

Soldiers escorted the Dakota men onto the platform, where they began to sing. As their voices found each other in a slow but rhythmic Dakota death song, their bodies started to sway in unison. Dakota oral history, handed down among Dakota Christian congregations, records that at least some also sang a familiar Christian hymn written by a congregationalist minister for use among Dakota converts.

When hoods were placed over their heads and nooses around

their necks, at least two of the men managed to clasp hands, and another, failing in the attempt, grasped the shirt of the man next to him. At 10:00 a.m., the first of three drumbeats sounded. The soldiers filed off the platform. The singing grew louder. The men then began calling out their names to each other, chanting in their Native tongue, "This is me." With the third drumbeat at 10:15, the axe was brought down on the triggering rope but failed to cut it. A second blow dropped the scaffolding under all thirty-eight men. Thirty-seven died instantly, the jolt at the end of the rope breaking their necks. One rope snapped. Soldiers rushed to retrieve the limp body of Rattling Runner and strung him back up. A final man struggled for nearly twenty minutes, slowly kicking and choking to death.[42]

Shouts of "huzza" and other ecstatic utterances pealed across the square. Multiple observers used the word *exultation* to describe the response of the mostly white Christian crowd to the largest mass execution in American history.

DAKOTA DEPORTATION

Although the war had been led principally by the Mdewakanton clan of the Dakota people, and two Dakota clans had no part of the violence, whites made no distinctions after the five-week Dakota War of 1862 drew to a close. Indians were Indians, and all would have to go. On February 16, 1863, a bill passed both houses of Congress that revoked the treaties made with each of the four Dakota clans, taking away "all lands and right of occupancy," terminating all annuity payments, and revoking any remaining Indian claims in the state.

Back in Minnesota, there was a consensus that a mass deportation effort to the West would begin as soon as the Mississippi River became navigable in the spring. As I narrated in the opening scene of the book, approximately 1,300 mostly women, children, and elderly men were crowded into two steamboats in unsanitary conditions and with insufficient food on May 4 and 5. After an arduous and deadly journey, what one white missionary likened to the "middle passage for the slaves," they arrived at Crow Creek on the upper Missouri River, where they found inadequate fresh water and rocky soil ill-suited to agriculture. They were left with few provisions. By the spring of 1864, more than two hundred—mostly children—had died of malnutrition and disease, and all but five hundred had abandoned the reservation in search of better conditions. Two years later, in 1866, the US government offered to move the remainder of the scattered group to a reservation at Santee, Nebraska. There the Mdewakanton band was reunited with the surviving remainder of the men Lincoln spared (approximately one-third of the men had perished during their three years of imprisonment), who had finally been released.[43]

WHITE SUPREMACY IN MINNESOTA

With statehood achieved in 1858, and with Native American lands seized and the Dakota people first decimated and then deported just five years later, Minnesota was poised to be the embodiment of the dream of an idealized new Zion, a new promised land for European Christian settler colonists.[44]

But to preserve this ethno-religious state identity, white Minnesotans also needed to limit the number of African American immigrants, particularly given that the Mississippi River was a conduit connecting St. Paul to the heart of the Confederacy and the South. In 1860, despite the fact that the census showed only 259 Black residents in the entire state, a bill was introduced in the Minnesota legislature to prevent the migration of free Blacks and mulattoes into the state and to require those already present to be registered.[45] Although the bill was defeated, its proposal nevertheless signaled how top of mind these concerns were among the state's early white population.

The disproportionate reactions in St. Paul to the arrival of Robert Hickman's small party of African Americans fleeing slavery, as described in the prologue, provides a preview of the power white supremacy would continue to hold in Minnesota. By towing Hickman's band farther upriver to Fort Snelling on May 5, 1863, Captain Woods and the *Northerner* had avoided white mob violence in St. Paul. Nevertheless, the mere appearance of this small group of African Americans caused enough white collective handwringing to make the St. Paul papers the following day. On May 6, even the liberal editor of the *Saint Paul Daily Press* gave voice to the widely shared idea that African Americans, like Native Americans, were an inferior race that would contribute little to the future prosperity of the state:

> What will be done with them? Women and pickaninnies will not render material assistance in driving mule teams over the plain, and they would probably show very large whites of their eyes on such an occasion. We presume they will be left to garrison the Fort, while the head of the family goes roaming among the mules.[46]

Significantly, European immigrants were viewed in an entirely different light. Just three days later, the *Daily Press* published this assessment of new German and Scandinavian arrivals:

> We record with satisfaction an unmistakable increase of immigration to the state. For a number of days we have observed, on the landing of the packet boats here, an unusual number of passengers on board.... The class of immigrants is another gratifying circumstance. They are nearly all agricultural and are all of a solid, intelligent and well-to-do class, who will make good settlers.... On a recent trip the *McLellan* left La Crosse with 98

bright-eyed little boys and girls, to become the future legislators, farmers, and merchants of Minnesota.[47]

We do not know whether those white children went on to fulfill the rosy destiny that the white newspaper editor envisioned for them, but Robert Hickman would live a remarkable life. After working at Fort Snelling for a few months, he settled in St. Paul, becoming a religious leader and pillar of the small Black community. Calling himself and his followers "pilgrims," he founded Pilgrim Baptist Church in 1866 (the oldest Black congregation still in existence in the state), became one of the first Black men to serve on a jury in 1869, and was finally recognized by the state as an ordained minister in 1874.[48]

Hickman's success notwithstanding, as the nineteenth century closed, Minnesota's Black population remained minuscule, particularly outside the Twin Cities. While the state's early European colonists managed to embrace a wide range of other European immigrants, including coming to terms with anti-Catholic prejudice that targeted the Irish lower classes and even prejudice against Finns because of their socialist leanings, they continued to see African Americans as outsiders and a potential threat.

WHITE SUPREMACY IN DULUTH

These statewide patterns were also evident in Duluth, although they were slightly delayed because of the city's remote location in the northern part of the state. Before the city first appeared on an 1856 map as "Duluth," the area was historically occupied first by the Dakota and then by the Ojibwe (Anishinaabe) people on the tip of Lake Superior. European powers referred to it in relationship to the lake and their other land holdings. It was Fond du Lac ("Bottom of the Lake") for the French, but it was "Head of the Lakes" for the British;

either way, it was the place where the great lake and the great river (the St. Louis River) converged.[49]

Even after statehood, the fledgling community of European colonists struggled with the decline of the fur trade and false hopes about copper deposits that never materialized. Fortunes finally shifted in 1869 when Philadelphia financier Jay Cooke decided to build the Lake Superior and Mississippi Railroad (LS&M) line to connect the two great bodies of water. He also financed a canal across the sandbar, providing a safe shipping lane from the open lake into the protected harbor.

In just a year, Duluth's population swelled from a few hundred—with Ojibwe outnumbering whites—to over 3,100, mostly immigrants. Over one-third were Swedish, with Norwegians, Germans, Irish, and Canadians (mostly of French descent) each comprising around 10 percent.[50] The infrastructure of a real city began to be evident by the 1890s, with sixty-five churches, several synagogues, and nearly thirty public schools. The Masons built a new temple and a public opera house. Duluth also boasted more than one hundred saloons and a dozen brothels.[51]

This growth pattern continued into the early twentieth century. By 1910, Duluth's population had swelled to 78,000, nearly 40 percent foreign-born citizens primarily of Swedish, Norwegian, Canadian, and German stock. As in the rest of the country, race relations in Duluth became tense following World War I, due to competition for unskilled labor jobs. In Duluth, the opening of the Minnesota Steel Company plant in 1916 included a recruitment program that brought dozens of African Americans to the area. Even this small number competing for jobs (often willing to work for lower wages than European immigrants) created a negative reaction among Duluth's white supermajority. According to historian David Vassar Taylor, many whites attempted to use the opportunity to establish a white supremacist new normal; after World War I, Black Duluthians found a humiliating and infuriating pattern: "restaurants, hotels, and theaters, which had reluctantly served blacks before the war, refused to do so or attempted to establish segregated seating."[52]

By 1920, Duluth was a city of 100,000 citizens, 99.3 percent of whom were of European descent. All but eighteen Native Americans had now moved away from Duluth. Despite the newer arrivals looking for opportunities at US Steel, the census counted only 495 African Americans.[53] Due to an influx of Eastern European, particularly Polish, immigrants, St. Louis County was about 40 percent Catholic; Lutherans dominated the Protestant landscape, comprising approximately 13 percent of the population, double the size of the next-largest Protestant groups, the Methodists and the Presbyterians.[54] That same year, one of the most widely attended lynchings in American history would occur not in the Deep South, where Black populations often rivaled or sometimes surpassed white populations, but in this far northern, nearly completely Caucasian city.

Chapter Five

THE LYNCHINGS
IN DULUTH

In 1920, fifty-seven years after Robert Hickman was threatened by Irish dockworkers in St. Paul, and one hundred years before George Floyd was murdered by a white police officer in Minneapolis, an enraged white mob of approximately ten thousand people lynched three Black men in Duluth, Minnesota.

THE ACCUSATION

Despite its cultural and geographic distance from the Deep South, the events leading to the lynchings in Duluth followed a familiar trope: a white woman accused a Black man of raping her. In this case, the accused were a group of Black men who were not residents of Duluth but were working as roustabouts for the John Robinson Circus, which was in town for a single day.

While the details of the story—like many white accusations against Black men at the time—are murky, the following are the basic precipitating events. In the early evening of June 14, 1920, nineteen-year-old Irene Tusken left her house for the circus with two friends. There she met up with eighteen-year-old Jimmy Sullivan, a handsome young man with a fast-lane reputation whom she had been seeing socially, against the expressed wishes of her parents. Sometime after 9:00 p.m., as the fairway activities were winding down, they ventured off beyond the well-lit fairway to a field behind the wagons and the tents. There they encountered a group of six Black circus workers hanging out behind one of the cook tents. During the next hour, there was a confrontation between the two parties, but the nature of it remains unclear.[1]

After leaving the circus, Jimmy and Irene caught the streetcar back to their working-class West Duluth neighborhood, and Jimmy walked her home. Opening the door around 10:30 p.m., Irene found her father in the front room reading the evening edition of the *Duluth Herald*. He nodded over his paper to acknowledge her arrival. She matter-of-factly told him she was going to bed and went upstairs. Before going into her room, she also told her mother good night and mentioned only that she had seen Jimmy at the circus. She was in bed by 11:00 p.m.

Jimmy went off to his night shift job at the docks. Around 1:00 a.m., he informed his father, P. B. Sullivan, a superintendent, that six Black men had held him at gunpoint and brutally raped Irene. He claimed she'd barely been able to walk back to the streetcar stop. Jimmy's father first called Irene's father and then Chief of Police John Murphy at his home. Once the drowsy officer grasped the magnitude of the accusation—in the parlance of many white Duluth residents of the time, that "six circus niggers raped a white girl"—Murphy sprang into action. He roused a group of officers and issued orders to stop the circus train, which was already heading north to its next destination. Officials caught up to the train at the Duluth, Winnipeg, and Pacific Railway yard just outside of town.

There, a tired and angry all-white Duluth police force roughly unloaded every African American on the train, many standing in their bare feet and nightgowns in the crisp night air. After interrogating them about their whereabouts at the time of the alleged rape, all but forty were released and allowed to return to the warmth of their sleeping cars. The rest were kept standing, shoulder to shoulder, in the grass. Jimmy Sullivan and his father were brought to the railyard and led twice down the line. Jimmy was asked repeatedly if he could identify any of the assailants, but he said he could not. Irene Tusken and her father were awakened and summoned to the spot, where her account of the evening switched from a mere clandestine meeting with Jimmy at the circus to confirming that she had been raped. Police repeated the same drill, walking them down the line of detained circus workers. Like Jimmy, Irene said she could not identify any faces, but she singled out six men based on their general build.

After intense questioning of the group, the officers initially detained seven additional men but soon released them. The circus train was released, and the remaining six were arrested, driven to the city jail, and locked in their cells around 7:00 a.m. on June 15. The accused were all between the ages of nineteen and twenty-two. Chief Murphy believed that five had been involved in the alleged rape: Elias Clayton, Elmer Jackson, Nate Green, Loney Williams, and John Thomas. The additional detainee, Isaac McGhie, was being held as a material witness.[2]

THE LYNCHINGS

The alleged crime and the arrests did not make the June 15 morning edition of the *Duluth News Tribune*, but rumors began to spread quickly through the city, picking up steam during the lunch hour, particularly in West Duluth. One of the most incensed residents was

Louis Dondino, a thirty-eight-year-old widower who owned a small auto transfer business in West Duluth, whose green one-ton Ford pickup truck was a familiar sight in the city.[3] By late afternoon, tempers were flaring, and Dondino drove through the streets recruiting like-minded men who climbed in the truck bed and then, when there was no more room, ran alongside.

At one point near the police station, a group ducked into Siegel Hardware, requesting several yards of rope. The clerk, who had been watching the procession, gave them the rope free of charge, telling them, "You're doing a good thing."[4] The macabre processional drove through the streets, dragging the long rope behind the truck, yelling, "Come on! Show what kind of men you are! The niggers raped the girl, and she might be dead! . . . What if she was your sister or daughter? . . . Join the necktie party!"[5] The group eventually became so large that it caused a traffic jam at Eighth Avenue and Superior Street, which a police officer had to disperse.

To Duluth's small Black population, the transformation of their white neighbors was immediately apparent. A Black truck driver and World War I veteran, Eddie Nichols, described his experience on his commute home from work that day. For the first time, he felt angry whites glaring at him on the streetcar, with one clenching his fist and yelling, "We're gonna get *all* the niggers in town."[6] Nichols, like many others in the small Black Duluth population, spent many of the next few nights sleepless, behind barricaded doors with army surplus weapons loaded just in case.

The June 15 early evening edition of the *Duluth Herald* dropped a match into this tinderbox with a front-page headline, "WEST DULUTH GIRL VICTIM OF NEGROES." Although the story was not the lead and consisted of only about 250 words, reactions to it soon revealed the widespread presence of racial bigotry in this city, where reserved Christian sensibilities and midwestern manners, combined with limited white interactions with the small Black population, typically tucked coarse racist language and prejudice out of view.

The evening edition of the *Duluth Herald* also ran another, less sensational story that contained evidence that should have poured cold water on the entire affair. That morning, Irene Tusken's mother had phoned the family physician, Dr. David Graham, and asked if he could examine Irene given the brutal sexual assault she claimed to have experienced the night before. Dr. Graham conducted a thorough psychological and gynecological examination the morning of June 15. He declared that he saw no signs of sexual trauma.[7] He told a detective flatly, "I don't think she was raped." He was even quoted in the evening edition of the *Herald*, saying, "I believe she is suffering more from nervous exhaustion than anything else."[8] But this exculpatory revelation was unable to compete with the ready willingness of white Duluthians to believe the scandalous accusations that a teenage white girl had been gang-raped by Black men.

With night falling, the skeleton crew of police officers were increasingly uneasy about the size of the undulating throng gathering outside the small city jail on Superior Street. Hearing of the potential mob activity, two district judges arrived around 7:00 p.m. to assess the situation, just as the first bricks were being hurled through the first-story windows of the jail. Judge William Cant tried to dissuade the crowd from further violence, declaring, "The honor of Duluth is at stake. Most of you are all law-abiding citizens, and if you do this thing, you will never live it down, and neither will Duluth." He was quickly shouted down. Seeing the mob's resolve, Judge Bert Fesler made no attempt of his own to speak.[9]

At 8:00 p.m., Sergeant Oscar Olson received calls from the police switchboard with reports of scattered shooting incidents around town. He could not afford to send men to investigate. By 8:40, the mob at the jail had grown to over ten thousand people—representing about 10 percent of the town's population.[10] It was mostly young men, but there were also entire families, including baby carriages and children hoisted on shoulders and playing around the edges of the crowd. Members of Duluth's upper class, in their evening finery, also joined the crowd after Duluth's downtown theaters let out at 9:45. Surveying the size and diversity of the crowd, William Murnian, Duluth's public safety commissioner, issued a fateful order, that officers were not to use firearms to protect the prisoners.[11] When *Duluth Herald* reporter Albert Tracy later found him in the midst of the attack on the jail and asked him to confirm that he had issued the order, Murnian replied, "I do not want to see the blood of one white person spilled for six blacks."[12]

Sometime around 9:00 p.m., the mob reached a fever pitch and rushed the jail from every direction. The first attempts came at the back door, but these were initially rebuffed by courageous hand-to-hand fighting by Sergeant Olson and a handful of officers. A group of men also rushed the front door and again were repulsed. Another group climbed the fire escape, attempting to chisel their way directly into the cell room. Sergeant Olson requested assistance from the fire department and was able for some time to push the mob back from the front door with the force of a powerful fire hose. In the end, prohibited from using their firearms, the beleaguered police were overrun by the bloodthirsty crowd. The mob seized the fire hose and turned it back on the police. Men poured into the wrecked jail building and pushed the drenched and dazed officers aside, ignoring their pleas to let justice be done in the courts.

The steel doors to the cell room and the individual cells were locked, however, and the police, to their credit, refused to hand over the keys. But the mob had prepared for this possibility. Men with all manner of industrial machinist saws, chisels, and heavy tools set to work, switching out when one became spent. Local attorney Hugh McClearn attempted to take advantage of this slowdown in activity, climbing a small ladder inside the building and imploring the mob to disperse. Over the din, he reminded the crowd that no official evidence had been presented against the six Black men and pleaded, "Give the courts a chance to administer justice according to the law." Sergeant Olson also spoke from the ladder, declaring, "We don't even know if we got the right negroes. That circus had nearly two hundred of them, and we arrested thirteen. And the girl and her young man couldn't identify a single one." But the men were undeterred. The reply came back, "We don't care if they are guilty or innocent! Kill the black snakes!" Then a chant began to build, coordinated with the rhythm of the work, "Let's go! Let's go!"[13]

The detained Black men behind those bars could hear this exchange but not yet see the commotion. The five accused of the crime were being held on the main adult floor. But twenty-year-old Isaac McGhie, the lone prisoner not being held as a suspect, had been placed alone on the level above them on what was known as the boys' floor. Each of these young men had southern roots and had lived enough years to know what terrors awaited them if the white mob broke through. But McGhie, all alone, must have been particularly panicked with no one to talk to, no one with whom to share his fears.

The mob got to McGhie first. They pulled him from the cell and pummeled him all the way down the stairs to the cell room with the others. As he landed on the main floor where the other men were being held, blood and a dislodged tooth fell from his mouth. The mob had not yet breached the other cells, so they held him against the wall. "Oh, God, oh, God—oh, God," he repeated. "I am only twenty years old. I have never done anything wrong. I swear I didn't. Oh, God, my God, help me."[14]

The mob got to Elias Clayton next. As his battered cell door swung open, he also received a barrage of punches that knocked him to the floor. But then some of the leaders pushed the other white men back, threw McGhie into the cell with him, and guarded the entrance. As the other four prisoners were yanked from their cells, they also were deposited into this single cell. Then several men stepped forward to declare that they were going to conduct an impromptu trial. "We're going to find out which nigger's guilty!" one man announced. "The rest of you stay back. We want to be fair!"[15]

But in the chaos of the increasingly cramped cell block, questions were coming from multiple directions, and the dazed and fearful Black men were either silent or continued to insist upon their innocence. Finally, someone yelled, "Give us *somebody*!" The self-appointed prosecutors finally saw the futility of the exercise and stepped aside. Those closest to the cell door grabbed McGhie by the hair and pulled him into the frenzied mob, and Jackson was pushed out close behind him. The mob immediately pounced and began beating them as they were carried out of jail and into the even larger mass of impatient whites who had been waiting in the street for hours with anticipation. Mayhem ensued. The two were carried along in a violent current, as people battered them and tore at their clothes. Many in the mob fought their way up to the front for the opportunity to personally strike the men, and women in high heels stomped them when they fell to the ground.[16] This continued for a city block until they stopped in front of the Shrine Auditorium at Second Avenue East and First Street.

A nineteen-year-old accountant named Albert Johnson had climbed a streetlamp pole to get a better view of the commotion. Someone in the crowd near the two Black victims noticed him and threw up a rope, instructing him to loop it over the top of the pole. He hesitated, but then obeyed.

As McGhie was being pushed toward the pole, Fr. William Powers, a Catholic priest at Duluth's Sacred Heart Cathedral, shoved his way through the crowd to the spot. Like the civic leaders and police officers earlier, Powers admonished the crowd to stop before they committed such a heinous crime. Climbing up the pole himself, both to block the action and to be heard, Powers reminded the crowd that there had been no determination of guilt for any of the Black suspects. Mustering the highest authority he could invoke, he shouted, "It's not too late to stop this tragedy, men. In the name of God and the church I represent, I ask you to stop."

Another Catholic priest, Fr. P. J. Maloney, was also on the scene, trying to find people he knew personally, taking them by the arm and saying, "You've no business here, boy. Go on to your home now. This is no place for a good Catholic young fellow." But these appeals to God and the church fell largely on deaf ears. Some yelled, "To hell with the church! To hell with the law!"[17] One man calmly replied to Maloney, "Stay out of this, Father. This has nothing to do with God."[18] Notably, there is no record that any Lutheran minister, representing the city's largest Protestant denomination—or any other Protestant minister—tried to stop the lynchings.

The Catholic priests' efforts did effect a momentary pause, before refrains rose again from the crowd: "Remember the girl!" and "String him up!" Several men then pulled Fr. Powers down from the pole and pushed McGhie forward. As a noose was tightened around his neck, he yelled, "God be with me. I'm not the right man." But no one in the crowd was listening. Hands pulled on the rope and his feet left the ground. The rope loosened and he temporarily fell back, only to be quickly hoisted up just a few feet off the ground, where he struggled until he died. Someone in the crowd yelled, "String him up so we can see." Next Elmer Jackson was dragged to the pole, along with a new rope. He could see McGhie's body and did not fight the crowd. He was hung slightly higher than McGhie's body to be more visible to the frenzied white mob.

Back in the jail cell, the remaining four prisoners had heard the two crescendos from the crowd. For reasons that are unclear, the leaders inside the cell pushed one more man, nineteen-year-old

Elias Clayton, into the hands of the mob. Like McGhie and Jackson, Clayton was shoved through a gauntlet of blows up the block to the pole. As he made out his friends' bodies hanging from the pole, he cried, "Please, oh God, don't kill me! I'm innocent!"[19] A blow to the face silenced his protest, and a man looped a noose around his neck. As he struggled and died, a man positioned up the pole kicked him repeatedly in the head, rewarded each time by cheers from the crowd.

With no other victim at hand, someone yelled, "Throw a little light on the subject!" The crowd parted to allow a car to come through and its headlights were focused on Clayton, the highest on the pole. Someone suggested that a photograph should be taken to commemorate the event. Because Clayton's body was higher than the rest, it was cut down so that all three victims could be in the camera frame. Ralph Greenspun, a photographer from nearby Superior, Wisconsin, took several shots while white residents of Duluth posed, some smiling. Another voice yelled, "Send them pictures to Alabama. Tell 'em to keep their niggers."[20] Within just a few days, these gruesome photographs were printed as postcards, which were available at a variety of retailers in Duluth and quickly sold out.[21]

The violent mayhem only ended when Fred Beecher, a major in the Minnesota National Guard with training in mob control, reorganized the battered police officers and equipped them with military rifles with fixed bayonets. Within an hour, they were able to expel the mob from the jail and set a perimeter around the building, saving the lives of the three remaining prisoners. With the mob partially sated by the lynchings, this decisive action broke its spirit, and it dispersed more quickly than it had gathered. Meanwhile, Chief Murphy loaded the three surviving prisoners into a dented police car and smuggled them across the bridge to Superior for safety.[22]

CONDEMNATIONS

In the immediate aftermath of the lynchings, condemnation of the lawlessness in Duluth was swift, both locally and nationwide. The morning *Duluth News Tribune* contained a 7,500-word story under a large banner headline reading, "DULUTH MOB HANGS NEGROES."[23] The story, detailing the brutality of the event, was written by reporter A. I. Carson, who had been on the scene at both the lynching site and the jail. Many white participants were so certain of the rightness of their cause that they left him unmolested and cooperated with his reporting. The *Minneapolis Journal* ran a June 17 editorial titled "The Duluth Disgrace," which put racial prejudice at the core of the story: "It was the color of the three prisoners that made them victims of the mob. Had they been white they might have been the objects of reprobation for the crime for which they were charged, but would no doubt have been left to the processes of the law."[24]

On June 19, the *New York Times* took aim at the emerging defense among some Duluthians that the mob had shown restraint by sparing three of the Black prisoners or that the mob had been fearful of a massive Black uprising: "No valid or even colorable claim on behalf of Duluth can be based on the fact that three of the six Negroes were spared by the executors of 'wild justice.' In that city and state there can be no pretense that the white population is under any general menace from a black majority."[25]

But in other prominent outlets, even condemnations of lynching were tempered with white supremacist sympathies. A June 19 *Chicago Tribune* editorial opened on a somber note, stating that "Duluth has now joined the American cities which have discovered how easily the safeguards of civilized justice can be leaped." It also noted that the race of the accused was "undoubtedly . . . an important factor in the psychology of outbreak." But it tellingly went on to argue that it was neither possible nor desirable to eliminate this "race instinct";

rather, the root of the problem was that such race instincts were not properly controlled.[26]

By Sunday, June 20, most Duluthians were hoping to move past Tuesday's awful events. But at least some prominent clergy were determined to address the issue from the pulpit. Rev. Dr. George Brewer, pastor of Duluth's First Presbyterian Church for the past four years, gave an impassioned and widely reprinted sermon titled, "Why This Crime, and Why These Lynchings?" in which he condemned the violence and further argued that the responsibility for the plight of African Americans should be laid at the feet of whites. Rev. O. W. Ryan, priest at St. Paul's Episcopal Church, also addressed the lynchings during his Sunday homily. "We are all humiliated by the disgraceful violence of the mob," he declared. "We trust that every good man and true will lift up his voice in bitter condemnation of such a disgraceful act. Duluth now stands shamed in the eyes of the world."[27]

Notably, there is no recorded public action or public statement from Duluth's prominent First Lutheran Church or from any Lutheran pastor or lay leader.[28]

THE TRIALS AND AFTERMATH

Even while the lynch mob was ending the lives of Clayton, Jackson, and McGhie, a separate contingency of Duluth police continued to round up additional suspects when the circus train arrived in Virginia, Minnesota. They arrested ten more men and drove them back to Duluth, where they were to face a grand jury along with the other three survivors of the mob. With blood spilled, the Duluth police were now under enormous pressure to produce a guilty party. Despite extended interrogations and threats, however, the thirteen men remained resolute about their innocence.

As the Black suspects languished in jail throughout June and July, prosecutors moved forward with cases against the white ringleaders of the mob. On August 8, a grand jury handed down indictments against nineteen white men on charges that ranged from rioting to first-degree murder. The trials moved swiftly, with the first starting on August 30. In the end, all the murder charges were dropped. There were only three convictions—Louis Dondino, Gilbert Henry Stephenson, and Carl Hammerberg—for the lesser charge of rioting, which carried a maximum sentence of five years. There was one hung jury, one agreement of immunity for turning state's evidence, and two acquittals; the remaining cases were dismissed by the end of September. Dondino and Stephenson were each paroled after serving just over two years of their sentences. Hammerberg served out his sentence not at Stillwater State Prison but at the state reformatory in St. Cloud.[29]

The first Black defendant, Max Mason, did not face trial until November 22, five months and six days after his arrest on June 16, 1920. The evidence against Mason was shaky. Irene Tusken had failed to identify him in the lineup in the early hours of June 15 and only later identified him by body type alone. The only other prosecution argument was an unfounded assertion that Mason had infected Irene with gonorrhea, which was based on an impossible epidemiological timeline and was called into question by the court's refusal of his request for an independent physical examination. Despite the weakness of the case against him, Mason's trial did not go well. He had a weak defense team that missed critical opportunities, such as failing to cross-examine Irene's doctor, who had recanted his earlier conclusion that there was no medical evidence of a physical assault and was now stating that his examination of Irene was "inconclusive." They also failed to effectively counter prosecutor Warren Greene's closing statement, which perniciously argued that convicting Mason would have symbolic value as a prophylactic against future white violence:

Why do we have mobs? It is because people think the Negroes won't be convicted. That's why they take the law into their own hands. People of Duluth and St. Louis County want to know through your verdict that when a white girl is ravished by a black or white man and the man is proven guilty, as in this case, the man is going to be found guilty.[30]

After deliberating for less than six hours, the jury returned the requested guilty verdict, and relieved white Duluthians possessed their proof that one of their white girls had indeed been raped by Black circus workers. Mason continued to assert his innocence even at sentencing, where he was remanded to Stillwater State Prison for thirty years, the maximum sentence under state law for rape.

The only other Black suspect to face charges was William Miller. Miller was represented by Charles Scrutchin, a well-respected African American attorney from Bemidji, Minnesota. Disturbed by the weak defense mounted in Mason's trial, Scrutchin was determined to do better for his client. He forced Irene's physician, Dr. Graham, to remove the equivocation from his statement. Asking Graham directly whether Irene's condition was consistent with what he would have expected if the girl had been raped multiple times, Graham conceded, "I do not think I would have found her in a normal condition the next morning." And when Greene again used his closing argument to prejudice the jury, Scrutchin called the bigotry out into the open: "If this boy on trial was a white boy, and the complaining witness a colored girl, there would be no occasion for me to argue the case before you. Prejudice? Certainly, there is prejudice. . . . Still, I believe that you are going to be fair in this case, that there is still a little spark of justice burning, and you will give this boy the presumption of innocence the law says is his."[31] This time a six-hour deliberation delivered a not guilty verdict. With this acquittal, Judge Cant dismissed charges against five of the other Black suspects, and Greene ceased pursuing cases against the rest.

Although the accused Black men were not local residents, the lynchings and the trials unleashed repressed racial prejudice among many white residents in Duluth and neighboring communities. In the days following the lynchings, Black families all over town reported threatening phone calls, bricks thrown through the street-facing windows of their homes in the middle of the night, physical assaults in public spaces, and verbal abuse. In nearby Superior, Chief of Police Louis Osborne was widely praised for his public promise to whites in his city, which echoed sentiments of Indian removal sixty years earlier: "We're going to run all idle Negroes out of Superior, and they're going to stay out."[32] Many terrified African Americans fleeing Superior on foot were turned away by Duluth police roadblocks before they could reach town. A nearby manager of a carnival fired all Black employees.

AFRICAN AMERICAN QUESTS FOR JUSTICE

Just weeks after the lynchings, on July 3, 1920, Elmer Jackson's father, Clifford Jackson, filed a suit against the Duluth police for negligence, seeking $7,500 in damages (approximately $100,000 in today's currency). But the city attorney, John E. Samuelson, dismissed it, stating simply, "This city is not liable." In the wake of this curt response and on the advice of his attorney, Jackson did not pursue the case further.[33] His Kansas-based attorney, Elisha Scott, however, continued to fight for Black equality and justice for the rest of his career; his sons, Charles and John Scott, were two of the three attorneys who filed the *Brown v. Board of Education* case, which ultimately desegregated America's public schools more than three decades later.[34]

Following the trials, in September 1920, a small group of Duluth's Black residents banded together to form the first Duluth branch of the NAACP. Together with NAACP leaders statewide, they began pushing for a state antilynching law. A central leader of this campaign was Nellie Griswold Francis, a resident of St. Paul who was a leader in Black Baptist circles and in the women's suffrage movement. She also served as director of the Republican Colored Women for Minnesota campaign. Nellie had been an outspoken leader from an early age. She was the only African American in her high school class of eighty-four people and won second prize in a national oratory competition for a presentation titled "Race Problems."[35]

Nellie and her husband, William, were both on the NAACP state board and were a formidable couple. William was a well-respected attorney, a member of the Minnesota Republican Central Committee, and a presidential elector in 1920. In July, he had written Minnesota governor Joseph Burnquist a letter enclosing the NAACP's investigative report on the Duluth lynchings and received a return letter from the governor thanking him. He was also a gifted speaker with the ability to cut to the chase. "The solution of the whole problem is simple justice," he declared, "a recognition of the fact that the rights of the humblest citizens are as worthy of protection as the highest."[36]

William wrote to W. E. B. Du Bois and the national NAACP office, which provided the couple with educational materials and a copy of Kentucky's 1897 antilynching law to use as a model. Together with a small group of Black attorneys in St. Paul, the Francises helped craft antilynching legislation for the state. Nellie also played a leading role in organizing events to build public support for the issue, including high-profile March 1921 appearances by Du Bois in both St. Paul and Duluth. Thinking long-term, Nellie designed these events not only to build support for this specific piece of legislation but also to create a sustainable community to work for Black civil rights. In addition to educational and strategy sessions, the gatherings featured Bible readings, folk songs, formal choral arrangements, and—at one rally—dancing until midnight.[37]

Introduced in the spring 1921 session, the Francises' antilynching bill easily passed both houses (41–0 in the House and 81–1 in the Senate) and was signed into law in April 1921, just ten months after the lynchings in Duluth; Governor Jacob Preus publicly stated that it would be a pleasure to sign it. The bill made any county in which a lynching occurred liable in a civil suit to the dependents of the victims. It also declared that any sheriff or other law enforcement officer who should "fail or neglect to use all lawful means to resist" a lynching would be removed from office by the governor. The bill, by design, set the maximum liability that could be recovered at $7,500, the same amount sought by Elmer Jackson's father in his failed suit against the city of Duluth. NAACP leaders celebrated this milestone, declaring it "the most important piece of legislation affecting our race that has ever passed in our state."[38]

In May, the Black community in St. Paul honored Nellie with a special event. They presented her with an engraved silver "loving cup" for her "untiring efforts" on behalf of justice and equality. Visibly moved by the recognition, Nellie passionately urged those in attendance to continue in the work. "Your children will reap the harvest of our solidarity—of our determination to stand together, to fight together, and if needs be, to die together," she declared, "for they are dying every day, the men and women of our race, martyrs to lynch-law." The event was held at Pilgrim Baptist Church in St. Paul, the congregation Robert Hickman founded, following his own emancipation journey, more than a half century earlier.[39]

While they were working on the passage of the Minnesota anti-lynching law, the powerhouse couple of William and Nellie Francis also worked diligently on Max Mason's behalf. With William's help, Mason appealed his case all the way to the Minnesota Supreme Court, which upheld his conviction. A judge in the minority, however, wrote in his dissent, "Convictions are not rested on possibilities. The story in its entirety is unusual and strikingly improbable."[40] For reasons that remain unknown—but in part due to the tireless work of Nellie, president of the Minnesota State Federation of Colored Women, which maintained a Max Mason Pardon Fund—Mason was released by the parole board after serving only four years, rather than the twelve-year minimum or the thirty-year maximum to be expected of a Black convict whose victim was white.[41] He was told, on condition of release, to leave the state and not to return to Minnesota. He returned to his home state of Alabama and died in Memphis, Tennessee, less than twenty years later, in 1942.

THE LEGACY OF WHITE SUPREMACY IN MINNESOTA

Consistent with trends across the US, the *Duluth Herald* reported in July 1922 that the Ku Klux Klan had organized a 1,500-member chapter in the city, which included many of its prominent citizens: Duluth's representative to the state legislature George W. Johnson (who later became the mayor), a municipal judge, county and city commissioners, members of the police and fire departments, a city clerk, a Methodist minister, school board members, schoolteachers, and small business owners whose names graced downtown retail shops. The group's publicly stated goals were "the preservation of American ideas and institutions and the maintenance of white supremacy"—objectives that were inseparable to its members.[42]

Whites who had been appalled by the lynchings and who opposed the overt tactics of violence and intimidation employed by the KKK publicly cleared their consciences by getting behind the 1921 anti-lynching law and getting on with business as usual. While the white supporters of the antilynching law rejected the use of vigilante justice to enforce white supremacy, most nevertheless supported laws and policies that sustained white supremacy both locally and statewide for decades to come.

As it became clear that whites in Duluth were, like their southern counterparts, committed to policies designed to perpetuate white supremacy, many African Americans simply left for places where there would be more security in numbers. According to the US Census Bureau, between 1920 and 1930, as Duluth grew overall by 2,000 persons, the city's already tiny Black population dropped 16 percent.[43]

Racial housing attitudes and restrictions hardened. In 1931, a Black family was attacked by an angry mob in their south Minneapolis home by whites who wanted them out of the neighborhood.[44] In the 1950s, Minnesota joined a dozen states in passing a constitutional amendment that required a general referendum before building a low-income family public housing project. This tool allowed middle-class whites to systematically veto any public housing proposals in their community. These proposals were race-neutral on their face but clearly racist in their intent. The amendment, for example, required a referendum on family public housing, which was more likely to be used by nonwhites, but not on senior citizen public housing, which was more likely to be used by whites.[45]

By 1940, like most cities in America, Duluth had instituted the formal practice of "redlining."[46] Collusion between real estate agents, mortgage lenders, and federal and state laws prevented Black Duluthians from living in neighborhoods that were designated "whites only" until the 1970s. The US Postal Service, which had about eighteen Black employees in Duluth at the time of the lynchings, did not hire any additional Black employees for four decades. And while Black residents were allowed to enroll at Duluth State Teachers College, they were not permitted to be placed as student teachers in the public school system, a requirement for certification.[47]

As for the story of the 1920 lynching of Elias Clayton, Elmer Jackson, and Isaac McGhie, after the passing of the antilynching law the following year, attention quickly waned. Most white Duluthians and Minnesotans seemed to agree with the sentiments a white resident expressed in a letter to the editor on June 21, 1920: "Last week's happening is indeed unfortunate—it cannot be undone, therefore it is better the quicker it is forgotten."[48] For the next six decades, the lynchings in Duluth would be mentioned occasionally by a teacher or an intrepid tour guide, or in private family conversations, but they mostly faded into a distant and unspeakable past.

Chapter Six

COMMEMORATION AND REPAIR IN MINNESOTA

FORGETTING

Like the mass execution of thirty-eight Dakota men and the forced Indian deportations of the nineteenth century, the erasure of the lynching of Elias Clayton, Elmer Jackson, and Isaac McGhie from collective memory in the twentieth century was achieved in informal and intentional ways. When Michael Fedo, a white Duluth native, first set out to write about the lynchings in the 1970s, based on a half-remembered story he had heard from his mother as a child, he found no existing books and few official records. Textbooks in Minnesota history, even those focused on a history of crime in the state, contained no mentions of the mob or the lynchings. The staff at the St. Louis County Historical Society told him that the society had maintained some records on the events but that a previous director had ordered them removed.[1] A St. Louis County court clerk claimed that a judge had ordered the records from the trials to be burned—a statement that subsequently turned out to be a lie designed to discourage curious students and journalists.[2]

A librarian at the Minnesota Historical Society in St. Paul was finally able to locate a single manila folder with faded newspaper clippings and a pamphlet summarizing the events.[3] These sparse materials opened the door to other sources, and Fedo coupled the historical accounts with interviews of residents to produce the first carefully researched book-length treatment of the lynchings. But Fedo's 1979 book, originally bearing the unfortunate title *They Was Just Niggers*, was published by a small press that went bankrupt just before the book hit the shelves. It sold few copies and had little impact on public awareness.

In his foreword to a second edition of Fedo's book, William D. Green, a professor of history at Augsburg University in Minneapolis and vice president of the Minnesota Historical Society, also expressed his surprise and dismay about the conspiracy of silence. Green noted, "It was as if the event had never occurred. I had never heard of the incident. No one I knew had heard of it. For most Minnesotans, the intervening years since the lynchings would obliterate their collective memory, leaving a diminishing handful to treat it, like all dirty little secrets, as something best left unspoken."[4]

REMEMBERING

The seventieth anniversary of the event, however, brought modest first attempts to lift the veil of silence. In the early 1990s, small groups began to hold "Day of Remembrance" vigils downtown at the lynching site. A group of local citizens began a quest to locate the three men's final resting places, which had widely been assumed to be in unmarked graves in a potter's field. Craig Grau, a political science professor at the University of Minnesota Duluth, discovered that, contrary to this mythology, First Lutheran Church had secretly arranged for the three Black victims to be buried in unmarked graves in a section of Norwegian Lutheran Cemetery (now Park Hill Cemetery) dedicated to indigent people.

The motivations for this act have been lost to time, but perhaps the 1920 leaders of the church may have sought to compensate in some small private way for what they failed to do publicly. The leadership at First Lutheran Church who knew of these interments in 1920 kept the secret to themselves. They certainly would have been concerned about the desecration of the graves. But they also knew that burying three African Americans—whom many whites believed guilty of a heinous crime—in a cemetery reserved for Norwegian Lutherans would undoubtedly have set off a storm of protest among many of their own members.

Equipped with the new evidence, Grau, along with leaders of First Lutheran Church and the Duluth branch of the NAACP, spearheaded an effort to increase awareness, raise funds, and mark the graves. On October 26, 1991, three granite markers were placed on the graves. Each headstone contained first and last name, the years of birth and death on either side of a cross, and, at the bottom, the defiant but curious phrase "Deterred But Not Defeated." Leftover funds were used to set up a small scholarship at the University of Minnesota in the victims' names.[5]

Rev. Stanley Olson, pastor of First Lutheran Church, spoke at the ceremony: "Somebody made the decision to welcome into this white, Scandinavian cemetery three black men who had suffered such indignity. This effort now to dignify the very undignified death of these men by putting gravestones there, builds on a tradition of compassion that was manifested in 1920 by the decision to move the bodies to Park Hill Cemetery."[6] While Olson's reference to a "tradition of compassion that was manifested in 1920" is an overreach, given the long silence of the church and its leaders, the marking of the graves was nonetheless an important first step on the path to truth-telling and a permanent commemoration of the lynchings.

That same year, the Duluth chapter of the NAACP also launched an effort to mark the site of the lynching. A wreath was laid at the site on the anniversary in 1991, an action that gave birth to small annual vigils throughout the 1990s.[7] These early efforts brought this suppressed history out of the shadows and anchored it in public memory with an accessible historical narrative, the first permanent physical markers, and a rhythm of shared commemoration.

THE CLAYTON-JACKSON-McGHIE MEMORIAL

Just ahead of the eightieth anniversary of the lynchings, Michael Fedo got a call from the Minnesota Historical Society with an offer to republish his book under the new title *The Lynchings in Duluth*. This time the momentum from the previous gravesite marking and the upcoming anniversary provided more fertile ground. In 2000, the book sold more briskly, and the story of the Duluth lynchings was featured on NPR's *All Things Considered* and in a column at the *Atlantic* by James Fallows. It even garnered international coverage in the London *Times* and Paris's *Le Monde*.[8]

Fedo's book also caught the attention of Duluth resident and local reporter Heidi Bakk-Hansen. While reading it, she realized that on her commute to work she regularly passed the prominent downtown corner where the lynchings happened. This daily juxtaposition of historical rupture and contemporary silence pushed her to put pen to paper. On June 7, 2000, her story about the forgotten lynchings was featured on the cover page of the local alternative weekly publication, the *Ripsaw*, under the title "Duluth's Lingering Shame."[9] In this short but moving piece, Bakk-Hansen laid out the story and called for the placement of a permanent marker at the lynching site to memorialize the victims.

The article concludes with the question, "Will the city step forward?" Bakk-Hansen implored city leaders to answer in the affirmative, quoting Henry Banks, a local Black civil rights leader, entrepreneur, and organizer of Martin Luther King Jr. Day events: "This city needs to live its truth. And show us this community is ours as well." Banks was adamant that the city needed to do more than just verbally acknowledge this history. The final sentence is a simple notice that "a vigil will be held on June 15, starting at 9 a.m., on the corner of First Street and Second Avenue East to support the placement of a permanent memorial."[10]

The article, together with the backing of Fedo's book by the Minnesota Historical Society, sparked a large turnout at the eightieth anniversary vigil and inspired additional conversations about the possibilities of doing more to help the community reckon with this ugly part of its history. Together, Bakk-Hansen, Banks, and Catherine Ostos, an educator who is Latina, spearheaded a campaign to create a public memorial that would tell the truth about this terrible event in the city's history—one that whites had largely tried to forget, and that the tiny minority of Black residents talked about only among themselves.

After more than two years of organizing marches, concerts, art exhibits, lectures, and other events to raise awareness—and convincing an initially skeptical Mayor Gary Doty to get behind the effort—their efforts resulted in the creation of the Clayton-Jackson-McGhie Memorial Committee. More than $267,000 in donations poured in from the community. One anonymous $10,000 donation came from a female relative of a man who had been working at the jail that fateful night, charged with ensuring the inmates' safety. She said his failure to fulfill that duty had haunted him for the duration of his life.

At noon on Friday, October 10, 2003, on a corner lot on First Street directly across from the lamppost where the 1920 lynching took place, the committee unveiled its memorial plaza, making Duluth one of the first major cities in the post–Jim Crow era to create an official public memorial to lynching victims. What had started as a campaign to add a modest plaque to the site of the violence ended with the creation of the Clayton-Jackson-McGhie Memorial, a fifty-three-by-seventy-foot plaza paved with bricks and accented with plantings, a memorial wall, and life-size bronze reliefs of Elias Clayton, Elmer Jackson, and Isaac McGhie.

More than three thousand people turned out for the unveiling. A massive processional, led by the leaders of the commission and the Tremé Brass Band, from New Orleans, followed the route the men had been forced to walk from the jail to the intersection. The program at the memorial site featured Mayor Doty, author Michael Fedo, members of the memorial committee, a state supreme court judge, local clergy, and schoolchildren. Mayor Doty opened his remarks by declaring that the event was "a celebration of the lives of three young men." But he also emphasized the importance of this difficult recognition for the contemporary residents of the city: "Yes, it happened in Duluth. No, we're not proud of it. But we're going to learn from it."[11]

Most of the attendees and speakers at the event were local, but one of the most stirring moments came from Warren Read, a fourth-grade teacher from Kingston, Washington. While doing genealogical research on his family, Read was horrified to discover that his great-grandfather Louis Dondino had been one of the ringleaders of the lynch mob. When he received the news about the monument unveiling, he asked if he could come to symbolically apologize to Elmer, Elias, and Isaac, and to their families and descendants. Ostos and the committee accepted his offer and gave him space on the program.

It was a complicated address. Read began by expressing his hope that the photographs of the 2003 crowd, gathered for the purpose of commemoration and reconciliation, would come to replace the infamous postcard image that had frozen the awful racial violence of 1920 in time. Read wanted the crowd to know that Dondino's actions that fateful night were not the sum of his family or even of Dondino himself. He told a story about a lifelong friendship Dondino had with a Black man. Read also honestly confessed that while he had no idea whether Dondino ever felt remorse for his role in the lynching, his family hoped "that the way in which he completed his life, the example he was for his granddaughter and his friends later in life spoke this for him." But Read did not equivocate about the culpability of Dondino's actions or about his own sense of connection to them: "I stand here today as a representative of [my great-grandfather's] legacy, and I willingly place that responsibility on my shoulders."[12]

His voice choking with emotion, he then offered an apology, on behalf of his family, to each of the victims and their families:

> For Elmer Jackson, I am sorry that unreason and bigotry disallowed you the right to prove your innocence and deprived you of the opportunity to create a legacy of your own choosing.
>
> For Elias Clayton, ignorance and self-righteousness were the fuel for your untimely and undignified death. For this, I offer my deepest apologies.
>
> For Isaac McGhie, I give you my heartfelt apology. Fear can never be used for an excuse for hysteria and passage of time can never be used as a reason for ignoring injustice.[13]

Read concluded, "As a family, we have used the discovery of this as a tool for continued discovery of ourselves. This means our past, present and future selves, and a lesson that true shame is not in the discovery of a terrible event such as this, but in the refusal to acknowledge and learn from that event."[14] His remarks were met with loud and long applause. As the crowd dispersed, Read felt a gentle hand on his arm. A woman about his age leaned in close. "My family was there that night too," she confided. "I want to thank you for speaking for me."[15]

Two decades later, the Clayton-Jackson-McGhie Memorial continues to bear witness to Duluth's confession of a shameful past and commitment to a brighter future. As you enter the plaza from First Street, the word "Respect," boldly painted in orange, marks the beginning of a curving brick-lined concrete pathway, inviting you to walk along two memorial walls that intersect in the far corner. Both walls are covered with inspirational and thought-provoking quotes from a wildly diverse group of famous people. If you don't allow yourself to be distracted by the opaque rationale behind their selection or the occasional dissonance with their original contexts, the inscriptions add a sense of gravity and universality to the memorial.

As you arrive at the first wall on your left, there are quotes by Oscar Wilde, the Buddha, Marian Wright Edelman, Anne Lamott, Euripides, and this from Albert Einstein: "The world is a dangerous place, not because of those who do evil, but because of those who do nothing." Below your feet, on the pathway anchoring the wall, is the word "Compassion." Curving to the right, the second wall contains another set of quotes from artists, leaders, and writers, including this from James Baldwin: "We are responsible for the world in which we find ourselves, if only because we are the only sentient force that can change it."

The far end of the second wall is anchored by the bronze reliefs of Elias Clayton, Elmer Jackson, and Isaac McGhie. On the pathway, the word "Atonement" lies directly under the figures. A concrete capstone spanning both walls contains these words by eighteenth-century Irish orator and member of the British Parliament Edmund Burke, inscribed in large, deeply carved letters: "An event has happened, upon which it is difficult to speak, and impossible to remain silent."

THE LEGACY OF THE CLAYTON-JACKSON-McGHIE MEMORIAL

If Duluth was once a city with collective amnesia, it is now very much a city with citizens willing to confront its past, admit its

sins, and move forward in a spirit of forgiveness and together-
ness. And in the process they hope to heal the city's open, unspoken wounds that had festered for decades.

—Michael Fedo, author of *The Lynchings in Duluth*[16]

The placing of a public monument hasn't solved all of Duluth's racial problems or prevented ongoing expressions of white supremacy.
But the commitment to tell this truth—and the community that assembled to make good on this promise—has created a precedent for
moral accountability and an enduring public forum for racial justice.

On Election Day in 2012, an effigy of President Barack Obama was
found hanging from a Duluth billboard. In response, the mayor's office,
along with the board of trustees from the Clayton-Jackson-McGhie
Memorial, declared that as stewards of that memorial, they were required to speak out. Their response looked to the memorial as a public
commitment "to build a more just and inclusive community." Based on
that down payment on a different future for the city in race relations,
they declared:

> As a community, we cannot tolerate bigotry and hate. We cannot
> ignore or remain indifferent to the heinous nature of this act. We
> can speak out and defy such behavior in our community. We can
> commit to actively eradicate racism and hatred in our midst.[17]

Fifteen years after the unveiling, these memorialization efforts
were still paying dividends. After the opening of the National Memorial for Peace and Justice in Montgomery, Alabama, in 2018, a group
of thirty-five Duluth residents gathered to make the 1,223-mile trip.
The group included many who had been present from the beginning
of this journey, including Bakk-Hansen, who checked people onto
the bus with a clipboard. But it also included some new faces, such

as Mike Tusken, Duluth's chief of police, the grandnephew of Irene Tusken, the white woman who falsely accused the African American men of raping her. Tusken didn't know about his own family's connection to the lynchings until the unveiling of the memorial in 2003. In an interview ahead of the trip, Tusken emphasized the importance of the pilgrimage. "This has been a journey for me, being that I didn't find out for years my family's history. . . . I can't miss this. It's too big for our nation, too big for our city."[18]

Between the 2003 unveiling of the Duluth memorial and the 2018 opening of the National Memorial for Peace and Justice, Warren Read continued to dig into his family's ties to the lynchings, publishing his personal journey in *The Lyncher in Me: A Search for Redemption in the Face of History* in 2008.[19] Along the way, he located the family of Elmer Jackson using online genealogical tools. He connected with Virginia Huston—Jackson's cousin, who was in her seventies and still living in his hometown of Pennytown, Missouri—and told her what he had discovered about that terrible night and his own family's connection to it.

After some email exchanges, the two agreed to meet in Montgomery during the Duluth delegation's visit and to tour the National Memorial together. Standing outside the Equal Justice Initiative's Legacy Museum in Montgomery, Huston introduced Read to others who didn't know the connection, saying:

> Warren is my baby brother now. He brought the research to us to let us know what happened. We didn't know what happened to Elmer, but with his research, we now know. We have closure. Warren's great-grandfather, he was instrumental in getting the lynch mob. But that's not Warren. He shouldn't have any guilty feelings or anything. We're going to look forward, we're not looking back. We're going to build ourselves up and live for today and live for tomorrow. He will always be my brother and I love him very much.[20]

Read and Huston later returned to Duluth and planted a black oak tree at the site of Jackson's grave in Park Hill Cemetery. The sapling had been grown from an acorn collected at Jackson's family home in Pennytown, Missouri.[21]

Following the tour of the National Memorial for Peace and Justice, Duluth police chief Mike Tusken was visibly moved. He explained that the experience of confronting this troubling past had convinced him that his initial feelings of grief or shame had to give way to commitments to action. "Leaving this memorial, I think everyone has to ask themselves, 'What are you personally going to do to confront racism? To make sure that people have access and equality?' And that really is the takeaway everyone should leave with: What are you going to do?"[22]

Three weeks before the planned centennial commemoration of the lynchings in Duluth, the nation was thrown into chaos over the murder of another Black man. On May 25, 2020, Minnesota was thrust into the international spotlight when Derek Chauvin, a white police officer, held his knee on the neck of George Floyd, after he was subdued and cuffed, for eight minutes and forty-six seconds, until he died of asphyxiation. The viral video demonstrating the disregard for a Black man's life by a white cop went viral, setting off months of protests throughout the country.

Floyd's murder was also shocking because the event did not take place in the Deep South but in the far north. Just as the Birmingham police became the ugly face of bigotry and white supremacy in May 1963, so did Minneapolis police in May 2020. And just as those images from Alabama propelled the civil rights movement six decades ago, the heartbreaking indifference and cruelty captured in that video from Minnesota has propelled the Movement for Black Lives in our era.

The Saturday after George Floyd was killed, more than one thousand people gathered in Duluth at the Clayton-Jackson-McGhie Memorial. After nearly two decades, the memorial had become an organic part of the city landscape. It served as an informal meeting spot, a gathering place, a forum to express grievances, and a launching point for marches for civil rights. So, when anger and dismay flooded into the streets in the wake of Floyd's death, the memorial plaza was the place Duluthians instinctively knew to come. Jordon Moses, a local activist who worked closely with the Clayton-Jackson-McGhie Memorial Committee, spoke at the rally, noting that the role the memorial was playing that day was a direct answer to those who had been skeptical about digging up the history of Duluth's worst days. The memorial was simultaneously serving as a place to come together to express grievances and functioning as a reminder that there is much work yet to be done.

> They ask, "Why do we still gotta talk about this, why does this still matter?" There's something in the roots of our community that needs to be dug out so that this can never happen again. And so that's the reality, we're talking about it because we never fixed the problem. We never solved the problem.[23]

The work of the memorial committee, with its personal connection to police chief Tusken, also importantly impacted community policing practices. Over three decades, Tusken had built a sense of trust with community leaders, including leaders of Duluth's small African American community. When Dylann Roof murdered nine African American worshippers at Mother Emanuel AME Church in Charleston, South Carolina, in 2015, Tusken showed up and spoke to the crowd gathered at the memorial. Tusken's experience with the memorialization work also impacted his work as police chief, where he implemented programs to diversify the composition of the police force and institute diversity training for white officers to help them better serve Duluth's racial minorities. After George Floyd's murder—when people gathered without permits, flowing into the streets and gathering at the memorial plaza almost daily for nearly a year—Tusken understood that a large police presence might unnecessarily escalate a peaceful protest. He deployed smaller groups of officers and utilized remote cameras to monitor the events for safety.

In an interview with me, Tusken described the Clayton-Jackson-McGhie Memorial plaza as vital shared civic space. "It's been really healing for our communities," he said. It's "a gathering space, space for times when there are tragedies across the country, for people to get up and to speak and to have a rallying cry—how do we build better people, better communities?"[24] This response by a police force to respectfully protect what had become a sacred public space was markedly different from the confrontational approaches seen in so many other cities across the country.

The lead-up to the centennial of the 1920 Duluth lynchings also saw some semblance of long-overdue justice for Max Mason, the lone Black man wrongfully convicted of raping Irene Tusken. After decades of work by Duluth activist Jordon Moses, the Clayton-Jackson-McGhie Memorial Committee, and Minneapolis attorney Jerry Blackwell, Mason was finally pardoned by the Minnesota Board of Pardons on June 12, 2020, nearly one hundred years to the day from his initial arrest. It was the first posthumous pardon issued in Minnesota state history.[25]

Blackwell argued that guilty white consciences from the lynching made Mason's conviction, as the first Black suspect brought to trial, near certain. Without "a scapegoat to exculpate the actions of the mob," he argued, it "would have meant that the lynch mob had not murdered rapists, but innocent men."[26] The pardon application was also supported by a wide range of public officials, including a rare letter issued by the chief judge of the US district court for Minnesota, John R. Tunheim. "I have read the entire transcript of the trial of Mr. Mason, and to say that he was convicted on the flimsiest of evidence is a vast understatement," he declared. "We can only do what we can now, and that is to try to address the injustices that can be remedied, and never, ever, forget this sad and awful history." Governor Tim Walz called the decision "100 years overdue."[27]

The 2020 centennial of the Duluth lynchings fell just three days after Mason's pardon and three weeks after the murder of George Floyd by Minneapolis police. It also fell approximately three months into the lockdown due to the COVID-19 pandemic. The original plan had been to gather more than ten thousand people, enough to rival or exceed the number present for the lynchings in 1920, but due to pandemic concerns, the Clayton-Jackson-McGhie committee announced a postponement of most events until 2021 (which were also modest due to the ongoing pandemic). Even so, when June 15 arrived, a few hundred people assembled outside at the Clayton-Jackson-McGhie Memorial plaza, including Governor Walz, state attorney general Keith Ellison, and Jerry Blackwell.[28]

At a press conference, Governor Walz acknowledged some serendipity, given that Mason's pardon was decades in the making, but he also noted the appropriateness of the alignment: "There is a direct line between what happened with Max Mason and Clayton, Jackson, and McGhie. There is a direct line to what happened to George Floyd on the streets of Minneapolis."[29] Ellison cautioned against easy dismissal of both events as one-off anomalies. "You may think that this is a matter of mean police doing mean things to people," he said. "This is a social disease buried deep in the core of our society."[30]

Abdul Hussein, a twenty-year-old African American student at the University of Minnesota Duluth, talked about his own fears and frustrations with the police, but he also saw hope in the diverse crowd that turned out even during the pandemic. "You see more people my age, but [of] different colors—white people—they're coming to support, and that gives me so much hope, that they care about me, they care about the same rights, they think I deserve the same rights." Blackwell, the attorney who fought for Mason's pardon, also sounded a hopeful note, combined with an admonishment to the crowd that progress is only possible when people decide to take action. "Do the right thing. Treat people fairly. Treat people justly," he said. "Let's all collectively declare that we are better than this. We are better than this. We deserve better."[31]

The importance of the memorial at the centennial of the lynchings, particularly in the wake of Floyd's murder by police, and the distance the city had come since the memorial's unveiling in 2003, was not lost on Carl Crawford, a founding Clayton-Jackson-McGhie Memorial Committee board member and the city's first human rights officer. Raised in Los Angeles, Crawford, who is Black, first arrived in the area in the late 1980s as a recruited basketball player for the University of Wisconsin–Superior. On his very first trip across the bridge to Duluth, he and some friends were approached by a white man on the sidewalk who made sure he imparted one piece of information about Duluth to the young Black men: "Did you know there was a lynching here in Duluth?"[32]

Since then, the lynchings in Duluth have moved from a sinister secret—and one that could be used to instill fear—to a public testimony of confession and repentance that has laid a foundation for a more inclusive future. "That's what we were able to do here, with many people of many walks of life, many races," Crawford told me with pride during an interview. "We've been able to come here and make this place a spot for healing, a spot for pain, but more importantly, a spot for reflection—that we never forget."[33]

Coda: Mendota Heights

At approximately 2:30 p.m. ET on Saturday, May 14, 2022, in Buffalo, New York, a white supremacist terrorist—motivated by a fear that whites were being "replaced" by immigrants and the growth of the nonwhite population in the US—massacred ten people and injured three others in a grocery store in a predominantly Black neighborhood. As this horrific racial violence was unfolding, I was sitting on a hill in Mendota Heights, Minnesota, overlooking the confluence of the Minnesota and Mississippi Rivers.

I had been invited to join a "Healing Minnesota Stories" tour led by Rev. Jim Bear Jacobs, a member of the Stockbridge-Munsee Mohican Nation and the director of racial justice for the Minnesota Council of Churches, and Native American theologian Kelly Sherman-Conroy of the Oglala Lakota Nation. I was appended to a group of approximately twenty-five people from a local white evangelical church. As we made our way around several sites near the Twin Cities across four hours, I was struck by how central and explicit the goal of demographic and cultural replacement has been to white supremacy in this country—a truth plainly evident in the systematic genocide and removal of Native Americans from their historic lands by white European settler colonists, who acted with the support of soldiers supplied by the government and moral justifications produced by the church.

We began the tour on the dandelion-carpeted green lawn of St. Peter's Catholic Church, founded in 1840, the oldest church in the state of Minnesota. Standing in this place, the legacy of white settler colonialism was all-enveloping. The church sits on high ground known as Mendota Heights (after a Dakota word *mdo-te*, meaning "meeting of the waters"), in view of Fort Snelling (originally called Fort Saint Anthony after the Catholic saint) just across the river, on a road named Sibley Memorial Highway (named after the man responsible for the mass executions and deportation of the Dakota people from the state).

One of the major stops on the tour was Fort Snelling State Park, a beautiful area that includes the historical military outpost perched on a bluff overlooking the confluence of the two rivers. We were given time to take a meditative walk on the hiking trails that loop through the river valley—the site where Robert Hickman's intrepid band finally disembarked from the *Northerner* to find emancipation, and the site where 1,600 mostly women, children, and elderly Dakota captives spent a miserable, deadly winter ahead of their deportation from the state. In one of the most moving experiences on my trip, Jacobs invited each of us to take an offering of loose tobacco and to sprinkle it along the path as we walked as a way of honoring this place as sacred ground.

The tour concluded on a 350-foot-high bluff in Mendota Heights with a commanding view of the two rivers, Fort Snelling, and St. Peter's Church, where the tour began. The competing names that have been assigned to that hill are also testimony to the violent logic of replacement. In documented history dating back to the early 1800s and in oral Native American traditions reaching back much further, this land was known as *Oheyawahi* ("the place much visited"). It served as a sacred burial and ceremonial space for the Dakota people. Early French fur traders acknowledged it as *La Butte des Morts* ("hill of the dead"). But as white settlements increased in Minnesota in the mid-1800s, the place became known in English as Pilot Knob, because its geographic distinctiveness allowed riverboats—with their cargoes of goods and guns, powerful symbols of white settler colonialism—to safely mark their position along the great rivers.

In 1925, most of the hill was purchased by the Masons and christened "Acacia Cemetery," after a sprig used in Masonic funeral ceremonies. Early advertisements declared that the land was now to be "dedicated to the exclusive and perpetual use of Masons and their families," with promises that "a perpetual fund will care for the entire cemetery for all time."[34] A monument construction plan, including a memorial temple, a large obelisk, and extensive landscaping, removed more than twenty vertical feet from the top of the hill, a process that conveniently purged the land of most Native American remains. A few remaining bones, most of which likely belonged to Dakota people, were collected haphazardly in a vault at the periphery of the property when they interfered with new landscaping plans or a purchased white burial plot.[35]

As our tour group rested weary feet on *Oheyawahi*, Jacobs and Sherman-Conroy delivered their closing remarks and then opened the floor for a last round of questions. There were a few queries related to historical details. An older man expressed his gratitude for the gift of the history, which most in the group, including myself, had not known. Then a woman who looked to be in her thirties asked the native tour leaders what they hoped groups of white Christians like them would take away from the experience. Rev. Jacobs's answer was the last thing I heard on the tour: "I don't need white Christians to be smarter. I need them to be better."

Nearly a century after the project was first advertised, the Masonic cemetery still sits on the left side of the access road that dead-ends just beyond pristine white mausoleums and manicured lawns. On the right side of the road, where I sat with the late-afternoon sun on my back on that unseasonably warm May afternoon, there is an unmarked and untended field. Jacobs had explained that through local preservation efforts, 125 scarred acres have been placed on the National Register of Historic Places, protected from future disturbance and development. The bones of Native peoples that were laid to rest here have been lost. But today, under the watch of a local nonprofit, the land is being restored to an oak savanna, slowly healing from the wounds of the past.

PART THREE

TULSA

Chapter Seven

BEFORE OKLAHOMA

In the beginning God created Oklahoma, with its broad, level, fertile prairies; its wooded valleys, its rich mineral mountains, and deep oil pools. White men forced the Indians to move into this territory, but later, when its wealth was discovered, began to covet what they had despised.

—Paul D. Mitchell, *From Tepees to Towers:*
A History of the Methodist Church in Oklahoma (1947)[1]

THE LAND AND EARLY PEOPLES

As a political entity, the land we know today as Oklahoma is a remnant. It was formed after other territories and states had been carved out of the vast Louisiana Purchase, of which it was a part. Before it too succumbed to the legal and extralegal machinations of white settler colonists, this area was imagined by the US government as a solution to the "Indian problem" east of the Mississippi River. Known as Indian Country, it served as a designated refugee zone for Indigenous peoples as they were forcibly driven out of the Southeast as European settler colonists pushed Red people west to make room for white crops and Black slaves.

The lines that create the unique profile of the state we today call Oklahoma, with only its southern border defined by a natural feature, did not appear in their final form on a map until its relatively recent statehood in 1907. Oklahoma's pronounced western panhandle, appended late in the state's history, provides a useful imaginative tool for understanding its topography. The highest point in the state, at Black Mesa in the panhandle's northwestern tip, is more than 5,000 feet above sea level. The state dips diagonally down to only 325 feet above sea level at its southeastern corner, an average drop of about seven feet per mile. The tilt of the state "pan" causes two major rivers to spill out of the state's eastern edge on their way to join the Mississippi River. The more northern Arkansas River flows from the eastern slopes of the Rocky Mountains, gathers the Cimarron and Canadian Rivers within the state, and finally empties into the Mississippi River in the Delta just above Greenville, Mississippi. The Red River, which forms the state's southernmost boundary, continues its southeasterly run, also reaching the Mississippi River just below Mississippi's state border at Angola, Louisiana.[2]

As a borderland and crossroads, Oklahoma can be a land of unpredictable extremes. Because it is a collision point for hot and cold air, it is subject to abrupt weather changes, including "northers" with blasts of cold air rushing down from the plains and violent thunderstorms spewing lightning and baseball-sized hailstones. While its northern neighbor Kansas is perhaps the most infamous state in tornado alley, thanks to *The Wizard of Oz*, Oklahoma is the state with the greatest number of violent (EF5/F5 rated) tornadoes since 1950—65 compared to 49 in Kansas. In western Oklahoma, due to a steady prevailing wind from the south, the scattered trees mature with their limbs permanently reaching north.

The first human activity in the area dates back more than ten thousand years. There is fossil evidence that Indigenous hunting clans traveled a seasonal circuit following game, including the woolly

184

mammoth and giant bison. From approximately 500 to 1300 CE, a people known as Spiro mound builders erected flourishing villages and ceremonial mounds in what is today eastern Oklahoma. The Spiro people were an advanced agricultural society, with sophisticated levees and crop management techniques, and they also produced beautiful pottery, jewelry, textiles, and metal goods.[3]

This society declined in the 1300s and was gradually absorbed into three other Indigenous groups that settled mostly along the area's major rivers and hunted the plentiful buffalo on the plains: the Caddoans (Caddo, Wichita, and Pawnee), Siouans (Quapaw and Osage), and Athapascans (Plains Apache). These were the principal people groups that Francisco Vázquez de Coronado encountered on his expedition in July 1541 from Spain. Although neither Coronado nor the Indigenous peoples of the area were aware of it, his countryman Hernando de Soto had already claimed the area for Spain just two months earlier when de Soto's party landed on the banks of the Mississippi River. Under the unbridled logic of the Doctrine of Discovery, that vast Spanish claim included territories drained by the great river, which included the Arkansas and Red Rivers of Oklahoma.

Like de Soto, Coronado's expedition was driven by the motives of colonial conquest, Christian missionary zeal, and the search for fabled cities of gold. King Charles V formally charged Coronado to "place the land under my rule and bring its natives to the knowledge of my Holy Catholic faith."[4] While de Soto approached the Mississippi River from Florida and the east, Coronado began his journey from the western coast of Mexico and moved up through today's New Mexico and Texas before heading north to Oklahoma. It was a brief foray. When he arrived at the Indigenous village on the Arkansas River known as Quivira, part of the Wichita tribe, he found a modest farming village made up of tattooed people living in dome-shaped grass huts rather than a magnificent city with walls of solid gold. He was so angry he ordered his Native American guide to be executed.

Before leaving, however, Coronado performed the rituals associated with the Doctrine of Discovery, which were necessary to establish Spanish claim to the region. He met with tribal leaders, allegedly securing their voluntary submission to Spain's distant king. One of the expedition's missionaries, Friar Juan de Padilla, along with two Indigenous people who had reportedly converted to Christianity and a soldier, stayed behind to work for the conversion of the Wichita tribe to Christianity.[5] This effort was unwelcome and short-lived. Padilla was ambushed and killed while traveling between villages the following year. His companions were held prisoner for nearly a year before finally escaping and returning to Spanish settlements in the south.

Having staked Spain's claim, Coronado began his return journey south and then back to the Spanish court. Upon arrival, he delivered the mixed news to his king. First, he reported that the Native chiefs had taken an oath pledging "obedience to Your Majesty and placing themselves under your Royal Lordship." But he also reported the disappointing news about the mythical, fabulously wealthy cities of the region: "What I am sure of is that there is not any gold nor any other metal in all this country."[6]

The lack of easily extractable treasure and its remote interior location meant that there was minimal and intermittent Spanish activity in the area now constituting Oklahoma during the period of Spanish claims from 1540 to 1700. Over the next century, interest in the area was largely driven by the fur trade along its major navigable rivers. European claims to the lands changed several times—it was alternatively New Spain and New France—until the US finally purchased the right of preemption from France in 1803 in the Louisiana Purchase.

INDIAN COUNTRY

Thus, Oklahoma, like the southwestern portion of Minnesota discussed earlier, was part of the vast tract of land west of the Mississippi River and east of the Rocky Mountains that was brought under US sovereignty with the Louisiana Purchase. After additional states and territories were carved out in the opening decades of the nineteenth century, the remaining area showed up on official maps of North America simply as "unorganized US territory" and later as "Indian Country." Even before the Indian Removal Act of 1830, three major eastern tribes had already been assigned nearly all of Oklahoma territory by treaties negotiated in 1825 and 1828. The Choctaws, for ceding eastern lands in Mississippi and Alabama, were granted roughly the southern half of Oklahoma. The Cherokee, for ceding their lands in northern Georgia, North Carolina, and eastern Tennessee, were granted the bulk of northeastern Oklahoma. The Creeks were granted lands in the center and northwestern corner of the state in exchange for lands in southern Georgia, Alabama, and Mississippi.[7]

Shortly thereafter, in 1833, the Seminoles, pushed out of Florida, agreed to join the Creeks in their territory, and in 1837, evicted Chickasaws took new homes in the Choctaw region. The Chickasaws and the Seminoles received their own domains in 1855 and 1856, respectively, resulting in each of the so-called "five civilized tribes" residing in independent republics. These new arrivals flooded into areas that were occupied by existing groups—Wichitas, Caddoes, Kiowas, Comanches, Quapaws, and Osages—leading to frequent and sometimes violent conflicts, and additional forced relocations by the US government.[8]

Each of the tribes received lofty promises from the US government.

The Treaty with the Western Cherokee, proclaimed on May 18, 1828, contained these pledges in its opening paragraph:

> WHEREAS, it being the anxious desire of the Government of the United States to secure to the Cherokee nation of Indians a permanent home ... , and which shall, under the most solemn guarantee of the United States, be, and remain, theirs forever a home that shall never, in all future time, be embarrassed by having extended around it the lines, or placed over it the jurisdiction of a Territory or State, nor be pressed upon by the extension, in any way, of any of the limits of any existing Territory or State.[9]

President Andrew Jackson wrote the following on March 23, 1829, in a letter to Creek leaders:

> Beyond the great river Mississippi, where a part of your nation has gone, your father has provided a country large enough for all of you, and he advises you to remove to it. There your white brothers will not trouble you; they will have no claim to the land, and you can live upon it, you and all your children, as long as the grass grows, or the water runs, in peace and plenty. It will be yours forever.[10]

These eternal guarantees lasted less than forty years. Following the Civil War, the US government took advantage of some tribes' alignment with the Confederacy, and the decimation of tribal well-being the war brought, to renege on earlier promises while advancing a national goal of continued Indian removal from eastern territories. In the Reconstruction Treaties of 1866, the US reclaimed the entire western half of Oklahoma from these five major tribes.[11] Lured by similar promises from the US government, and under various degrees of duress, in all more than twelve thousand people from dozens of tribes were removed from their homelands and resettled within this western section of Oklahoma as the march of white colonization in the East continued unabated. As late as 1889, with the exception of the panhandle and a small southeastern area in dispute with Texas, all of Oklahoma remained designated as an Indian re-settlement zone. More than eighty thousand Native Americans were building new lives on twenty-one separate reservations.[12]

But this too was about to change. In less than twenty more years, rapacious white settler colonists, envious of these Indigenous hold-ings, launched campaigns in virtually every domain—political, legal, cultural, and public opinion—to wrest control of even these lands. Native Americans in Oklahoma were subjected to an onslaught of disingenuous overtures by white leaders, specious legal maneuver-ings, political power plays, and outright thievery at the hands of bankers, railway companies, land speculators, churches, and others seeking to profit from opening Native American lands.

Professional promoters called "Boomers" were hired to mobi-lize potential white colonists. They were buoyed by a novel legal theory, promoted by two attorneys, T. C. Sears, who worked for the Missouri-Kansas-Texas Railroad, and Elias C. Boudinot, an attorney for the Cherokee and member of the tribe, that fourteen million acres of land in Indian Territory belonged to the public domain of the United States and was therefore open to white settlers. Part of this newly imagined free land included two million acres of "Unas-signed Lands" that had been taken from the Cherokee to resettle other tribes but had not yet been used for that purpose.[13]

The duo began promoting this idea in newspapers throughout the East, creating enough interest that potential settler colonists began arriving on the borders of Indian Country to gain first access when these lands opened. By 1879, there were three "Oklahoma colonies" in Kansas and Texas near the Cherokee borders. The leaders of these colonies energized their followers with appeals to the religious lan-guage of divine discovery. David Payne, a former Union military leader, organized the most robust of these Boomer encampments and regularly quoted the Old Testament and harnessed Christian hymnody in support of his cause.[14] His favorite verse was: "And the Lord commanded unto Moses, 'Go forth and possess the Promised Land.'" The anthem of his movement was "On to Beulah Land," which opens with this stanza:

I've reached the land of corn and wine,
And all its riches freely mine;
Here shines undimmed one blissful day,
For all my night has passed away.[15]

Unwilling to wait for legal permission, Boomers regularly organized unlawful incursions into Cherokee territory, sometimes going as far as platting towns and breaking ground for farms. When they were reported to federal authorities by Native Americans or discovered by federal officials, they were ejected as trespassers, but these incursions created fantastical national press stories and ultimately strengthened the movement by keeping the issue before land-hungry white Americans and sympathetic members of Congress.

In 1889, the Boomer movement managed to get a rider added to the Indian Appropriations Bill that officially opened the two million acres of "Unassigned Lands" for white settlement.[16] This law produced the first colonial island of white-owned land to appear amid the sea of Indian Country. It also set the stage for perhaps the wildest spectacle in the history of white colonial settlement on the continent: the land run. Federal officials decided to allocate the lands with a free-for-all race on April 22, 1889. They lifted the ban on trespassing on Native American territory three days prior to allow Boomers to gather around the borders of the "Unassigned Lands." As the sun rose to its apex, a member of the US Cavalry mounted a small hill with a bugle and a flag. At precisely twelve noon, he blew a long, piercing blast and dropped the flag. Mayhem ensued. Approximately fifty thousand colonists raced at breakneck speed to reach the choicest lands and plant their stake in the ground to register their claim. Many of the hopeful were killed or maimed by overturned wagons or downed horses. Some fought to the death over claims. When the dust settled that evening, nearly every parcel and town lot had been claimed.[17]

The die had been cast. The very next year, Congress passed the Oklahoma Organic Act, which contained two critical provisions. First, it attached the "no man's land" panhandle and the newly seized and settled "Unassigned Lands" to Oklahoma Territory under the jurisdiction of the federal government. Second, it passed a provision that signaled the US government's clear intentions; it specified that all reservations existing in western Oklahoma Territory, whenever opened to settlement in the future, would automatically be annexed into Oklahoma Territory.

Back in Washington, a group of senators drafted "An Act to Provide for the Allotment of Lands in Severalty to Indians on the Various Reservations," also known as the "General Allotment Act" or the "Dawes Act," after its principal sponsor, Senator Henry Dawes of Massachusetts.[18] Dawes was a complicated figure. He had been supportive of Reconstruction and antislavery laws, but he was also an expansionist and investor in railroad construction. Dawes was also chairman of the US Senate Committee on Indian Affairs.

His views on Native Americans had been strongly shaped by his association with a group of wealthy Protestant Christian reformers who, beginning in 1883, met each fall at a resort on Lake Mohonk in the Catskill Mountains north of New York City. While they thought of themselves as progressive reformers working in the best interests of Native Americans, this group's aspirations operated within the sturdy framework of the Doctrine of Discovery, with its paternalistic understandings of the superiority of Christianity and European civilization. The consensus of the group was that there was no future for Native Americans without full assimilation into the dominant

European culture, a path that mandated the abandonment of Indian religions, dress, languages, food acquisition practices, and, most of all, their relationship to the land. Their approach hewed to the Doctrine of Discovery's strategy of Indigenous domination—kill, confine, individuate, and convert—in the name of lofty humanitarian virtue. Historian Robert Utley concluded that Dawes and the Lake Mohonk Christian reformers "saw nothing worth saving from the past, and they had not the slightest doubt of the rightness and righteousness of their vision of tribal destiny."[19] In other words, these optimistic reformers envisioned a future path for the remnant Indian people in the land, but one predicated on Indian cultural genocide.

Remarkably, Dawes and other members of this influential group saw a lack of greed and envy among Native American communities not as a virtue but as an impediment to their progress toward Christian civilization.[20] Two years before the passage of the Dawes Act, he gave this assessment of the state of Native American societies:

> The head chief told us that there was not a family in that whole nation that had not a home of its own. There was not a pauper in that nation, and the nation did not own a dollar. It built its own capitol, and it built its schools and its hospitals. Yet the defect of the system was apparent. They have got as far as they can go because they own their land in common. . . . There is no enterprise to make your home any better than that of your neighbour's. There is no selfishness, which is at the bottom of civilisation. Til this people will consent to give up their lands, and divide them among their citizens so that each can own the land he cultivates, they will not make much more progress.[21]

Another prominent member of this group of Christian reformers was Merrill Gates, president of Amherst College, whose mission was to provide free education to men who "manifest a desire to obtain a liberal education with a sole view to the Christian ministry."[22] At one of the Lake Mohonk retreats, Gates argued that Native Americans, for their own good, needed to be taught to be "intelligently selfish" and that they should be "got out of the blanket and into trousers, and trousers with a pocket in them, *and with a pocket that aches to be filled with dollars!*" (emphasis in original).[23]

But other congressional leaders objected to this vision on moral grounds. Members of the House Committee on Indian Affairs who disagreed with the proposed legislation put their strong dissent on record in a minority report. "The real aim of the bill is to get land out of Indian hands and into the hands of white settlers," they wrote. "If this were done in the name of Greed, it would be bad enough, but to do it in the name of Humanity, and under the cloak of an ardent desire to promote the Indian's welfare by making him like ourselves, whether he will or not, is infinitely worse."[24] Despite these objections, the sweeping vision and self-assuredness of the prominent Protestant reformers held sway. On February 8, 1887, the Dawes Act became law, effectively giving the president the authority to unilaterally dissolve centuries of treaties with Indigenous nations.

To eliminate tribal land claims, the Dawes Act created and imposed a devastating legal device called "allotment." Rather than recognizing communal tribal claims to land as original treaties did, the new tactic allotted specific amounts of land for each individual member of the tribe. In addition to transforming communal land rights into individual private property rights, this scheme was designed to dramatically reduce Indigenous landholdings. By setting individual allotments to modest portions, even after accounting for everyone's claims, the commission ensured there would be significant "surplus lands," which could then be claimed by the US government. While the details varied from tribe to tribe, the typical arrangement was to provide for a 160-acre allotment for each man, woman, and child whose name was on the official tribal roll. The remaining land, declared a surplus, was then purchased by the US government and opened for colonization by white settlers.

In the wake of the Dawes Act, Congress authorized various commissions to carry out the work in Indian Country. In the early 1890s, the congressionally authorized Jerome Commission, named after its chairman, David H. Jerome, former governor of Michigan, was formed to pressure Native American leaders in western Oklahoma to relinquish land. The Jerome Commission extracted allotment agreements with most of the tribes in western Oklahoma. When the standard allotment metrics did not result in reducing tribal holdings, such as on Kickapoo nation landholdings that were already small, the commission arbitrarily reduced individual allotments by half to only eighty acres.

In western Oklahoma, this scheme generated massive "surplus lands" adjacent to the island of white settlement in the previously Unassigned Lands.[25] By 1901, Native American land claims in western Oklahoma had been drastically reduced. An act of Congress in 1904 opened the remaining smaller reservations in western Oklahoma for white colonization. By 1906, on the eve of statehood, the population of Oklahoma Territory had increased to 700,000 people, more than ten times the population in 1890.[26]

What the Jerome Commission did in western Oklahoma, the Dawes Commission—another newly authorized body—accomplished among the "five civilized tribes" in eastern Oklahoma. The work of the Dawes Commission was more difficult—particularly since these Indian nations had been explicitly exempted from being subject to allotment in the Dawes Act of 1887. In addition to the problem of communal ownership of land, the five Indian republics in eastern Oklahoma already had, by virtue of guarantees in previous treaties, independently functioning courts, laws, and governmental bodies.

Understanding the tribal courts and governments as obstacles to the goal of further Indian dispossession, the federal government set about dismantling them. The most crushing blow was the passage of the Curtis Act of 1898, which abolished tribal courts in all five Indian republics and brought all residents under the jurisdiction of US federal law or the law of the neighboring state of Arkansas, as applicable. It also granted all male residents the right to vote, shifting political control on Indian lands to whites, since whites substantially outnumbered Native Americans and Native Americans were often denied the right to vote.[27]

The Dawes Commission then went to work on the land issue. In 1894, commission members met with the leaders of the five Indian republics and were met with stiff opposition; Indian leaders simply refused to discuss the possibility of allotment. In response, Congress gave the commission authority to survey tribal lands and begin enrolling allottees without tribal permission. Under increasing pressure and without further recourse, each of the eastern Oklahoma tribes finally acquiesced to individual allotment of their communally held lands between 1897 and 1901. As part of these negotiations, all five Indian republics agreed that their tribal governments would phase out and cease operations by the end of 1906.[28]

The allotment and enrollment process did not go smoothly. The commission was unprepared for the complexity of the process and continued Indian resistance. The commission set itself up as the arbiter of who qualified as a member of each tribe—a task complicated by generations of intermarriage between Indigenous people with people of European and African descent, adoptions across racial and ethnic lines, and the presence of former slaves and their descendants who had been previously granted tribal membership. Between 1898 and 1907, when they were closed, the Dawes Commission entered 101,526 persons on the official allotment rolls—about one-third of the more than 300,000 people who claimed membership. In other words, they denied the membership claims—and the accompanying benefit of land allotment—of roughly two out of three people who came before them.

Unlike the Jerome Commission, the Dawes Commission did not officially generate "surplus lands" with their allotment scheme, but the five Indian republics nonetheless lost nearly four million acres of land taken for town sites, schools, and designated coal and timber lands. The latter were sold at public auction with the proceeds held in trust by the government on behalf of the tribes previously holding these lands.

Even the granting of citizenship to Native Americans was contentious. The Dawes Act of 1887 had provided that tribal members would automatically receive US citizenship as a condition of receiving their land allotments, but this provision still left out most Indigenous peoples in the territory. In 1890, Congress passed a law allowing Native Americans to apply for citizenship, but few wished to trade tribal citizenship for US citizenship. Finally, a 1901 law made all Native American residents of Indian Territory citizens of the United States—a move that seemingly extended rights on its face but had the purpose of extinguishing Indian sovereignty and extending US laws over Indian bodies.[29]

As the walls were closing in, leaders of the five tribes began organizing, making one last attempt to thwart Oklahoma statehood, with its planned fusion of their republics with Oklahoma Territory. After three years of planning, the chiefs called a meeting of 182 delegates at Muskogee on August 21, 1905, to create a constitution for an alternative: a united separate Indian state to be called Sequoyah. They produced a detailed, thirty-five-thousand-word document that followed the basic patterns of American constitutional government and circulated it among each of the tribes. Although turnout was light, the proposal was overwhelmingly approved, with 56,279 votes in favor and 9,073 against.[30]

But the delegation received a cool reception in Washington, DC. While they managed to get two bills introduced to consider their proposal, Congress refused to take up either. Instead, with the backing of President Theodore Roosevelt, Congress passed the Oklahoma Enabling Act on June 16, 1906, ending any hopes of an independent Indian state. The bill specified that the Oklahoma Territory would be joined with Indian Territory to form the new state of Oklahoma. Over the next seventeen months, delegates met to create a constitution for the new state, borrowing generously from the Sequoyah document. They held elections to approve the new constitution and to fill statewide offices in September 1907. On November 16, 1907, President Roosevelt signed the official proclamation to make Oklahoma, with its now majority-white population of 1.5 million, the forty-sixth state.

With statehood came the need for grand proclamations and symbols. One writer from the *Muskogee Phoenix* described the jubilant mood among white Oklahomans:

> But yesterday, we were a million and a half of political orphans, misunderstood, misgoverned in administration.... Today, we have entered into our inheritance ... to take our place in Columbia's household as the most favored of all of the nation's children.... Today, we begin a new era with the ideal government of the immortal Lincoln, "a government of the people, by the people, and for the people," ... secure in the belief that tomorrow will bring to us but additional triumphs.[31]

One of the earliest state symbols, used when Charles N. Haskell took the oath of office as Oklahoma's first governor, depicted a Native American woman, representing Indian Territory, and a European man, representing Oklahoma Territory, being bound in marriage. Perhaps because that symbol was too intimate, the state seal ultimately came to feature a five-pointed white star, with each ray of the star containing symbols representing one of the "five civilized tribes." In the center of the star, there is a scene depicting a European settler in farming attire shaking hands with a Native American man in buckskin and full headdress. They are standing before Columbia, the female personification of the United States, who is clothed in the American flag; she holds up the scales of justice, which are balanced. On the ground below them lie the cornucopia of plenty and the olive branch of peace. Above them are the words *Labor Omnia Vincit*, meaning "Work Conquers All."

THE OSAGE

The most well-known stories of the theft, violence, and disregard for the humanity of Indigenous peoples by the US government are the removals of Native Americans east of the Mississippi River known collectively as the "Trail of Tears" (more accurately, trails of tears, given the repeated waves and different routes of forced migrations). But the story of the Osage, one of the tribes native to Oklahoma, provides insight into the lengths to which white Americans—well into the twentieth century—have gone to dispossess, and dispossess again, our country's original inhabitants.

In 1804, one year after the Louisiana Purchase, a delegation of Osage chiefs traveled to Washington to meet with President Thomas Jefferson. At that time, their lands stretched across the middle of that territory to the Rockies in the west, including much of what is now Oklahoma, Missouri, and Kansas. Addressing the chiefs as "my children," Jefferson asserted the inevitability of white westward expansion but also declared, "We are all now of one family." At the close of their conversation, Jefferson left them with these words: "On your return tell your people that I take them all by the hand; that I become their father hereafter, that they shall know our nation only as friends and benefactors."[32]

That promise was broken just four years later, when the US government began pressuring the Osage to cede land to make room both for white colonists and for tribes like the Cherokee who were being uprooted and relocated from the Southeast. By 1825, the US government successfully pressured the Osage to cede more than 100 million acres of their tribal lands, including all lands in present-day Oklahoma, in exchange for a 50-by-125-mile plot in southeastern Kansas. Less than four decades later, after Kansas statehood in 1861, white settler colonists in Kansas were encroaching on these Osage lands and pressuring the federal government to push the tribe back south into Indian Country.

As part of the Cherokee Reconstruction Treaty of 1866, the Osage were authorized to purchase nearly 1.6 million acres from the Cherokee.[33] These lands were originally Osage, but they were also lands that the Cherokee were subsequently promised would remain "forever a home" for them. The law also contained a provision for Osage who were of "mixed blood" to accept individual land allotments from the Kansas reservation, becoming citizens of the United States. Many mixed-heritage Osage chose to avail themselves of this provision, having established prosperous farms and extensive family ties with both Indigenous and white residents of the area.

Almost immediately after news of the law became public, however, land-hungry white Kansans descended like locusts on the properties of mixed-race Osage, disregarding their new standing as fellow citizens and the attendant legal rights to the land. The commissioner of Indian Affairs reported this appalling account of the aftermath:

> Outrages and persecutions perpetrated upon them ... shames humanity. All except eight have abandoned their homes, or taken what they could get for them. Some of their homes were burnt by mobs of white men; and one half-breed died from injury received. ... The murderers were arrested, went through the forms of a trial, and were discharged. The eight still remaining will probably lose their land, as they have not the means to engage in a long contest of law.[34]

Even those departing were not spared by impatient hordes of settler colonists. Several Osage were killed as they were preparing to leave, their bodies mutilated and scalped. One Indian Affairs agent noted, "The question will suggest itself, which of these people are the savages?"[35]

Between 1871 and 1872, between 1,500 and 3,000 Osage—about one-third of what their population had been in the early 1800s—moved back to Indian Country. Rather than the vast ranges they had enjoyed, they found themselves relegated to a rocky upland meadow and hill country, unsuitable for farming and marginally able to accommodate livestock grazing.[36] Despite the challenges, Wah-Ti-An-Kah, an Osage chief, saw an advantage in the barren landscape: "My people will be happy in this land. White man cannot put iron thing in ground here. White man will not come to this land. . . . If my people go west where land is like floor of lodge, white man will come to our lodges and say, 'We want your land. . . .' Soon land will end and Osages will have no home."[37]

By the late 1870s, however, conditions were grim for the Osage. A deliberate white settler practice of exterminating the vast herds of buffalo as a means of robbing Native Americans of a source of food and thereby independence had been largely successful. And as the "Indian removal" policy was accomplishing its goals, US government aims evolved from forced emigration to forced assimilation, following the Doctrine of Discovery formula of imposing Christianity and civilization on the Osage. Practically, that meant discouraging the use of tribal languages and religion in favor of English and church membership; the establishment of boarding schools where these ideals would be enforced while children were separated from their families and communities; discouraging traditional clothing in favor of European dress; and demanding that the Osage take up farming despite the barren soil.

The government was able to enforce these practices because it held the funds for the sale of the tribe's Kansas lands in trust. Although it was required by law to distribute regular annuity payments to the tribe, it withheld them until all able-bodied men took up farming. Even when payments were released, the government often did so in the form of food and clothing rations rather than money. "We are not dogs that we should be fed like dogs," one Osage chief protested, but his complaints fell on deaf ears. The results were predictably disastrous, leaving many Osage in Oklahoma living at the edge of survival.[38]

Through the skills and determination of their leaders, and the lessons learned from government dealings with other tribes, the Osage did manage to secure better legal terms than most other tribes. Chief James Bigheart—who spoke seven languages, including French, English, and Latin, and who wore European suits—had skillfully delayed the allotment process for the Osage, leaving it the last to be negotiated in Indian Country. Bigheart also recruited an enterprising young lawyer, John Palmer, the orphaned son of a Sioux woman and a white trader who had been adopted by the Osage, to help with legal strategies and to serve as an additional envoy to Washington.

Bigheart and Palmer leveraged the eagerness of US officials to clear the way for Oklahoma statehood to secure favorable terms for the Osage, at least within the confines of their limited options. The pair succeeded in securing an agreement that divided the entire territory solely among members of the tribe, expanding the typical allotment of 160 acres to 657 acres and thereby avoiding the creation of any "surplus lands." And they inserted this provision: "That the oil, gas, coal, or other minerals covered by the lands ... are hereby reserved to the Osage Tribe." The result of this shrewd provision was that while the surface land had been turned into private property allotments owned by individuals, Bigheart and Palmer had preserved the Indigenous ideal of communal ownership of the mineral rights.

These rights were distinguished by two terms: "allotment," a private property right to an equal share in the surface land; and "headright," a claim to an equal share of proceeds produced by mineral rights. Under the agreement, anyone could purchase a land allotment from any individual Osage who was willing to sell. But the communal headrights, the value of what was beneath the land, could not be sold. Headrights could only be inherited from the original 2,229 Osage recipients.[39] All mineral proceeds were collected by the tribe and divided into equal portions, distributed quarterly to all headright share owners.[40] In short, the Osage had acquiesced to European rights controlling the surface of the land, but Indian ideals ruled below.

OSAGE OIL AND PROSPERITY

The delaying tactics by Bigheart and Palmer to avoid allotment also had another fortuitous effect. By the first decade of the twentieth century, the nascent but burgeoning automobile industry had created an increasingly insatiable appetite for oil. Bigheart and Palmer had some knowledge that there was oil beneath Osage lands. A decade earlier, an Osage Indian had discovered a rainbow sheen floating on a creek near Gray Horse in the eastern part of Osage lands. But no one imagined the fortune these rocky, barren tribal lands would produce.

Between 1917, when one of the first major oil "gushers" erupted, and the early 1920s, the riches of the Osage oilfields garnered the attention, and the investment, of the world's largest oil companies. Early leases granted by the Osage in 1912 for a single 160-acre drilling tract could be had for as little as $500, but by 1923 the most valuable of these tracts went for as much as $2 million. The auction of the Osage leases, which occurred three or four times a year and were overseen by the Department of the Interior, drew oil barons from all over the country. Arriving in their own luxurious railcars, the likes of Harry Sinclair (Sinclair Oil) and Frank Phillips (Phillips Petroleum) made the trip personally to stand under the branches of what became known as "the Million Dollar Elm," a tree on a hill in Pawhuska where the auctions were held, and bid on the choicest leases.[41]

In 1923 alone, the tribe received more than $30 million for their leases, equivalent to about $520 million today. This communal income translated into thousands of dollars in quarterly payments for each member of the tribe, enormous sums at the time, and they were increasing every year. In a little more than a decade, the Osage had moved from the brink of starvation to being described as the wealthiest people per capita in the world by outlets like the *New York Times*.[42] This transformation was met with dismay not only by envious local white residents but by observers across the country. Reporters wrote fabulous stories about the lavish lifestyles of "red millionaires." The equivalent of the "reality TV" of their day, these voyeuristic accounts depicted chauffeured luxury automobiles and servant staffs, particularly the existence of white servants, who were derided as "Indian pot-lickers" for their willingness to do "all the menial tasks about the house to which no Osage would stoop."[43]

"Where will it end?" a reporter from *Harper's Monthly Magazine* mused. "Every time a new well is drilled the Indians are that much richer. The Osage Indians are becoming so rich that something will have to be done about it."[44]

INCOMPETENCE AND GUARDIANSHIP

The dismay of the *Harper's* reporter was transformed into outrage among many white Oklahoma residents and government officials. With the allotment scheme's purposes of diminishing Indian power thwarted by headright wealth, officials turned to other bureaucratic and legal procedures designed to keep dollars out of the hands of the Osage. The annual lease auctions were held under the supervision of the US Department of the Interior, who collected the huge sums paid by oil companies and held the funds in trust for the tribe. Even when quarterly payments were made for the benefit of individual headright beneficiaries, few members were given full control over their own wealth. This system was accomplished by the imposition of a racist system of guardianship, based on an assertion of Indian inferiority and irresponsibility. By law, the Department of the Interior held the right to declare an American Indian "incompetent" to handle their own wealth. Indeed, this was the default assumption. In those cases, a white guardian would be appointed by a judge and given the power to control access to the funds. One guardian justified the arrangement by declaring that an Osage adult was "like a child six or eight years old, and when he sees a new toy he wants to buy it."[45]

In practice, and by design, this policy interposed white people between the Osage and their own money and was part of a strategy of coercive assimilation. Full-blooded Osage were nearly always declared incompetent and appointed a white guardian, while mixed-race tribal members rarely received this restriction. In 1920, Osage attorney John Palmer argued the injustice of this arrangement to members of Congress, pleading, "Let not that quantum of white blood or Indian determine the amount that you take over from the members of this tribe. It matters not about the quantum of Indian blood. You gentlemen do not deal with things of that kind."[46]

Rather than taking Palmer's appeal under consideration, Congress sided with a government inspector who had been dispatched to scrutinize Osage spending habits and who urged Congress to take even further actions to curb Osage financial independence. "Every white man in Osage County will tell you that the Indians are now running wild," he reported. "The day has come when we must begin our restriction of these moneys or dismiss from our hearts and conscience any hope we have of building the Osage Indian into a true citizen."[47] In 1921, Congress obliged, passing a new law that declared Osage Indians with guardians were now "restricted" from receiving more than a few thousand dollars per year from their trust fund regardless of the purpose.

Hearing of the new policy, Fred Lookout, the last hereditary chief of the Osage, issued a strong objection to the policy to the press:

> We have many little children. We want to raise them and educate them. We want them to be comfortable, and we do not want our money held up from us by somebody who cares nothing for us. We want our money now. We have it. It is ours, and we don't want some autocratic man to hold it up so we can't use it. . . . It is an injustice to us all. We do not want to be treated like a lot of little children. We are men and able to take care of ourselves.[48]

If federal micromanagement and restrictions weren't enough, Osage were constantly swarmed by swindlers of all kinds: white land speculators, unethical bankers and accountants, merchants and even undertakers who charged them special (that is, exorbitant) Indian rates for basic goods and services from groceries to burials, and missionaries who promised to educate their children but whose larger purposes entailed harsh programs of religious conversion and cultural assimilation that alienated children from parents.[49] Just as white settler colonists had launched decades of ever-changing ploys to separate Indigenous people from their lands, there seemed no end to the gambits white Oklahomans would employ to separate the Osage from their money.

THE REIGN OF TERROR

The bigoted system of restrictive guardianship, with its long-term genocidal intent, also provided the context for exposing the truly perverse lengths to which many whites would go to divert Indian wealth into their own hands and into the control of their white descendants. Because headrights could only be inherited, the most certain strategy for gaining control of them, if you were white, was to be both appointed as a guardian over one or more wards and to be married into an Osage family. Under these conditions, an evil logic presented itself. If an Osage familial line was terminated—for example, through untimely deaths—the white intermarried member of the family could petition to legally inherit the headright.

The darkest era, which became known among the Osage as the "Reign of Terror," was a period between 1918 and 1931, when wealthy Osage were systematically targeted for marriage and murder by whites who wanted control of their headrights. As David Grann documented in his bestselling *Killers of the Flower Moon: The Osage Murders and the Birth of the FBI*, while federal authorities documented twenty-four murders during this period, contemporary scholars and investigators believe the numbers to be much higher, certainly dozens and perhaps even hundreds.[50]

When Grann examined the US Office of Indian Affairs logbooks containing the names of guardians and their wards during the Reign of Terror, a disturbing pattern appeared. For example, Scott Mathis, owner of the Big Hill Trading Company in Pawhuska, had been the guardian of nine Osage, seven of whom had died, including two that were proven homicides. Other listings confirmed horrific patterns that defied actuarial natural death rates: eight of eleven wards dead from one guardian; more than half of thirteen wards dead from another; and all five wards dead from yet another. Almost none of these suspicious deaths were investigated as possible premeditated murders.

While a few Osage were violently killed, other more covert methods were common during this period. Many were slowly poisoned by their own white spouses or other trusted family members. The Shoun brothers, local doctors, were known to procure poisons for their white clients and even substitute poison for insulin to speed the deaths of Osage diabetics in their care.[51] Osage who had been drinking were taken to a doctor who officially declared them intoxicated and then were forcibly injected with a morphine overdose under the armpit, where it was less detectable; coroners would readily list the cause of death as "alcohol poisoning." One guardian deliberately denied medical treatment to a ward with tuberculosis because it would have required expensive out-of-state hospital care, for want of which she died.

The wealthiest Osage, especially women, were the most preyed upon, even by whites who became their spouses or parents. In the early 1920s, Mary Elkins, with seven inherited headrights, was considered the wealthiest member of the tribe. When she was twenty-one years old, in 1923, she married a white man. A report from the Office of Indian Affairs documents that her husband, a professional boxer, repeatedly and systematically abused her and concluded that he gave her "drugs, opiates, and liquor in an attempt to hasten her death so that he could claim her huge inheritance."[52] Sybil Bolton was a young Osage woman living in Pawhuska under the guardianship of her white stepfather. She was reported dead with a single gunshot wound to the chest in what was recorded as a suicide, without an autopsy or investigation. Dennis McAuliffe Jr., a *Washington Post* editor and her direct descendant, investigated her death in 1994 and determined that the evidence suggests she was assassinated on her lawn with her sixteen-month-old baby (his mother, who survived) beside her. Sybil's stepfather also had four other Osage wards, all of whom died during this period.[53] One guardian robbed his ward, a widow, of most of her possessions and falsely told her there was no more money in her trust account. Even when her baby became sick, the guardian refused to send her money, leading to the child's death.[54]

These evil acts were not carried out by desperate ruffians on the fringes of society. Rather, they were perpetrated by some of eastern Oklahoma's most prominent and respected white citizens, who were widely considered to be pillars of the community and exemplars of Christian civilization. What was unimaginable to the Osage became a premeditated strategy consciously pursued by many whites. As one Osage interviewed by Grann asked incredulously, "Who would believe that anyone would marry you and kill your family for your money?"[55]

EARLY TULSA

Tulsa is located just outside the southwest corner of Osage County, less than sixty miles from Pawhuska. It sits on land where the Lower Creek tribes were resettled beginning in 1833, after being forcibly removed from their lands in Alabama. By the late 1800s, the incursions of the railroad into Tulsa to serve cattle interests and the process of allotment opened white settlement in the area. At the turn of the twentieth century, before statehood, Tulsa was a sleepy frontier town, comprising a few thousand residents and without a single paved street. But in late 1905, the massive Glenn Pool oil reserve was discovered, followed in quick succession by the Cushing Field and the Osage reserves. This oil was key in powering the US engagement in World War I, and the town grew in fifteen years to a city of 75,000, supported by a web of pipelines, refineries, and railroads, along with other business infrastructure such as banks, law offices, restaurants, and hotels. It called itself the Magic City.[56]

A small population of African Americans lived in early Tulsa, some arriving as slaves to either white settler colonists or Native American peoples who arrived via the Trail of Tears from the Southeast; some arriving later as freedmen following the Civil War; and some coming for the economic opportunity the oil boom promised. The African American population in Tulsa benefited from the unique dynamics of Oklahoma territorial history, which was described this way in a 1907 article in a national scholarly magazine called the *Independent*:

> [T]he negro of Indian Territory is also a land-owner. The ex-slaves of the Five Tribes are protected in their holdings as are the Indians. And in the Oklahoma, or Western half of the new state, the negro was as free to homestead land as the whites.... So in both divisions of the State there are probably a larger percentage of negroes who own their own homes and are in comfortable circumstances than elsewhere in the United States.[57]

Tulsa's Black population dates to 1905, before statehood, when African Americans acquired a parcel of land in what became known as the Greenwood District, in the northeast quadrant of the segregated city. While lagging behind the development of white Tulsa in terms of basic infrastructure like sewage treatment and paved streets, the fledgling African American community nonetheless participated in the economic growth during the first two decades of the twentieth century.[58]

Mary Jones Parrish, a young Black teacher and entrepreneur, arrived in Tulsa from Rochester, New York, in 1918, lured by economic opportunity and "because of the wonderful co-operation ... among our people" she had observed during an earlier visit. She described the scene in the 1910s near the Frisco railroad tracks, which served as the dividing line between white and Black Tulsa: "On leaving the Frisco Station, going north to Archer Street, one could see nothing but Negro business places. Going east on Archer for two or more blocks, there you would behold Greenwood Avenue, the Negro's Wall Street."[59]

While this area north of the Frisco railroad tracks was disparaged by white Tulsans as "Little Africa" or "Niggertown," Greenwood was also known among African Americans across the nation as "Black Wall Street," a shining example of a Black middle-class community. Greenwood developed rapidly from this single parcel of land into a vibrant community of Black residences and businesses just fifteen years later. While some side streets had elements of poverty, crime, and illegitimate enterprises one might see in any rapidly developing urban area, by 1921 the main strip contained retail outlets, grocers, doctors and dentists, funeral parlors, restaurants, barbershops, and a confectionary. In addition to the businesses, Greenwood held an impressive array of cultural and civic institutions: twenty-three churches, a public library, an eight-hundred-seat theater, a thirteen-acre park with a swimming pool and dance hall, a hospital, two schools, two newspapers, and three fraternal lodges.[60]

But with the close of the war in November 1918, the demand for oil and other commodities plummeted, pulling wages down with them. The nation was also pummeled by the 1918–19 influenza pandemic, which claimed more than 675,000 lives nationwide and further stifled economic recovery. Nationwide, unemployment jumped more than three percentage points in 1920 alone, hitting places like Tulsa, with its heavy reliance on the oil industry, particularly hard. In Tulsa, the value of building permits fell by 30 percent, and workers in an Ocmulgee glass plant walked out after their wages were slashed by 60 percent.[61]

Soldiers returning home, both Black and white, encountered a drastically different economic reality from the bounty reflected in wartime letters, including many broken promises of awaiting employment. Competition for the dwindling number of jobs, even those with substandard pay, became fierce. And after being called upon to give and risk their lives to defend the nation, many Black soldiers and their families were no longer willing to accept second-class citizenship at home. On May 12, 1921, for example, the *Tulsa World* reported that an elderly Black couple, Mr. and Mrs. Gilbert Irge, had refused to sit at the back of a segregated streetcar and had been fined ten dollars, approximately $160 in today's currency.[62]

The Osage and African Americans in Oklahoma had two things in common that proved intolerable to their white neighbors: the achievement of economic prosperity and the expectation that the promises recorded in the Constitution and in federal treaties would be honored. The white response to both communities was the same: a reassertion of divinely ordained white supremacy and a willingness to kill to defend it. While white residents of Osage County were waging a slower, thirteen-year Reign of Terror to kill and disenfranchise Native Americans, just down the road, in the late spring of 1921, white Tulsans unleashed unspeakable violence against African Americans, killing hundreds and displacing thousands in just two days.

Chapter Eight

THE TULSA
RACE MASSACRE

On Sunday evening, June 5, 1921, Bishop Ed D. Mouzon rose to the pulpit of Tulsa's prominent Boston Avenue Methodist Church. He was not its regular occupant, but he made the nearly three-hundred-mile journey from his home in Dallas, Texas, to personally address the anxious white congregation. On the north side of the Frisco railroad tracks that bifurcate the town, the Greenwood District, a thirty-five-block sector of the city with a vibrant African American middle class, was still smoldering. After two days of violence perpetrated by Tulsa's white citizens the previous week, hundreds of African Americans had been killed or were missing, thousands were displaced, and hospitals were still treating patients, with the Red Cross handling the overflow.

Rev. Mouzon's bold sermon title was "The Tulsa Race Riot and the Teachings of Jesus Christ." The sermon was a master class in doublespeak. Rather than focusing on white violence, Mouzon's sermon located the source of the troubles within Tulsa's African American community. While he denounced mob violence, he went on to speculate that "if it is true that our wives and children and the people

212

of Tulsa were threatened with being at the mercy of armed negroes, then the white man who got his gun and went out in defense with it did the only thing that a decent white man could have done." While the early part of the sermon expressed ambivalence about the causes of the violence, he pointed an accusing finger at the "bitterest race hatred" of Black newspapers and a recent visit to Tulsa by W. E. B. Du Bois, whom he called "the most vicious negro man in this country."[1] He denounced the contemporary KKK but explicitly justified its nineteenth-century actions and raison d'être.[2]

His primary criticism of white Christians in Tulsa fell comfortably within the worldview of the Doctrine of Discovery: as members of the superior race and religion, they had shirked their paternalistic duties by allowing Black deviance in their homes and Black vice in their city to thrive unchecked.

> We Christian white people have not expected enough from the colored people who worked for us. We have allowed all sorts of pilfering to go on in our kitchens; and we have winked at immorality in our servants' rooms. We would not have allowed white servants to do these things; but we put up with our colored people when they are openly guilty. And we have not expected the law to be enforced in such places as "Little Africa." "Little Africa" had become one of the blackest spots in Oklahoma—and we all knew it. . . . In "Little Africa" were low dives where black and whites, men and women, mingled freely. I insist that we must have a higher standard of decency and morality for these colored people who live in our midst.[3]

If there was a lesson to be learned from the bloodshed, it was not that the Jim Crow worldview was wrong, but that segregation and law and order had not been adequately enforced. The climax of his sermon was a clarion endorsement of white supremacy: "There is one thing upon which I should like to make myself perfectly clear. That is racial equality. There never has been and never will be such a thing. It is divine [*sic*] ordained. This is something that the negroes should be told very plainly. Steps toward social equality are the worst possible thing for the negro man and the white."[4]

He closed his sermon with a comforting declaration for the white, well-to-do congregation: the foundation of civilization is a strong assertion of law and order, and "the hope of civilization is Christ."

Mouzon's presence as an authority in the pulpit that Sunday was important. He was a widely respected bishop in the Methodist Episcopal Church South, the branch of Methodism that split from its northern brethren in 1845 to maintain and defend slavery, and which—along with Southern Baptists who also split with their northern brethren the same year—provided much of the moral justification and energy that ultimately gave birth to the Confederacy.[5] Mouzon was also the founder and dean of the theology department at Southern Methodist University. He knew that the message emanating from this influential pulpit would shape understandings of the week's mayhem, not only among the white parishioners of Boston Avenue Methodist Church, which served as home to many of Tulsa's elite, but also among local white civic leaders and a broader national public.

In Mouzon's telling, the violence in Tulsa was a "race riot" born out of widespread corruption and immorality in Tulsa's segregated Black district, which became a "powder magazine waiting to blow up when some sparks might fall into it."[6] The sparks were provided by agitators like editors of local Black newspapers and outsiders like Du Bois. And they were brought to full flame by murderous Blacks who fired on a group of unarmed white citizens who were merely curious "to see what might happen" at the jail after a nineteen-year-old Black man was arrested for allegedly assaulting a seventeen-year-old white girl. Mouzon did allow that the widespread burning of Greenwood "was not necessary" and "ought never to be done," but he blamed these actions on a mob mentality among "white trash" elements that Black Tulsans ultimately unleashed on themselves.

His gambit paid off handsomely. The *Tulsa Daily World* reprinted his sermon on the front page of the Monday paper under bold-face headlines that occupied five lines: "Black Agitators Blamed for Riot: Bishop Mouzon Cites Visit of Radical Negro as One Cause of Battle / Citizens Criticized: Says City Government Reflects the Moral and Spiritual Desires of its Electors / Whites Overlooked Crime: Allowed Little Africa to Become Festering Sore and Wonder at Results."[7] When the Tulsa mayor addressed the city commissioners a week later, he echoed these sentiments, entering this interpretive frame into the minutes of the Tulsa City Commission meeting as the official city position. For his part, Mouzon expanded his sermon and published it the following month as part of a series he authored in the *Christian Advocate*, a Methodist weekly magazine with national circulation.[8]

This narrative—blessed by a bishop from one of the largest Protestant denominations in the country, propagated from one of the city's most respected pulpits, published by the city's most measured newspaper, and validated by the mayor—became the official account of the event for whites, both in Tulsa and beyond. This myth of white innocence stood for half a century, challenged only by new scholarship and public investigations in the last fifty years, and only fully relinquished after a century of resistance.

THE TULSA RACE MASSACRE

The Tulsa Race Massacre took place on May 31 and June 1, 1921, when mobs of white residents systematically attacked Black residents and businesses of the Greenwood District in Tulsa,

Oklahoma. The precipitating event was the accusation by Sarah Page, a white seventeen-year-old, that she had been assaulted by a Black nineteen-year-old, Dick Rowland, while she was working as an elevator operator on May 30. Rowland, who worked shining shoes nearby, had ridden the elevator with Page regularly because it was the only way to get to the "colored" restroom on the fourth floor of the Drexel Building, near his stand. No one knows exactly what happened on that elevator ride. By Rowland's account, he tripped and fell into Sarah by accident, stepping on her already injured toe and grabbing her arm. Incensed and in pain, she began beating him with her purse. Rowland responded by holding her arms back until he could get out of the car. When the elevator hit the bottom floor, Page screamed, "I've been assaulted!" A clerk ran after Rowland, but he escaped across the Frisco railroad tracks to Greenwood, where he lived.[9]

The next day, Rowland returned downtown to see friends, where he was recognized. He was arrested and taken to the city jail on Second Street. From the beginning, police were skeptical that a violent assault, much less a sexual assault as runaway rumors cast it, had taken place, since Page's version of events differed little from Rowland's. Given police ambivalence, the *Tulsa Daily World* declined to run a story, but the competing *Tulsa Tribune* ran a sensational front-page headline, "NAB NEGRO FOR ATTACKING GIRL IN ELEVATOR," containing racially charged language, including a biasing characterization of Rowland as "Diamond Dick" and a misleading description of Page as an orphan working her way through business school.[10]

The *Tribune* afternoon edition was released at 3:00 p.m. Within hours, a growing mob of hundreds of whites—men, women, and even children—had gathered outside the courthouse. Sheriff William McCullough warned the crowd that anyone attempting to lynch Rowland would be met with lethal force and urged the crowd to disperse. Undaunted, the crowd persevered, with leaders shouting, "The honor and purity of white women everywhere is at issue right here in Tulsa!" and chanting, "Give us the nigger! Give us the nigger!"[11]

There is no evidence of any coordinated effort by Tulsa's white civic or religious leaders to stop the violence. But there is documentation of a few courageous individual efforts to calm the bloodlust in the white mob. Around 7:00 p.m., Rev. Charles Kerr, senior minister at Tulsa's influential First Presbyterian Church, made an unsuccessful attempt to disperse the increasingly agitated white lynch mob gathering outside Dick Rowland's jail cell. Standing on the courthouse steps, he pleaded with the crowd to go home, but he was quickly "hooted down," with a member of the crowd saying, "Pastor, go home. This is our concern and not yours."[12] Rev. J. W. Abel and Rev. Leslie Miller of First Methodist Church, who served within Bishop Mouzon's jurisdiction, stood on boxes attempting to dissuade the rioters but were similarly dismissed.

Word of the undeterred mob spread to the north side of the tracks in Greenwood. Younger African Americans in the pool halls and other public gathering places began organizing a resistance, yelling, "They'd better not even try to lynch a Negro here, because if they do, we're going to be right in the middle of it." O. B. Mann, an imposing figure and World War I veteran, interrupted a movie at the eight-hundred-seat Dreamland Theatre, declaring, "The whites are getting ready to hang a Negro boy downtown, and I say Tulsa niggers ain't about to let that happen. We're going to go down to stop it, and if you want to join us, come on!" As he left, the theater emptied behind him in minutes.

Around 9:00 p.m., three carloads of armed Black men from Greenwood arrived at the courthouse, declaring their intent to prevent the mob from lynching Rowland. Sheriff McCullough assured the men that he had barricaded the courthouse and that he was personally ensuring the prisoner's safety and delivery to trial. Convinced, the men returned to Greenwood. But their bold appearance, their willingness to openly defy whites in an armed confrontation, sent a shock wave through Tulsa's white community. Many whites responded first by trying to break into the National Guard armory, and when that failed, they supplemented gathered weapons from their homes with more easily obtained weapons looted from local hardware stores.

By 10:00 p.m., the heavily armed white mob had grown to over two thousand. Hearing of this white response, a larger group of armed Black men arrived at the courthouse to assess the situation, and once again Sheriff McCullough persuaded them to leave. But as they were marching back to their cars, an older white man attempted to disarm O. B. Mann, and in the struggle Mann's pistol discharged. Following that report, hundreds of shots rang out. At least twenty died in the opening melee, and chaos ensued.[13]

Tulsa's police department was ill-equipped to respond with integrity. Just two weeks before, the Oklahoma attorney general had opened an investigation of the Tulsa Police Department in response to charges that little was being done to control crime and that the police were themselves operating an auto theft ring, all while lacking a single fully functioning car themselves. A police officer had been fired for punching the rector of Trinity Episcopal Church during a routine traffic stop but had been subsequently rehired. And one of the few Black police officers, Staley Webb, had been fired for complaining about white officers' abusive treatment of African Americans.[14]

Tulsa law enforcement also had, as recently as August 1920, failed to stop two lynchings, one of a white man and one of a Black man, who were each taken from jail cells by mobs. When asked about the failings of his men to protect the prisoners, Tulsa police chief John Gustafson replied, "In my honest opinion, the lynching . . . will prove of real benefit to Tulsa and the vicinity."[15] As the crisis escalated that night, Tulsa's police responded by rapidly deputizing virtually any white man who requested it, issuing makeshift badges at first and ribbons when those ran out, to approximately four hundred men.[16] These new recruits were reportedly given just one mandate: "Get a gun and get a nigger."[17]

By midnight, Rowland was an afterthought. White rage erupted, and bands of white Tulsans indiscriminately targeted the entire Black population and Greenwood. Dozens of Black domestics who lived in white employers' houses were dragged from their beds and imprisoned at Convention Hall, and the National Guard sealed off the streets leading across the tracks to Greenwood to prevent any Black incursions. Bands of armed whites made forays into Greenwood, dousing everything within easy reach with kerosene and putting it to the torch. When firefighters arrived, they were prevented from putting out the flames. Families were burned alive or shot as they fled burning homes.

But the destruction of life and livelihood in that long night did not sate the appetite for violence. At 5:08 a.m., a whistle—either from a steam engine or a factory—signaled a massive new coordinated assault by whites on Greenwood. There were reports of a machine gun firing indiscriminately onto Greenwood Avenue as whites advanced from all directions, putting the remaining neighborhood buildings to the torch. Any Blacks who resisted or were suspected of being armed were shot. Thousands were forcibly and publicly marched through jeering white neighborhoods to makeshift holding pens at Convention Hall and McNulty Park, the local baseball venue. White looters, including well-dressed women with shopping bags, then ransacked Black homes and businesses before they succumbed to the flames.

It was not uncommon to see a Black body being dragged behind a car full of whites. Even the old and disabled were shown no mercy. In one horrific episode, a blind, double-amputee Black man—who was familiar as a homeless beggar who pushed himself along sidewalks in the white part of town using a small cart—was tied to the back of a late-model convertible and dragged to his death. A white eyewitness, E. W. Maxey, recalled, "He was hollering. His head was bashed in, bouncing on the steel rails and bricks.... All in broad daylight on June 1, right through the center of town on Main Street."[18]

The violence only subsided late in the day when the last Black fighters had been dispatched. In the end, the roving white mobs on the ground and, in some reports, even private biplanes shooting or dropping makeshift incendiary devices from the air destroyed more than thirty-five square blocks of what was at the time arguably the wealthiest Black community in the United States. Hundreds of businesses and twenty-three African American churches were destroyed. The *Tulsa World* described the destruction on June 2 this way: "Only gas and water pipes, bath fixtures, bedsteads or other metal fixtures remain to mark the places where homes once stood. The negro residences remaining intact can almost be counted on one's hand. There is not an undamaged business building owned by negroes in the entire district."[19] More than eight hundred people were admitted to hospitals and more than five thousand Black residents were arrested and detained—many for several days at Convention Hall and McNulty Park, and when those were full, at the pig and cow barns at the Tulsa State Fairgrounds.[20]

Tulsa hospitals were overwhelmed, and the American Red Cross reported treating 531 people the week of the massacre, fewer than fifty of them white.[21] A fire official estimated the Black death toll to be 185, noting that many had been burned in their own homes. The Oklahoma Bureau of Vital Statistics first recorded 78 dead (9 white, 68 Black) but quickly cut this estimate by more than half, posting a final official recorded death toll at only 36 dead (10 white, 26 Black). Only in 2001 did the bureau concede that the official death toll was likely between 100 and 300 in the African American community alone. Not a single white person was sent to jail for the massacre or the burning, and no Black victims were compensated for their losses.

REACTIONS

Tulsa's two competing newspapers offered wildly different accounts of the events. The *Tulsa Tribune*, which had printed the article that had incited the violence, published a story titled "Blacks Taken into Custody Form Motley Parade to Ballpark." It gloated that the prisoners held their hands in the air as "a token of their submission to the white man's authority," and that they would "return not to their homes they had on Tuesday afternoon, but to heaps of ashes, the angry white man's reprisal for the wrong inflicted on them by the inferior race."[22]

By contrast, the *Tulsa Daily World* made an unusual and somewhat remarkable decision, one that gives us rare firsthand insight into the plight of Tulsa's Black population in the wake of the massacre. Publisher Eugene Lorton assigned the paper's June 2 coverage of the aftermath to Faith Hieronymus, a young female reporter, because he thought a female reporter would best convey the plight of the survivors in the aftermath of the violence. Hieronymus spent the day interviewing Black Tulsans in McNulty Park who had suddenly become refugees in their own city. Her front-page story tendered a moving account of the suffering of the displaced victims, many of whom were desperately searching for information about missing family members. Her firsthand accounts are heartbreaking. She described "an old woman with a gray handkerchief tightly knotted about a wrinkled face" who was so overcome with grief and shock, she was rocking back and forth and unable to eat. When a Red Cross volunteer asked the woman why she wasn't eating, Hieronymus described her response in Black dialect:

> Oh, Lawdy, Me an ole woman what has worked so hard all huh life, and now eve'thing gone! Mah house burned, mah chaihs [chairs] burned, mah chickens burned. Nuthin' have I got but the

clothes on mah back. Oh, Lawdy, that I should live to see such trouble come to me![23]

But even the compassionate eye of Hieronymus was blurred by the racial prejudices of her day. She took pains to assure her white readers that the people she interviewed were good Negroes, not those involved with the "uprising." She referred at one point to a woman reading a Bible to a group of "pickaninnies," a racist term for Black children. In the final layout of her column, her editor inserted a bold descriptive comment between two paragraphs, intended to signal the sympathetic tone of the article to its white readers; it read: "Black—but human."[24]

Nationwide, the violence and conflagration was widely condemned in virtually every major newspaper in the country. While most white journalists were willing to grant that the initial violence at the courthouse and the fighting that resulted in Black residents retreating across the tracks to Greenwood were perhaps justified, they broadly decried the systematic assault and burnings of June 1. The *New York Times* editorial, for example, concluded, "The ruthless demolition of virtually the entire Negro quarter south [*sic*] of the tracks is condemned as indefensible violence."[25]

In the wake of this wave of scathing coverage, Tulsa's Chamber of Commerce held an emergency public meeting and press conference on June 2 to try to mitigate the damage to the city's reputation. Tulsa's leaders were sure to place the principal blame squarely with some "lawless" Black leaders, but they also knew the white community had to express some regret. To loud applause, Tulsa's former mayor, Loyal J. Martin, delivered a polished statement promising an ambitious response by white civic leaders. "Tulsa can only redeem herself from the country-wide shame and humiliation into which she is today plunged by complete restitution and rehabilitation of the destroyed black belt," he boldly declared.[26] By the end of the meeting,

Martin had been named head of a committee of influential white Tulsans to spearhead the Greenwood recovery efforts. It was originally
informally referred to as the "reconstruction committee" but soon
adopted the more ambiguous name of the "Public Welfare Board."[27]

But the national attention span was brief, and by the weekend the
Tulsa Race Massacre was no longer leading national news. If Black
Tulsans' hopes were dimming with the fading national media spotlight, they were all but extinguished by the near-universal reassertion
of white supremacy and Black culpability in the pulpits of Tulsa's
most influential white Christian churches.

Aside from Rev. Mouzon, the loudest testimonies to the continued
vitality of the Doctrine of Discovery worldview came, ironically, from
two of the three clergymen who tried to disperse the lynch mob, Rev.
J. W. Abel at First United Methodist Church and Rev. Charles Kerr
at First Presbyterian Church.[28] Despite their courageous attempts to
tamp down the violence, their subsequent sermons ultimately echoed
Bishop Mouzon's. Abel had this to say from the pulpit the Sunday
after the massacre:

> We must not make a martyr of the negro, even though many
> hundreds of them have suffered innocently. . . . What other na-
> tion in all human history has done as much . . . as the white race
> has done for the race which but a brief half-century ago emerged
> from slavery? A race which even in slavery was a thousand times
> better off than the Black princes who ruled their race in Africa.
> We tax ourselves to educate him; we help him to build churches,
> we are careful to keep him supplied with work at a good wage,
> and trust him with a ballot, and all we ask of him is to behave
> himself and prove himself worthy of our trust.[29]

Abel went so far as to suggest that the African American residents of Tulsa could have more properly executed their civic duties

by offering themselves as an alternative lynch mob: "How much more respect we would have had for the leaders of the race had they presented themselves to the authorities and asked for the privilege of meting out their wrath on the criminal who had disgraced their race."[30]

Even the widely respected and typically moderating Rev. Kerr preached a sermon at First Presbyterian Church of white innocence and Black blame: "The colored people must understand they started it. The fact of their arming and coming up through the city was an outrage to the citizenship of Tulsa."[31] Moreover, Kerr's use of the terms "the city" and "the citizenship" as synonymous with white Tulsans is a clear indication of the status he accorded Black residents. And there were other telling contradictions. While First Presbyterian was proud of sheltering African Americans during the riot, historian and former church member Scott Ellsworth noted that, afterward, the church leadership also quickly took pains to assure their white congregants and other potential visitors, via advertisements in the local papers, that the building had subsequently been "well fumigated."[32]

We have a clear record that these racist themes were consistently preached across the most prominent white churches the Sunday after the massacre. The *Tulsa Daily World* carried two parallel front-page stories with extensive sermon excerpts in its Monday morning edition, and the afternoon *Tulsa Tribune* featured a similar story, each confirming that Tulsa's white churches were of one mind.

The *World* also closed their coverage with a telling final paragraph describing the afternoon services arranged by white clergy for African Americans being held at the fairgrounds and in a tent adjacent to Booker T. Washington High School. The paper assured its anxious white readers that "the negroes seemed responsive and attentive" in these services, in which only "simple gospel sermons, with no allusion to the events of last week, were preached."[33]

THE AFTERMATH

As the days clicked by, white city leaders quickly turned over the work of assisting displaced African American residents to the Red Cross. On June 5, the same day the wall of white Christian defense was erected by Mouzon and others across the city, municipal leaders announced that the city would not accept outside assistance with the rebuilding, despite numerous and substantial offers, including a $1,000 gift from the *Chicago Tribune*. Instead, former mayor Loyal Martin's vaunted Public Welfare Board invited one thousand Tulsa businessmen to underwrite an initial $500,000. None took up the challenge. The *Tulsa World* donated $5,447, but only $775 came in from all other sources combined in the first week.

All of this contrasted sharply with the $1.5 to $2 million that white real estate appraisers and insurance companies estimated the Greenwood losses to be and fell far short of the $5 million in losses filed with the city by Black property owners themselves.[34] By the next week, the Public Welfare Board quietly turned over relief fundraising to the Red Cross.[35] The Public Welfare Board continued to help raise funds for the Red Cross but publicly confirmed that "the question of permanent reconstruction or housing will not be considered by this committee, which is named solely to gather funds for temporary relief work of an urgent nature."[36] Squabbling between city leadership and the Public Welfare Board led to an abandonment of even this limited mission. By the fall, these differences were put aside to sell the public on an unrelated $6.8 million bond issue for a water infrastructure project that would disproportionately benefit white Tulsans.[37]

The absence of any serious municipal or even private funding was not the only obstacle to rebuilding. On June 7, the city issued Fire Ordinance No. 2156, which contained requirements that any building being rebuilt in Greenwood had to meet expensive construction criteria. On June 14, public awareness of the extent of the damage was limited when police commissioner J. M. Adkison announced that anyone photographing the smoldering remains of Greenwood would be arrested.[38] Finally, at the Tulsa City Commission meeting that same night, city leaders announced their intention to prohibit the rebuilding of Greenwood altogether. Mayor T. D. Evans asserted: "A large portion of this district is well suited for Industrial purposes: better adapted for these purposes than for residences.... Let the negro settlement be placed farther to the north and east."[39]

The *Tulsa Tribune* ran a declarative headline, "Negro Section Abolished by City's Order," announcing the anticipated results of this action by the city as a fait accompli: "Thirty-five blocks south of Standpipe Hill now in ruins following the fire Wednesday morning will never again be a Negro quarter but will become a wholesale and industrial center."[40] Only after a summer of struggle and a raft of lawsuits filed by a courageous and dogged interracial team of three Black attorneys and one white attorney was the city's fire code declared illegal, allowing Black residents to begin rebuilding in Greenwood.[41]

Like efforts at restitution, the quest for criminal justice was also half-hearted. On June 9, a hastily assembled all-white grand jury returned eighty-eight indictments, fifty-seven of which named African Americans, including a charge of attempted rape against Dick Rowland, who was still incarcerated safely outside Tulsa. However, reflecting the white population's desire to move quickly past this stain on its reputation, few convictions followed. One Black man went to jail for thirty days for carrying a concealed weapon. The white police chief was convicted, sentenced to pay a fine, and lost his job. But by the beginning of September, just three months after the events, nearly all the charges—including those against Rowland—were summarily either dismissed or ignored.

If the grand jury did not seek justice, its final report offered an illuminating insight into the worldview of Tulsa's white citizens.

Closely echoing Bishop Mouzon's sentiment, the report asserted that the deepest roots of the conflict lay in the fact that Black people had found the audacity to challenge the basic tenets of white supremacy. Those who advocated for racial equality were the true source of the problem. The report concluded: "This agitation resulted in the accumulation of firearms among the people and the storage of quantities of ammunition, all of which was accumulative in the minds of the Negro, which led them as a people to believe in equal rights, social equality, and their ability to demand the same."[42] The grand jury's recommended solution? More stringent segregation and more law enforcement. Specifically, they recommended that the "colored town be policed by white officers," that social mingling of the races be "positively prohibited" everywhere, and that "every law be rigidly enforced to the end that a proper relationship may be maintained between the two races."[43]

Rather than chastening white Tulsans, once national scrutiny waned, the wholesale destruction of the Black community intensified racist activity in Tulsa. Throughout the early 1920s, local white entrepreneurs sold postcards commemorating the massacre, many with graphic images of charred Black bodies in the streets. As Tulsa's remaining Black citizens were living in tents through the summer and fall of 1921 and into the winter of 1922, Tulsa's white citizens—including many of its civic and religious leaders—were joining the revived KKK by the thousands, celebrating their reinforced belief in the demonstrable superiority of the white race. *The Birth of a Nation*, with its glorification of the Klan, opened in Tulsa the same day charges against Dick Rowland were dropped. It enjoyed a five-day, sold-out run at Convention Hall.[44]

Chapter Nine

COMMEMORATION AND REPAIR IN OKLAHOMA

FORGETTING

As the years passed and the white Tulsa business establishment began to see the value in promoting Tulsa as a more polished and cultural town, a conspiracy of silence began to take hold. As historian Scott Ellsworth documented, the *Tulsa Tribune* did not mention the Tulsa race massacre in its regular "Fifteen Years Ago Today" feature on June 1, 1936. But it found noteworthy that on that day "Miss Carolyn Skelly was a charming young hostess" who had thrown a successful luncheon and theater party. The events were also not mentioned in the *Tribune*'s "25 Years Ago Today" column, or in the *Tulsa World*, at their twenty-fifth anniversary in 1946.[1] Most notably, when the *Tulsa Tribune*'s file copies were microfilmed in the 1940s, some unidentified person attempted to redact the paper's coverage; the May 31, 1921, "NAB NEGRO FOR ATTACKING GIRL IN ELEVATOR" story was torn from the bottom right corner of the front page, along with about half of the back page containing editorials.[2]

Even well into the second half of the twentieth century, denial and silence were still the norm, even among those entrusted to keep the annals of Tulsa history. In a 1978 interview with Ellsworth, the president of the Tulsa County Historical Society, Beryl Ford, incredulously claimed, "There weren't any white rioters. They were all Mexicans and Indians."[3]

REMEMBERING

The first book written about the Tulsa Race Massacre was a contemporaneous eyewitness account by Mary Parrish, who went from optimistic new resident of Greenwood to a survivor of the terror. *Events of the Tulsa Disaster* was privately published in 1923,[4] but the small print run allowed only a few copies to circulate in Tulsa and those only on the Black side of town.[5]

The Tulsa "race riot" was mentioned in an Oklahoma history book in 1941 in a single paragraph and in a few subsequent texts, but only in passing. The *Tulsa Tribune*'s 1941 profile of police captain George Blaine discussed his role in the "negro race riot," but it got both the date and year wrong.[6] In 1946, Loren Gill wrote a master's thesis at the University of Oklahoma on the history of the riot, but it received no public attention. In 1968, Don Ross, a young columnist for the African American newspaper the *Oklahoma Eagle*, drew on these early sources to pen a ten-week series detailing the violence and destruction. This broke the silence among Tulsa's African American residents, but the topic was still taboo on the white side of the tracks.[7]

In 1971, at the fiftieth anniversary of the atrocities, local white writer and radio personality Ed Wheeler determined to pull the events out of "a kind of speculative limbo," as Ellsworth described its uncomfortable place in the minds of most white Tulsans.[8] After seven months of research, Wheeler presented the article to the *Tulsa*

World's Sunday magazine, only to be told by the editor that "there is an unwritten rule at this paper that we don't touch this subject with an eleven-foot pole."[9]

As word got out about his article during his research process in the spring of 1971, Wheeler endured a number of personal threats; he received ominous phone calls to his house at all hours, and in May someone had even scrawled a death threat on the windshield of his car in soap: "Best look under your hood from now on."[10] As a Vietnam veteran with military intelligence experience and an active-duty captain in the Oklahoma National Guard, Wheeler was not one to be easily deterred, but he was concerned. For the next month, while he completed the story, he moved his wife and two-year-old son across town with relatives.

As he interviewed survivors of the massacre, he was struck by how present the fears remained five decades on. Those who agreed to talk typically insisted on meeting him at night, many in the sanctuary of their churches and in the company of their pastor.[11] White interviewees were also circumspect, insisting on anonymity not only because of embarrassment but because of an awareness that there is no statute of limitations on murder.

Turned down by multiple white outlets, Wheeler finally found a home for his piece in a new Black magazine, the *Oklahoma Impact*, which was edited by Don Ross, now not just a columnist but a local Black entrepreneur. The story ran as a special insert in the June 1971 edition of the magazine, with the headline, "Profile of a Race Riot," appearing against a red background within a ring of fire.[12] While Wheeler's narrative feels a bit restrained fifty years on—it refused to name names, for example—it was the first to estimate the death toll at three hundred, and it clearly named "prejudice, suspicion, ignorance, and hate" rather than "Negroes of the lower class" as the causes of the violence. The magazine doubled its normal print run to five thousand copies, which were quickly consumed by Tulsa's

Black population. But on Wheeler's white side of town, it created only modest buzz in private conversations, and most, including the white-controlled mainstream media outlets, took no notice.

A decade later, another voice attempted to set the official record straight. Scott Ellsworth, a native Tulsan and member of its white upper middle class, devoted his graduate studies in Duke University's history department to creating the first scholarly account of the massacre. His advisor was the renowned historian John Hope Franklin, also a Tulsa native.[13] The dissertation project developed into the 1982 book *Death in a Promised Land*, which provided sturdy documentation of the atrocities committed by Tulsa's white population.[14] Turned down by Oklahoma University Press but eventually published by Louisiana State University Press, the book generated a national story in the *Washington Post*, but not enough coverage to bring the events fully out of the shadows.[15]

The same year *Death in a Promised Land* was published, Don Ross was elected to the Oklahoma House of Representatives, representing the Greenwood District, and by the 1990s he was a senior member and leading Democratic voice. As part of his continued efforts to bring the facts into public consciousness and to create accountability for the violence and property damage, he introduced a bill calling for $5 million in reparations for the survivors and descendants of the victims of the Tulsa Race Massacre. Ross's bill was met with widespread skepticism from his white colleagues, many of whom either had no idea what he was talking about or denied the extent of the violence.

But then he switched tactics. Leveraging momentum from modest media coverage of the seventy-fifth anniversary of the massacre in 1996, he asked the legislature for a report, arguing that there had never been an official study of one of the most violent episodes in the history of the state. Ross convinced the Republican governor, Frank Keating, and enough of his colleagues to support the effort, and in 1997 the legislature earmarked a modest amount of funding and passed legislation forming what became known as the Tulsa Race Riot Commission (TRRC).[16] But Ross remained clear that he was not looking primarily for an apology but for the acceptance of responsibility. "An apology without recompense, in my view, is subterfuge if not altogether hot air," he declared.[17]

The commission comprised an eleven-member, interracial body of community leaders, state legislators, and scholars, including Scott Ellsworth as a consultant. It produced a remarkable set of scholarship establishing the facts of the events and put forward concrete recommendations for an appropriate public response. In late November 1999, the TRRC subcommittee on reparations presented its recommendations, which included direct reparations of up to $150,000 per family to massacre survivors, five hundred endowed scholarships for Black Tulsa youth, and other provisions that were estimated to be a minimum of $33 million. In February 2000, the full TRRC voted 7–4 in favor of these reparation provisions.[18]

The commission's final report, running 178 pages and delivered February 28, 2001, corroborated higher estimates of between 100 and 300, much closer to Wheeler's conclusions. It documented the deliberate destruction of property, coordinated in many cases by those in police uniform or those who had been hastily deputized and issued temporary badges or ribbons. And the report's official existence created widespread media interest in telling this story, which was covered by major outlets like the *New York Times* and CBS's *60 Minutes*.

The final chapter of the report documents the coordinated acts of violence by the city's white residents, the police, and the National Guard against the Black residents of Greenwood. It establishes culpability for the city's failure to protect its Black citizens' lives and property during the two days of violence and for its deliberate implementation of policies to prevent rebuilding by the city's Black residents. The report concludes that the payment of reparations "would be good public policy and do much to repair the emotional and physical scars of this terrible incident in our shared past." It concludes by putting the question directly back to local and state elected officials: "Now the question is whether the city and state wish to acknowledge that as a debt and to pay it."[19]

The state legislature and the governor provided a swift answer just three months later. Despite a fervent call to include reparations in the final bill that translated the commission report into action, the legislature passed, and the governor signed, the 1921 Tulsa Race Riot Reconciliation Act of 2001 without any such provisions.[20] The buck got passed down the line. Governor Keating announced that he did not believe the commission report made the case for reparations payments. Tulsa mayor M. Susan Savage declared that the city's hands were tied without a court order, but she announced a private effort led by the city's Chamber of Commerce to pay each of the 138 living survivors $5,000 each. That effort quickly dissipated. Tulsa Metropolitan Ministry, underwritten primarily by the Unitarian Universalist Association, was the only entity that distributed funds, raising $28,000 that allowed them to send roughly $200 checks to each survivor.

Even a proposed $5 million in state funding for business incentives and a memorial resulted in only a fraction of that support. The most tangible outcome was the $405,000 purchase of three acres that eventually became John Hope Franklin Reconciliation Park, which broke ground in 2008 and opened in 2010.[21] The state did make one concrete provision for the survivors. It commissioned the creation of a gold-plated "Medallion of Distinction"—embossed with the seal of the state of Oklahoma on one side and a representation of "Black Wall Street" on the other, suspended on a red, white, and blue ribbon. The state announced that it would present the medals to several survivors in a ceremony to be held, of all places, at the National Cowboy & Western Heritage Museum in Oklahoma City.[22]

COMMEMORATING: THE ONE HUNDREDTH ANNIVERSARY OF THE TULSA RACE MASSACRE

> For fifty years, the story of the massacre had been suppressed. Then for fifty more, that story was brought to light. In the next fifty, we will learn what it means.
>
> —Scott Ellsworth, *The Groundbreaking: An American City and Its Search for Justice*[23]

The saga of the public commemoration of the one hundredth anniversary of the Tulsa Race Massacre is winding, and it is clear that the centennial events mark a new, rather than a final, chapter. In 2021, a century after the atrocities, Tulsa seemed finally ready to acknowledge, citywide, the white mass racial violence that had marred their community. Signaling its commitment, four years ahead of the anniversary, the city formed the 1921 Tulsa Race Massacre Centennial Commission—consisting of representatives from government, as well as business, religious, and civic groups—to plan an appropriate approach.

The public commitment of the city to commemorate the hundredth anniversary of these events, along with the zeitgeist produced by the Movement for Black Lives and the nationwide protests for racial justice following the murder of George Floyd by police in the spring of 2020, resulted in significant national and even international attention. Fictional depictions of the massacre appeared in two HBO series, *Watchmen* and *Lovecraft Country*. The *New York Times* produced a three-dimensional interactive walk-through of 1921 Greenwood titled "What the Tulsa Race Massacre Destroyed."[24] And not one but three nationally distributed documentary films were released in 2021 by the History Channel, CNN/HBO Max, and PBS.[25]

The Centennial Commission planned a multipronged approach that included not only events marking the one hundredth anniversary but a major fundraising campaign for long-term investments in Greenwood. It successfully raised $30 million, $18.2 of which was invested in Greenwood Rising, a major new history center anchoring the historic entrance to the Greenwood neighborhood. The commission also organized the Black Wall Street Legacy Festival, a series of major arts, music, and educational programs, running from May 26 through May 31. Events included the unveiling of the Greenwood Arts Project and a mural, a *Legacy of Survival* exhibit opening at Gilcrease Museum, marches and parades, lectures on contemporary issues such as "the case for reparations," and a worship service at First Baptist Church, a historically Black congregation on Greenwood Avenue. On May 31, Rev. Jesse Jackson helped dedicate a prayer wall at Vernon AME Church, created from the only part of the church that survived the burning a century ago.[26]

Tulsa's white churches, which had historically served as the chief moral legitimizers of white supremacy and white mob violence, also stepped up. Boston Avenue United Methodist Church, Bishop Mouzon's platform in 1921, used the season of Lent in 2021 to launch one hundred days of reflection and repentance for their congregation's part in supporting white supremacy and racial segregation in Tulsa. At the invitation of Rev. David Wiggs, senior pastor at the church, I found myself a part of this work. During these days of reflection and repentance, the church organized a study group of eighty people to read my book *White Too Long: The Legacy of White Supremacy in American Christianity.*[27] I also delivered a sermon to the full congregation at the end of Lent, wherein I reflected on the impact of Bishop Mouzon's white supremacist sermon, delivered from that same pulpit a century earlier.

The predominantly white First Baptist Church, affiliated with the Southern Baptist Convention, set up a "Tulsa Race Massacre Prayer Room" containing photographs and facts, including excerpts from numerous racist sermons preached the Sunday following the 1921 violence by the pastors of Tulsa's most prominent white churches. In addition to the historical material, they placed a prominent plaque on the wall featuring a joint rebuttal from the current pastors of each of these churches: "Racism, in any form and at any level, is incompatible with being a follower of Jesus Christ."[28] On the last Sunday in May 2021, marking the one hundredth anniversary, most of these churches held moments of acknowledgment and repentance in their services, incorporating resources such as scripture readings, prayers, songs, and a proclamation that were developed by Black pastors working with the Centennial Commission.[29]

But even a century later in a city largely dedicated to telling the truth about a troubled past, the Centennial Commission found the road forward bumpy. Just two weeks ahead of the centennial celebrations, the commission voted to eject Oklahoma governor J. Kevin Stitt from its ranks because of his active support for a bill in the state legislature that would have discouraged teaching about the legacy of racism in Oklahoma's public schools.[30] Despite sitting on the commission, which stated it "believes strongly in reparations," and signing a city council resolution of apology by the city that included a commitment to making "tangible amends," Tulsa mayor G. T. Bynum voiced his opposition to any cash payments to survivors, saying it would divide the city.[31]

Most tragically, the "Remember and Rise" capstone centennial event—which was to feature a nationally televised keynote by Georgia representative Stacey Abrams and a performance by musician John Legend on Memorial Day—unraveled just days before it was to air, entangled in internal disagreements about reparations. Just a few weeks ahead of the centennial, Damario Solomon-Simmons, an attorney for the known survivors, sent a letter to the Centennial Commission demanding that $1 million be set aside from commission funds for each of the three known survivors and that the commission pledge to raise $50 million for a fund for survivors and descendants. According to state senator Kevin Matthews, the Centennial Commission indicated that this demand wasn't possible but reached an alternate agreement of setting aside $100,000 paid directly to each survivor and $2 million to establish a reparation fund—only to have Solomon-Simmons demand more the following day. Solomon-Simmons claimed his reply was part of ongoing negotiations.[32]

No agreement was reached. Solomon-Simmons accused the Centennial Commission of forgetting about the very victims of the violence. The commission countered that funds had not been raised for reparations and therefore could not legally be diverted to those purposes at the requested scale. Further, the commission asserted that reparations were ultimately owed by the city, the county, and the state, the responsible civic entities. Word got out about the dispute, and both Abrams and Legend withdrew, depriving the city of what promised to be the pinnacle event of the commemoration.[33]

The three remaining survivors of the Tulsa Race Massacre did finally receive some cash payments at the centennial, but only from private funds. The largest were $100,000 payments from Justice for Greenwood, a nonprofit organization run by Solomon-Simmons. And, like two decades before, Tulsa Metropolitan Ministry (TMM) raised modest amounts itself, nearly $80,000 in what it called an "Atonement Project." TMM disbursed checks of $10,000 each to each of the survivors and planned to direct the remaining funds to other projects "that would be restorative in the Greenwood District, ideally through work that would have a long-term impact." As of this writing, TMM had also contributed $13,000 to the "Beyond Apology Project," an initiative led by Councilor Vanessa Hall-Harper, Tulsa's lone Black city council representative, to "determine what making amends for the devastation should include, and then steps to make those amends a reality."[34]

In 2021, Tulsa had largely succeeded in telling the truth about its history. But even a city genuinely committed to acknowledging and remembering its past has yet to be able to make meaningful acts of repair and restitution a reality. The city has yet to redeem the public promise made by former Tulsa mayor Loyal J. Martin just one day after those awful events in 1921:

> The rest of the United States must now know that the real citizenship of Tulsa weeps at this unspeakable crime. And will make good the damage, so far as it can be done, to the last penny. We have neglected our duties and our city government has fallen down. We have had a failing police protection here, and now we have to pay the costs of it. The city and county is [*sic*] legally liable for every dollar of the damage which has been done. Other cities have had to pay the bill of race riots, and we shall have to do so probably because we have neglected our duty as citizens.[35]

HEALING AND CHANGE

On May 18, 2021, just days ahead of the hundredth anniversary, the three known remaining survivors of the massacre—aged 107, 106, and 100—were invited to testify before the House Judiciary Committee of the US Congress as part of its own work considering reparations for survivors and descendants of the incident.[36] Viola Ford Fletcher, who had just celebrated her 107th birthday, recalled just how vividly the awful events of that day remain with her and called for justice:

> I'm here seeking justice, and I'm asking my country to acknowledge what happened in Tulsa in 1921. I will never forget the violence that looked like a mob when we left our home. I still see

Black men being shot, Black bodies lying in the street. I hear the screams. I have lived through the massacre every day. Our country may forget this history, but I cannot.[37]

Lessie Benningfield Randle, 106, likewise lamented the glacial pace of recognition and justice, which hindered survivors and their families from finding peace and some closure. "It seems like justice in America is always so slow or not possible for Black people," she declared. "I am asking you today to give us some peace; please give me, my family, and my community some justice."[38]

Authentic healing flows from, and true repentance is built on, the twin pillars of truth-telling and repair. It's notable that in a city like Tulsa, which has led the way with this public commemoration, healing is very much in process. At the time of this writing, despite the promises by city leaders in 1921 and the clear recommendations of the Tulsa Race Riot Commission in 2001, not a single penny has moved from the coffers of the city, the county, or the state to the survivors of the massacre and their descendants. The question of reparations for these massive, multigenerational losses remains unanswered.

At the same time, the work of truth-telling and acknowledgment has produced other important fruits. This achievement has made a difference, not just for the residents of Tulsa but for the African American community generally, and for all of us, as we face together this appalling part of our history and its legacy among us today. Ellsworth elegantly noted what is at stake in America's history wars and why telling a truer story about ourselves is key to living into a better future:

History isn't just a chronicle of events. Rather, it is a mirror of both who we are and who we want to be. For us to learn from the past, we have to look at and wrestle with *all* of it—the sad and the ugly as well as the good and the great.[39]

On the one hundredth anniversary of the Tulsa Race Massacre, President Joe Biden made history with a strongly worded presidential proclamation titled "A Proclamation on Day of Remembrance: 100 Years After the 1921 Tulsa Race Massacre." It declared May 31, 2021, a national "Day of Remembrance" for the massacre, and opened with this unequivocal acknowledgment about what happened:

> One hundred years ago, a violent white supremacist mob raided, firebombed, and destroyed approximately 35 square blocks of the thriving Black neighborhood of Greenwood in Tulsa, Oklahoma. Families and children were murdered in cold blood. Homes, businesses, and churches were burned. In all, as many as 300 Black Americans were killed, and nearly 10,000 were left destitute and homeless. Today, on this solemn centennial of the Tulsa Race Massacre, I call on the American people to reflect on the deep roots of racial terror in our Nation and recommit to the work of rooting out systemic racism across our country.[40]

Biden also acknowledged that the injustices inflicted on the Black residents of Greenwood did not stop with the killing and burning. The proclamation importantly notes that the violence was "followed by laws and policies that made recovery nearly impossible" at both the local and federal levels, such as redlining, zoning, and interstate highway construction in the 1970s that—under the guise of "urban renewal"—plowed through Greenwood and cut it off from the rest of the city. He declared flatly, "The attack on Black families and Black wealth in Greenwood persisted across generations."[41]

Biden also personally traveled to Tulsa, delivering a speech in which he recognized all three survivors—Viola Ford Fletcher, Hughes Van Ellis, and Lessie Benningfield Randle—by name. At the heart of his remarks, he made the link between acknowledgment and the process of healing, declaring, "My fellow Americans, this was not a riot. This was a massacre—[applause]—among the worst in our history, but not the only one. And for too long, forgotten by our history. . . . And only—as painful as it is, only in remembrance do wounds heal. We just have to choose to remember."[42]

A year after the commemoration events, I asked Rev. Wiggs what difference he thought all the activity had made. Wiggs's answer came easily: "Truth-telling about the horror of what actually happened has raised awareness, and the facts are now widely accepted."[43] This broad agreement was not always present. Ellsworth also counted this consensus a considerable accomplishment: "that a great wrong had been done was no longer up for serious debate."[44]

Today, there are more than two dozen books in print documenting the 1921 atrocities in Tulsa, and the events have become integrated into the public memory of America. When the National Museum of African American History and Culture opened in 2016, for example, it featured a prominent exhibit on the massacre and Greenwood.[45] However imperfect and incomplete the efforts, Tulsa has succeeded in excavating the truth and exposing it to the light for all to see. After more than half a century of silence, establishing a consensus about what happened—backed by official public recognitions, expressed in prominent monuments and exhibits, commemorated in a world-class museum and history center, preached in prominent white pulpits, and proclaimed by a sitting US president—is an important, and certainly not an inevitable, achievement. And it benefits not just Tulsans, but us all.

In my conversation with Rev. Wiggs, he noted that the discussions and activities leading up to the commemoration had also produced something even more elusive: an improvement in the ability of white Tulsans to see the long tendrils of systemic racism. The historical documentation of the commissions and the citywide discussions made plain the ways in which white Tulsans had exploited the tragedy to advance their own interests, such as "city rezoning to prevent Black entrepreneurs from rebuilding, insurance claims not being paid—the ongoing ways that powerbrokers used the carnage to enrich the white community at expense of the Black community."[46] Whatever future conversations happen around issues of race, the improved ability to perceive systemic racism is new social capital that can be tapped, an asset in building bridges across the racial divide.

The long process of truth-telling has also impacted other decisions that are changing the civic landscape in Tulsa. A prominent founding father of the city, Wyatt Tate Brady, cast a long shadow over swaths of the city well into the twenty-first century. He was memorialized in the names of a neighborhood called "Brady Heights" and a commercial district downtown informally known as "the Brady district," which included the Brady Theater and a major thoroughfare named Brady Street. As the momentum of commemorating the hundredth anniversary of the Tulsa Race Massacre increased, citizens and civic leaders began to question the continued use of Brady's name, given his open associations with the Sons of Confederate Veterans and the Ku Klux Klan, along with his known participation in the massacre.

In 2013, the city first responded with a disingenuous half measure, awkwardly renaming Brady Street to M. B. Brady Street after the Civil War photographer Mathew Brady, who had no connection to Tulsa. Five years later, they overwhelmingly voted to change the name to Reconciliation Way, effective July 1, 2019. In 2017, business owners renamed the commercial district the Tulsa Arts District, which is now a thriving, eclectic section of town boasting museums, philanthropic organizations, galleries, and restaurants. In 2019, the owner of the Brady Theater—formerly Tulsa Convention Hall, where Black Tulsans had been interned following the massacre and where *The Birth of a Nation* was shown in the fall of 1921—changed its name to the Tulsa Theater.[47] The neighborhood carved from the Tate family's massive landholdings also changed its name from "Brady Heights" to "The Heights."

In a final turning of the page, Wyatt Tate Brady's three-story mansion, originally constructed to mimic Robert E. Lee's Arlington, Virginia, home, was purchased in 2016 by retired NFL running back Felix Jones, a graduate of Tulsa's Booker T. Washington High School. Jones renamed it Skyline Mansion after his childhood neighborhood and opened it as an event venue. In 2020, Jones invited hip-hop artist and Tulsa native Steph Simon to lead a "Born on Black Wall Street: Unplugged" concert at the mansion, which was covered by *Rolling Stone*.[48]

The momentum from the hundredth anniversary has also breathed new life, and new racial justice frameworks, into existing coalitions in the civil society sector. The Oklahoma Center for Community and Justice, an offshoot of the older National Conference of Christians and Jews, has launched a regular Advancing Oklahoma meeting, which gathers a diverse group of two hundred business, community, and religious leaders. Each month, leaders look to address community problems, now within a racial equity frame that Wiggs summarized this way: "How can we work together across sectors to improve race relations, be more inclusive, empower people, remove barriers?"[49]

Boston Avenue United Methodist Church is harnessing the momentum from their own involvement with the commemoration to build a commitment to racial justice and healing into the DNA of their congregational life. The church has formed a Justice and Reconciliation Strategic Initiative and a task force, cochaired by an older white male member and a younger Black female member, to move that work forward. As of early 2022, the task force had developed a multiyear plan for continued truth-telling, coupled with acts of justice, repair, and reconciliation.

One arm of that work has involved developing a partnership

with Vernon AME Church, one of the historic churches right on Greenwood Avenue that was destroyed in 1921 and struggled for decades to rebuild.[50] This partnership is symbolically significant, pairing a Black church that was burned by white Tulsans with a white church that justified it and deflected blame for the violence onto the victims.

Programmatically, the churches have established shared worship experiences and educational programs, including a study of their shared Methodist tradition. Their denomination became divided by race in nineteenth-century America because of white supremacist attitudes among white Methodists, resulting in a United Methodist Church that remains predominantly white and the African Methodist Episcopal (AME) Church, which remains mostly Black. As part of the partnership, Boston Avenue has contributed modest financial assistance and volunteers for building renovation work at Vernon, and has supported a food program Vernon set up to assist struggling families during the COVID-19 pandemic. As Wiggs notes, even this small act—a white church supporting a program that was initiated and run by a Black church—contributes to improving healing and creating relationships of trust: "It has helped white people decenter our power by supporting Vernon projects—joining them there at their site—and not leading them. *We* have to support *their* work. It helps us learn about how whiteness has historically been the power center, and how that's not helpful."[51]

Wiggs also told me a moving story about how challenging building real relationships across the racial divide can be, particularly because even well-meaning white people have trouble grasping how painful and palpable the experience of racism remains today. As the Boston Avenue leadership was thinking of ways for their congregation to engage the Vernon congregation, someone proposed a joint viewing and discussion of the 2016 movie *Hidden Figures*, which chronicles the stories of African American women who faced racial and gender discrimination while working at NASA in the 1960s. In an emotional recounting, Wiggs described the disconnect when he posed the idea to Vernon's pastor, Rev. Robert Turner:

> At lunch, I tossed that idea to Dr. Turner. And he got very quiet. And he's not a quiet man. Clearly something was going on I wasn't keen to. He very gently said, "That's probably not the place to start for us." It dawned on me in a painful way that we [at Boston Avenue] were looking at [racial discrimination] as history, but for him and his congregation it was very much a lived experience. It became very clear how painful that was, even though it was a triumphant story, how painful it was for those people then and how painful it still was for him and his congregation. For us it was going to be a theoretical exercise. We were thinking, "Oh, all that bad stuff happened back there. It's all good now, and we can talk about it and celebrate those women who triumphed." You know, that's not what it feels like if you're Black.[52]

Wiggs described this awkward, painful experience as "a paradigm shift" that sensitized both him and the Boston Avenue church leadership to how much work white people, and particularly white Christians who think of themselves as racial justice allies, still must do. Wiggs, who has been a leader on racial justice issues among white churches in Tulsa and who has seen himself as someone supporting racial equality for most of his life, noted his own surprise that he had such a blind spot. He confessed, "I've been doing this work since I was twelve years old. I was part of the first integrated junior high school in my hometown. But somehow over all those decades I missed how real the wounds and trauma of racism in America still are."[53]

Boston Avenue's example also provides a reality check, revealing the significant challenges that are still with us, even among whites who accept the realities of systemic racism today. When I asked where his congregation was on the issue of reparations, Wiggs replied that the church was in the "very early stages" of that conversation. Just ahead of the one hundredth anniversary of the massacre, the church leadership had raised the possibility of participating in Tulsa Metropolitan Ministry's push to raise $100,000 in reparations from the faith community, an effort strongly supported by Rev. Turner and Vernon AME.[54]

The immediate pushback Wiggs received from some 255 congregants made him realize that, despite their proactive work and support for the commemoration, significant work still lay ahead. He explained: "I had a few people immediately call me up and object, saying, 'This is a political issue,' and 'They're just trying to take money out of my pocket for no good reason,' and 'The church should not be involved in this.' It signaled that we'll need to create a context where reparations can be one track of a wider conversation." His hope is that the Justice and Reconciliation Strategic Initiative can provide that context. Under the banner of "Acts of Justice," it includes a charge "to foster healing for the injustices done to people of other races and cultures by the church and our community" and lists three potential avenues for this work: 1) financial gifts such as direct payments or grants; 2) mission activities such as home building; and 3) direct service projects such as providing mobile dental clinics.[55] Despite the resistance among the congregation, Wiggs is convinced that reparations, financial redress of financial wrongs, must be part of any response that has integrity, declaring, "If you're serious about this, it's part of the work that has to be done."[56] It remains an open question how the church will respond to this challenge.

However clumsy, however inconsistent, and however insufficient, these experiences are nonetheless building self-understanding and humility among white leaders and participants who are engaging in this work. And they are contributing both to present efforts to heal from this awful rending of the social fabric and to capacities for future success. For Black Tulsans, some healing flows from the death of denial among their white neighbors about these atrocities, even if frustration and residues of distrust remain because of an unwillingness to repair the damage that has now been acknowledged. For white Tulsans and Oklahomans, there is healing in telling the truth about who they have been and how that has impacted who they are. And white Americans owe white Oklahomans—citizens of the only state in which not a single county voted for our first Black president in either 2008 or 2012—a debt of gratitude for their example.[57] Truth-telling is the key that opens the door to a new place, one that better expresses who we want to be, to ourselves and in relationship to our fellow citizens.

The survivors and descendants of the 1921 Tulsa Race Massacre have received something important, something few other victims of white racial violence have had in American history: official and widely accepted acknowledgment of the truth of the atrocities committed by their white neighbors, both a century ago and for decades in their wake. But even with confession on the lips of the president and Tulsa's civic and religious leaders, a willingness to repair the damage continues to be elusive. As long as justice and repair remain arrested, failing to be realized even in some symbolic way, the process of healing cannot be fully consummated.

Despite its important successes, Tulsa's story, and our own, remain incomplete. This, then, is where we find ourselves today, in medias res, knowing our forward momentum requires us to follow the vital first step with another, lest we fall.

Coda: Land Back

Oklahoma's legacy as "Indian Country," a refugee zone for displaced Indian nations from across the eastern half of the country, as well as its distinction today as the state with the highest percentage of Native Americans (16 percent) among its population, make it a visible symbol of our nation's treacherous dealings with the land's original inhabitants.[58] While most of the promised reservation lands for the scores of tribes forcibly resettled within the state's boundaries have been subsequently either eliminated or decimated, there remain thirty-nine officially recognized Indian nations in Oklahoma today, only five of which are historically from the area.[59]

In 2020, the US Supreme Court ruling in *McGirt v. Oklahoma* generated eyebrow-raising nationwide headlines, such as "US Supreme Court Rules Half of Oklahoma Is Native American Land," even from typically measured outlets like the BBC and NPR.[60] In one of the most significant decisions upholding Native American rights in decades, the US Supreme Court ruled that because the eastern half of Oklahoma sits on Native American lands protected by treaty agreements, the state could not bring criminal prosecutions for crimes on those lands without consent of the Native American tribes.

As is typical within the convoluted world of Indian Law, the high court's ruling relied on historical treaties between the federal government and Indian nations, which address sovereignty and land rights, but it restricted its concerns to the question of legal jurisdiction. In other words, for legal jurisdictional purposes, the treaties defining "Indian Country" still apply. For land ownership determinations, they do not. Still, the *McGirt* ruling was a clear victory for Native American sovereignty.

Celebrations in Native American circles, however, were short-lived. Oklahoma governor J. Kevin Stitt secured a $10 million fund from the state legislature in 2021 to launch what Supreme Court justice Neil

Gorsuch described as a "media and litigation campaign" to portray reservations as "lawless dystopias" and asked the court to reconsider its decision.[61] In *Oklahoma v. Castro-Huerta* (2022), the Supreme Court partially granted this request, narrowing the earlier ruling and declaring that the state had jurisdiction over crimes involving non–Native Americans in Native American territory. Conservative justice Gorsuch penned a scathing dissent, which was joined by the three liberal justices. "Truly, a more ahistorical and mistaken statement of Indian law would be hard to fathom," he wrote. "Tribes are not private organizations within state boundaries. Their reservations are not glorified private campgrounds. Tribes are sovereigns."[62]

While the struggles over Native American sovereignty continue within Oklahoma, nationwide, Native American leaders are increasingly pushing the issue that the US Supreme Court sidestepped in *McGirt*: land. The realities are stark. Native Americans controlled all of the 2.4 billion acres of what is today the United States in 1492, but only 56 million acres of that land, or about 2 percent, is under Native American control today.[63]

While the idea of reclaiming stolen lands has always been a part of Native American activism, over the last few years the term "Land Back" (or on social media, #LandBack) has gained new resonance. One of the earliest precedents in the modern era was the return of Blue Lake, forty-eight thousand acres of land in the mountains of northwest New Mexico, to the Taos Pueblo tribe. After more than sixty years of activism, Native American leaders secured the initial transfer of the bulk of the lands with the support of President Richard Nixon in 1970 and a smaller tract with the support of President Bill Clinton in 1996.[64]

B. "Toastie" Oaster (Choctaw), a reporter for *High Country News*, described the recent evolution of the #LandBack movement:

> In mid-2019, the hashtag gained traction in North America during the Tiny House Warriors' blockade of the Trans Mountain

Pipeline in unceded Secwepemc territory. Soon after, the Yellowhead Institute, an Indigenous-led policy research center at Toronto Metropolitan University, released a report called "Land Back" that examined settler-colonialism at work in present-day Canada. In August 2020, the advocacy group NDN Collective launched landback.org with a brief "LandBack Manifesto."[65]

The LandBack movement has resulted in a number of significant victories. In 2019, the city of Eureka, California, returned Indian Island (now Tuluwat Island) in Humboldt Bay to the Wiyot people. The transfer of the 280-acre island came nearly 160 years after it was taken by white settler colonists following a massacre of approximately two hundred Wiyot, mostly women and children, while the men were away hunting.[66]

In June 2022, the state of New York approved the transfer of more than one thousand acres of land in and around Onondaga Creek near modern-day Syracuse to the Onondaga Nation, the largest such transfer in New York history. These lands were guaranteed to the tribes of the Haudenosaunee Confederacy, of which the Onandaga were a part, by America's first president, George Washington, in the 1794 Treaty of Canandaigua. Sid Hill, the Tadodaho (chief) of the Onondaga and Keeper of the Flame of the Six Nations Haudenosaunee Confederacy, penned a measured celebration of the long-overdue and partial recognition of their treaty rights. "We organize our lives around the belief that what we do today is designed to benefit those seven generations into the future, as we build on what was left for us seven generations into the past," he wrote. "We owe it to ourselves, and to them, to seize the opportunity to return our stewardship to this land—with more land to come."[67]

In 2022, other LandBack efforts have taken root from coast to coast. In April, a collaboration between a conservation organization and the US Fish & Wildlife Service returned 465 acres to the

Rappahannock Tribe in Virginia. The city of Oakland, California, is in the process of returning five acres of parkland to the Sogorea Te' Land Trust, the East Bay Ohlone tribe, and the Confederated Villages of Lisjan Nation.

Conviction has also spawned creative approaches beyond government actions. With many government efforts stalled or anemic, some individuals and community organizations are creating their own ways of contributing to the LandBack movement. In Seattle, for example, a group of white residents launched the Duwamish Solidarity Group (DSG) in 2009 to work for racial justice and to create an authentic relationship with the Duwamish Tribe.[68] DSG launched a program called "Real Rent Duwamish," with a straightforward call:

> Real Rent calls on people who live and work in Seattle to make rent payments to the Duwamish Tribe. Though the city named for the Duwamish leader Chief Seattle thrives, the Tribe has yet to be justly compensated for their land, resources, and livelihood.[69]

After more than a decade, the program has more than 22,000 voluntary "Real Renters." The website challenges participants to make a meaningful but sustainable commitment. Some, for example, contribute $18.55 per month to symbolize the broken promises since the Treaty of Point Elliott in 1855; others contribute $54 per month as a reminder of the 54,000 acres of homeland that the Duwamish Tribe were forced to cede to white settler colonists that year. All funds are deposited directly to the nonprofit Duwamish Tribal Services, which is run by the tribe. On their website, the Real Rent Duwamish group declares, "Our government hasn't honoured the treaty, but WE can."

Reminiscent of Ta-Nehisi Coates's 2014 "The Case for Reparations" article in the *Atlantic*, David Treuer (Leech Lake Ojibwe) wrote "Return the National Parks to the Tribes" for the *Atlantic* in 2021.[70]

Treuer starts with the historical fact that all US national parks were carved out of Native American lands that were lost by force or ceded under duress. Native Americans were promised continued access to these lands, guarantees that were quickly abrogated when the parks opened to the white public.

Treuer makes a compelling case:

> We live in a time of historical reconsideration, as more and more people recognize that the sins of the past still haunt the present. For Native Americans, there can be no better remedy for the theft of land than land. And for us, no lands are as spiritually significant as the national parks. They should be returned to us. Indians should tend—and protect and preserve—these favored gardens again.

Treuer proposes that all 85 million acres of national park sites should be turned over to a consortium of the 574 federally recognized tribes in the US. Most concretely, this move would ensure that all Native Americans have direct access to these parts of their ancestral lands. But Treuer also argues that such a large symbolic act would accomplish much more. "To be entrusted with the stewardship of America's most precious landscapes would be a deeply meaningful form of restitution," he writes. "Alongside the feelings of awe that Americans experience while contemplating the god-rock of Yosemite and other places like it, we could take inspiration in having done right by one another."[71]

PART FOUR

THE RIVERS BEFORE US

Chapter Ten

THE SEARCH FOR
HOPE IN HISTORY

History says, Don't hope
On this side of the grave . . .
But then, once in a lifetime
The longed-for tidal wave
Of justice can rise up
And hope and history rhyme.

—"The Cure at Troy," Seamus Heaney[1]

The work of truth-telling and repair in the Mississippi Delta, Duluth, and Tulsa finds its own path in each place, tracing the scars that white supremacy and violence have carved across that land. Looking upstream, we see the connections between the torture and murder of a fourteen-year-old boy and the genocide and dispossession of Indigenous people. On the not-too-distant horizon, beyond the lynching of three African American circus workers, we discern the silhouettes of thirty-eight Dakota men hanging from the gallows.

And the flames that engulfed Black Wall Street cast light on the Trail of Tears and the reign of terror brought upon the Osage people just a few miles away.

These episodes feature their own unique characters and settings. But, together, they reveal an archetypal plot. Every US state contains similar legacies of white racial violence because every US state was built on the same foundation, anchored by the Doctrine of Discovery: the conviction that America was divinely ordained to be a new promised land for European Christians. In each of the thirteen original colonies and in eight additional slave states, this deep founding myth justified the enslavement and exploitation of Africans in pursuit of white flourishing. In all, it justified the killing and dispossession of Native Americans and the claiming of their lands by good white Christian people, who alone possessed the virtues necessary for sustaining "civilization."

We are just beginning, over the last two decades, to see widespread efforts to tell the truth about this troubling past, not just in the history books, but on the ground in local communities. Prior to the turn of the twenty-first century, although Emmett Till's name was known around the world, there was virtually no tangible acknowledgment of his murder in the Mississippi Delta. There was no public space in downtown Duluth commemorating the lynching of Elias Clayton, Elmer Jackson, and Isaac McGhie. And the Tulsa Race Riot Commission had not yet published their groundbreaking fact-finding report. The UN Declaration on the Rights of Indigenous Peoples had not been passed, and no Christian denominations had seriously considered, much less repudiated, the Doctrine of Discovery.

But today, the landscape is marked by promising efforts at both truth-telling and repair. In the Mississippi Delta, the Emmett Till Interpretive Center has not only established a presence on the town square across from the infamous Sumner County Courthouse, but it may soon become part of a new national park. In Tulsa, the

Greenwood Rising center serves not only as the leading educational center about Black Wall Street and the Tulsa Race Massacre but also as an anchor to the Greenwood neighborhood's redevelopment. In downtown Duluth, the Clayton-Jackson-McGhie Memorial plaza has served as an important community rallying point during Black Lives Matter protests and continues to function as a site for communal reflection and organizing to combat racial inequality.

These meaningful efforts may not constitute the "tidal wave" of justice so eloquently described by Seamus Heaney above, but they could not have been undertaken by a people without hope.

ELEMENTS OF CHANGE

While activists in each of these three locations are addressing their own unique histories, it is possible to identify some common elements. These observations do not constitute anything like a blueprint or a ten-step checklist for social change, particularly given a white supremacy as deeply rooted as ours. But leaders in three key roles have been critical in moving these communities from silence and amnesia to truthfulness and repair.

First, there have been *witnesses* who testified about the events themselves. In the Mississippi Delta, figures like Moses Wright, Emmett Till's uncle, and Wheeler Parker Jr., his cousin and best friend, spoke courageously and steadfastly preserved the story of Till's life and murder. Wright's courage was captured in a 1955 Associated Press photo, as he lifted his finger to point out Till's murderers, becoming the first Black man in the Delta that anyone could remember who was willing to risk his life to accuse a white man of murder in a court of law. Parker, who became a minister and is now the last living witness to Till's abduction, has continued, throughout his life, to tell Emmett's story. Currently eighty-three years old, he and his wife run the Emmett Till & Mamie Till-Mobley Institute, which has this statement at the top of its home page: "Racial reconciliation begins by telling the truth."[2]

Sometimes a witness provided a single detail that illuminated the true dynamics of events.[3] For example, Albert Tracy, a reporter for the *Duluth Herald*, buttonholed Duluth's public safety commissioner, William Murnian, at 11:00 p.m. on the night of the lynchings to ask him why the police were not using force to disperse the mob that was breaking into the jail. He confirmed that Murnian had forbidden police to use lethal force and captured this explanation from the commissioner: "I do not want to see the blood of one white person spilled for six blacks."

In Tulsa, Mary Jones Parrish, a trained journalist who fled the violence with her young daughter, provided a detailed eyewitness account of the 1921 Tulsa Race Massacre, published as *Events of the Tulsa Disaster* in 1923. While it received little attention during her lifetime, it serves as a critical primary source document today. Jones Parrish not only saw the importance of documenting the events for local history, but she also eloquently expressed the national significance of the horror unfolding before her eyes:

> Tonight as I write and think of Tulsa . . . my eyes well with tears
> and my soul cries for justice. Oh, America! Thou Land of the
> Free and Home of the Brave! The country that gave its choicest
> blood and bravest hearts to make the world safe for democracy!
> How long will you let mob violence reign supreme? Is democracy a mockery?[4]

In each place, the movement for social change was sparked and sustained by *prophets*. These people broke the silence and pierced the veil of collective amnesia in the dominant white culture. In Mississippi, Jerome Little, the first Black president of the Tallahatchie

Board of Supervisors, was such a person. Despite growing up in the Delta, he only learned of Emmett Till's story after being deployed overseas in the army. When he returned home, he went on a mission to make sure the next generation would know Emmett Till's name. He described his decades-long efforts at telling Emmett Till's story as a calling, something that was "just in me."[5]

Duluth's prophets were Michael Fedo, along with a multiracial trio of activists—Heidi Bakk-Hansen, Henry Banks, and Catherine Ostos. Each brought complementary skills to the work of commemoration and repair. Fedo was a white Duluth native whose relentless efforts resurrected the story of the lynchings in a 1979 book that was republished by the Minnesota Historical Society just ahead of the eightieth anniversary of the event in 2000. Bakk-Hansen was a local white reporter who, after reading Fedo's book, wrote a viral account of the lynchings that called for local residents to support a memorial; Banks was an African American entrepreneur and civil rights activist; and Ostos was a Latina educator. These three continued to ask whether the community would step forward to address and heal from what Bakk-Hansen had dubbed "Duluth's Lingering Shame."

Tulsa had the indefatigable Don Ross. Ross was an African American entrepreneur and elected official who pushed Tulsans to reckon with the legacy of what is likely the largest destruction of African American property and the largest massacre of African Americans in our history. As a young reporter in 1968, Ross wrote a ten-part series on the Tulsa Race Massacre. Three years later he had risen to be the editor of a new Black magazine, which published "Profile of a Race Riot," a deeply researched account by white local radio personality and writer Ed Wheeler. From 1982 to 2003, Ross served in the Oklahoma House of Representatives, where he spearheaded the effort in 1989 to make Oklahoma the first state (among those guilty of this offense) to remove the Confederate battle flag flying over its government buildings. He also shepherded legislation that created the Tulsa

Race Riot Commission, which delivered a report in 2001 officially documenting the killings and destruction. Additionally, Ross secured funding for the establishment of John Hope Franklin Reconciliation Park and the Greenwood Cultural Center and achieved recognition of the living survivors of the massacre.

These movements for truth-telling and repair were able to take root in the wider white community with the help of white *allies*. Betty Bobo Pearson, a seventh-generation member of a white planter family who attended Emmett Till's trial as a young woman, provided a critical bridge across the deeply segregated Black and white social worlds of the Delta. As cochair of the inaugural body of the Emmett Till Memorial Commission, along with Robert Grayson, an African American mayor of Tutwiler who grew up as a sharecropper, she was vital to the group's success. Patrick Weems, executive director of the Emmett Till Interpretive Center, and Susan Glisson, the first executive director of the William Winter Institute for Racial Reconciliation and later a longtime consultant to the commission, have also played important ally roles in recent years.

Warren Read, whose great-grandfather Louis Dondino had been one of the ringleaders of the lynch mob in Duluth, joined the memorialization effort and was an important ally and model for other white residents. At the unveiling of the Clayton-Jackson-McGhie Memorial, he declared, "True shame is not in the discovery of a terrible event such as this, but in the refusal to acknowledge and learn from that event."[6] Duluth police chief Mike Tusken, the grandnephew of Irene Tusken, the white woman who falsely accused the African American men of raping her, used his position to protect the memorial plaza as a kind of civic sacred space and to reform policing practices.

In Tulsa, Ed Wheeler's determination to publish the story of the Tulsa Race Massacre provided early momentum in bringing the story out of more than half a century of silence. Scott Ellsworth's 1982 book, *Death in a Promised Land*, documented the events in a university press book and generated the first national media story of the event. A white native of Tulsa, Ellsworth served as a consultant to the Tulsa Race Riot Commission and has continued, over four decades of scholarship, to raise awareness of the events in Tulsa, not only for what they mean for his hometown but for what they mean for the nation. He has steadfastly encouraged his readers to understand history as "a mirror of both who we are and who we want to be."[7] And veteran journalist Randy Krehbiel, who has written for the *Tulsa World* since 1979, tirelessly documented the long push to finally tell the truth in Tulsa.

There are no longer any living witnesses to the dispossession and genocide of Indigenous people perpetrated by white settler colonists to create the country we know today. But a chorus of Native American descendants—almost entirely unknown or dismissed by white Americans—continue to testify to the injustices inflicted upon the original inhabitants of this land by our federal and state governments, Christian missionaries, and white settler colonists. Modern prophets—such as Vine Deloria Jr., Joy Harjo, Wilma Mankiller, and George "Tink" Tinker—have played an indispensable role in holding those memories before America, with slow, partial, but certain impacts on our national conscience.

STUMBLING TOWARD CHANGE

The efforts in the Mississippi Delta, Duluth, and Tulsa discussed in these pages are illustrative of the cultural churn we are experiencing in our time, a collective effervescence produced by a cyclical process of momentum and resistance. In such times, courageous acts of truth-telling and sincere efforts to repair past damage are met with defensive and often frantic attempts to protect the social and economic status quo. There is measurable progress, but it often comes at a price, and it is rarely linear.

Confederate Monuments and Statues

In the wake of the nationwide protests for racial justice following the murder of George Floyd, the Southern Poverty Law Center recorded the removal of 168 Confederate monuments in 2020 alone. In Richmond, Virginia, the former capital of the Confederacy, the empty pedestals in traffic circles that previously contained massive Confederate monuments stand as silent witnesses to this change. With the removal of Richmond's massive statue of Confederate general Robert E. Lee in 2021 from public property to a Black history museum, the last man standing on Richmond's Monument Avenue, long a defiant Lost Cause pilgrimage site, is the late Black international tennis star, civil rights activist, and Richmond native son Arthur Ashe Jr. But while cities like New Orleans and Richmond have taken the lead, hundreds of communities have still to wrestle with this legacy.[8] The SPLC report also documents more than 2,100 Confederate symbols, including more than seven hundred monuments, still standing on public property in the US.

In late June 2021, the US House of Representatives voted to remove statues honoring Confederate or white supremacist leaders from public display in the US Capitol. Sixty-seven Republicans joined all Democrats supporting the legislation, but a majority (120) of GOP representatives opposed it. Although House minority leader Kevin McCarthy (R-CA) voted for the measure, he used his floor speech to accuse the Democratic Party of trying to replace the "racism of the past" with "the racism of critical race theory."[9] While this bill ultimately died in the Senate, Congress approved a narrower law in December 2022 that authorized the removal of a bust of Roger Brooke Taney, the Supreme Court justice who wrote the racist *Dred Scott* decision, which will be replaced by a bust of Justice Thurgood Marshall, the first Black man to serve on the country's highest court.[10]

Juneteenth and Indigenous Peoples' Day

On June 16, 2021, Congress voted to make Juneteenth a federal holiday—the first new federal holiday since the creation of Martin Luther King Jr. Day in 1983—celebrating the end of slavery in Texas in 1865. While the legislation passed the Senate unanimously, fourteen white Republicans in the House voted against it. "Let's call an ace an ace," said Representative Matthew M. Rosendale Sr. (R-MT). "This is an effort by the Left to create a day out of whole cloth to celebrate identity politics as part of its larger efforts to make Critical Race Theory the reigning ideology of our country."[11]

In October 2021, after decades of legislative action at the city and state levels across the country, Joe Biden became the first sitting president to commemorate Indigenous Peoples' Day along with Columbus Day. "Today, we also acknowledge the painful history of wrongs and atrocities that many European explorers inflicted on Tribal Nations and Indigenous communities," Biden wrote in the first-ever presidential proclamation of Indigenous Peoples' Day. "It is a measure of our greatness as a Nation that we do not seek to bury these shameful episodes of our past—that we face them honestly, we bring them to the light, and we do all we can to address them." President Biden's proclamation marked a strong contrast to former president Trump's repeated characterization of Columbus as one of our "intrepid heroes" and his lament that "radical activists" were seeking "to replace discussion of his vast contributions with talk of failings, his discoveries with atrocities, and his achievements with transgressions."[12] Indigenous leaders cautiously welcomed Biden's proclamation as an important event. "Big changes happen from each small step," said John Echohawk, executive director of the Native American Rights Fund. But Echohawk also emphasized how much work was left to do. "We hope this administration intends to continue making positive steps towards shaping a brighter future for all citizens."[13]

White Christian Institutions Funding Reparations

Significant steps have also been taken by Christian religious institutions to begin repairing the damage done by centuries of allegiance to the racist tenets of the Doctrine of Discovery. The Episcopal Church in America, with roots in the Church of England, had supported and justified the dispossession of Indigenous people from the land and had upheld slaveholding from its inception in America. The denomination had also claimed prominent members of the Confederacy, such as Confederate president Jefferson Davis and General Robert E. Lee, as members. Beginning in 2019, state bodies and a seminary of the Episcopal Church have voted to commit nearly $27 million to create reparations funds to benefit groups that have been injured by the denomination's support for white supremacy and settler colonialism.

These efforts by the Episcopal Church have been led by the Diocese of New York ($1.1 million in 2019), the Diocese of Maryland ($1 million in 2020), and the Diocese of Texas ($13 million in 2020).[14] The denomination's Virginia Theological Seminary, where enslaved people from George Washington's Mount Vernon estate were rented out to work, also joined the effort, making a $1.7 million pledge in 2019 that grew to $2.2 million by late 2022.[15]

Most recently, in November 2021, the Diocese of Virginia, the body overseeing churches in the capital of the Confederacy in Richmond during the Civil War, voted to create a $10 million reparations fund. The resolution confesses that "the Episcopal Church and the Diocese of Virginia have a long history of support for and complicity with chattel slavery, violence against Indigenous peoples and land, segregation and other racist systems." It requires the diocese "to identify and propose means by which repair may begin for those areas of our structures, patterns, and common life by which Black, Indigenous, People of Color . . . still carry the burden of injustices, exclusions, and biases born out of white supremacy and the legacy of slavery."[16] While supporters in the Diocese of Virginia celebrated the resolution's historic passage, they noted its fragility, even within one of the most progressive white mainline Protestant denominations in the country; earlier reparations resolutions had been defeated, and 30 percent of the diocese voted against the most recent effort.

In March 2021, the Jesuits, a prominent order of Catholic priests, announced an initiative to raise $100 million to atone for their role in slavery and to benefit the descendants of the enslaved people they had once owned. Rev. Timothy P. Kesicki, president of the Jesuit Conference of Canada and the United States, noted that the efforts would aim at both truth-telling and reconciliation, stating, "Our shameful history of Jesuit slaveholding in the United States has been taken off the dusty shelf, and it can never be put back." That history had been unshelved five years earlier in a series of 2016 *New York Times* articles revealing that the priestly order had owned, used, and sold enslaved people to build and sustain their churches and schools, such as the flagship Georgetown University.[17] Importantly, the new reparations funds will be placed in a new foundation, co-administered by descendants of enslaved people.

Despite this progress toward confession and repair among predominantly white Christian denominations and institutions, other Christian groups have responded to this time of reckoning with decidedly more defensive moves. The Southern Baptist Convention, the nation's largest Protestant denomination and the denomination in which

I grew up, doubled down *against* efforts at truth-telling and repair. Following months of protests for racial justice across the summer of 2020, the white male presidents of all six Southern Baptist seminaries came together to issue an unprecedented joint statement. While it paid lip service to condemning "racism in any form," its main thrust—and clear purpose—was the defensive condemnation of "any version of Critical Race Theory" as incompatible with the denomination's confession of faith.[18] The president of the SBC, J. D. Greear, also endorsed the statement, adding, "The Gospel gives a better answer."[19]

To my knowledge, no other issue in the denomination's nearly 180-year history has warranted a joint official statement by its seminary presidents—neither poverty, nor hunger, nor slavery, nor racial prejudice, nor the discovery of widespread sexual abuse perpetrated by clergy trained in their seminaries. Not even evangelism. But the exposure of the complicity of Christianity with white supremacy, to those charged with perpetuating an organization that was explicitly founded in 1845 to defend the compatibility of slaveholding and the gospel, warranted such a response. There would be no troubling of those waters on their watch.

White Christian Institutions Repudiating the Doctrine of Discovery

White Christians have only recently begun to recognize the devastating implications of the Doctrine of Discovery for both Indigenous peoples and their own theology. As late as the turn of the twenty-first century, there were no public acknowledgments of this impact by white Christian groups, despite decades of overt calls for accountability by Indigenous leaders. In 1972, for example, Vine Deloria Jr.—scholar, activist, and former executive director of the National Congress of American Indians—penned "An Open Letter to the Heads of the Christian Churches in America," calling on Christian clergy and denominational leaders to begin "an honest inquiry by yourselves into the nature of your situation."[20] The heart of Deloria's indictment was that white Christians had fabricated a dishonest history that denied the impact of the Doctrine of Discovery on Indigenous people, and by doing so, continued to harm them. Deloria's missive was piercing:

> We have been placed beyond the remedies of the Constitution of the United States because the Doctrine of Discovery has never been disclaimed either by the government of the Christian nations of the world or by the leaders of the Christian churches of the world. And more especially by the leaders of the Christian churches of this country. No effort has been made by Christians to undo the wrongs that were done, albeit mistakenly, and which are perpetuated because Christians refuse to . . . appraise the present situation in its true historical light.
>
> The American experience would not then appear inevitable. The novelty of the establishment of a democracy would be understood in its own light. The mythology of American history would be seen as mere mythology. The Custers, Chivingtons and Calleys would be seen for what they were. We could all come to the necessity of facing ourselves for what we are. We would no longer have a God busily endorsing and applauding the things that we are doing. We would have to be on God's side in our dealings with other peoples instead of being so sure that God is automatically on our side.[21]

Deloria passed away in 2005 and never witnessed a significant response from white Christians. But shortly after his death, the decades of organizing and advocacy that he and other Indigenous leaders around the world tirelessly led began to bear fruit. In 2007, the Declaration on the Rights of Indigenous Peoples was passed by the United Nations following twenty-five years of steadfast lobbying. Its final passage concluded the longest negotiation period of any resolution in UN history.

The UN declaration is a nonbinding human rights standard that contains forty-six articles that serve as guidelines for member states for affirming and considering the rights of Indigenous peoples in their countries.[22] While it does not reference the Doctrine of Discovery by name, the document clearly addresses its underlying ideology. One of the first paragraphs in the UN declaration affirms, for example, that "all doctrines, policies and practices based on or advocating superiority of peoples or individuals on the basis of national origin or racial, religious, ethnic or cultural differences are racist, scientifically false, legally invalid, morally condemnable and socially unjust." It also highlights a concern that "indigenous peoples have suffered from historic injustices as a result of, inter alia, their colonization and dispossession of their lands, territories and resources, thus preventing them from exercising, in particular, their right to development in accordance with their own needs and interests."[23] As I noted in the prologue, the UN resolution passed 143–4, with the United States, Canada, Australia, and New Zealand casting the only initial votes against its passage.

In the wake of the UN declaration's passage, more than a dozen Christian denominations and institutions have taken actions to formally repudiate the Doctrine of Discovery and confess their complicity in perpetuating the white supremacy and Christian dominionism embedded in its worldview. As with reparations, one of the earliest to act was the Episcopal Church in America, historically the denomination of the nation's Protestant elite who sat at the helm of America's universities, churches, corporations, and government.

At its 2009 General Convention, the denomination declared that it "repudiates and renounces the Doctrine of Discovery as fundamentally opposed to the Gospel of Jesus Christ and our understanding of the inherent rights that individuals and peoples have received from God." The resolution called on its members and the US government, as well as Queen Elizabeth II, head of the Anglican Church in England, to review their history and change "contemporary policies that contribute to the continuing colonization of Indigenous Peoples."[24] Notably, the Episcopal Church statement also called on the United States to rescind its vote against the UN Declaration on the Rights of Indigenous Peoples. On December 16, 2010, bowing to international and domestic pressure, President Barack Obama announced that the United States would reverse its position, becoming the last of the four holdout states to affirm the declaration.[25]

In 2012, the World Council of Churches, a fellowship of more than 350 member churches who represent more than half a billion Christians around the world, renounced the Doctrine of Discovery in language virtually identical to the 2009 Episcopalian resolution. Additionally, the WCC resolution urged "various governments in the world to dismantle the legal structures and policies based on the Doctrine of Discovery and dominance, so as better to empower and enable Indigenous Peoples to identify their own aspirations and issues of concern"; it also urged its member bodies to support the 2007 UN Declaration on the Rights of Indigenous Peoples.[26]

Over the last thirteen years, among the US-based groups that have repudiated the Doctrine of Discovery are the largest white mainline Protestant denominations (Christian Church/Disciples of Christ, Evangelical Lutheran Church in America, Episcopal Church, Presbyterian Church in the USA, United Church of Christ, United Methodist Church), peace churches such as the Quakers and the Mennonites, the Evangelical Covenant Church, and the Unitarian Universalist Association. In the Catholic world, between 2007 and 2022, more than a dozen Roman Catholic–affiliated groups—such as the Leadership Conference of Women Religious (the association of the leaders of congregations of Catholic women religious in the US), several religious orders of nuns, and Pax Christi—issued statements repudiating it.[27]

These actions by major white Christian organizations, and the affirmation of the UN Declaration on the Rights of Indigenous Peoples by the US government, are significant milestones on our nation's journey to acknowledge the historical impact of the Doctrine of Discovery and its continued influence on our thinking, policies, and laws today. While there is still much work to be done—most congregants have still heard little to nothing about the Doctrine of Discovery in their local churches—these official organizational actions are an improvement over the anemic responses Deloria encountered during his lifetime. They provide momentum for future progress. But the relative newness of these efforts also reminds us that we are only on the first steps of a long journey to achieve, as Deloria put it, "an honest inquiry" into our past and present situations.

The Penitential Pilgrimage Tour of Pope Francis

Even while there is movement on the part of leaders of Christian institutions with European roots to acknowledge and atone for past injustices, there remains significant reticence to accept full responsibility for the disastrous Doctrine of Discovery. On July 25, 2022, Pope Francis arrived in Maskwacis, Alberta, Canada, at the former site of a Catholic-run boarding school for Indigenous children, to deliver an apology as part of his five-day "penitential pilgrimage" of Indigenous sites in Canada. The apology was long overdue, coming fully seven years after a Canadian "Truth and Reconciliation Commission" determined that the conduct of the schools was tantamount to "cultural genocide" and formally requested an apology from the Catholic Church. Nevertheless, the pope's effort was sincere.[28]

> Today I am here, in this land that, along with its ancient memories, preserves the scars of still open wounds. I am here because the first step of my penitential pilgrimage among you is that of again asking forgiveness, of telling you once more that I

am deeply sorry. Sorry for the ways in which, regrettably, many Christians supported the colonizing mentality of the powers that oppressed the Indigenous Peoples.

I am sorry. I ask forgiveness, in particular, for the ways in which many members of the Church and of religious communities cooperated, not least through their indifference, in projects of cultural destruction and forced assimilation promoted by the governments of that time, which culminated in the system of residential schools.

Although Christian charity was not absent, and there were many outstanding instances of devotion and care for children, the overall effects of the policies linked to the residential schools were catastrophic. What our Christian faith tells us is that this was a disastrous error, incompatible with the Gospel of Jesus Christ. It is painful to think of how the firm soil of values, language and culture that made up the authentic identity of your peoples was eroded, and that you have continued to pay the price of this. In the face of this deplorable evil, the Church kneels before God and implores his forgiveness for the sins of her children. I myself wish to reaffirm this, with shame and unambiguously. I humbly beg forgiveness for the evil committed by so many Christians against the Indigenous Peoples.[29]

This penitential tour was a remarkable action by the head of the Roman Catholic Church, one without precedent in the Americas. Pope Francis himself was visibly emotional. Many members of the crowd of several thousand Indigenous people gathered wiped away tears and hugged each other as they listened to the apology. Afterward, a photographer captured an image of Pope Francis kneeling to kiss the hand of an Indigenous woman.[30] Local Indigenous leaders placed a headdress on Francis's head.

But a close look at the apology reveals the insidious power that the Doctrine of Discovery still holds over even authentic efforts by church leaders with integrity and sincere intentions. Most significantly, Pope

Francis places the responsibility for the evil on "many Christians," "many members of the Church and of religious communities," and the church's "children." But the church itself escapes indictment. In fact, in each instance, Francis attempts to make an untenable distinction between misguided Christians and a church whose virtue remains unblemished. This disingenuous line of reasoning implies that if Christians are at fault, it is because they stopped following the church's pure teachings and became misled by various external forces: "the colonizing mentality of the powers that oppressed the Indigenous Peoples" or "the projects of cultural destruction and forced assimilation promoted by the governments of that time."

Francis's most jarring claim was this: "What our Christian faith tells us is that this was a disastrous error, incompatible with the Gospel of Jesus Christ." This conjuring of an abstract "Gospel of Jesus Christ" by the head of the Roman Catholic Church, whose direct predecessors created the Doctrine of Discovery in collusion with the Christian monarchs of their day, is literally nonsensical in light of the clear historical record. The entire purpose of the papal bulls of the fifteenth century—their very raison d'être—was to use papal authority to establish and declare, to the entire Christian world, their verdict that the domination and enslavement of Indigenous peoples were in fact demanded by the gospel and therefore had the moral blessing of the Christian church.

This evasive language was not lost on an Indigenous reporter for Canada Broadcasting Commission (CBC) Radio, Jessica Ka'nhehsíio Deer. During a press briefing on the plane home to Rome at the end of the tour, she asked Francis this direct question: "As a descendant of a residential school survivor, I know that survivors and their families want to see concrete actions following your apology, including the rejection of the 'Doctrine of Discovery,'" she said. "Considering that this is still enshrined in the Constitution and legal systems in Canada and the United States, where Indigenous peoples continue to be defrauded of their lands and deprived of power, was it not a missed opportunity to make a statement to this effect during your trip to Canada?"

Pope Francis was, shockingly, unprepared for this question. His first response was, "I didn't understand the second part of the question. Could you explain what you mean by Doctrine of Discovery?" Even after getting a basic explanation and some examples from Deer, Francis still seemed confused and, according to Deer, "didn't really answer the question." Francis also fumbled a question from the only other Indigenous reporter on the plane, about why he didn't use the word *genocide* in his remarks. Francis again demurred, saying simply that "I didn't use the word because it didn't come to my mind."[31] Given how long Indigenous people, including Indigenous Catholics, have been raising these questions, Thomas Reese, a veteran Jesuit reporter for Religion News Service, was incredulous. Reese called Francis's response "scandalous," concluding that these exchanges left Francis "looking like a student who had not done his homework."

This bungled response, along with continued lobbying on the part of Indigenous activists inside and outside of the church, ultimately led to historic action. On March 30, 2023, the Vatican finally issued a statement repudiating the Doctrine of Discovery.[32] It declared, "In no uncertain terms, the Church's magisterium upholds the respect due to every human being. The Catholic Church therefore repudiates those concepts that fail to recognize the inherent human rights of indigenous peoples, including what has become known as the legal and political 'doctrine of discovery.'" While the statement was not issued personally by Pope Francis, it includes these powerful words from him: "Never again can the Christian community allow itself to be infected by the idea that one culture is superior to others, or that it is legitimate to employ ways of coercing others."

This official Vatican response is undoubtedly a watershed moment. But the full statement is also unfortunately plagued by equivocations about the past. As with Pope Francis's apology during his "penitential pilgrimage" eight months before, the subsequent Vatican statement deploys deceptive rhetorical strategies to avoid accepting full ecclesiastical responsibility. The statement begins with a defensive rehearsal of papal virtue, declaring that "in the course of history the Popes have condemned acts of violence, oppression, social injustice and slavery, including those committed against Indigenous peoples." It emphasizes that previous popes have asked for forgiveness "on numerous occasions" for evil acts committed against Indigenous peoples.

Most perniciously, the Vatican statement continues to draw an untenable distinction between an unblemished church on the one hand and the evil acts committed against Indigenous peoples by "many Christians" on the other. Disappointingly, before the statement arrives at its purported penitential purpose, it contains this lengthy drumbeat of denial.

> The "doctrine of discovery" is not part of the teaching of the Catholic Church. Historical research clearly demonstrates that the papal documents in question, written in a specific historical period and linked to political questions, have never been considered expressions of the Catholic faith. At the same time, the Church acknowledges that these papal bulls did not adequately reflect the equal dignity and rights of indigenous peoples.

The mental gymnastics on display here are remarkable. Even though these public declarations were issued under the authority of sitting popes, whose proclamations were sought by European monarchs precisely because of the religious and legal authority they carried, the Vatican statement implausibly denies that they reflected "the Catholic faith." And it is an understatement of epic proportions to say that calls for the domination and perpetual enslavement of Indigenous peoples "did not adequately reflect the equal dignity and rights of Indigenous peoples."

If that flat denial of theological and ecclesiastical responsibility weren't enough, the statement continues:

> The Church is also aware that the contents of these documents were manipulated for political purposes by competing colonial powers in order to justify immoral acts against indigenous peoples that were carried out, at times, without opposition from ecclesiastical authorities. It is only just to recognize these errors, acknowledge the terrible effects of the assimilation policies and the pain experienced by indigenous peoples, and ask for pardon.

By the time we arrive at the end of this paragraph, it's not exactly clear on what grounds the church would need to ask for a pardon. *Whose* "errors" is the statement really acknowledging? If the papal bulls that constituted the foundation of the Doctrine of Discovery were not expressions of the Catholic faith, if the evil acts perpetrated by Christians against Indigenous peoples were committed by rogue believers suffering from human weakness and failings, if those truly responsible were the political leaders of the colonial powers who manipulated these documents for their own ends, there is very little culpability left for the church to assume. Indeed, the only admission of responsibility that stands without qualification is a weak one. At worst, Indigenous people were killed and enslaved "without opposition from ecclesiastical authorities"—a sin of omission rather than commission.

The ambivalence of the statement was not lost on those who have long been advocating for a repudiation of the Doctrine of Discovery. Phillip B. Arnold, professor of religious studies at Syracuse University and president of the Indigenous Values Initiative, said that while the statement was a "good first step," the Vatican had still "not owned up to a worldview" reflected in these papal statements. Most pointedly, he noted that there is "not much of an emphasis on self-reflection," particularly about how the assumptions in the Doctrine of Discovery are "still active in the church."[33]

To make good on the stated goals of his "penitential pilgrimage" and to make both the repudiation and his apology credible, Pope Francis and the church still need to say something much more specific: that these previous popes and the church were simply *wrong* about their theological conceptions of Indigenous peoples and their own racial and religious superiority. The legitimacy of any church apology, and the possibility of repentance, hangs on this clear admission of error.

For repentance to be authentic, sinful acts must attach to the proper subject. As the head of the Roman Catholic Church, the body that originally produced and promulgated an interpretation of the gospel of Jesus Christ that underwrote colonial violence, it is vital that the pope acknowledge the sins and errors of the church itself. Otherwise, the entire exercise is premised on a rhetorical sleight of hand.[34] By defending the purity of the church, even while acknowledging the damage "many Christians" did in the past, Pope Francis and church leaders are squandering the opportunity for healing to fully take root.

BETWEEN HOPE AND HISTORY

I grew up with a sense of America as a divinely chosen nation, and of my people as its rightful inhabitants. Over the last decade of my adult life particularly, I've struggled to reorient as I've redrawn terrain on that self-serving map. I've realized that I needed a more complex and mature understanding of not only history but justice. From the chosen's vantage point on the high bluff overlooking the promised land, the river of history runs true from the headwaters to its terminus. Its waters are always navigable and calm. And its banks are never eroded.

The chosen's view of justice is similarly satisfying. "But let justice roll down as waters, and righteousness as a mighty stream." This image—voiced by the prophet Amos in the Hebrew Bible and secured in American political memory by Rev. Dr. Martin Luther King Jr.'s 1963 "I Have a Dream" speech—all too often functions as a naïve understanding of social change. It can imply that the injustices of the past and the powerful systems of present oppression will, naturally, when confronted with the facts, experience a catastrophic failure, like a dam suddenly breaking. A favorite text in progressive white Christian churches, its attractiveness derives from the unrealistic hope that confession of past wrongs will trigger the flood of justice, which will, by its own mysterious power, wash away the old and make all things new. Justice and righteousness, personified, rather than people, are the agents of change. There is no struggle or conflict, no costs to the powerful, only the magical appearance of a new world.

But real rivers meander. They gather tributaries carrying rain and soil from distant mountains. They flood. Some are seasonal. Others dry up altogether when environmental conditions shift. When rivers are fortunate enough to endure, they carve horseshoe bends whose increasing curvature finally causes them to sever their own bodies, leaving behind orphaned oxbow lakes as a testimony to former lives. This organic image provides a sounder metaphor for history and the work of justice.

The epigraph at the beginning of this chapter from Irish poet Seamus Heaney also evokes the power and unpredictability of water. Heaney wrote these lines as Nelson Mandela was being released from prison and the South African regime was falling in 1991. As an Irish poet, Heaney was also drawing on his own experience of the impacts of brutal British settler colonialism in Northern Ireland (where, by the way, the British and not Native Americans invented the practice of scalping as an efficient way for vigilantes to collect bounties for Irish killings); he was certainly not naïve. But like us, Heaney felt the pulse of new possibilities, the opportunity to wrestle with the challenges of our history while holding the hope of our ideals.

The contradictions between hope and history are palpable, perhaps even irreconcilable. In *The Substance of Hope: Barack Obama and the Paradox of Progress*, writer and dean of the Columbia Journalism School Jelani Cobb wrestled with the harsh lessons that history has for those hoping to see progress toward racial justice. He titled the preface to the 2020 paperback, written ten years after the first edition of the book appeared during Obama's first term, "On Hopes & Histories." Looking back, Cobb notes with anguish the reactionary lurch the country took in 2016: "If Obama was the opening statement of a new age, it was now clear that there would be a vitriolic and contemptible response, one whose roots lie deep in American history."[35] Cobb also issues one of the most concise, poignant explanations of Donald Trump I've ever read. "Absent Barack Obama [Trump] had no rationale for his own existence," Cobb wrote. "The forty-fourth president operates as a kind of inverse guiding star for the forty-fifth, a mechanism by which he can look north to travel south."[36]

Near the end of President Barack Obama's second term in 2015, writer Ta-Nehisi Coates also penned a reflection on these themes, titled "Hope and the Historian," in the *Atlantic*.[37] His jumping-off point was the jarring juxtaposition of Obama-era optimism—memorialized in the title of Obama's autobiography, *The Audacity of Hope: Thoughts on Reclaiming the American Dream*—and the disturbing conclusion reached in 2010 by preeminent Princeton historian Nell Irvin Painter that white supremacy was likely a permanent feature of American culture.[38] For Coates, Painter's words contradicted not only the prevailing national mood but the faith in the efficacy of politics that has been an orthodox tenet of the Black political tradition.

"The problem is history," he wrote. "The more I studied, the more I was confronted by heroic people whose struggles were not successful in their own time, or at all."[39]

It wasn't that activism by persecuted groups was irrelevant. These efforts, Coates was increasingly convinced, were just never sufficient on their own to secure liberation from the group in power. Frederick Douglass was right that "power concedes nothing without a demand";[40] but, by Coates's lights, history also seems to indicate that even such shifts are made on the oppressor's timetable and for one reason: when a threat to white interests demanded it. "'Hope' struck me an overrated force in human history," Coates wrote. "'Fear' did not."[41]

LIGHTS HELPING US FIND OUR WAY

At many moments throughout this project, history has left me, like Coates, feeling cynical and even hopeless. Of the twin streams of American history—one representing America as a white Christian nation and one as a pluralistic democracy—the former has for too long been the dominant current. At this point in the American story, a tidal wave of equity and justice, if that is what it might become, still seems a building swell far offshore. Nonetheless, I remain convinced that the waters of justice are rising in a way that indeed feels different from any other in my adult lifetime.

Buoyed on those waters are lights that are helping us find our way. A racially diverse group of kids fanning out in Sumner, Mississippi, filming documentary projects that tell their stories alongside Emmett Till's. Daughters of plantation owners standing beside sons of sharecroppers to tell the truth in the Mississippi Delta. A white, Black, and Latino trio determined to commemorate the lynchings in Duluth, and the three thousand Duluthians who showed up for the unveiling of a city's memorial and pledged their commitment to create a new history. A white church in Tulsa confessing its role in covering up acts of mass white racial terrorism. The leader of the worldwide Roman Catholic Church kneeling to kiss an Indigenous woman's hand. A Black international tennis star as the last man standing on Monument Avenue in the former capital of the Confederacy. A president issuing a proclamation honoring Indigenous Peoples' Day. A Native American Christian minister working on behalf of the Stockbridge-Munsee Mohican Nation and with the Minnesota Council of Churches to help white Christians be not just smarter but better people. The determination, against all odds, of Native American leaders across generations to hold the US to its word and treaty obligations and to maintain their dignity amid endless broken promises and dismissals by our government and leaders.

The efforts highlighted in these pages show us what can happen when just a few dedicated souls decide to tell a truer story about who we are and then harness the energy unleashed by that confession for creative action. Taken together, along with the myriad of other efforts across the country, they reveal unrealized possibilities for our nation. While the destination seems scarcely discernible on the horizon, these beacons are sufficient, if we persist, to help us chart a different course.

Chapter Eleven

DISCOVERY AND DEMOCRACY IN AMERICA

INDIANS AND COWBOYS

"I don't want to be the Indians again," my younger brother complained. "I want to be the cowboys."

It was a familiar argument between us, repeated nearly every time we reset the pieces of our Big Western Town play set. We had dog-eared the page on which it was featured in the much-anticipated Sears Wish Book Christmas catalog, and the large box appeared, to our delight, on Christmas morning in 1972.[1] Santa had come through.

When our family relocated from Georgia for a brief stint in the Lone Star State during my preschool years, our grandparents equipped us with complete outfits of boots, smart leather chaps (mine were red, my brother's blue), matching fringed vests, hats, and holsters securing shiny chrome cap pistols. We also, though less frequently, donned stereotypical Native American costumes, with faux eagle feather headdresses and rubber tomahawks we had picked up at

"Cherokee Village" during a vacation drive through North Carolina's Great Smoky Mountains.

The objection to "being the Indians" was not just rooted in a sense that the cowboys always won, although that lesson was driven home in TV series like *Bonanza* and *Gunsmoke* that were favorites of my grandfather and in the big Hollywood westerns that John Wayne was still cranking out late in his career. Rather, the biggest frustration, to our young minds, was how constrained the options were for playing with the Indian figures.

The cowboys, as the name of the play set indicated, came with an entire town you could assemble. There was a green bank building, a brown general store, a two-story blue building that housed a saloon below and a hotel above, and a yellow building identified as "City Hall," where the sheriff also hung out his shingle. The set contained remarkable attention to detail. The white block-letter signs, which declared the function of the buildings, also identified fictional proprietors with decidedly European names such as "Braun," "Davis," and "Miller." Each building had a chimney, paned windows, articulating doors, and an attached front porch with its own distinctive pattern of white support posts and railings. The cowboys also possessed a covered wagon and a stagecoach, pulled by a team of four horses and topped by cargo boxes and steamer trunks belonging to new settlers presumably arriving from the East.

The Indians, by contrast, had no structures or shelters. They were, apparently, a homeless roving band. The image on the front of the box features the town, the stagecoach, and all the cowboys in the foreground. Behind that scene, there are a string of boulders spread across the horizon in front of a red setting sun. Four mounted Indians are perched, in silhouette, on the rocks, while a raiding party spills down toward the rear of the unsuspecting but heavily armed cowboy town.

There was only one logical script for any play episode: assemble the white cowboy men and then attack their little outpost of civilization with the Indian warriors who arrived with hostile intent from the hinterlands.

For me, as a member of the dominant ethno-religious group, this play set, manufactured in West Germany for Sears's America, reinforced deep assumptions about our history and our standing in this land. It presented Indigenous people as uncivilized others; and it produced a flattering image of the superiority of my people. The inanimate figures firmly locked Native Americans into a distant past, allowing us to admire and appropriate aspects of their culture while remaining oblivious to the conditions of, and calls for justice by, their living descendants.

In the same year my brother and I gleefully unwrapped our Big Western Town, for example, the modern American Indian Movement organized the "Trail of Broken Treaties," a march to demand the US honor its treaty obligations to Native Americans, and forcibly occupied the Bureau of Indian Affairs headquarters in Washington, DC.[2] But that news did not make it into our white Baptist enclave in southwest Jackson, Mississippi. A few years later, when I discovered a flint arrowhead on the playground at Oak Forest Elementary School, I added it to my rock collection, placing it beside my samples of petrified wood, as more evidence of living things that once occupied these lands but were long extinct. When I received the Cub Scouts' highest rank, the Arrow of Light, symbolized by a Native American arrow, I felt proud to accept this award, and participated in what felt like an exotic substitute rite of passage that was absent from my own culture. At my Southern Baptist alma mater, Mississippi College, the athletic teams' name was taken from the original inhabitants of the land the campus now occupies, a fact that never troubled my mind during my four-year sojourn on campus. And when our football cheerleaders led the crowd in singing fake Native American chants, while raising their arms at the elbow to mimic a tomahawk strike (as tens of thousands of Kansas City Chiefs fans recently did on national television at the 2023 Super Bowl)—chanting "Scalp 'em, Choctaws, scalp 'em!"—I enthusiastically joined in.[3]

DEMOCRACY IN AMERICA

For most of my life, the enchanting power of the Christian Doctrine of Discovery has endowed me with a comfortable obliviousness. Indigenous people were conceptually present but held at bay in my moral imagination, like those posed plastic figures just outside of Big Western Town. Black people were more firmly part of the landscape, but they were minor characters with unpleasant and unfortunate backstories. While their proximity to the white world meant that they could not be ignored, their narrative needed to be distanced from the central plotline, lest they complicate the character of America's founders and sully the exploits of the real American heroes.

As I reflect on these realities, I am stunned by the sheer amount of energy and capital required to maintain this worldview in the presence of so much counterevidence. And I am transfixed by the command it has had on white American psyches from the founding to the present. The contradictions between professed American principles and plain American actions have all too often been compartmentalized and rationalized, even among some of the most astute observers of early American culture.

The power of the Doctrine of Discovery to hide this hypocrisy is evident, for example, in the work of Alexis de Tocqueville, who famously wrote *Democracy in America* following his travels across the fledgling United States over nine months between May 11, 1831, and February 20, 1832.[4] Tocqueville wrote with a sense of urgency, "with a mind constantly occupied by a single thought—that the advent of democracy as a governing power in the world's affairs, universal and irresistible, was at hand."[5] He was convinced that he was witnessing an important evolutionary moment, as American democracy was maturing and European democracies were struggling to emerge.

For the twenty-six-year-old French aristocrat, the age of revolution, the throwing off of monarchy and the rise of the concept of individual equality, was no mere abstraction. His great-grandfather's family had met their end at the guillotine, and part of the motivation for his overseas trip was to escape the chaos that enveloped the French politics of his day. Close observation of American democracy, he hoped, might lead to universal insights that could guide the turn toward democracy in Europe. "Let us look to America," he urged his French readers.[6]

My first introduction to Tocqueville was in the pages of *Habits of the Heart: Individualism and Commitment in American Life*, the best-selling crossover book published in 1985 by sociologist Robert N. Bellah and four colleagues, which takes its title from a Tocquevillian phrase.[7] Like most contemporary treatments of Tocqueville, *Habits* focuses on what Tocqueville identifies as the peculiar elements that have led to the emergence of a vital American democracy:

> Tocqueville argues that while the physical circumstances of the United States have contributed to the maintenance of a democratic republic, laws have contributed more than those circumstances and mores (*moeurs*) more than the laws. Indeed, he stresses throughout the book that their mores have been the key to the Americans' success in establishing and maintaining a free republic.[8]

For Tocqueville, mores are the religious and ethical foundation of a people's worldview. He describes them as the opinions and ideas that "shape mental habits" and as "the sum of moral and intellectual dispositions of men in society." In Tocqueville's most eloquent description, mores are the "habits of the heart" that orient a citizenry toward both individual and communal life. These mores were also, in the American context, inextricably entwined with religion. Tocqueville declared, "I think I can see the whole destiny of America contained in the first Puritan who landed on these shores."⁹

When Tocqueville is cited in contemporary work, he is typically invoked to set the table in a way that is consistent with *Habits*. The argument goes like this. The problem to be addressed is excessive individualism that stems from the conceptualization of people as citizens in democracies. This newfound individualism threatens the social cohesion needed for a functioning society. The American solution, which Tocqueville documented in his travels, is the blossoming of a vibrant set of voluntary associations, including churches and other religious organizations. These associations, and the individual and civic virtues they produce and nourish, are the balancing forces that integrate individuals into the social body. The central concern, then, is whether such a web of voluntary associations is up to the task of civic integration in our day.

But this reading of Tocqueville—which is, to be sure, consistent with his understanding of the central political problem—is far too philosophical and idyllic to accurately portray the mores of the citizenry of the United States he encountered in the 1830s. President Andrew Jackson's brutal and popular Indian Removal policy, for example, was well under way. As I noted in chapter one, just before his return to France, Tocqueville himself witnessed the "frightful sufferings" produced by the forced march, during the dead of winter, of hundreds of Choctaw men, women, and children from Mississippi to Oklahoma along the Trail of Tears. Slavery was in full swing, with the population of enslaved people topping two million at the turn of the decade. During Tocqueville's sojourn in America, enslaved Baptist minister Nat Turner led an armed rebellion that resulted in the deaths of more than fifty white residents and the retaliatory deaths of up to two hundred Black residents in Southampton, Virginia.[10] The slave rebellion rocked the nation, and the state of Virginia responded by restricting education and movement among enslaved Africans and banning their religious meetings after sundown. In 1834–35, as the nascent abolitionist movement was being launched and Tocqueville's book was being published, violent anti-abolitionist riots broke out in cities across the Northeast.[11]

To his credit, Tocqueville did not ignore these contradictions in *Democracy in America*, although most contemporary treatments of Tocqueville and most course syllabi (including those in my own graduate courses) skip over his most sustained treatment of them. In fact, the final chapter of volume one, which brought Tocqueville fame after its publication in 1835, is titled "The Present and Probable Future Condition of the Three Races that Inhabit the Territory of the United States."[12]

Tocqueville did not hold back harsh judgments about the duplicitous behavior of European settler colonists and the US government, which made a mockery of the nation's self-proclaimed noble values. Tocqueville pointed out that none other than George Washington declared to Congress, "We are more enlightened and more powerful than the Indian nations; we are therefore bound in honor to treat them with kindness, and even with generosity." But Tocqueville immediately noted that "this virtuous and high-minded policy" had not been followed. "The rapacity of the settlers is usually backed by the tyranny of the government," he observed. "If an Indian nation happens to be so encroached upon as to be unable to subsist on their territory, they kindly take them by the hand and transport them to a grave far from the land of their fathers."[13]

Tocqueville unflinchingly dubbed these deeds by white Americans "great evils" but recognized that they were likely "irremediable," given that the "civilized people" committing them were "also (it must be owned) the most grasping nation on the globe."[14] Tocqueville also recognized that these actions were always covered with a thin veneer of legality. They were carried out by state and federal governments "deficient in good faith" and determined to either exterminate Native Americans or deprive them of their rights. Tocqueville summarized his impressions of the disingenuous US treatment of Native Americans in a stinging final statement: "It is impossible to destroy men with more respect for the laws of humanity."[15]

Tocqueville was also deeply critical of American race-based chattel slavery, a system he traced back to European Christian origins.

> Generally speaking, men must make great and unceasing efforts before permanent evils are created; but there is one calamity which penetrated furtively into the world. . . . That calamity is slavery. Christianity suppressed slavery, but the Christians of the sixteenth century re-established it, as an exception, indeed, to their social system, and restricted it to one of the races of mankind; but the wound thus inflicted upon humanity, though less extensive, was far more difficult to cure.[16]

Tocqueville talked about slavery as an institution in conflict with the Laws of Nature and criticized the slavery laws of the southern states as "unparalleled atrocities" that "show that the laws of humanity have been totally perverted." He saw the American system of slavery as exceptionally pernicious, even when compared to slavery in ancient times, since American enslavers endeavored not only to dominate human bodies but to employ "their despotism and their violence against the human mind." Even as he wrote sympathetically about the Gordian knot that the problem of southern slavery, once established, presented, he took pains to declare, "God forbid that I should seek to justify the principle of Negro slavery, as has been done by some American writers!"[17]

Still, Tocqueville's own moral imagination remained strongly shaped by the worldview of the Doctrine of Discovery. Intermixed with his commitment to the rising principle of equality, and coexisting with his sensitive portrayals of the injustices committed against Indigenous peoples and enslaved Africans, were firm convictions of European and Christian supremacy. His opening description of the "three races" inhabiting the United States depicts a clear hierarchy:

> Among these widely differing families of men, the first that attracts attention, the superior in intelligence, in power, and in enjoyment, is the white, or European, the MAN pre-eminently so called; below him appear the Negro and the Indian. . . . If we reason from what passes in the world, we should almost say that the European is to the other races of mankind what man himself is to the lower animals: he makes them subservient to his use, and when he cannot subdue he destroys them.[18]

In his description of "the Negro" and "the Indian," Tocqueville's cultural prejudices overwhelm his moral sensibilities. He reduces these two races to philosophical types, which is each in its own way incapable of embodying the ideal balance of societal integration and individual freedom that the emerging form of modern democracy requires. Tocqueville portrays the enslaved African as a being whose "understanding is degraded to the level of his soul." Despite abundant evidence to the contrary, he believed that the psychological damage from oppression was so complete that enslaved Africans barely perceived the calamity of their own situation and were unable to benefit from emancipation. Tocqueville concludes, "In short, he is sunk to such a depth of wretchedness that while servitude brutalizes, liberty destroys him."[19]

Tocqueville also adhered to the racist, romanticized view of Native Americans common to Europeans of his day. He describes them as living "quietly in their woods, enduring the vicissitudes and practicing the virtues and vices common to savage nations." If the Negro's deficiency stemmed from the extinguishing of the flame of individual liberty, the Indian's vice was that it burned out of control: "As he delights in this barbarous independence and would rather perish than sacrifice the least part of it, civilization has little hold over him."[20] In the end, in Tocqueville's eyes, only Europeans were capable of mastering the proper balance of individualism and social bonds demanded by modern civilization. And the shortcomings of African Americans and Native Americans promised a dim future for each: "the servility of the one dooms him to slavery, the pride of the other to death."[21]

Tocqueville was an especially gifted sociological observer. The sensitivity, honesty, and transparency in his work leave us with a complex portrait of the promise and contradictions in early Euro-American democracy and culture, which he himself embodied. Tocqueville may have been correct—but not only in the way he intended—that he could see the destiny of America in the first Puritan who landed on these shores. The mores of those descended from the Puritans may have produced vibrant associations among themselves, but their habits of the heart also justified genocide, dispossession, and enslavement. This has always been the contradiction of democracy in America.

THE DOCTRINE OF DISCOVERY IN AMERICA TODAY

We have not traveled such a great distance from Tocqueville's America. The spirit of the Doctrine of Discovery continues to haunt us today. We remain torn by two mutually incompatible visions of the country. Are we a pluralistic democracy where all, regardless of race or religion, are equal citizens? Or are we a divinely ordained promised land for European Christians? The confounding paradoxes, constant confusions, and violent convulsions of the present are signs that we have yet to choose between these two streams of American history.

Over the last two decades, our nation has experienced several shocks to the system that have threatened the fiercely guarded narrative of white American innocence and white Christian virtue. These include:

- The demographic decline of white Christians, particularly the transition of the country during this period from being a majority-white Christian country to one in which there is no single dominant ethno-religious majority.

- The election, and then reelection, of our first African American president, followed by the backlash election of Donald Trump, who engaged in ongoing racist attacks on Obama, challenged his American citizenship, and suggested that he was Muslim rather than Christian by drawing attention to his middle name, Hussein (even tracing the *H* in the air for emphasis in one infamous interview).

- The Black Lives Matter movement, launched in 2015 in the wake of the mass murder of nine worshippers at Mother Emanuel AME Church in Charleston, South Carolina, by white Christian nationalist Dylann Roof. The movement gained nationwide momentum after the 2017 white supremacist marches in Charlottesville, Virginia, and especially after the 2020 murder of George Floyd in Minneapolis.

- The 1619 Project, launched in 2019, which has importantly challenged assumptions about an American genesis story focused on the European male "founding fathers" gathered in Philadelphia in 1776.

These events have disrupted what had seemed to be an impervious dominant narrative of Euro-Christian supremacy that flowed from the Doctrine of Discovery. The shrill, breathless protestations of these changes by many white Christian conservatives is itself an indication of the persistence of this anti-democratic, ethno-religious ideology in our laws, our politics, and our culture.

The Doctrine of Discovery in American Law

The first formal consideration of Indian land rights by the US Supreme Court occurred in *Fletcher v. Peck* (1810).[22] In a condescending unanimous decision, the court declared that Indian land title was "a mere occupancy" title. The court explained: "It is not like our tenures; they have no idea of a title to the soil itself. It is overrun by them, rather than inhabited. It is not true and legal possession. . . . It is a right not to be transferred but extinguished." The court justified this assertion by declaring that "the Europeans always claimed and exercised the right of conquest over the soil."[23]

As I noted in the prologue, the Doctrine of Discovery primarily enters US law in Chief Justice John Marshall's sweeping majority opinion in *Johnson v. M'Intosh* (1823). Despite Marshall's later attempt to repudiate the doctrine and limit the implications of the decision, it proved too powerful a force to be tamed. The Doctrine of Discovery fueled President Andrew Jackson's Indian Removal policies of the 1830s and continued to pick up steam, creating the foundation of Indian Law that persists two centuries later.[24]

The Doctrine of Discovery underwrites the claim made in *Cherokee Nation v. Georgia* (1831) that Native American tribes were not "denominated foreign nations" but "domestic dependent nations" whose relationship to the United States resembles "that of a ward to his guardian."[25] A decade later, *Martin v. Waddell* (1842) affirmed that "the Indian tribes of the new world were regarded as mere temporary occupants of the soil" and that "the territory they occupied was disposed of by the governments of Europe, at their pleasure, as if it had been found without inhabitants."[26]

The long shadow of the *Johnson v. M'Intosh* decision extends well beyond the nineteenth century. *Northwest Band of Shoshone Indians v. US* (1945) affirmed that "even where a reservation is created for the maintenance of Indians, their right amounts to nothing more than a treaty right of occupancy." That ruling defined "Indian title" as "aboriginal usage without definite recognition of the right by the United States" and declared that the extinguishing of such title by "the white man's government" has justly proceeded "without any admitted legal responsibility in the sovereign to compensate the Indian for his loss."[27] Ten years later, *Tee-Hit-Ton Indians v. US* (1955) affirmed the idea of "Indian title" as "permission from the whites to occupy" and contained this strikingly glib, racist assertion: "Every American schoolboy knows that the savage tribes of this continent were deprived of their ancestral ranges by force and that, even when the Indians ceded millions of acres by treaty in return for blankets, food and trinkets, it was not a sale but the conquerors' will that deprived them of their land."[28]

The Doctrine of Discovery has even been cited in US Supreme Court cases in the twenty-first century. In *Sherrill v. Oneida* (2005), liberal justice Ruth Bader Ginsburg authored the majority 8–1 opinion rejecting the Oneida Nation's attempt to reincorporate, for tax purposes, land that was historically lost and recently repurchased into their current reservation holdings. The first footnote grounding Ginsburg's argument declared, "Under the 'doctrine of discovery' . . . fee title to the lands occupied by Indians when the colonists arrived became vested in the sovereign—first the discovering European nation and later the original States and the United States.'"[29] Notably, Justice John Paul Stevens's solo dissenting opinion did not part ways with his colleagues over the invocation of the Doctrine of Discovery;

rather, he more narrowly argued that only Congress, not the courts, held the authority to "abrogate or extinguish tribal sovereignty."[30]

Clearly, the spirit of the Doctrine of Discovery still animates our nation's highest court and is positively cited by justices across the ideological spectrum. While the language brought forth today is often more subtle, reliance on *Johnson v. M'Intosh* evokes the settler colonist prejudices embedded in that decision. Amid all the legal argumentation, for example, Chief Justice John Marshall gave this description of Native Americans, an attitude that cannot be separated from the legal conclusions: "But the tribes of Indians inhabiting this country were fierce savages, whose occupation was war, and whose subsistence was drawn chiefly from the forest. To leave them in possession of their country, was to leave the country a wilderness."[31] Our current legal apparatus, which can only be justified by a Euro-Christian supremacy that most white Christian Americans would recoil from today, continues to diminish Native American rights and justify the violation of US treaty obligations to Native American nations.

The Doctrine of Discovery in American Politics

The contemporary conflict between the worldview of the Doctrine of Discovery and the principles of a pluralistic democracy has also produced reactive governmental actions and legislative efforts. Some have been farcical, such as Trump's feeble, short-lived attempt at a 1776 Project. Some have been episodic, such as new efforts to ban books—including in some cases award-winning classics such as Toni Morrison's *The Bluest Eye* and even a contemporary adaptation of *The Diary of Anne Frank*—in public schools and libraries across the country.[32] But some have been more muscular, such as a coordinated national effort to introduce vague bills designed to restrict education on the history of slavery and racism, LGBTQ identity, or the contributions of specific racial or ethnic groups to US history.[33] These bills, which claim to oppose so-called "critical race theory" (CRT), are best understood as a new front in the old war to defend the worldview of the Doctrine of Discovery. They are culture war weapons disguised as legislation.

It is tempting to dismiss these efforts out of hand. There is, after all, no credible evidence of the existence of the problem they purport to address (that is, the widespread teaching of CRT in K–8 public schools). But if we listen closely enough, behind all the newspeak, legislative activity, and white Christian handwringing, we can make out the familiar cadence of this old worldview. We can hear it, for example, in the key provisions of a Florida law, preposterously titled "An Act Relating to Individual Freedom," which has served as a template for others around the country. The law specifies that all public school instruction must be consistent with its delineation of six "principles of individual freedom." The final three principles are particularly instructive:

- Meritocracy or traits such as a hard work ethic are not racist but fundamental to the right to pursue happiness and be rewarded for industry.

- An individual, by virtue of his or her race or sex, does not bear responsibility for actions committed in the past by other members of the same race or sex.

- An individual should not be made to feel discomfort, guilt, anguish, or any other form of psychological distress on account of his or her race.[34] *what about sex?*

The real purpose of these bills is twofold: 1) to erect a platform for political grandstanding by white Republican candidates and officials; and 2) to create a climate of uncertainty and fear for public school teachers and librarians that will in turn have a chilling effect on the teaching of an honest and full history of the US. There is evidence that these weapons are having their desired effect.

In the wake of the raft of anti-CRT bills introduced across the country in 2021 and 2022, the organization I founded, Public Religion Research Institute (PRRI), examined current trust in public school teachers and librarians. On our 2022 American Values Survey, we asked Americans which of two statements came closest to describing their beliefs about public school teachers and librarians: 1) "They provide our kids with appropriate curriculum and books that teach the good and bad of American history"; or 2) "They are indoctrinating our kids with inappropriate curriculum and books that wrongly portray America as a racist country."[35]

By a margin of more than two to one (66 percent to 29 percent), Americans believe that public school teachers and librarians are appropriately teaching the good and the bad of American history. But majorities of two groups—Republicans (54 percent) and white evangelical Protestants (51 percent), who comprise the religious base of the GOP—have now lost faith in our public school teachers and librarians, suspecting them of indoctrinating our kids with messages about America being a racist country. Republicans are wildly out of step on this question, even compared to independents (only 27 percent of whom believe public school teachers and librarians are indoctrinating students). And white evangelicals look starkly different from all other religious Americans (only 29 percent of whom believe public school teachers and librarians are indoctrinating students).[36]

These anti-CRT bills contain an implicit confession of what conservative white Christian people want, even demand at this moment of reckoning in America: the protection of an American origin story of innocence. The movement for racial reckoning today is restaging the American story—changing the set, throwing old plotlines into disarray, and introducing new characters that dethrone old heroes. The current defensive actions we are witnessing from some white Christian quarters are desperate attempts to shore up the teetering worldview of the Doctrine of Discovery.

FIGURE 11.1 Perceptions of Public School Teachers and Librarians, by Party and Religious Affiliation

Public school teachers and librarians . . .

■ Are indoctrinating our kids with inappropriate curriculum and books that wrongly portray America as a racist country.

▢ Skipped/Don't Know

■ Provide our kids with appropriate curriculum and books that teach the good and bad of American history.

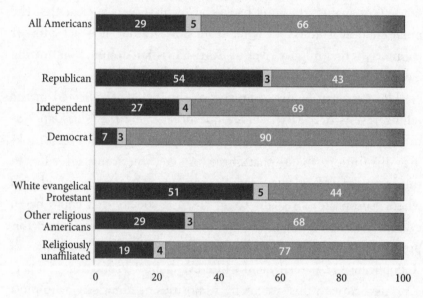

Source: PRRI, American Values Survey, 2022.

The Doctrine of Discovery in American Culture

Over the last few years, the term "white Christian nationalism" (WCN) has emerged in the social sciences and the media to describe the worldview behind Trumpism and the "Make America Great Again" movement. We've clearly seen the blending of white identity politics with Christianity, not only in the rhetoric from former president Trump and Republican leaders like Florida governor Ron DeSantis and Georgia congresswoman Marjorie Taylor Greene, but also in the symbols participants have carried at Trump rallies and at the insurrection at the US Capitol on January 6, 2021. WCN is a more accurate and useful term—an important improvement over euphemisms like "white nationalist"—because it properly identifies the movement as an ethno-religious one, a reality often lost on the mainstream media and even those assessing domestic threats, like the Department of Justice and the FBI. But if we see WCN against the long backdrop of history, it is clear that the phenomenon it describes is far from new. Rather, it is yet another tributary of that mighty river of Euro-Christian domination flowing from the Doctrine of Discovery.

The currency of five centuries of this belief is reflected in the telling results of a PRRI survey question. The 2023 Christian Nationalism Survey, conducted by PRRI in partnership with the Brookings Institution, found that three in ten Americans agreed with this statement: "God intended America to be a new promised land where European Christians could create a society that could be an example to the rest of the world."[37] Americans overall rejected this premise by a margin of two to one. Notably, however, majorities of Republicans (52 percent) and white evangelical Protestants (56 percent) agreed with this statement. Majorities of Americans who most trust Fox News (55 percent)—and seven in ten of those who most trust far-right news sources such as One America News (OAN) or Newsmax—also agreed.

Moreover, among white Americans, this belief in America as a divinely ordained white Christian nation—one that has blessed so much brutality in our history—is strongly linked to denials of structural racism, anti-immigrant sentiment, anti-Semitism, anti-LGBTQ sentiment, support for patriarchal gender roles, belief in conspiracy theories such as QAnon, and even support for political violence.

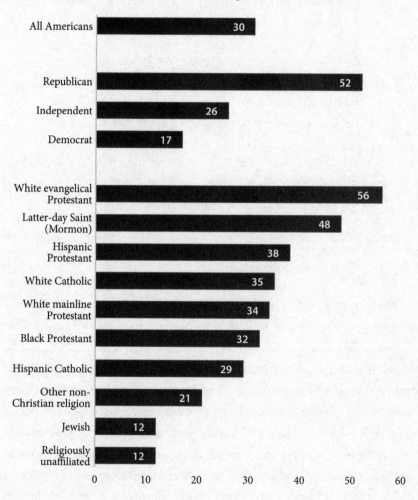

FIGURE 11.2 Support for the Core Tenet of the Doctrine of Discovery, by Party and Religious Affiliation

Percent who Agree

God intended America to be a new promised land where European Christians could create a society that would be an example to the rest of the world.

Source: PRRI/Brookings, Christian Nationalism Survey, 2023.

Compared to white Americans who reject it, white Americans who agree with this core tenet of the Doctrine of Discovery are:

- Two and a half times as likely to believe that the impact of America's history of slavery and racism on the present is exaggerated (58 percent vs. 23 percent);

- More than three times as likely to believe in the so-called "great replacement theory," which contends that immigrants are "invading our country and replacing our cultural and ethnic background" (68 percent vs. 21 percent); and

- Most disturbingly, whites who embrace the core tenet of the Doctrine of Discovery are nearly three times as likely as those who reject it to believe that "true American patriots may have to resort to violence to save our country" (26 percent vs. 9 percent).

The contemporary white Christian nationalist movement flows directly from a cultural stream that has run through this continent since the first Europeans arrived five centuries ago. The photographs of the insurrectionists storming the US Capitol on January 6, 2021, bear an uncanny resemblance to the painting of Hernando de Soto marshaling Christian symbols to claim Indigenous lands for Spain on May 8, 1541, which still hangs prominently in the Rotunda of that same building. On the Capitol steps, a massive wooden cross was erected, standards emblazoned with the name of Jesus were flown, and Biblical passages were read. Hands were raised in both prayer and violence. Seen in this light, the symbols brandished by the insurrectionists were not incidental; they were the centuries-old ritual implements of the Doctrine of Discovery, summoned to do the work they have always done.

FROM THE INDIAN PROBLEM AND THE NEGRO PROBLEM TO THE WHITE CHRISTIAN PROBLEM

Our current conflicts and contradictions are clear signs that we are experiencing a significant new moment in our nation's history. It is telling, for example, that even the 2022 Supreme Court decision in *Dobbs v. Jackson Women's Health Organization*, which overturned a right to abortion—one of the hottest flashpoints in contemporary American politics—hinged primarily on the high court's normative understanding of "history and tradition" (which the court arbitrarily defined as some indistinct period prior to the 1970s) rather than arguments about the morality of abortion itself.[39] Across the spectrum of issues, and from national presidential elections to local school board meetings, the most visceral disagreements and vehement fights to come will likely center not on policy but on historical narratives, public rituals, and civic spaces.

The work commemorating the histories of white racial violence against African Americans in the Mississippi Delta, Duluth, and Tulsa are beginning to reinscribe a different history in public spaces. Each of these public achievements serves as a cultural toehold, helping future generations tell a more honest history and take another step along the path to a more inclusive future.

But even with these significant accomplishments, there is more to be done. One important piece of that work, to which I hope this book contributes, is collectively recognizing that the histories of oppression in our country flow from the same source. Emmett Till's story doesn't typically get told against the backdrop of the Choctaw people's forced removal west of the Mississippi River to Indian Country via the Trail of Tears. The lynching of three Black men in Duluth isn't usually connected to the genocide-fueled mass execution of thirty-eight Dakota men and exile of thousands of their relatives beyond the bounds of the state. The Tulsa Race Massacre is rarely understood alongside the Reign of Terror experienced by the Osage.

The compartmentalization of history has some advantages for specific people groups, insofar as it centers their particular struggle for justice. But the real beneficiaries of siloed history are white Christian people. These stories, told in isolation, fracture the historical gaze among the victims of violence, theft, slavery, and oppression. Even well-intentioned accounts, told in this way, encourage a partial reckoning. These fragmented narratives demarcate America's so-called "Indian problem" and so-called "Negro problem" as distant islands, neither one visible from the shores of the other. But if we do the hard work of pushing upriver, we find that the same waters that produced the Negro problem also spawned the Indian problem. If we dare to go further, at the headwaters is the white Christian problem.

CONFESSION AND CALL: A WORD TO MY FELLOW WHITE CHRISTIANS

The following is my attempt to give voice to the half-conscious narrative I inherited and relied upon, for far too many years, to dispel the ghosts of other American histories haunting the edges of my awareness. I believe it is not too far off the mark from the history many contemporary white Christians are demanding at this moment, or at least the history we actually *want* to claim even if we cannot bring ourselves to assert it as straightforwardly as our forebears.

We would like to hold these truths to be self-evident:

That we bear no responsibility for the actions of our ancestors, nor for the effects of their actions on the present. That hard work and individual merit are the keys to understanding both the path to the present and the possibilities of the future; the haves and the have-nots of today received what they deserved based on the virtues of their individual past actions. It follows that no one, particularly hardworking white Christian people, should be made to feel uncomfortable because of what we now have. If anyone asserts otherwise, we are the ones being discriminated against.

This land is our land, from California to the New York island. We deserve to keep everything we've worked so hard to take. We have deeds in safe-deposit boxes with our names on them, the veracity of which are guaranteed by a notary seal and a state we created for this purpose. As for the vast amount of wealth locked away in individual trusts and institutional endowments, we have histories that document our industriousness and our cunning, along with quarterly and annual statements that testify to our now long-held legal ownership. Furthermore, what we have done, we have done with the ultimate authority. Jesus is one of us. In case there was any doubt, we made a likeness of Jesus in our image the most widely distributed portrait in human history.

We insist, both for ourselves and for others, on an inevitable present, one in which what was leads to what is, and what is will always be. It is not that we are against history. We know the importance of a good origin story. History, done rightly, explains how we got here—with our fences transforming land into property, our ledgers turning labor and crops into capital, and our hands holding the receipts. The history of America, founded in 1776, is a genesis story justifying the divinely ordained now, not a sloppy mess of narratives with multiple beginnings and contingent outcomes.

Those who looked like us owned the publishing companies who hired our writers to tell us the story of how we came to be America. Those executives also had the right connections to sell those packaged narratives to our public school boards, who handed books and lesson plans to our teachers, who in turn faithfully taught these stories to our children. And the circle remained unbroken, by and by, Lord, by and by.

We know that slavery was a blemish on the country's record and that this was, mostly, the cause of the Civil War. Still, there were good and noble people fighting on both sides. Even though slavery wasn't always as brutal as Hollywood depicts it, we're glad that that sinful practice has ended and that the whole unfortunate episode is behind us now. What we didn't get right after the Civil War was finally rectified by the good Rev. Martin Luther King Jr., whose eloquent words we now read in our churches and whose birthday we celebrate alongside Robert E. Lee's.

On the occasions when we think about it, we also feel bad about what happened to the Indians. But we also share Laura Ingalls Wilder's sentiments about the land in the early days of the country: "[T]here were no people there. Only Indians lived there."⁴⁰ In any case, we weren't personally a part of all that. And it was, after all, our missionaries who brought the Indians, with their primitive and savage ways, out of the darkness and into the light of Christian salvation. It was our government and our churches that coaxed those lost children out of the woods and into boarding schools, saving their souls and disciplining their bodies for more industrious pursuits like farming and factory work. We still honor their history with our athletic team names, mascots, and, more recently, with the occasional "land acknowledgment" ritual at public events. We did finally give the Indians reservations of their own, and they seem to be doing fine now with their casinos and government-provided health care and welfare subsidies.

Finally, though of course there have been times when some Christians acted badly, they were acting against and not with the spirit of our faith. No true Christian would kill or steal or lie.

This is the history we want our tax dollars to teach public school children. (Many of our children are already getting this history in private Christian academies.) We want our children to know that America is good. Just like us.

How do we cope responsibly with our history as the descendants and beneficiaries of perpetrators of unspeakable violence done in the name of the country and faith we still claim? After all, we have been the cowboys, not the Indians. We have been the occupiers and the enslavers, not the displaced or enslaved. We have been the violent, not the violated. Even when we have been one or two social classes removed from the true economic heirs of white supremacy—as was true for my family, who scratched out a living as Georgia sharecroppers and later labored in the Bibb County textile mill—we still reaped the relative benefits of whiteness and comforted ourselves with the notion that our lighter skin signified our superior place in a divine pecking order. The segregation of Jim Crow had the twin purposes of disenfranchising Black Americans and ensuring working-class whites of our place in an imaginary hierarchy, a promise to which we paradoxically clung all the more tightly as that system failed to secure our economic futures. We, at least, did not suffer the curse of Ham.

Our precarious position demands that we remain vigilantly ignorant of our own origin story. Up until very recently, history books have been full of the lies necessary to defend an impossibly innocent and glorious past. The crimes were so monstrous and the evidence so near at hand that we desperately built theologies, philosophies, and entire cultural worlds designed to obscure the facts and to produce, propagate, and protect these mythic origins. This worldview washed over our churches and seeped into our sermons, liturgies, and hymnals. It created its own grammar that renders the most clarion testimonies of our accusers silent. Euphemisms like *explorer*, *pioneer*, and *homesteader* created a respectable veneer that smoothed over the jagged valence of terms like *invader*, *occupier*, and *colonizer*. The ubiquitous use of the passive voice in our histories protected responsible subjects. We were so successful in masking the truth that even one of our most enlightened artists could sing to us, without a pang of conscience, "This Land Is Your Land."

Every map of every US state is a living witness to our massive land theft and occupation. The states featured in these pages—Mississippi, Minnesota, and Oklahoma—have names derived from native peoples. Place-names in the Mississippi Delta, where Emmett Till was lynched, cannot be spoken without the tongues of the conquistador and the Choctaw (DeSoto and LeFlore counties; the Tallahatchie River), the family names of former enslavers (Mitchener, Bobo,

Webb, and countless other multigenerational plantation names), or the legacies of former slaves (Mound Bayou, the remarkable town founded by freed slaves).

In Minnesota, place-names testify to bloody historical conflicts and occupations. The valorization of European domination is preserved in the derivation of Duluth from the nobility title of an early French explorer, *Sieur du Lhut*. The "Twin Cities" of Minneapolis (*minne* meaning water in the Dakota language) and St. Paul (named after the apostle Paul in the New Testament) eternally tie together the deadly Indigenous–Christian conflict.

In Oklahoma, Tulsa sits on the Arkansas River (a French reference to the Quapaw tribe), and the city's name, likely derived from a contraction of Tallahassee (an Apalachee word meaning "ghost town" or "abandoned fields"), was carried on the Trail of Tears by the Creek people, along with ashes from the last fires that were burned in their ancestral homes.

Here is the question that must illuminate the path forward for us and our children: *How can we meaningfully respond to being beneficiaries of a crime so plain it cannot be denied and so large it can never be fully righted?* It is easy to be overwhelmed by such a question. Even those conversations about restitution or reparations that get off the ground are quickly sandbagged by assertions about the impossibility of the task or red-herring objections to extreme solutions that no one has proposed. But if we're honest, we also know that the paralysis that often cripples discussions of justice is a defense mechanism stemming from a lack of real motivation. Up to this point in our history, the lesson seems to be this: While we are endlessly creative in fashioning novel ways to kill, dispossess, and defraud others, we are hopelessly unimaginative in our efforts to balance the scales of justice. Greed spawns a million schemes, while repentance throws up its hands.

Indeed, the challenge before us is formidable. To account for the lives, land, and labor that have been stolen, we'll need a broadened "moral imaginary," as Rev. Dr. Kelly Brown Douglas so eloquently describes in *Resurrection Hope: A Future Where Black Lives Matter*. We will need to relinquish the ethno-religious hierarchies embedded in the Doctrine of Discovery in favor of a transcendent vision in which "the sacred humanity of each person is honored and respected."[41] And we'll need a moral imaginary that is not amnesic, one that will hold on to the memory of the systemic injustices that have accrued to Black and Indigenous people and their forebears.

We'll also need to expand our vocabulary. For example, while *reparations* may be the right term to describe what justice looks like for African Americans who are descendants of enslaved people and who have experienced generations of disenfranchisement by discriminatory US laws, this term may not capture what Native Americans want and deserve. Here, *restitution* may be a more apt response. As the American Indian Movement and more recently the #LandBack movement have insisted, at root, justice toward Native Americans cannot be met simply with monetary payments; it must be worked out in the context of honoring the promises in US government treaties with regard to land and sovereignty.

This is a tall order, but we cannot shrink before the difficulty of the task. The creativity of our solutions is directly proportional to, and a measure of, the strength of our convictions. Our better angels must energize us now as much as our worst have in the past.

We white Christians no longer represent the majority of Americans. We are no longer capable of setting the nation's course by sheer cultural and political dominance. But there are still more than enough of us to decisively derail the future of democracy in America. If we wish to do otherwise, we can no longer disengenuously pretend that democracy and the Doctrine of Discovery are, or ever were, compatible. We can no longer pay tribute to one while benefiting from the other. We must choose. And if we choose democracy, it will require more than just confession by an unflinching few. It will require joining the work already underway to repair the damage done by this malignant cultural legacy. Through that transformative engagement, we might finally illuminate the path that leads to a shared American future.

ACKNOWLEDGMENTS

The Hidden Roots of White Supremacy, my fifth book, is a continuation of my journey to navigate the tumultuous currents of racial reckoning in America and to discern the possible courses we might chart toward a more inclusive future. I've benefited from generosity and guidance from so many lights along the way. First, I want to express my gratitude to Chris Scharen and Ted Smith, to whom the book is dedicated, fellow travelers for more than twenty-five years now.

In Mississippi, I am indebted to the hospitality of April Grayson, director of community and capacity building at the Alluvial Collective; Brother Rogers, director of programs and communication at the Mississippi Department of Archives and History; and Patrick Weems, cofounder and director of the Emmett Till Interpretive Center, who granted interviews, provided introductions, and shared their intimate knowledge of developments on the ground. Thanks also go to Jennifer Ford, senior curator of manuscripts at the University of Mississippi Libraries, for facilitating access to the archives of the William Winter Institute for Racial Reconciliation.

I am also grateful for my fellow Mississippians who agreed to talk with me about their work with the Emmett Till Interpretive Center in the Delta: Donna Burton Sanders, Gloria Dickerson, Jessie Jaynes-Diming, Devona Jones-Chambers, Sykes Sturdivant,

Jackson Webb, and Willie Williams. Additionally, I was privileged to see Susan Glisson—author and poet, gifted consultant, and founding former director of the William Winter Institute for Racial Reconciliation—in action, moderating a meeting of the Emmett Till Interpretive Center board, where she composed an impromptu poem based on the aspirations expressed in that meeting that I feature in chapter three.

In Minnesota, I am grateful to Anthony Galloway for inviting me to worship at the historic St. Mark's AME Church in Duluth and teaching me about the congregation's long history of advocating for civil rights. Rev. Galloway also connected me with past president of the Duluth NAACP Claudie Washington, who helped put the last twenty years of memorial work into context. Human rights officer Carl Crawford, city councilor Janet Kennedy, and police chief Mike Tusken provided valuable perspectives about how the work of racial repair and healing has made its way into the official halls of the city of Duluth.

Several current and past members of the Clayton-Jackson-McGhie Memorial board helped me understand the impact of nearly two decades of racial reconciliation work in the city: Henry Banks, Lynn Goerdt, Kim Green, Roger Gregoire, and Treasure Jenkins. Finally, I want to thank Jim Bear Jacobs, a member of the Stockbridge-Munsee Mohican Nation and the director of racial justice for the Minnesota Council of Churches, along with native theologian Kelly Sherman-Conroy of the Oglala Lakota Nation, for a moving daylong tour of Native American sacred sites in the Minneapolis-St. Paul area.

In Oklahoma, I am grateful for David Wiggs, pastor of Boston Avenue United Methodist Church, for the experience of speaking to the congregation during its "One Hundred Days of Repentance" program during Lent in 2021, ahead of the one hundredth anniversary of the Tulsa Race Massacre. Rev. Wiggs also granted me several interviews and provided critical introductions to local activists.

Michelle Place, director of the Tulsa Historical Society, also generously facilitated introductions and helped me understand the Tulsa Race Massacre anniversary against the backdrop of the city's growth and development. The struggles white Tulsa churches have had reckoning with the legacy of white racial violence were illuminated by insightful conversations with Carlton Pearson, Gary Peluso-Verdend, Chris Moore, Jean Neal, Amanda Chastang, and Richard Wansley.

My understanding of the work of the Tulsa Race Massacre Centennial Commission (TRMCC) was deepened by the in-depth reporting of Randy Krehbiel in the *Tulsa World* and an interview with Phil Armstrong, former program director of the TRMCC and interim director of the Greenwood Rising Black Wall Street History Center, along with Glenda Love-Williams, Moises Echeverria, and Francisco Trevino. Finally, I witnessed councilwoman Vanessa Hall-Harper's unrelenting efforts to bring the economic benefits of racial reckoning and commemoration work to her constituents in North Tulsa's District One, which she shared in both a personal interview and a public conversation with me on a podcast for the Tulsa Metropolitan Ministry.

I also could not have completed the book without my steadfast colleagues at Public Religion Research Institute (PRRI)—especially Melissa Deckman, Natalie Jackson, and Sean Sands—who not only served as thought partners but also kept the wheels turning at PRRI, giving me the space to research and write. Graphics designer Tim Duffy also lent his considerable skill to making complex charts clear and understandable on the black-and-white printed page. I am grateful for a group of gifted scholars, writers, and colleagues who have provided vital intellectual community and support both for my work at PRRI and on this project: Wajahat Ali, Ruthie Braunstein, Kelly Brown Douglas, Anthea Butler, Diana Butler Bass, Michael Cressler, Paul Djupe, E. J. Dionne Jr., Bill Galston, Greg Garrett, Andra Gillespie, Eddie Glaude Jr., Simon Greer, Obery Hendricks Jr., Kristin

Kobes Du Mez, Rachel Laser, Jacqui Lewis, Gerardo Marti, Bryan Massingale, Pierre Moon, Eboo Patel, Sam Perry, Sarah Posner, Stella Rouse, Angela Sims, Katherine Stewart, Jemar Tisby, Emilie Townes, Nate Walker, Jim Wallis, Andrew Whitehead, Jonathan Wilson-Hartgrove, and Janelle Wong.

I am grateful for the generous support of the Carnegie Corporation of New York, the Ford Foundation, Open Society Foundations, Stand Together Trust, and the Unitarian Universalist Veatch Program at Shelter Rock, which underwrote the PRRI public opinion survey research cited in the prologue and chapter eleven. Additionally, I am grateful for insightful conversations with Tom Glenn and for multiyear research support for PRRI's work related to religion and racial justice provided by the Wilbur and Hilda Glenn Family Foundation, the Hearthland Foundation, the Henry Luce Foundation, the Mellon Foundation, and the Stiefel Freethought Foundation.

I owe a special word of thanks to Phil Arnold and Sandy Bigtree (Bear Clan, Mohawk Nation), of the Indigenous Values Initiative, who reached out after reading a piece I wrote for Religion News Service/ the *Washington Post* on the problem of white Christian innocence and Independence Day celebrations. They encouraged me to deepen my understanding of the contemporary ramifications of the Doctrine of Discovery. I am also grateful for George "Tink" Tinker (Osage Nation), the Clifford Baldridge Emeritus Professor of American Indian Cultures and Religious Traditions at the Iliff School of Theology, for advice and for introducing me to his former student and colleague Roger Green, a scholar of rhetoric and Native American religion. Roger read the entire manuscript and provided invaluable guidance on Native American history, culture, and religion—areas that were new to me. I am especially grateful to Roger for introducing me to the work of Vine Deloria Jr. (Standing Rock, Sioux Nation), whose "Open Letter to the Heads of the Christian Churches in America" still resonates as loudly today as it did half a century ago when it was penned.

ACKNOWLEDGMENTS

The Hidden Roots of White Supremacy is the third book on which I've worked with Bob Bender, vice president and executive editor at Simon & Schuster. I'm grateful for his guidance and advice on storytelling and adapting quantitative research for a general audience. Associate editor Johanna Li has been exceptionally efficient and attentive as the book has moved through production on a tight timeline. I first connected with my agent, Roger Freet, at a book exhibit at the American Academy of Religion in 2012. Roger was a critical early voice urging me to think about shaping my research and writing for a wider public, and the seeds planted in those early conversations have blossomed into three books over the last decade. He continues to be a valued conversation partner and trusted advocate. Thank you, Roger, and the team at Folio Literary Management.

Finally, I'd like to thank my family for supporting the project by listening to far too many stories and deliberations over dinner and by understanding not only the time spent away in Mississippi, Minnesota, and Oklahoma, but also the time spent away at the little antique desk in our guest room. My spouse and partner, Jodi Kanter, professor of theater and dance at George Washington University, is also a gifted scholar and writer. She generously read every page, often at the end of a day's writing, helping me to keep the story moving and the language tight. She is always my first, last, and best editor.

As I learn more about our troubling past, and especially the role that my Christian faith has played in most of our worst moments, I'm often tempted toward despair. But when I see the work of racial reckoning and repair being done in local communities across the country, and the organically diverse and inclusive friendship circles of my children, Riley and Jasper, I am buoyed with hope that we might yet find the way to live into the promise of our nation.

APPENDIX

Recommended Reading Related to the Doctrine of Discovery

Churchill, Ward. *A Little Matter of Genocide: Holocaust and Denial in the Americas 1492–Present*. San Francisco: City Lights, 1997.

Conroy-Krutz, Emily. *Christian Imperialism: Converting the World in the Early American Republic*. Ithaca, NY: Cornell University Press, 2015.

Deloria, Vine, Jr. *Custer Died for Your Sins: An Indian Manifesto*. Norman: University of Oklahoma Press, 1969.

———. *For This Land: Writings on Religion in America*. New York: Routledge, 1999.

———. *God Is Red: A Native View of Religion*. Wheat Ridge, CO: Fulcrum, 1973.

Dunbar-Ortiz, Roxanne. *Not "A Nation of Immigrants": Settler Colonialism, White Supremacy, and a History of Erasure and Exclusion*. Boston: Beacon Press, 2021.

Heath, Joseph J. "The Doctrine of Discovery: Its Fundamental Performance in United States Indian Law and the Need for Its Repudiation and Removal." *Albany Government Law Review* 10 (2017): 112–56.

Jennings, Willie James. *The Christian Imagination: Theology and the Origins of Race*. New Haven, CT: Yale University Press, 2011.

Miller, Robert J. *Native America, Discovered and Conquered: Thomas Jefferson, Lewis and Clark, and Manifest Destiny*. Lincoln: University of Nebraska Press, 2008.

Miller, Robert J., et al. *Discovering Indigenous Lands: The Doctrine of Discovery in the English Colonies*. Oxford, UK: Oxford University Press, 2010.

Newcombe, Steven T. *Pagans in the Promised Land: Decoding the Doctrine of Christian Discovery*. Chicago: Chicago Review Press, 2008.

Robertson, Lindsay G. *Conquest by Law: How the Discovery of America Dispossessed Indigenous Peoples of Their Lands*. Oxford, UK: Oxford University Press, 2005.

Seed, Patricia. *Ceremonies of Possession in Europe's Conquest of the New World: 1492–1640*. New York: Cambridge University Press, 1995.

Tinker, George E. *American Indian Liberation: A Theology of Sovereignty*. New York: Orbis, 2008.

———. *Missionary Conquest: The Gospel and Native American Cultural Genocide*. Minneapolis: Fortress Press, 1993.

Williams, Robert A., Jr. *The American Indian in Western Legal Thought*. Oxford, UK: Oxford University Press, 1990.

Additionally, for primary source documents (and English translations) related to the Doctrine of Discovery, see the website maintained by the Indigenous Values Initiative: https://doctrineofdiscovery.org/.

BIBLIOGRAPHY

Adams-Heard, Rachel. "Land Is Power, and the Osage Nation Is Buying Theirs Back." Bloomberg. October 12, 2022. https://www.bloomberg.com/news/features/2022-10-12/osage-nation-fights-to-buy-back-land-after-reign-of-terror.

Anderson, Devery S., and Julian Bond. *Emmett Till: The Murder That Shocked the World and Propelled the Civil Rights Movement.* Jackson: University Press of Mississippi, 2017.

Anderson, Gary Clayton. *Massacre in Minnesota: The Dakota War of 1862, the Most Violent Ethnic Conflict in American History.* Norman: University of Oklahoma Press, 2019.

"Anniversary of the Apology to Emmett Till's Family." Video. Emmett Till Interpretive Center, 2017. https://vimeo.com/237209316.

Anti-Defamation League. "QAnon." May 4, 2020. https://www.adl.org/resources/backgrounder/qanon.

AP/Votecast. "National Exit Poll, Presidential Election." Exit poll. AP/Votecast, 2020.

Architect of the Capitol. "Discovery of the Mississippi by De Soto." Accessed July 18, 2022. https://www.aoc.gov/explore-capitol-campus/art/discovery-mississippi-de-soto.

Austen, Ian. "Canada's Forced Schooling of Aboriginal Children Was 'Cultural Genocide,' Report Finds." *New York Times*, June 2, 2015. https://www.nytimes.com/2015/06/03/world/americas/canadas-forced-schooling-of-aboriginal-children-was-cultural-genocide-report-finds.html.

Avila, Bryan. Florida CS/HB 7: An Act Relating to Individual Freedom (2022). https://www.flsenate.gov/Session/Bill/2022/7/BillText/er/PDF.

Bakk-Hansen, Heidi. "Duluth's Lingering Shame." *Ripsaw*, June 7, 2000. https://www.perfectduluthday.com/2010/06/14/duluths-lingering-shame/.

Baldwin, James. *The Fire Next Time*. New York: Vintage International, 1993.

Barnett, James F. *Mississippi's American Indians*. Heritage of Mississippi Series, vol. 6. Jackson: University Press of Mississippi, 2012.

Bell, Jerri. "Clinton Massacre of 1875: Four Days of Violence Ushered in 'Mississippi Plan' to Halt Black Vote." *Mississippi Free Press*, August 5, 2021. https://www.mississippifreepress.org/14364/clinton-massacre-of-1875-four-days-of-violence-ushered-in-plan-to-halt-black-vote.

Bellah, Robert N., Richard Madsen, William M. Sullivan, Ann Swidler, and Steven M. Tipton. *Habits of the Heart: Individualism and Commitment in American Life*. Updated with a new introduction. Berkeley: University of California Press, 1996.

Bentley, Mac. "39 Tribes Call State Home." *Oklahoman*, February 16, 2003. https://www.oklahoman.com/story/news/2003/02/16/39-tribes-call-state-home/62057840007/.

Bercaw, Nancy. "Black Codes." Mississippi Encyclopedia, July 10, 2017. https://mississippiencyclopedia.org/entries/black-codes/.

Bessler, John D. *Legacy of Violence: Lynch Mobs and Executions in Minnesota*. Minneapolis: University of Minnesota Press, 2003.

Biden, Joseph. "A Proclamation on Day of Remembrance: 100 Years After the 1921 Tulsa Race Massacre." The White House, May 31, 2021. https://www.whitehouse.gov/briefing-room/presidential-actions/2021/05/31/a-proclamtion-on-day-of-remembrance-100-years-after-the-1921-tulsa-race-massacre/.

Biggs, Mouzon. Interview by John Erling. Audio, June 22, 2011. https://voicesofoklahoma.com/interviews/biggs-mouzon/.

Bigtree, Sandy, and Philip P. Arnold. "Why Removing Columbus Matters: From Foundational Narratives of Domination to Inclusivity." Association for Public Religion and Intellectual Life Online. March 10, 2021. https://www.aprilonline.org/why-removing-columbus-matters/.

Boorstein, Michelle. "Va. Episcopal Diocese to Spend $10 Million for Reparations. But How?" *Washington Post*, August 14, 2022. https://www.washingtonpost.com/religion/2022/08/14/va-episcopal-diocese-spend-10-million-reparations-how/.

Brant, Steve. "Site of Racial Showdown in Minneapolis Heading to National Register." *Star Tribune*, July 24, 2014.

Breen, Patrick H. *The Land Shall Be Deluged in Blood: A New History of the Nat Turner Revolt*. New York: Oxford University Press, 2015.

Broadwater, Luke. "Congress Set to Replace Dred Scott Author's Statue with Thurgood Marshall." *New York Times*, December 22, 2022. https://www .nytimes .com/2022/12/14/us/politics/taney-thurgood-marshall-statue-capitol.html.

Broom, Brian. "Grandmothers, Grandfathers 'From Long Ago': Miss. Returns Remains to Chickasaw Nation." *Clarion-Ledger*, March 30, 2021. https://www.clarionledger.com/story/news/local/2021/03/31/mississippi-re turns-remains-403-native-americans-chickasaw-nation-repatriation-bur ial/6978798002/.

Cameron, Guy and Steven Vermette. "The Role of Extreme Cold in the Failure of the San Miguel de Gualdape Colony." *Georgia Historical Quarterly* 96:3 (Fall 2012): 291–307.

Carley, Kenneth. *The Dakota War of 1862: Minnesota's Other Civil War*. 2nd ed. St. Paul: Minnesota Historical Society Press, 1976.

Cartier, Jacques. *A Memoir of Jacques Cartier, Sieur de Limoilou, His Voyages to the St. Lawrence*. Translated by James Phinney Baxter. New York: Dodd, Mead, 1906. https://libsysdigi.library.illinois.edu/oca/Books2009-06/mem oirofjacquesc00baxt/memoirofjacquesc00baxt.pdf.

Chaffee, John. "Repudiate the Doctrine of Discovery." *Journal of the General Convention of the Episcopal Church* (2009): 371–72.

Charles, Mark, and Soong-Chan Rah. *Unsettling Truths: The Ongoing, Dehumanizing Legacy of the Doctrine of Discovery*. Downers Grove, IL: IVP, 2019.

Chicago Tribune. "The Duluth Lynching." Editorial, June 19, 1920.

———. "Renamed Roads Honor Rights Victims." March 22, 2005. https://www .chicagotribune.com/news/ct-xpm-2005-03-22-0503220101-story.html.

Chokshi, Niraj. "Prestigious Laura Ingalls Wilder Award Renamed Over Racial Insensitivity." *New York Times*, June 26, 2018. https://www.nytimes .com/2018/06/26/books/laura-ingalls-wilder-book-award.html.

Churchill, Ward. *A Little Matter of Genocide: Holocaust and Denial in the Americas 1492–Present*. San Francisco: City Lights, 1997.

Clayton-Jackson-McGhie Memorial Committee. "Election Day Statement." November 12, 2012.

Coates, Ta-Nehisi. "Hope and the Historian." *The Atlantic*, December 10, 2015.

Cobb, James C. *The Most Southern Place on Earth: The Mississippi Delta and the Roots of Regional Identity*. New York: Oxford University Press, 1994.

Cobb, Jelani. *The Substance of Hope: Barack Obama and the Paradox of Progress*. New York: Bloomsbury, 2020.

Cohn, David. *Where I Was Born and Raised*. Boston: Houghton-Mifflin, 1948.

Convery, William. "Duluth's Clayton Jackson McGhie Memorial Aims to Ensure a Dark Episode in the City's History Isn't Forgotten." *MinnPost*, October 19, 2020. https://www.minnpost.com/mnopedia/2020/10/duluths-clayton-jackson-mcghie-memorial-aims-to-ensure-a-dark-episode-in-the-citys-history-isnt-forgotten/.

Cornish, Audie. "County Apologizes to Emmett Till Family." *All Things Considered*, NPR, October 2, 2017. https://www.npr.org/2007/10/02/14904083/county-apologizes-to-emmett-till-family.

Crawford, Carl. Interview by Robert P. Jones. Audio, May 18, 2022.

"CRT MAP: Critical Race Theory Legislation and Schools." Chalkbeat, February 2, 2022. https://www.chalkbeat.org/22525983/map-critical-race-theory-legislation-teaching-racism.

Custalow, Dawn. "Opinion: Native Americans Still Overlooked in Debates about U.S. History." *Virginian-Pilot*. Accessed August 31, 2022. https://www.pilotonline.com/opinion/columns/vp-ed-column-custalow-0927-20200926-aof7b2j4brgbzmwbess7ywhirm-story.html.

Davey, Monica. "LETTER FROM DULUTH; It Did Happen Here: The Lynching That a City Forgot." *New York Times*, December 4, 2003.

Dawes, Henry. An Act to Provide for the Allotment of Lands in Severalty to Indians on the Various Reservations, Pub. L. No. Statutes at Large 24, 388–91, NADP Document A1887 (1887). https://www.archives.gov/milestone-documents/dawes-act.

DeBonis, Mike. "Congress Votes Overwhelmingly to Make Juneteenth a Federal Holiday. The Day Commemorates the End of Slavery in Texas in 1865." *Washington Post*, June 16, 2021. https://www.washingtonpost.com/politics/juneteenth-federal-holiday/2021/06/16/7be284d8-ceba-11eb-a7f1-52b8870bef7c_story.html.

Deloria, Philip Joseph. *Playing Indian*. New Haven, CT: Yale University Press, 2022.

Deloria, Vine, Jr. *Custer Died for Your Sins: An Indian Manifesto*. Norman: University of Oklahoma Press, 1988.

———. *God Is Red: A Native View of Religion*. 3rd ed. Golden, CO: Fulcrum, 2003.

Deloria, Vine, Jr., and James Treat. *For This Land: Writings on Religion in America*. New York: Routledge, 1999.

Dierckins, Tony. *Duluth: An Urban Biography*. Saint Paul: Minnesota Historical Society Press, 2020.

———. "Park Hill Cemetery." Zenith City Press, April 18, 2017. http://zenithcity .com/archive/parks-landmarks/park-hill-cemetery/.

Doss, Erika. *Memorial Mania: Public Feeling in America*. Chicago: University of Chicago Press, 2010.

Douglas, Kelly Brown. *Resurrection Hope: A Future Where Black Lives Matter*. Maryknoll, NY: Orbis Books, 2021.

Douglass, Frederick. "West India Emancipation." Archive. University of Rochester, Frederick Douglass Project Writings, August 3, 1857. https://rbscp.lib .rochester.edu/4398.

Dunbar-Ortiz, Roxanne. *An Indigenous Peoples' History of the United States*. ReVisioning American History. Boston: Beacon Press, 2014.

Duwamish Solidarity Group. "Real Rent Duwamish." December 11, 2022. https:// www.realrentduwamish.org/.

Edwards, Elsie. "Interview with Elsie Edwards." *Indian-Pioneer History* (Oklahoma History Society) 23 (September 17, 1937): 255.

Ellsworth, Scott. *Death in a Promised Land: The Tulsa Race Riot of 1921*. Baton Rouge: Louisiana State University Press, 1982.

———. *The Ground Breaking: An American City and Its Search for Justice*. New York: Dutton, 2021.

Emmett Till & Mamie Till-Mobley Institute. Accessed December 9, 2022. https://www.thetillinstitute.org.

Episcopal Diocese of Virginia. "Reparations." November 2021. https://www.the diocese.net/resources/ministries/racial-justice-and-healing/reparations/.

Epstein, Jake, and Oma Seddiq. "Justice Neil Gorsuch Fumes That the Supreme Court 'Failed' to 'Honor This Nation's Promises' as It Rolled Back Tribal Authority in Oklahoma." *Business Insider*, June 29, 2022. https://www.busi nessinsider.com/gorsuch-slams-supreme-court-decision-reducing-tribal-au thority-in-oklahoma-2022-6.

Fandos, Nicholas. "House Votes to Purge Confederate Statues from the Capitol." *New York Times*, June 29, 2021. https://www.nytimes.com/2021/06/29/us/poli tics/house-confederate-statues-vote.html.

Fedo, Michael W. *The Lynchings in Duluth*. 2nd ed. Saint Paul: Minnesota Historical Society Press, 2016.

———. *Zenith City: Stories from Duluth*. Minneapolis: University of Minnesota Press, 2014.

Flew, Antony. *Thinking About Thinking*. New York: HarperCollins, 1975.

"Fourteenth Census of the United States Taken in the Year 1920." Washington, DC: US Bureau of the Census, 1922.

Francis, Pope. "Full Text: Pope Francis' Apology to Indigenous Peoples in Canada." *America Magazine*, July 25, 2022. https://www.americamagazine.org/faith/2022/07/25/pope-francis-apology-canada-243411.

Fuller, A. James. *Chaplain to the Confederacy: Basil Manly and Baptist Life in the Old South*. Southern Biography Series. Baton Rouge: Louisiana State University Press, 2000.

Galloway, Patricia Kay. *Choctaw Genesis, 1500–1700*. Indians of the Southeast. Lincoln: University of Nebraska Press, 1998.

Giangravé, Claire. "In Canada, Pope Francis Apologizes to Indigenous Peoples, Says It's Only 'First Step.'" Religion News Service, July 25, 2022. https://religionnews.com/2022/07/25/in-canada-pope-francis-apologizes-to-indigenous-peoples-says-its-only-first-step/.

Gibson, Arrell Morgan. *Oklahoma: A History of Five Centuries*. Norman: University of Oklahoma Press, 2010.

Gilder Lehrman Institute of American History. "De Soto's Discovery of the Mississippi, 1541." Accessed July 18, 2022. https://www.gilderlehrman.org/history-resources/spotlight-primary-source/de-sotos-discovery-mississippi-1541.

Glisson, Susan. "What We Can't Yet See but Still Believe: A Demos Found Poem by Community Leaders of Tallahatchie County, Mississippi, and Susan Glisson." June 23, 2022.

Gorn, Elliott J. *Let the People See: The Story of Emmett Till*. New York: Oxford University Press, 2018.

"Governor Reeves Takes Action Against Critical Race Theory." Video. Jackson, MS, 2022. https://www.facebook.com/tatereeves/videos/771428113837269/.

Grann, David. *Killers of the Flower Moon: The Osage Murders and the Birth of the FBI*. New York: Vintage Books, 2018.

Green, William D. *A Peculiar Imbalance: The Fall and Rise of Racial Equality in Minnesota, 1837–1869*. Minneapolis: University of Minnesota Press, 2015.

Guasco, Michael. "The Fallacy of 1619: Rethinking the History of Africans in

Early America." African American Intellectual History Society (AAIHS), September 4, 2017. https://www.aaihs.org/the-fallacy-of-1619-rethinking-the-history-of-africans-in-early-america/.

Hannah-Jones, Nikole. "The 1619 Project." *New York Times Magazine*, August 14, 2019. https://pulitzercenter.org/sites/default/files/full_issue_of_the_1619_project.pdf.

Hannah-Jones, Nikole, Caitlin Roper, Ilena Silverman, Jake Silverstein, and New York Times Company, eds. *The 1619 Project: A New Origin Story*. New York: One World, 2021.

Harjo, Joy. *An American Sunrise: Poems*. New York: Norton, 2019.

Hayasaki, Erika. "How Book Bans Turned a Texas Town Upside Down." *New York Times Magazine*, September 8, 2022. https://www.nytimes.com/2022/09/08/magazine/book-bans-texas.html.

Heaney, Seamus, and Sophocles. *The Cure at Troy: A Version of Sophocles's Philoctetes*. New York: Farrar, Straus & Giroux, 1991.

Heath, Joseph J. "The Doctrine of Discovery: Its Fundamental Performance in United States Indian Law and the Need for Its Repudiation and Removal." *Albany Government Law Review* 10 (2017): 112–56.

———. "Statement on the Historical Use of the Doctrine of Christian Discovery by the United States Supreme Court Since 1823." Syracuse, NY: Doctrine of Discovery Project, 2014. https://doctrineofdiscovery.org/statement-on-the-historical-use-of-the-doctrine-of-christian-discovery-by-the-united-states-supreme-court-since-1823/.

Hedgpeth, Dana. "The Week Hundreds of Native Americans Took Over D.C.'s Bureau of Indian Affairs." *Washington Post*, January 24, 2021. https://www.washingtonpost.com/history/2021/01/24/native-americans-occupied-bureau-indian-afffairs-nixon/.

Henry VII, King. "Patent Granted by Henry VII to John Cabot," March 5, 1496. https://doctrineofdiscovery.org/patent-cabot-henry-vii/.

Hill, Sid. "Why We Accepted a Thousand Acres of Land Back From New York State." *Nation*, July 6, 2022. https://www.thenation.com/article/environment/onondaga-land-new-york/.

Hochschild, Adam. "A Landmark Reckoning with America's Racial Past and Present." *New York Times*, November 15, 2021. https://www.nytimes.com/2021/11/15/books/review/the-1619-project-nikole-hannah-jones-caitlin-roper-ilena-silverman-jake-silverstein.html.

Hogan/Albach, Susan. "Dedicating Headstones: City to Memorialize Lynching Victims, Acknowledge Graves." *Duluth News Tribune*, October 26, 1991, sec. B.

Holy See Press Office. "Joint Statement of the Dicasteries for Culture and Education and for Promoting Integral Human Development on the 'Doctrine of Discovery.'" March 30, 2023. https://press.vatican.va/content/salastampa/en/bollettino/pubblico/2023/03/30/230330b.html.

Horowitz, Jason. "Francis Begs Forgiveness for 'Evil' Christians Inflicted on Indigenous People." *New York Times*, July 25, 2022. https://www.nytimes.com/live/2022/07/25/world/pope-francis-canada-visit.

Huie, William Bradford. "The Shocking Story of Approved Killing in Mississippi." *Look*, January 24, 1956.

Indigenous Values Initiative. *Dum Diversas*. Doctrine of Discovery Project, July 23, 2018. https://doctrineofdiscovery.org/dum-diversas/.

———. *Inter Caetera*. Doctrine of Discovery Project, June 13, 2022. https://doctrineofdiscovery.org/inter-caetera/.

———. "Repudiations of the Doctrine of Discovery by Faith Communities." Doctrine of Discovery Project, July 30, 2018. https://doctrineofdiscovery.org/faith-communities/.

Jackson, Andrew. "President Jackson's Message to Congress 'On Indian Removal.'" Speech presented at the United States Senate, Washington, DC, December 6, 1830. https://www.nps.gov/museum/tmc/manz/handouts/andrew_jackson_annual_message.pdf.

Johnson, Brooks. "'100 Years Overdue': Minnesota Grants First Posthumous Pardon in Case Connected to Duluth Lynchings." *Star Tribune*. Accessed January 28, 2022. https://www.startribune.com/100-years-overdue-man-who-was-scapegoat-in-1920-duluth-lynchings-pardoned/571215122/.

Johnson, Hannibal B. *Black Wall Street: From Riot to Renaissance in Tulsa's Historic Greenwood District*. Austin, TX: Eakin Press, 2007.

———. *Black Wall Street 100: An American City Grapples with Its Historical Racial Trauma*. Fort Worth, TX: Eakin Press, 2020.

Jones, Robert P. "Columbus Day or Indigenous Peoples' Day? The Damaging Christian 'Doctrine of Discovery' at the Heart of the American Identity Crisis." Substack newsletter. *White Too Long by Robert P. Jones* (blog), October 8, 2021. https://robertpjones.substack.com/p/columbus-day-or-indigenous-peoples.

———. *Photograph of Confederate Monument, Sumner, Mississippi*. June 24, 2022.

———. *Photograph of Emmett Till Historical Marker, Courthouse Lawn, Sumner, Mississippi*. June 22, 2022.

———. *Photograph of Graball Landing Sign, near Glendora, Mississippi.* June 25, 2022.

———. *The End of White Christian America*. New York: Simon & Schuster, 2016.

———. "This Supreme Court's Dangerous Vision of 'History and Tradition.'" Substack newsletter. *White Too Long by Robert P. Jones* (blog), July 1, 2022. https://robertpjones.substack.com/p/this-supreme-courts-dangerous-vision.

———. *White Too Long: The Legacy of White Supremacy in American Christianity*. New York: Simon & Schuster, 2021.

Julin, Chris. "Dedicating a Memorial." Minnesota Public Radio, October 10, 2003. https://news.minnesota.publicradio.org/features/2003/10/10_julinc_lynch ingdedicati/.

Kaur, Harmeet. "More than 160 Confederate Symbols Came Down in 2020, SPLC Says." CNN, February 24, 2021. https://www.cnn.com/2021/02/24/us /confederate-symbols-removed-2020-splc-trnd/index.html.

King, Rev. Dr. Martin Luther, Jr. "Pride Versus Humility: The Parable of the Pharisee and the Publican." Sermon presented at the Dexter Memorial Baptist Church, Montgomery, AL, September 25, 1955. https://nmaahc.si.edu /explore/stories/emmett-tills-death-inspired-movement.

Kraker, Dan. "Echoes of 1920 Duluth Lynching Persist at Centennial." Minnesota Public Radio News, June 15, 2020. https://www.mprnews.org /story/2020/06/15/we-never-solved-the-problem-echoes-of-1920-duluth -lynching-persist-as-city-marks-centennial.

———. "Hope, Call for Changes on Duluth Lynching Anniversary." Minnesota Public Radio News, June 15, 2020. https://www.mprnews.org /story/2020/06/15/centennial-remembrance-of-duluth-lynchings-subdued -but-hopeful.

Krehbiel, Randy. "Pair of Lynchings Shake Tulsa." *Tulsa World*, May 30, 2021.

———. "Pride Before the Fall." *Tulsa World*, May 30, 2021.

———. *Tulsa, 1921: Reporting a Massacre*. Norman: University of Oklahoma Press, 2019.

Kunze, Jenna. "'The United States Lags Behind' on the Rights of Its Indigenous Peoples, Natives Say." Native News Online, May 8, 2022. https://nativenews online.net/currents/the-united-states-lags-behind-on-the-rights-of-its-indig enous-peoples-natives-say.

Ladner, Joyce, and Dorie Ann Ladner. Oral history interview conducted by Joseph

Mosnier in Washington, DC, September 20, 2011. https://www.loc.gov /item/2015669153/.

Lee, Robert. "Accounting for Conquest: The Price of the Louisiana Purchase of Indian Country." *Journal of American History* 103, no. 4 (March 1, 2017): 921–42.

Leonard, Ben. "Biden Issues Proclamation on Tulsa Race Massacre." *Politico*, May 31, 2021. https://www.politico.com/news/2021/05/31/joe-biden-tulsa -proclamation-491450.

Lepore, Jill. *These Truths: A History of the United States*. New York: W. W. Norton, 2018.

Levenson, Michael. "Tulsa Race Massacre Commission Ousts Oklahoma Governor." *New York Times*, May 15, 2021. https://www.nytimes.com/2021/05/14 /us/Oklahoma-critical-race-theory-Tulsa-massacre.html.

Loaysa, Francisco Garcia de. "Spain Authorizes Coronado's Conquest in the Southwest, 1540." Gilder Lehrman Institute of American History, February 28, 2012. https://www.gilderlehrman.org/node/2199.

Madigan, Tim. *The Burning: Massacre, Destruction, and the Tulsa Race Riot of 1921*. New York: Thomas Dunne Books, 2001.

"Mamie Till Mobley." *American Experience*, PBS. Accessed July 20, 2022. https:// www.pbs.org/wgbh/americanexperience/features/emmett-biography-mamie-till -mobley/.

Mann, Charles C. *1493: Uncovering the New World Columbus Created*. New York: Vintage Books, 2012.

"Mapping Inequality: Redlining in New Deal America (Duluth, MN)." Accessed January 30, 2022. https://dsl.richmond.edu/panorama/redlining/.

Max Mason Pardon Fund. "Report of Max Mason Pardon Fund." *Minnesota Messenger*, January 26, 1924.

May, John D. "Osage County." *The Encyclopedia of Oklahoma History and Culture*. Oklahoma City: Oklahoma Historical Society, 2012. https://www.okhistory .org/publications/enc/entry.php?entry=OS004.

McCloud, Tom, and Tara Lynn Thompson. *Journey: Tulsa's Century of Christian Faith, Leadership, and Influence*. Tulsa, OK: McCloud Media, 2006.

McLendon, Michael. Mississippi Senate Bill No. 2113, Pub. L. No. 2113 (n.d.). http://billstatus.ls.state.ms.us/documents/2022/pdf/SB/2100-2199/SB 2113IN.pdf.

Michaeli, Ethan. *The Defender: How the Legendary Black Newspaper Changed America*. Boston: Mariner Books, 2018.

Miller, Robert J., ed. *Discovering Indigenous Lands: The Doctrine of Discovery in the English Colonies*. Oxford, UK: Oxford University Press, 2012.

———. *Native America, Discovered and Conquered: Thomas Jefferson, Lewis & Clark, and Manifest Destiny*. Lincoln: University of Nebraska Press, 2008.

Miller, Zeek, and Ellen Knickmeyer. "Biden Is First President to Mark Indigenous Peoples' Day." AP News, October 8, 2021. https://apnews.com/article/joe-bi den-lifestyle-holidays-columbus-day-a1ad30d52ad7ff80aa8e7621e2f9a425.

Minnesota-Acacia Park Cemetery Association. "For Departed Masons and Their Families of Minnesota and Northwest." *Minneapolis Star Tribune*, November 7, 1926.

Minnesota Indian Affairs Council, Minnesota Humanities Center, and National Museum of the American Indian. "Basis of Civilization? Dakota and Ojibwe Treaties." Treaties Matter, December 8, 2008. https://treatiesmatter.org/rela tionships/basis-of-civilization.

Minnesota State Archaeologist. "Minnesota Archaeology: Prehistoric Period." 2020. https://mn.gov/admin/archaeologist/educators/mn-archaeology/prehis toric-period/.

Mitchell, Paul D. *From Tepees to Towers: A History of the Methodist Church in Oklahoma*. Verden, OK, self-published, 1947. https://divinityarchive.com /bitstream/handle/11258/2615/fromtepeestotowe01mitc.pdf?sequence=1&is Allowed=y.

Mize, Richard. "Sequoyah Convention." *The Encyclopedia of Oklahoma History and Culture*. Oklahoma City: Oklahoma Historical Society, 2009. https://www .okhistory.org/publications/enc/entry.php?entry=SE021.

Moore, Chris. Interview by Robert P. Jones, February 21, 2022.

Morgan, David. "Archaeology and Prehistoric Mississippi." *Mississippi History Now*, October 2002. https://www.mshistorynow.mdah.ms.gov/issue/archaeol ogy-and-prehistoric-mississippi.

Morrison, John. "NEGROES DID NOT RAPE GIRL: Examination by Doctor Discredits Girl's Story." *Duluth Rip-Saw*, June 26, 1920.

Mouzon, Ed. "Tulsa's Race Riot and the Teachings of Jesus." *Christian Advocate*, July 14, 1921.

National Association for the Advancement of Colored People. *M Is for Mississippi and Murder*. Pamphlet. Mississippi: NAACP, November 1955. https://usm.access .preservica.com/uncategorized/IO_d7161caf-caac-4d51-92d0-7b97effc5533/.

National Congress of American Indians. "President Obama Announces U.S.

Support for United Nations Declaration on the Rights of Indigenous Peoples." December 6, 2010. https://www.ncai.org/news/articles/2010/12/16/president-obama-announces-u-s-support-for-united-nations-declaration-on-the-rights-of-indigenous-peoples.

National Election Poll. "National Exit Poll, Presidential Election." 2016.

National Park Service. "Notice of Inventory Completion: Mississippi Department of Archives and History, Jackson, MS; Correction." Washington, DC, January 22, 2021. https://www.federalregister.gov/documents/2021/01/22/2021-01340/notice-of-inventory-completion-mississippi-department-of-archives-and-history-jackson-ms-correction.

Neill, Edward Duffield. "Sieur Du Luth: The Explorer between Mille Lacs and Lake Superior." *Collections of the Minnesota Historical Society* 1 (1872): 314–18.

Newcomb, Steven T. *Pagans in the Promised Land: Decoding the Doctrine of Christian Discovery*. Golden, CO: Fulcrum, 2008.

———. "On the Papal Bull, *Sublimis Deus*." *Indian Country Today*, September 12, 2018. https://ictnews.org/archive/on-the-papal-bull-sublimis-deus.

New York Times. "Tulsa." Editorial, June 3, 1921.

———. "Video: Survivors of Tulsa Race Massacre Testify in Congress." May 19, 2021. https://www.nytimes.com/video/us/100000007771821/tulsa-race-massacre-survivor.html.

Oaster, B. "Toastie." "Questions about the LandBack Movement, Answered." *High Country News*, August 22, 2022. https://www.hcn.org/issues/54.9/indigenous-affairs-social-justice-questions-about-the-landback-movement-answered.

Obama, Barack. *The Audacity of Hope: Thoughts on Reclaiming the American Dream*. New York: Three Rivers Press, 2006.

Oklahoma Commission to Study the Tulsa Race Riot of 1921. "Tulsa Race Riot: A Report by the Oklahoma Commission to Study the 1921 Tulsa Race Riot." Oklahoma City, February 28, 2001.

"On the 100th Anniversary of the Tulsa Race Massacre, Here Are 3 Docs to Watch." *All Things Considered*, NPR, May 30, 2021. https://www.npr.org/2021/05/30/1000923192/3-documentaries-you-should-watch-about-the-tulsa-race-massacre.

Ornelas, Kristy. "Reverend Robert Hickman." National Park Service, 2019. https://www.nps.gov/people/reverend-robert-hickman.htm.

Oshinsky, David M. *"Worse than Slavery": Parchman Farm and the Ordeal of Jim Crow Justice*. New York: Free Press, 1997.

Painter, Nell Irvin. *The History of White People*. New York: Norton, 2011.

———. "How We Think about the Term 'Enslaved' Matters." *Guardian*, August 14, 2019. https://www.theguardian.com/us-news/2019/aug/14/slavery-in
-america-1619-first-ships-jamestown.

Parrish, Mary E. Jones, John Hope Franklin, Scott Ellsworth, and Anneliese M. Bruner. *The Nation Must Awake: My Witness to the Tulsa Race Massacre of 1921*. San Antonio, TX: Trinity University Press, 2021.

Parshina-Kottas, Yuliya, Anjali Singvi, Audra D. S. Burch, Troy Griggs, Mika Grondahl, Lingdong Huang, Tim Wallace, Jeremy White, and Josh Williams. "What the Tulsa Race Massacre Destroyed." *New York Times*, May 24, 2021.

Paul, Maria Luisa. "Anne Frank Adaptation, 40 More Books Pulled from Texas School District." *Washington Post*, August 21, 2022. https://www.washington
post.com/nation/2022/08/18/anne-frank-book-school-texas/.

Paulsen, David. "As Dioceses Pursue Reparations, General Convention Poised for Churchwide Racial Justice Discussion." Episcopal News Service, June 9, 2022. https://www.episcopalnewsservice.org/2022/06/09/as-dioceses-pursue-repa
rations-general-convention-poised-for-churchwide-racial-justice-discussion/.

Percy, William Alexander. *Lanterns on the Levee: Recollections of a Planter's Son*. Library of Southern Civilization. Baton Rouge: Louisiana State University Press, 1973.

Povoledo, Elisabetta. "Vatican Repudiates 'Doctrine of Discovery,' Used as Justification for Colonization." *New York Times*, March 30, 2023. https://www
.nytimes.com/2023/03/30/world/europe/vatican-repudiates-doctrine-of-dis
covery-colonization.html.

PRRI. "The Divide Over America's Future: 1950 or 2050? Findings from the 2016 American Values Survey." Washington, DC: PRRI, October 25, 2016. https://www.prri.org/research/poll-1950s-2050-divided-nations-direction
-post-election/.

———. "Challenges in Moving Toward a More Inclusive Democracy: Findings from the 2022 American Values Survey." Washington, DC: PRRI, October 27, 2022. https://www.prri.org/research/challenges-in-moving-toward-a-more-in
clusive-democracy-findings-from-the-2022-american-values-survey/.

———. "A Christian Nation? Understanding the Threat of Christian Nationalism to American Democracy and Culture." Washington, DC: PRRI, February 8, 2023. https://www.prri.org/research/a-christian-nation-understand
ing-the-threat-of-christian-nationalism-to-american-democracy-and-cul
ture/.

———. "Census of American Religion, 2022 Supplement." Washington, DC: PRRI, March 2, 2023. https://www.prri.org/research/2020-census-of-ameri can-religion/.

Ramsey, Alexander. "Message of Governor Ramsey to the Legislature of Minnesota, Delivered at the Extra Session, September 9, 1862." Minnesota Historical Society, September 9, 1862. https://www.usdakotawar.org/history /multimedia/message-governor-ramsey-legislature-minnesota-delivered-ex tra-session-september-9.

Read, Warren. *The Lyncher in Me: A Search for Redemption in the Face of History.* St. Paul, MN: Borealis Books, 2008.

Reese, Debbie. "Renaming the Laura Ingalls Wilder Award Isn't Disturbing, William Shatner—It's Necessary." *Guardian*, July 10, 2018. https:// www.theguardian.com/books/2018/jul/10/renaming-the-laura-ingalls-wild er-award-isnt-disturbing-william-shatner-its-necessary.

Reese, Thomas. "Pope Francis Not Fully Briefed Prior to Canadian Visit." Religion News Service, August 2, 2022. https://religionnews.com/2022/08/02 /pope-not-fully-briefed-prior-to-canadian-visit/.

Reyes-Aguirre, Eve, and Betty Lyons. "It's Time to Give Indigenous Land Back." *The Nation*, November 18, 2022. https://www.thenation.com/article/world/its -time-to-give-indigenous-land-back/.

Rezal, Adriana. "The States Where the Most Native Americans Live." *U.S. News & World Report*, November 26, 2021. https://www.usnews.com/news /best-states/articles/the-states-where-the-most-native-americans-live.

Robertson, Campbell, and Audra D. S. Burch. "Anniversary Event for Tulsa Race Massacre Unraveled Over Reparations." *New York Times*, May 29, 2021. https:// www.nytimes.com/2021/05/28/us/tulsa-race-massacre-commission.html.

Robertson, Lindsay Gordon. *Conquest by Law: How the Discovery of America Dispossessed Indigenous Peoples of Their Lands.* Oxford, UK: Oxford University Press, 2005.

Ross, Bobby. "Tulsa Race Massacre Prayer Room Highlights Churches' 1921 Sins, Seeks Healing." Oklahoma Watch, May 30, 2021. http://oklahomawatch .org/2021/05/30/tulsa-race-massacre-prayer-room-highlights-churches -1921-sins-seeks-healing/.

Rothstein, Richard. *The Color of Law: A Forgotten History of How Our Government Segregated America.* New York and London: Liveright, 2018.

Rutherford, Adam. "A New History of the First Peoples in the Americas." *The*

Atlantic, October 3, 2017. https://www.theatlantic.com/science/archive/2017 /10/a-brief-history-of-everyone-who-ever-lived/537942/.

Saunt, Claudio. *Unworthy Republic: The Dispossession of Native Americans and the Road to Indian Territory*. New York: Norton, 2020.

Schroeder, George. "Seminary Presidents Reaffirm BFM, Declare CRT Incompatible." *Baptist Press*, November 30, 2020. https://www.baptistpress.com /resource-library/news/seminary-presidents-reaffirm-bfm-declare-crt-incom patible/.

Schuessler, Jennifer. "The Ideas Behind Trump's 1776 Commission Report." *New York Times*, January 19, 2021. https://www.nytimes.com/2021/01/19 /arts/1776-commission-claims-trump.html.

Seed, Patricia. *Ceremonies of Possession in Europe's Conquest of the New World: 1492– 1640*. Cambridge, UK: Cambridge University Press, 1995.

Serwer, Adam. "The Fight Over the 1619 Project Is Not About the Facts." *The Atlantic*, December 23, 2019. https://www.theatlantic.com/ideas/archive/2019 /12/historians-clash-1619-project/604093/.

Sheridan, Jake. "67 Years after Emmett Till's Chicago Funeral, His Best Friend Remembers Him." *Chicago Tribune*, September 6, 2022. https://www.chi cagotribune.com/news/ct-emmett-till-funeral-chicago-wheeler-park er-20220906-n7e4vysaajbltaochx3f4a54ua-story.html.

Shimron, Yonat. "Southern Baptist Seminary Presidents Nix Critical Race Theory." Religion News Service, December 1, 2020. https://religionnews.com/2020/12/01 /southern-baptist-seminary-presidents-nix-critical-race-theory/.

Silver, James W. *Mississippi: The Closed Society*. Jackson: University Press of Mississippi, 2012.

Silverstein, Jake. "The 1619 Project and the Long Battle Over U.S. History." *New York Times Magazine*, November 9, 2021. https://www.nytimes .com/2021/11/09/magazine/1619-project-us-history.html.

———. "An Update to the 1619 Project." *New York Times Magazine*, March 11, 2020. https://www.nytimes.com/2020/03/11/magazine/an-update-to-the-16 19-project.html.

———. "On Recent Criticism of The 1619 Project." *New York Times Magazine*, October 16, 2020. https://www.nytimes.com/2020/10/16/magazine/criti cism-1619-project.html

"Slavery and the Making of America, Timeline." PBS, Thirteen/WNET, New York, 2004. https://www.thirteen.org/wnet/slavery/timeline/1831.html.

Southern Poverty Law Center. "Rev. George Lee." Accessed July 22, 2022. https://www.splcenter.org/rev-george-lee.

Spears, Alan. "Honoring Emmett Till and Mamie Till-Mobley." National Parks Conservation Association. Accessed July 30, 2022. https://www.npca.org/advocacy/104-honoring-emmett-till-and-mamie-till-mobley.

———. Interview with Alan Spears, senior director for cultural services, National Parks Conservation Association, by Robert P. Jones, July 2, 2022.

Stahr, Beth. "Doak's Stand, Dancing Rabbit Creek and Pontotoc Creek, Treaties of." Mississippi Encyclopedia. Accessed July 18, 2022. https://mississippiencyclopedia.org/entries/doaks-stand-dancing-rabbit-creek-and-pontotoc-creek-treaties-of/.

Stanley, Tim. "Interfaith Leaders Raising $100K for Tulsa Race Massacre Reparations." *Tulsa World*, June 16, 2021. https://tulsaworld.com/news/local/race massacre/interfaith-leaders-raising-100k-for-tulsa-race-massacre-reparations/article_79c1308a-ae96-11eb-80f3-9b5a7d23b9a8.html.

Steens, Bret. "The 1619 Chronicles." *New York Times*, October 9, 2020. https://www.nytimes.com/2020/10/09/opinion/nyt-1619-project-criticisms.html.

Stites, Edgar Page. *Beulah Land*. 1876. Music composition. https://hymnary.org/text/ive_reached_the_land_of_corn_and_wine.

Stone, I. F. *The Best of I. F. Stone*. Edited by Karl Weber. New York: PublicAffairs, 2006.

Sturdivant, Sykes. Interview by Robert P. Jones. Audio, June 24, 2022.

"Survivor Medals for Race Riot Victims." Associated Press, March 27, 2001. https://www.newson6.com/story/5e3683472f69d76f62098171/survivor-medals-for-race-riot-victims.

Swarns, Rachel L. "Catholic Order Pledges $100 Million to Atone for Slave Labor and Sales." *New York Times*, March 15, 2021. https://www.nytimes.com/2021/03/15/us/jesuits-georgetown-reparations-slavery.html.

Taylor, David Vassar. *African Americans in Minnesota*. The People of Minnesota. St. Paul: Minnesota Historical Society Press, 2002.

Tell, Dave. *Remembering Emmett Till*. Chicago: University of Chicago Press, 2021.

Thomason, Sally Palmer. *Delta Rainbow: The Irrepressible Betty Bobo Pearson*. Jackson: University Press of Mississippi, 2016.

Thompson, Darren. "Chickasaw Nation of Oklahoma Repatriates 403 Human Remains from Mississippi." Native News Online, April 14, 2021. https://www.nativenewsonline.net/currents/chickasaw-nation-of-oklahoma-repatriates-403-human-remains-from-mississippi.

Till-Mobley, Mamie, and Chris Benson. *Death of Innocence: The Story of the Hate Crime That Changed America*. New York: One World, 2005.

Tocqueville, Alexis de. *Democracy in America*. Vol. 1. New York: Vintage Books, 1990.

Trahant, Mark. "Remembering the Return of Blue Lake." Indian Country Today, July 9, 2022. https://indiancountrytoday.com/news/remembering-the-return -of-blue-lake.

Tramel, Jimmie. "Turning the Page: Former Brady Mansion, Now Owned by Retired NFL Player, to Host 'Born on Black Wall Street' Concert." *Tulsa World*, February 8, 2020. https://tulsaworld.com/entertainment/music/turning-the -page-former-brady-mansion-now-owned-by-retired-nfl-player-to-host -born/article_15663f9f-333b-5f82-b368-4e18d6db54f5.html.

Treuer, David. "Return the National Parks to the Tribes." *The Atlantic*, April 12, 2021. https://www.theatlantic.com/magazine/archive/2021/05/return-the-na tional-parks-to-the-tribes/618395/.

"The Trial of J. W. Milam and Roy Bryant." *American Experience*, PBS. Accessed July 25, 2022. https://www.pbs.org/wgbh/americanexperience/features/em mett-trial-jw-milam-and-roy-bryant/.

Trudel, Marcel. "Donnacona, Chief of Stadacona." *Dictionary of Canadian Biography*, vol. 1 (1000–1700), 2022. http://www.biographi.ca/en/bio/donna cona_1E.html.

Tulsa Daily World. "Black Agitators Blamed for Riot." June 6, 1921.

———. "5,000 Negro Refugees Guarded in Camp at County Fairgrounds." June 2, 1921.

Tulsa 2021. "1921 Tulsa Race Massacre Centennial Commission." Accessed March 11, 2022. https://www.tulsa2021.org.

Tusken, Mike. Interview by Robert P. Jones, Zoom, June 8, 2022.

Tyson, Timothy B. *The Blood of Emmett Till*. New York: Simon & Schuster, 2017.

United Nations. United Nations Declaration on the Rights of Indigenous Peoples. Resolution. New York, September 13, 2007. https://www.un.org /development/desa/indigenouspeoples/wp-content/uploads/sites/19/2018/11 /UNDRIP_E_web.pdf.

US Bureau of the Census. Twenty-Fourth Census of the United States: 2020. Washington, DC, 2021.

———. American Community Survey, 2020. Washington, DC, 2021. https://data .census.gov/table?tid=ACSST5Y2020.S1701&g=0100000US$0400000.

———. United States Census of Religious Bodies, County File, 1926. Washington, DC, 1926. https://www.thearda.com/data-archive?fid=1926CEN SCT&tab=3.

US Government. 1820 Treaty of Doak's Stand. https://www.choctawnation.com /wp-content/uploads/2022/03/1820treaty-of-doaks-stand.pdf.

———. Treaty with the Western Cherokee (1828). https://treaties.okstate.edu /treaties/treaty-with-the-western-cherokee-1828-0288.

US Supreme Court. Cherokee Nation v. Georgia, No. 30 US (5 Pet.) 1 (US Supreme Court 1831).

———. City of Sherrill v. Oneida Indian Nation of N. Y., No. 544 US 197 (US Supreme Court March 29, 2005).

———. Fletcher v. Peck, No. 10 US 87 (1810) (US Supreme Court March 16, 1810).

———. Johnson & Graham's Lessee v. M'Intosh, No. 21 U.S. 543 (US Supreme Court 1823).

———. Martin v. Waddell, 41 U.S. 367 (1842), No. 41 US 367 (US Supreme Court 1842).

———. Shoshone Indians v. United States, No. 324 US 335 (US Supreme Court March 12, 1945).

———. Tee-Hit-Ton Indians v. United States, No. 348 US 272 (US Supreme Court February 7, 1955).

"US Supreme Court Rules Half of Oklahoma Is Native American Land." BBC News, July 10, 2020. https://www.bbc.com/news/world-us-canada-53358330.

Utley, Robert Marshall. *The Indian Frontier, 1846–1890*. Rev. ed. Histories of the American Frontier Series. Albuquerque: University of New Mexico Press, 2003.

Veal, Aliyah. "More than Bones and Science: Stolen Chickasaw Remains Finally Returning Home to Rest." Native News Online, July 3, 2021. https://native newsonline.net/currents/more-than-bones-and-science-stolen-chickasaw-re mains-finally-returning-home-to-rest.

Vicksburg Post. "Mississippi Levee Board: EPA's Reversal of Yazoo Backwater Determination Based on Fundamentally Flawed Findings, Runs Counter to Key Facts." December 15, 2021. https://www.vicksburgpost.com/2021/12/15 /mississippi-levee-board-epas-reversal-of-yazoo-backwater-determination -based-on-fundamentally-flawed-findings-runs-counter-to-key-facts/.

Victor, Daniel. "At 107, 106 and 100, Remaining Tulsa Massacre Survivors

Plead for Justice." *New York Times*, May 20, 2021. https://www.nytimes.com/2021/05/20/us/tulsa-massacre-survivors.html.

Vlamis, Kelsey. "Oklahoma Spent Millions on a Legal and PR Campaign to Paint Reservations as 'Lawless Dystopias' and Persuade the Supreme Court to Weaken Tribal Sovereignty, Experts Say." *Business Insider*, July 4, 2022. https://www.businessinsider.com/oklahoma-tribal-land-as-lawless-dystopias-for-scotus-sovereignty-experts-2022-7.

Wamsley, Laurel. "Supreme Court Rules That About Half of Oklahoma Is Native American Land." NPR, July 9, 2020. https://www.npr.org/2020/07/09/889562040/supreme-court-rules-that-about-half-of-oklahoma-is-indian-land.

Wansley, Richard, and Amanda Chastang. Interview, Boston Avenue United Methodist Church. Audio, February 22, 2022.

Washington, Robin. "The Duluth Lynching's Lasting Legacy." Marshall Project, May 3, 2018. https://www.themarshallproject.org/2018/05/03/the-legacy-of-a-lynching.

Webb, Jackson. Interview by Robert P. Jones, June 21, 2022.

Wharton, Vernon L. *The Negro in Mississippi, 1865–1890*. New York: Harper & Row, 1965.

Wideman, John Edgar. *Writing to Save a Life: The Louis Till File*. New York: Scribner, 2017.

Wiggs, David. Interview by Robert P. Jones, Zoom, August 21, 2021.

Willingham, Leah. "Years Later, Chickasaw Remains Returning to Mississippi Home." AP News, April 20, 2021. https://apnews.com/article/museums-mississippi-native-americans-afc7b58ea5f1a1516f70a34dd71a39e8.

Wilson, Charles Reagan. "Winans, William." *Mississippi Encyclopedia*. Center for the Study of Southern Culture, April 15, 2018. https://mississippiencyclopedia.org/entries/william-winans/.

Winans, William. *Rev. William Winans, Describing the Abolition of the Choctaw Tribal Government and the Extension of Mississippi Laws over Choctaw Lands, ca. 1829*. December 1, 2019. Museum display. Mississippi Department of Archives and History.

Winter, Rachel M. "Analysis of a Commingled Skeletal Sample from Acacia Park Memorial Cemetery." *Departmental Honors Projects* 52 (Spring 2016): 52.

Woodruff, Judy. "What Trump Is Saying about 1619 Project, Teaching U.S. History." *PBS NewsHour*, September 17, 2020. https://www.pbs.org/newshour/show/what-trump-is-saying-about-1619-project-teaching-u-s-history.

World Council of Churches Executive Committee. "Statement on the Doctrine of Discovery and Its Enduring Impact on Indigenous Peoples." Resolution,

Bossey, Switzerland, February 17, 2012. https://doctrineofdiscovery.org/as sets/pdfs/wcc-document-021712.pdf.

Wyoming Historical Society. "Fragmenting Tribal Lands: The Dawes Act of 1887." WyoHistory.org, October 30, 2018. https://www.wyohistory.org/ency clopedia/fragmenting-tribal-lands-dawes-act-1887.

Yesno, Riley, and Xicotencatl Maher Lopez. "Four Case Studies of Land Back in Action." Briarpatch, September 10, 2022. https://briarpatchmagazine.com /articles/view/four-case-studies-land-back-in-action.

Zinn Education Project. "Aug. 13, 1955: Lamar Smith Murdered." Accessed July 22, 2022. https://www.zinnedproject.org/news/tdih/lamar-smith-murdered/.

NOTES

PROLOGUE: BEFORE AMERICA

1. William D. Green, *A Peculiar Imbalance: The Fall and Rise of Racial Equality in Minnesota*, 1837–1869 (Minneapolis: University of Minnesota Press, 2015), 130–37.
2. Gary Clayton Anderson, *Massacre in Minnesota: The Dakota War of 1862, the Most Violent Ethnic Conflict in American History* (Norman: University of Oklahoma Press, 2019), 278; Kenneth Carley, *The Dakota War of 1862: Minnesota's Other Civil War*, 2nd ed. (St. Paul: Minnesota Historical Society Press, 1976), 79.
3. Robert P. Jones, *The End of White Christian America* (New York: Simon & Schuster, 2016).
4. PRRI, "Census of American Religion, 2022 Supplement" (Washington, DC: PRRI, March 2, 2023), https://www.prri.org/research/2020-census-of-amer ican-religion/.
5. PRRI, "The Divide Over America's Future: 1950 or 2050? Findings from the 2016 American Values Survey" (Washington, DC: PRRI, October 25, 2016), https://www.prri.org/research/poll-1950s-2050-divided-nations-direction -post-election/.
6. Robert P. Jones, *White Too Long: The Legacy of White Supremacy in American Christianity* (New York: Simon & Schuster, 2021), https://www.vlebooks .com/vleweb/product/openreader?id=none&isbn=9781982122881.
7. National Election Pool, "National Exit Poll, Presidential Election," 2016; AP/Votecast, "National Exit Poll, Presidential Election," 2020.
8. Nikole Hannah-Jones, "The 1619 Project," *New York Times Magazine*, August 14, 2019, https://pulitzercenter.org/sites/default/files/full_issue_of_the_1619 _project.pdf.
9. Hannah-Jones, "The 1619 Project," 5.

10. Hannah-Jones, "The 1619 Project," 4. Jake Silverstein, editor in chief of the *New York Times Magazine*, faced significant criticism for removing, in digital editions of the 1619 Project, some of the strongest claims from the original print edition. For example, the statement "America was not yet America, but this was the moment it began," and the phrase "the country's true birthdate" no longer appear online. However, Silverstein confirmed that these changes did not indicate any change in the central claim of the 1619 Project. "We did not see this as a significant alteration, let alone concession, in how we presented the project," Silverstein wrote. "Within the project's essays, the argument about 1619's being the nation's symbolic point of origin remained." See Bret Stephens, "The 1619 Chronicles," *New York Times*, October 9, 2020, https://www.nytimes.com/2020/10/09/opinion/nyt-1619-project-criticisms.html; Jake Silverstein, "On Recent Criticism of The 1619 Project," *New York Times Magazine*, October 16, 2020, https://www.nytimes.com/2020/10/16/magazine/criticism-1619-project.html.

11. Facing continued criticism that the 1619 Project had overstated the role protecting slavery played as a precipitating factor in the American Revolution, the *New York Times* issued a correction in March 2020, stating, "We recognize that our original language could be read to suggest that protecting slavery was a primary motivation for all of the colonists. The passage has been changed to make clear that this was a primary motivation for some of the colonists." See Jake Silverstein, "An Update to the 1619 Project," *New York Times Magazine*, March 11, 2020, https://www.nytimes.com/2020/03/11/magazine/an-update-to-the-1619-project.html.

12. Adam Serwer, "The Fight Over the 1619 Project Is Not About the Facts," *The Atlantic*, December 23, 2019, https://www.theatlantic.com/ideas/archive/2019/12/historians-clash-1619-project/604093/.

13. Nell Irvin Painter, "How We Think about the Term 'Enslaved' Matters," *The Guardian*, August 14, 2019, https://www.theguardian.com/us-news/2019/aug/14/slavery-in-america-1619-first-ships-jamestown. The creators of the 1619 Project were not alone in using the term "slave" rather than "indentured servants" to describe the Africans arriving on Virginia shores in 1619. Writing the year prior to the launch of the 1619 Project, Jill Lepore, professor of history at Harvard University, also described them as slaves, but, being cognizant of precedents, she specified that they were the first in *British* America. See Jill Lepore, *These Truths: A History of the United States* (New York: W. W. Norton, 2018), 38.

14. Guy Cameron and Steven Vermette, "The Role of Extreme Cold in the Failure of the San Miguel de Gualdape Colony," *Georgia Historical Quarterly* 96:3

(Fall 2012), 291–307; Charles C. Mann, *1493: Uncovering the New World Columbus Created* (New York: Vintage Books, 2012), 389.

15. Jake Silverstein, "The 1619 Project and the Long Battle Over U.S. History," *New York Times Magazine*, November 9, 2021, https://www.nytimes .com/2021/11/09/magazine/1619-project-us-history.html.

16. Adam Hochschild, "A Landmark Reckoning with America's Racial Past and Present," *New York Times*, November 15, 2021, https://www.nytimes .com/2021/11/15/books/review/the-1619-project-nikole-hannah-jones -caitlin-roper-ilena-silverman-jake-silverstein.html.

17. Nikole Hannah-Jones et al., eds., *The 1619 Project: A New Origin Story* (New York: One World, 2021).

18. Silverstein, "The 1619 Project and the Long Battle Over U.S. History."

19. Judy Woodruff, "What Trump Is Saying about 1619 Project, Teaching U.S. History," *PBS NewsHour*, September 17, 2020, https://www.pbs.org/news hour/show/what-trump-is-saying-about-1619-project-teaching-u-s-history.

20. Jennifer Schuessler, "The Ideas Behind Trump's 1776 Commission Report," *New York Times*, January 19, 2021, https://www.nytimes.com/2021/01/19 /arts/1776-commission-claims-trump.html.

21. Silverstein, "The 1619 Project and the Long Battle Over U.S. History."

22. James Baldwin, *The Fire Next Time* (New York: Vintage International, 1993), 101.

23. Baldwin, 101–102.

24. Serwer, "The Fight Over the 1619 Project Is Not About the Facts."

25. Hannah-Jones, "The 1619 Project," 4–5.

26. The most substantive treatment of Native Americans appears in the second essay by Tiya Miles, professor of history at Harvard University, titled, "Chained Migration: How Slavery Made Its Way West." Even here, Native Americans appear in only a single paragraph discussing the 1830 Indian Removal Act, which set the stage for further white colonization and the spread of slavery to areas like Mississippi. Other essays note briefly that the US Constitution excluded Native Americans and that white colonizers in New England regularly forced captured Native Americans to work without compensation. A single-page poem, by Pulitzer Prize winner Tyehimba Jess, is dedicated to "Black Seminoles," a Native American nation of Creek refugees and Black people who were both free and fugitives from slavery, many of whom were massacred in Florida by American troops. See Hannah-Jones, 22, 26, 33, 40, 58.

27. Adam Rutherford, "A New History of the First Peoples in the Americas," *The Atlantic*, October 3, 2017, https://www.theatlantic.com/science/archive/2017 /10/a-brief-history-of-everyone-who-ever-lived/537942/.

28. Two years before the publication of the 1619 Project, Michael Guasco,

professor of history at Davidson College, wrote a hard-hitting piece for "Black Perspectives," a project of the African American Intellectual History Society. He argued that "as a historical signifier, 1619 may be more insidious than instructive," and lamented that a growing focus on the year 1619 in history classrooms was having a distorting effect: "Privileging that date and the Chesapeake region effectively erases the memory of many more African peoples than it memorializes. The 'from-this-point-forward' and 'in-this-place' narrative arc silences the memory of the more than 500,000 African men, women, and children who had already crossed the Atlantic against their will, aided and abetted Europeans in their endeavors, provided expertise and guidance in a range of enterprises, suffered, died, and—most importantly—endured." See Michael Guasco, "The Fallacy of 1619: Rethinking the History of Africans in Early America," African American Intellectual History Society, September 4, 2017, https://www.aaihs.org/the-fallacy-of-1619-rethinking-the-history-of-africans-in-early-america/.

29. Dawn Custalow, "Opinion: Native Americans Still Overlooked in Debates about U.S. History," *Virginian-Pilot*, accessed August 31, 2022, https://www.pilotonline.com/opinion/columns/vp-ed-column-custalow-0927-20200926-aof7b2j4brgbzmwbess7ywhirm-story.html.

30. Historian Jill Lepore similarly chose to begin her magisterial one-volume history of America with 1492. She notes that her book sets out to tell "the story of American history, beginning in 1492, with Columbus's voyage, which tied together continents, and ending in a world not merely tied together but tangled, knotted, and bound." Lepore, xviii.

31. Mann, *1493*, 7.

32. For a discussion of the connection between Columbus and the Doctrine of Discovery, see Sandy Bigtree and Philip P. Arnold, "Why Removing Columbus Matters: From Foundational Narratives of Domination to Inclusivity," Association for Public Religion and Intellectual Life Online, March 10, 2021, https://www.aprilonline.org/why-removing-columbus-matters/.

33. Robert J. Miller, ed., *Discovering Indigenous Lands: The Doctrine of Discovery in the English Colonies* (Oxford: Oxford University Press, 2012), 2. Despite its near-total absence from white educational curricula in the fields of history, religion, and law, Native American scholars have been highlighting the impact of the Doctrine of Discovery for at least half a century. One of the earliest scholars to draw attention to the Doctrine of Discovery was Vine Deloria Jr. (Lakota/Standing Rock Sioux), in works first published in the early 1970s. See Vine Deloria Jr., *God Is Red: A Native View of Religion*, 3rd ed. (Golden, CO: Fulcrum, 2003), 258–69; Vine Deloria Jr. and James Treat, *For This*

Land: Writings on Religion in America (New York: Routledge, 1999), 77–83. Two other major books on the Doctrine of Discovery by Indigenous authors, Robert J. Miller (Eastern Shawnee of Oklahoma) and Steven T. Newcomb (Shawnee/Lenape), were published in 2008: Steven T. Newcomb, *Pagans in the Promised Land: Decoding the Doctrine of Christian Discovery* (Golden, CO: Fulcrum, 2008); Robert J. Miller, *Native America, Discovered and Conquered: Thomas Jefferson, Lewis & Clark, and Manifest Destiny* (Lincoln: University of Nebraska Press, 2008). For reflections on the Doctrine of Discovery from a somewhat narrow and at times defensive evangelical Christian perspective, see the recent work of Mark Charles (Diné) and Soong-Chan Rah. While they denounce the Doctrine of Discovery, their commitment to defending a version of evangelical Christianity leads them to turn the term "colonization" into a metaphor as well as some tortured conclusions, such as the claim that legal abortion is "furthering colonialism." Mark Charles and Soong-Chan Rah, *Unsettling Truths: The Ongoing, Dehumanizing Legacy of the Doctrine of Discovery* (Downers Grove, IL: IVP, 2019), 94.

34. English translations of each of the three major papal bulls that established the Doctrine of Discovery can be found at a site maintained by the Indigenous Values Initiative and the American Indian Law Alliance: https://doctrine ofdiscovery.org/papal-bulls/.

35. Indigenous Values Initiative, *Dum Diversas*, Doctrine of Discovery Project, July 23, 2018, https://doctrineofdiscovery.org/dum-diversas/.

36. Indigenous Values Initiative, *Inter Caetera*, Doctrine of Discovery Project, June 13, 2022, https://doctrineofdiscovery.org/inter-caetera/.

37. Indigenous Values Initiative.

38. Miller, *Discovering Indigenous Lands*, 12–13.

39. King Henry VII, "Patent Granted by Henry VII to John Cabot," March 5, 1496, https://doctrineofdiscovery.org/patent-cabot-henry-vii/. While Cabot disappeared during his return trip on this expedition, this posture by the English crown endured. See Lepore, *These Truths*, 25.

40. Deloria, *God Is Red*; Vine Deloria Jr., *Custer Died for Your Sins: An Indian Manifesto* (Norman: University of Oklahoma Press, 1988).

41. Deloria, *God Is Red*, 261.

42. It is notable that on May 29, 1537, Pope Paul III issued a papal bull, *Sublimis Deus*, which declared that "the Indians are truly men" and that they should by no means "be deprived of their liberty or the possession of their property . . . nor should they be in any way enslaved." While some defenders of the Catholic church claim this edict nullified the Doctrine of Discovery, there are serious problems with this assertion. First, it did not explicitly revoke

the previous bulls that constitute the Doctrine of Discovery. Second, it made no remedy for the decades of genocide and enslavement unleashed by the Doctrine of Discovery. It did not call for the liberation of Indigenous people from the Euro-Christian system of domination already in place, nor did it call for land and sovereignty to be returned to Indigenous peoples. Third, and most importantly, it stood for less than a year. Emperor Charles V, who immediately ordered all copies of the edict retrieved and returned to Spain, successfully pressured the pope first to remove all ecclesiastical penalties for violating it and then to rescind it altogether. In *Non Indecens Videtur*, issued June 19, 1538, Pope Paul III flatly declares, by "apostolic authority," that all provisions of the previous edict were to "be considered as canceled, invalidated and null." Finally, the historical record testifies to the continued power and ongoing influence of the Doctrine of Discovery in both European politics and the western Christian church long after *Sublimis Deus*. See Steven Newcomb, "On the Papal Bull, *Sublimis Deus*," *Indian Country Today*, September 12, 2018, https://ictnews.org/archive/on-the-papal-bull-sublimis-deus.

43. In addition to their concerns about their own rights and freedoms within the colonies, the Founding Fathers were also frustrated that the British crown would not allow them to expand their land claims west of the Appalachian Mountains because it had reserved those lands for Native Americans following the French and Indian War in 1763. See Lindsay Gordon Robertson, *Conquest by Law: How the Discovery of America Dispossessed Indigenous Peoples of Their Lands* (Oxford: Oxford University Press, 2005), 95.

44. Miller, *Discovering Indigenous Lands*, 74–75.

45. US Supreme Court, Johnson & Graham's Lessee v. M'Intosh, No. 21 U.S. 543 (US Supreme Court 1823).

46. Marshall subsequently denounced the way the decision was used to justify President Andrew Jackson's "Indian Removal" policy, but by then the decision had taken on a life of its own. Robertson notes the irony: "When courts now cite to *Johnson v. M'Intosh*, what they invoke is the repudiated product of multiple contingencies." Robertson, *Conquest by Law*, 113, 144.

47. Miller, *Discovering Indigenous Lands*, 53–56. See also Robertson, *Conquest by Law*.

48. Miller, *Discovering Indigenous Lands*, 2.

49. Miller, 1; Roxanne Dunbar-Ortiz, *An Indigenous Peoples' History of the United States*, ReVisioning American History (Boston: Beacon Press, 2014), 204.

50. Miller, *Discovering Indigenous Lands*, 9.

51. Scott Ellsworth, *The Ground Breaking: An American City and Its Search for Justice* (New York: Dutton, 2021), 272.

NOTES

CHAPTER ONE: BEFORE MISSISSIPPI

1. Elsie Edwards, "Interview with Elsie Edwards," *Indian-Pioneer History* (Oklahoma History Society) 23 (September 17, 1937): 255.

2. David Morgan, "Archaeology and Prehistoric Mississippi," Mississippi History Now, October 2002, https://www.mshistorynow.mdah.ms.gov/issue/archaeology-and-prehistoric-mississippi.

3. James F. Barnett, *Mississippi's American Indians*, Heritage of Mississippi Series, vol. 6 (Jackson: University Press of Mississippi, 2012), 90.

4. Patricia Kay Galloway, *Choctaw Genesis, 1500–1700*, Indians of the Southeast (Lincoln: University of Nebraska Press, 1998).

5. Staff reports, "Mississippi Levee Board: EPA's Reversal of Yazoo Backwater Determination Based on Fundamentally Flawed Findings, Runs Counter to Key Facts," *Vicksburg Post*, December 15, 2021, https://www.vicksburgpost.com/2021/12/15/mississippi-levee-board-epas-reversal-of-yazoo-backwater-determination-based-on-fundamentally-flawed-findings-runs-counter-to-key-facts/.

6. Architect of the Capitol, "Discovery of the Mississippi by De Soto," accessed July 18, 2022, https://www.aoc.gov/explore-capitol-campus/art/discovery-mississippi-de-soto.

7. For analysis and English translations of key excerpts of the *Requerimiento*, see Newcomb, *Pagans in the Promised Land*, 32–33.

8. Newcomb, 34.

9. Newcomb, 35.

10. Newcomb, 35–36.

11. Gilder Lehrman Institute of American History, "De Soto's Discovery of the Mississippi, 1541," accessed July 18, 2022, https://www.gilderlehrman.org/history-resources/spotlight-primary-source/de-sotos-discovery-mississippi-1541.

12. David Cohn, *Where I Was Born and Raised* (Boston: Houghton_Mifflin, 1948).

13. US Government, "1820 Treaty of Doak's Stand" (1820), https://www.choctawnation.com/wp-content/uploads/2022/03/1820treaty-of-doaks-stand.pdf.

14. For an in-depth discussion of US Indian policy and genocide, see Ward Churchill, *A Little Matter of Genocide: Holocaust and Denial in the Americas 1492–Present* (San Francisco: City Lights, 1997).

15. US Government, "1820 Treaty of Doak's Stand."

16. Andrew Jackson, "President Jackson's Message to Congress 'On Indian Removal,'" speech, United States Senate, Washington, DC, December 6, 1830, https://www.nps.gov/museum/tmc/manz/handouts/andrew_jackson_annual_message.pdf.

17. Claudio Saunt, *Unworthy Republic: The Dispossession of Native Americans and the Road to Indian Territory* (New York: Norton, 2020), 200.

18. Charles Reagan Wilson, "Winans, William," in *Mississippi Encyclopedia*, Center for the Study of Southern Culture, April 15, 2018, https://mississippiency clopedia.org/entries/william-winans/; William Winans, *Rev. William Winans, Describing the Abolition of the Choctaw Tribal Government and the Extension of Mississippi Laws over Choctaw Lands, ca. 1829*, December 1, 2019, museum display, Mississippi Department of Archives and History.

19. Saunt, *Unworthy Republic*, 207.

20. Alexis de Tocqueville, *Democracy in America*, vol. 1 (New York: Vintage Books, 1990), 339.

21. Tocqueville, 1:340.

22. Saunt, *Unworthy Republic*, 110–11.

23. Beth Stahr, "Doak's Stand, Dancing Rabbit Creek and Pontotoc Creek, Treaties of," *Mississippi Encyclopedia*, accessed July 18, 2022, https://mis sissippiencyclopedia.org/entries/doaks-stand-dancing-rabbit-creek-and -pontotoc-creek-treaties-of/.

24. James C. Cobb, *The Most Southern Place on Earth: The Mississippi Delta and the Roots of Regional Identity* (New York: Oxford University Press, 1994), 23.

25. Cobb, 8.

26. Cobb, 31.

27. Cobb, viii.

28. A. James Fuller, *Chaplain to the Confederacy: Basil Manly and Baptist Life in the Old South*, Southern Biography Series (Baton Rouge: Louisiana State University Press, 2000), 292.

29. Fuller, 294. I elaborate on the Christian underpinnings of the Confederacy and subsequent efforts at Black disenfranchisement here: Jones, *White Too Long*, 36–38.

30. Cobb, *The Most Southern Place on Earth*, 39.

31. Vernon L. Wharton, *The Negro in Mississippi, 1865–1890* (New York: Harper & Row, 1965), 117.

32. David M. Oshinsky, *"Worse than Slavery": Parchman Farm and the Ordeal of Jim Crow Justice* (New York: Free Press, 1997), 11.

33. Nancy Bercaw, "Black Codes," Mississippi Encyclopedia, July 10, 2017, https://mississippiencyclopedia.org/entries/black-codes/.

34. Oshinsky, *"Worse than Slavery,"* 27.

35. Cobb, *The Most Southern Place on Earth*, 51.

36. Oshinsky, *"Worse than Slavery,"* 22.

37. Jerri Bell, "Clinton Massacre of 1875: Four Days of Violence Ushered in

'Mississippi Plan' to Halt Black Vote," *Mississippi Free Press*, August 5, 2021, https://www.mississippifreepress.org/14364/clinton-massacre-of-1875-four -days-of-violence-ushered-in-plan-to-halt-black-vote.

38. Cobb, *The Most Southern Place on Earth*, 66.
39. Cobb, 66.
40. Cobb, 71.
41. Cobb, 86.
42. Cobb, 87, 90.
43. William Alexander Percy, *Lanterns on the Levee: Recollections of a Planter's Son*, Library of Southern Civilization (Baton Rouge: Louisiana State University Press, 1973), 61–67.
44. Cobb, *The Most Southern Place on Earth*, 104–6.
45. Cobb, 113.
46. Cobb, 91, 114.
47. Cobb, 113.
48. James W. Silver, *Mississippi: The Closed Society* (Jackson: University Press of Mississippi, 2012).
49. Cobb, *The Most Southern Place on Earth*, 115.
50. Cobb, 106. The colorful phrase "light a shuck" means to leave surreptitiously and with some haste. It derives from the practice of creating a makeshift torch from dried corn husks, which could be used in a pinch to facilitate travel at night.
51. Cobb, 115–17.
52. Ethan Michaeli, *The Defender: How the Legendary Black Newspaper Changed America* (Boston: Mariner Books, 2018), 85.
53. Michaeli, 122.
54. National Association for the Advancement of Colored People, *M Is for Mississippi and Murder*, pamphlet, November 1955, Mississippi, https:// usm.access.preservica.com/uncategorized/IO_d7161caf-caac-4d51-92d0 -7b97effc5533/.
55. Southern Poverty Law Center, "Rev. George Lee," accessed July 22, 2022, https://www.splcenter.org/rev-george-lee.
56. Zinn Education Project, "Aug. 13, 1955: Lamar Smith Murdered," accessed July 22, 2022, https://www.zinnedproject.org/news/tdih/lamar-smith-mur dered/.

CHAPTER TWO: THE MURDER OF EMMETT TILL

1. Mamie, the mother of Emmett Till, had the surname "Till Bradley" at the time of Emmett Till's death and trial in 1955 but is best known by her surname

"Till-Mobley," which she took after marrying Gene Mobley in 1957. For the sake of clarity, I refer to her and Emmett by their first names in this section.

2. "Mamie Till Mobley," *American Experience*, PBS, accessed July 20, 2022, https://www.pbs.org/wgbh/americanexperience/features/emmett-biography -mamie-till-mobley/.

3. Mamie Till-Mobley and Chris Benson, *Death of Innocence: The Story of the Hate Crime That Changed America* (New York: One World, 2005), 21.

4. Till-Mobley and Benson, 3, 18.

5. Till-Mobley and Benson, 3.

6. Mamie Till-Mobley only found out more details about the death of Louis Till after the trial for the murder of her son, when those wanting to paint Emmett as a sexual predator dug up the details: that Louis Till, along with another African American enlisted man, had been court-martialed and hung for raping two Italian women and murdering one during an air raid in 1944. While Louis Till clearly had a record of violent behavior against women, MacArthur fellow and author John Edgar Wideman argues persuasively that the two men were convicted without sufficient evidence by a racially biased military court that was part of a segregated US Army. John Edgar Wideman, *Writing to Save a Life: The Louis Till File* (New York: Scribner, 2017).

7. Till-Mobley and Benson, *Death of Innocence*, 17.

8. Till-Mobley and Benson, 66.

9. Till-Mobley and Benson, 100. As I write this sentence in August 2022, I'm struck that my own twelve-year-old son is currently down in my home state of Mississippi without me or his mother, visiting his grandparents and cousins. Even steeped in this history and Emmett Till's story, it's difficult for me to imagine the anxiety I would feel at this moment if we were Black in 1955.

10. Till-Mobley and Benson, 101.

11. Till-Mobley and Benson, 101.

12. Till-Mobley and Benson, 105.

13. Elliott J. Gorn, *Let the People See: The Story of Emmett Till* (New York: Oxford University Press, 2018), 26.

14. Till-Mobley and Benson, *Death of Innocence*, 107–9.

15. Till-Mobley and Benson, 114.

16. Till-Mobley and Benson, 116.

17. Till-Mobley and Benson, 120.

18. Because there are many conflicting accounts, I rely in this section primarily on Devery S. Anderson and Elliot J. Gorn, who have provided the most reliable composite picture based on primary evidence and firsthand testimonies. Devery S. Anderson and Julian Bond, *Emmett Till: The Murder That Shocked the*

World and Propelled the Civil Rights Movement (Jackson: University Press of Mississippi, 2017); Gorn, *Let the People See.*

19. Gorn, *Let the People See*, 27.
20. Till-Mobley and Benson, *Death of Innocence*, 125.
21. Gorn, *Let the People See*, 57.
22. Till-Mobley and Benson, *Death of Innocence*, 137.
23. Gorn, *Let the People See*, 42.
24. Gorn, 63.
25. Gorn, 73.
26. Gorn, 79.
27. Robert P. Jones, *Photograph of Confederate Monument, Sumner, Mississippi*, June 24, 2022.
28. Gorn, *Let the People See*, 96.
29. Gorn, 85.
30. "The Trial of J. W. Milam and Roy Bryant," *American Experience*, PBS, accessed July 25, 2022, https://www.pbs.org/wgbh/americanexperience/features/emmett-trial-jw-milam-and-roy-bryant/.
31. Gorn, *Let the People See*, 151–55.
32. Gorn, 93.
33. Gorn, 86.
34. Gorn, 96.
35. Gorn, 123–27.
36. Gorn, 42.
37. Gorn, 146.
38. Gorn, 169.
39. Gorn, 142.
40. Gorn, 168.
41. Timothy B. Tyson, *The Blood of Emmett Till* (New York: Simon & Schuster, 2017), 183.
42. Gorn, *Let the People See*, 183.
43. Gorn, 183.
44. Tyson, *The Blood of Emmett Till*, 188.
45. Tyson, 188–89.
46. Tyson, 192.
47. Gorn, *Let the People See*, 198.
48. Gorn, 62.
49. Joyce Ladner and Dorie Ann Ladner, oral history interview conducted by Joseph Mosnier in Washington, DC, September 20, 2011, https://www.loc.gov/item/2015669153/.

50. Tyson, *The Blood of Emmett Till*, 213.
51. Till-Mobley and Benson, *Death of Innocence*, xii.
52. Anderson and Bond, *Emmett Till*, 368–80.
53. Bryant and Milam certainly did not tell the whole truth. They told a modified version of the story that would carefully avoid implicating Carolyn Bryant and at least two other white men and two Black men likely involved in Till's murder. Anderson and Bond, 368–80.
54. William Bradford Huie, "The Shocking Story of Approved Killing in Mississippi," *Look*, January 24, 1956.
55. Anderson and Bond, *Emmett Till*, 241.
56. Tyson, *The Blood of Emmett Till*, 165.

CHAPTER THREE: COMMEMORATION AND REPAIR IN MISSISSIPPI

1. Tyson, *The Blood of Emmett Till*, 189.
2. Gorn, *Let the People See*, 176.
3. Dave Tell, *Remembering Emmett Till* (Chicago: University of Chicago Press, 2021), 22.
4. Anderson and Bond, *Emmett Till*, 287.
5. Anderson and Bond, 289.
6. Anderson and Bond, 290.
7. Anderson and Bond, 255.
8. Anderson and Bond, 256.
9. Anderson and Bond, 256.
10. Anderson and Bond, 345.
11. Tell, *Remembering Emmett Till*, 100.
12. The bill also named a portion of Mississippi State Route 19 near Philadelphia for James Cheney, Andrew Goodman, and Michael Schwerner, who were killed by the Ku Klux Klan while working to register Black Mississippians to vote during "Freedom Summer" in 1964.
13. "Renamed Roads Honor Rights Victims," *Chicago Tribune*, March 22, 2005, https://www.chicagotribune.com/news/ct-xpm-2005-03-22-0503220101 -story.html.
14. Tell, *Remembering Emmett Till*, 104.
15. Anderson and Bond, *Emmett Till*, 350.
16. Tell, *Remembering Emmett Till*, 106.
17. Sally Palmer Thomason, *Delta Rainbow: The Irrepressible Betty Bobo Pearson* (Jackson: University Press of Mississippi, 2016), 45.
18. Anderson and Bond, *Emmett Till*, 267.

19. Sykes Sturdivant, interview by Robert P. Jones, audio, June 24, 2022.

20. Tell, *Remembering Emmett Till*, 102.

21. Tell, 20.

22. Anderson and Bond, *Emmett Till*, 352.

23. Anderson and Bond, 352.

24. The full apology can be read here: https://www.emmett-till.org/apology.

25. "Anniversary of the Apology to Emmett Till's Family," video, Emmett Till Interpretive Center, 2017, https://vimeo.com/237209316.

26. Anderson and Bond, *Emmett Till*, 352.

27. Audie Cornish, "County Apologizes to Emmett Till Family," *All Things Considered*, NPR, October 2, 2017, https://www.npr.org/2007/10/02/14904083 /county-apologizes-to-emmett-till-family.

28. Anderson and Bond, *Emmett Till*, 353.

29. Anderson and Bond, 353–54.

30. Robert P. Jones, *Photograph of Emmett Till Historical Marker, Courthouse Lawn, Sumner, Mississippi*, June 22, 2022.

31. "Anniversary of the Apology to Emmett Till's Family."

32. Tell, *Remembering Emmett Till*, 80.

33. Tell, 107.

34. Jackson Webb, interview by Robert P. Jones, June 21, 2022.

35. There remains considerable controversy over where Emmett Till's body was discovered. While Graball Landing is one plausible location, multiple newspaper accounts suggested that Till's body was found near Pecan Point, 3.5 miles downstream from Graball Landing. A 2006 FBI investigation concluded the body was likely recovered nearly five miles downstream from this point. Tell, *Remembering Emmett Till*, 248.

36. Tell, 242.

37. Tell, 245.

38. Robert P. Jones, *Photograph of Graball Landing Sign, near Glendora, Mississippi*, June 25, 2022.

39. Bayou Bend is itself an interesting Delta artifact. It's low on curb appeal, consisting of a gravel parking lot, a converted old rural farmhouse with overgrown landscaping as the "clubhouse," a modest pool, and a golf course. Originally segregated at its founding in 1967, it is now integrated, and has had in the past an African American president of the board. Bayou Bend also boasts as a member actor and Delta native Morgan Freeman, who joined at the invitation of Sykes Sturdivant after the more upscale country club in Clarksdale told him they'd make a membership exception for him, but not for any of his local Black friends. With Sturdivant as its current president,

Bayou Bend regularly hosts the biracial meetings of the ETMC. Interview with Sykes Sturdivant.

40. To learn more about the national park campaign, visit http://TillNationalPark .org, accessed July 30, 2022.

41. Alan Spears, "Honoring Emmett Till and Mamie Till-Mobley," National Parks Conservation Association, accessed July 30, 2022, https://www.npca.org /advocacy/104-honoring-emmett-till-and-mamie-till-mobley.

42. Alan Spears, senior director for cultural services, National Parks Conservation Association, interview by Robert P. Jones, July 2, 2022.

43. Susan Glisson, "What We Can't Yet See But Still Believe: A Demos Found Poem by Community Leaders of Tallahatchie County, Mississippi, and Susan Glisson," June 23, 2022.

44. American Community Survey, 2020, Washington, DC, US Bureau of the Census, https://data.census.gov/table?tid=ACSST5Y2020.S1701&g=0100000US$0400000.

45. Additional evidence that the law was meant more as a political stunt and a campaign tool is its vacuous nature. The law merely prohibits teaching "that any sex, race, ethnicity, religion or national origin is inherently superior or inferior." Michael McLendon, "Mississippi Senate Bill No. 2113," Pub. L. No. 2113 (n.d.), http://billstatus.ls.state.ms.us/documents/2022 /pdf/SB/2100-2199/SB2113IN.pdf.

46. "Governor Reeves Takes Action Against Critical Race Theory," video, Jackson, MS, 2022, https://www.facebook.com/tatereeves/videos/771428113837269/.

47. "Governor Reeves Takes Action Against Critical Race Theory."

48. Tell, *Remembering Emmett Till*, 105. We have Susan Glisson, who advised on both projects and drafted both statements, to thank for keeping systemic racism in view.

49. Tell, 87–88.

50. Martin Luther King Jr., "Pride Versus Humility: The Parable of the Pharisee and the Publican," sermon, Dexter Memorial Baptist Church, Montgomery, AL, September 25, 1955, https://nmaahc.si.edu/explore/stories/emmett-tills -death-inspired-movement.

51. Huie, "The Shocking Story of Approved Killing in Mississippi," 46. Just before he died in 1974, Leslie Milam, the brother of J. W. Milam and half brother of Roy Bryant, also sought out the pastor of First Baptist Church in Cleveland, Mississippi, to confess his role in Till's murder. Tell, *Remembering Emmett Till*, 58.

52. Anderson and Bond, *Emmett Till*, 266–68.

53. Thomason, *Delta Rainbow*, 134.

54. Interview with Sykes Sturdivant.

55. I. F. Stone, *The Best of I.F. Stone*, ed. Karl Weber (New York: PublicAffairs, 2006), 173.

56. National Park Service, "Notice of Inventory Completion: Mississippi Department of Archives and History, Jackson, MS; Correction," notice, Washington, DC, January 22, 2021, https://www.federalregister.gov/docu ments/2021/01/22/2021-01340/notice-of-inventory-completion-mississippi -department-of-archives-and-history-jackson-ms-correction.

57. Leah Willingham, "Years Later, Chickasaw Remains Returning to Mississippi Home," AP News, April 20, 2021, https://apnews.com/article/museums -mississippi-native-americans-afc7b58ea5f1a1516f70a34dd71a39e8.

58. Darren Thompson, "Chickasaw Nation of Oklahoma Repatriates 403 Human Remains from Mississippi," Native News Online, April 14, 2021, https:// www.nativenewsonline.net/currents/chickasaw-nation-of-oklahoma-repatri ates-403-human-remains-from-mississippi.

59. Brian Broom, "Grandmothers, Grandfathers 'From Long Ago': Miss. Returns Remains to Chickasaw Nation," *Clarion-Ledger*, March 30, 2021, https://www .clarionledger.com/story/news/local/2021/03/31/mississippi-returns-remains -403-native-americans-chickasaw-nation-repatriation-burial/6978798002/. While Mississippi has moved quickly, there is still much work to be done nationwide. While 83,000 remains have been repatriated by universities and museums across the nation, the National Park Service estimates that there are 116,000 more Native American human remains waiting to be returned to their descendants. At the current pace, repatriation of these ancestors may take as long as two hundred years.

60. Willingham, "Years Later, Chickasaw Remains Returning to Mississippi Home."

61. Willingham.

62. Aliyah Veal, "More than Bones and Science: Stolen Chickasaw Remains Finally Returning Home to Rest," Native News Online, July 3, 2021, https://native newsonline.net/currents/more-than-bones-and-science-stolen-chickasaw -remains-finally-returning-home-to-rest. Because of past abuses, most Native American nations who have received remains, including the Chickasaw, are not publishing the locations of the burials.

CHAPTER FOUR: BEFORE MINNESOTA

1. Joy Harjo, *An American Sunrise: Poems* (New York: Norton, 2019), 39.

2. Tony Dierckins, *Duluth: An Urban Biography* (St. Paul: Minnesota Historical Society Press, 2020), 3; Minnesota State Archaeologist, "Minnesota Archaeology: Prehistoric Period," 2020, https://mn.gov/admin/archaeologist/educators /mn-archaeology/prehistoric-period/.

3. Minnesota State Archaeologist, "Minnesota Archaeology: Prehistoric Period."

4. Dierckins, *Duluth*, 6–8.

5. Jacques Cartier, *A Memoir of Jacques Cartier, Sieur de Limoilou, His Voyages to the St. Lawrence*, trans. James Phinney Baxter (New York: Dodd, Mead, 1906), 112–13, https://libsysdigi.library.illinois.edu/oca/Books2009-06/memoirof jacquesc00baxt/memoirofjacquesc00baxt.pdf.

6. Cartier, 112.

7. Cartier, 112. Even in his account of Donnacona's protests, Cartier imposes a European understanding of land ownership. Donnacona may have been protesting what he understood as Cartier's audacious claim of ownership based on mere arrival at a particular place or he may have been protesting the marring of the landscape with the massive cross. But he would not have based his objections on a claim to land ownership, a concept foreign to Indigenous people.

8. Cartier, 114.

9. Patricia Seed, *Ceremonies of Possession in Europe's Conquest of the New World: 1492–1640* (Cambridge: Cambridge University Press, 1995), 56.

10. Marcel Trudel, "Donnacona, Chief of Stadacona," *Dictionary of Canadian Biography*, vol. 1 (1000–1700), 2022, http://www.biographi.ca/en/bio/donna cona_1E.html.

11. Edward Duffield Neill, "Sieur Du Luth: The Explorer between Mille Lacs and Lake Superior," *Collections of the Minnesota Historical Society* 1 (1872): 314–18.

12. Robert Lee, "Accounting for Conquest: The Price of the Louisiana Purchase of Indian Country," *Journal of American History* 103, no. 4 (March 1, 2017): 921–42.

13. Anderson, *Massacre in Minnesota*, 17–18.

14. Anderson, 30.

15. Anderson, 31–32.

16. Anderson, 32.

17. Anderson, *Massacre in Minnesota*, 48.

18. Anderson, 55.

19. Anderson, 67.

20. Anderson, 78–79.

21. Anderson, 84; John D. Bessler, *Legacy of Violence: Lynch Mobs and Executions in Minnesota* (Minneapolis: University of Minnesota Press, 2003), 33.

22. Anderson, *Massacre in Minnesota*, 110.

23. Anderson, 187.

24. Anderson, 187.

25. Alexander Ramsey, "Message of Governor Ramsey to the Legislature of Minnesota, Delivered at the Extra Session, September 9, 1862," Minnesota Historical Society, September 9, 1862, https://www.usdakotawar.org/history

/multimedia/message-governor-ramsey-legislature-minnesota-delivered-extra-session-september-9.

26. Anderson, *Massacre in Minnesota*, 225.

27. Ramsey, "Message of Governor Ramsey to the Legislature of Minnesota, Delivered at the Extra Session, September 9, 1862," 215.

28. Anderson, *Massacre in Minnesota*, 225.

29. Anderson, 228.

30. Anderson, 229.

31. Bessler, *Legacy of Violence*, 55.

32. Anderson, *Massacre in Minnesota*, 233.

33. Anderson, 234.

34. These actions, taken collectively, would qualify today as genocide under United Nations standards the US has ratified. See Churchill, *A Little Matter of Genocide*.

35. Anderson, 245.

36. Anderson, 245.

37. Bessler, *Legacy of Violence*, 46.

38. Anderson, *Massacre in Minnesota*, 252–53.

39. The unprecedented mass execution presented daunting logistical challenges. Because Sibley wanted all the men executed at once, special gallows had to be designed. The solution was a square donut design, with each side measuring twenty feet long and three feet wide—large enough to fit ten men. The gallows, which would support the ropes with nooses, consisted of a large timber frame extended above the platform on all sides. A tall center pole, pitched in the middle of the square, would gather another set of ropes through an iron ring and down to the ground, so that the single blow of an axe could drop the platform out from under all thirty-eight men. See Anderson, 257.

40. Anderson, 260.

41. Carley, *The Dakota War of 1862*, 75.

42. Anderson, *Massacre in Minnesota*, 262; Bessler, *Legacy of Violence*, 61.

43. Anderson, *Massacre in Minnesota*, 279.

44. Steven Newcomb has examined the deep connections between the Doctrine of Discovery and the theological concept of a "promised land." See Newcomb, *Pagans in the Promised Land*.

45. Green, *A Peculiar Imbalance*, 131.

46. Green, 132.

47. Green, 132.

48. Kristy Ornelas, "Reverend Robert Hickman," US National Park Service, 2019, https://www.nps.gov/people/reverend-robert-hickman.htm.

49. Dierckins, *Duluth*, 9–17.

50. Dierckins, 34–39.

51. Dierckins, 70–71.

52. David Vassar Taylor, *African Americans in Minnesota*, The People of Minnesota (St. Paul: Minnesota Historical Society Press, 2002), 61.

53. Dierckins, *Duluth*, 78, 93.

54. United States Census of Religious Bodies, County File, 1926, Washington, DC, US Bureau of the Census, 1926, https://www.thearda.com/data -archive?fid=1926CENSCT&tab=3.

CHAPTER FIVE: THE LYNCHINGS IN DULUTH

1. Michael W. Fedo, *The Lynchings in Duluth*, 2nd ed. (St. Paul: Minnesota Historical Society Press, 2016), 10–11.

2. Fedo, 17–26.

3. Fedo, 36.

4. Warren Read, *The Lyncher in Me: A Search for Redemption in the Face of History* (St. Paul, MN: Borealis Books, 2008), 60.

5. Fedo, *The Lynchings in Duluth*, 47.

6. Fedo, 50.

7. Fedo, 26.

8. Read, *The Lyncher in Me*, 60.

9. Fedo, *The Lynchings in Duluth*, 55.

10. Fedo, 66.

11. Fedo, 66.

12. Fedo, 90.

13. Fedo, 85.

14. Fedo, 97.

15. Fedo, 98.

16. Fedo, 101.

17. John Morrison, "NEGROES DID NOT RAPE GIRL: Examination by Doctor Discredits Girl's Story," *Duluth Rip-Saw*, June 26, 1920.

18. Fedo, *The Lynchings in Duluth*, 105.

19. Fedo, 109.

20. Fedo, 111.

21. Robin Washington, "The Duluth Lynching's Lasting Legacy," Marshall Project, May 3, 2018, https://www.themarshallproject.org/2018/05/03/the -legacy-of-a-lynching.

22. Fedo, *The Lynchings in Duluth*, 111.

23. Fedo, 123.

24. Fedo, 117.

25. Fedo, 116.

26. Editorial, "The Duluth Lynching," *Chicago Tribune*, June 19, 1920.

27. Susan Hogan/Albach, "Dedicating Headstones: City to Memorialize Lynching Victims, Acknowledge Graves," *Duluth News Tribune*, October 26, 1991, sec. B.

28. Hogan/Albach.

29. Fedo, *The Lynchings in Duluth*, 171–72.

30. Fedo, 161.

31. Fedo, 165.

32. Fedo, 126.

33. Fedo, 142.

34. Hogan/Albach, "Dedicating Headstones."

35. Bessler, *Legacy of Violence*, 216.

36. Bessler, 217.

37. Bessler, 217.

38. Bessler, 220.

39. Bessler, 220.

40. Fedo, *The Lynchings in Duluth*, 171.

41. Max Mason Pardon Fund, "Report of Max Mason Pardon Fund," *Minnesota Messenger*, January 26, 1924.

42. Dierckins, *Duluth*, 96.

43. Fourteenth Census of the United States Taken in the Year 1920, Washington, DC, US Bureau of the Census, 1922; Twenty-Fourth Census of the United States: 2020, Washington, DC, US Bureau of the Census, 2021.

44. Steve Brant, "Site of Racial Showdown in Minneapolis Heading to National Register," *Star Tribune*, July 24, 2014.

45. Richard Rothstein, *The Color of Law: A Forgotten History of How Our Government Segregated America* (New York: Liveright, 2018), 32–33.

46. "Mapping Inequality: Redlining in New Deal America (Duluth, MN)," accessed January 30, 2022, https://dsl.richmond.edu/panorama/redlining/.

47. Fedo, *The Lynchings in Duluth*, 172–73.

48. Heidi Bakk-Hansen, "Duluth's Lingering Shame," *Ripsaw*, June 7, 2000, https://www.perfectduluthday.com/2010/06/14/duluths-lingering-shame/.

CHAPTER SIX: COMMEMORATION AND REPAIR IN MINNESOTA

1. Fedo, *The Lynchings in Duluth*, 172.

2. Michael W. Fedo, *Zenith City: Stories from Duluth* (Minneapolis: University of Minnesota Press, 2014), 162.

NOTES

3. Fedo, *The Lynchings in Duluth*, xxvii.
4. Fedo, vii.
5. Bakk-Hansen, "Duluth's Lingering Shame."
6. Hogan/Albach, "Dedicating Headstones."
7. Bakk-Hansen, "Duluth's Lingering Shame."
8. Fedo, *The Lynchings in Duluth*, xxxi.
9. Bakk-Hansen, "Duluth's Lingering Shame."
10. Bakk-Hansen.
11. Chris Julin, "Dedicating a Memorial," Minnesota Public Radio, October 10, 2003, https://news.minnesota.publicradio.org/features/2003/10/10_julinc _lynchingdedicati/.
12. Erika Doss, *Memorial Mania: Public Feeling in America* (Chicago: University of Chicago Press, 2010), 310.
13. Read, *The Lyncher in Me*, 130–31.
14. Monica Davey, "LETTER FROM DULUTH; It Did Happen Here: The Lynching That a City Forgot," *New York Times*, December 4, 2003, National ed., sec. A.
15. Read, *The Lyncher in Me*, 131.
16. Fedo, *The Lynchings in Duluth*, xxxiii.
17. "Election Day Statement, Clayton-Jackson-McGhie Memorial Committee," November 12, 2012.
18. Washington, "The Duluth Lynching's Lasting Legacy."
19. Read, *The Lyncher in Me*.
20. Washington, "The Duluth Lynching's Lasting Legacy."
21. Tony Dierckins, "Park Hill Cemetery," Zenith City Press, April 18, 2017, http://zenithcity.com/archive/parks-landmarks/park-hill-cemetery/.
22. Washington, "The Duluth Lynching's Lasting Legacy."
23. Dan Kraker, "Echoes of 1920 Duluth Lynching Persist at Centennial," Minnesota Public Radio News, June 15, 2020, https://www.mprnews.org /story/2020/06/15/we-never-solved-the-problem-echoes-of-1920-duluth -lynching-persist-as-city-marks-centennial.
24. Interview with Mike Tusken by Robert P. Jones, Zoom, June 8, 2022.
25. Brooks Johnson, "'100 Years Overdue': Minnesota Grants First Posthumous Pardon in Case Connected to Duluth Lynchings," *Star Tribune*, accessed January 28, 2022, https://www.startribune.com/100-years-overdue-man -who-was-scapegoat-in-1920-duluth-lynchings-pardoned/571215122/.
26. Johnson.
27. Kraker, "Echoes of 1920 Duluth Lynching Persist at Centennial."
28. William Convery, "Duluth's Clayton Jackson McGhie Memorial Aims to

Ensure a Dark Episode in the City's History Isn't Forgotten," *MinnPost*, October 19, 2020, https://www.minnpost.com/mnopedia/2020/10/duluths -clayton-jackson-mcghie-memorial-aims-to-ensure-a-dark-episode-in-the -citys-history-isnt-forgotten/.

29. Johnson, "'100 Years Overdue.'"
30. Dan Kraker, "Hope, Call for Changes on Duluth Lynching Anniversary," Minnesota Public Radio News, June 15, 2020, https://www.mprnews.org/story/2020/06/15 /centennial-remembrance-of-duluth-lynchings-subdued-but-hopeful.
31. Kraker.
32. Interview with Carl Crawford by Robert P. Jones, audio, May 18, 2022.
33. Kraker, "Echoes of 1920 Duluth Lynching Persist at Centennial."
34. Minnesota-Acacia Park Cemetery Association, "For Departed Masons and Their Families of Minnesota and Northwest," *Minneapolis Star Tribune*, November 7, 1926.
35. Rachel M. Winter, "Analysis of a Commingled Skeletal Sample from Acacia Park Memorial Cemetery," *Departmental Honors Projects* 52, Spring (2016): 52.

CHAPTER SEVEN: BEFORE OKLAHOMA

1. Paul D. Mitchell, *From Tepees to Towers: A History of the Methodist Church in Oklahoma* (Verden, OK, self-pub., 1947), 7, https://divinityarchive.com /bitstream/handle/11258/2615/fromtepeestotowe01mitc.pdf?sequence=1& isAllowed=y.
2. Arrell Morgan Gibson, *Oklahoma: A History of Five Centuries* (Norman: University of Oklahoma Press, 2010), 4.
3. Gibson, 13.
4. Francisco Garcia de Loaysa, "Spain Authorizes Coronado's Conquest in the Southwest, 1540," Gilder Lehrman Institute of American History, February 28, 2012, https://www.gilderlehrman.org/node/2199.
5. It is likely that the two Indigenous people whom Coronado characterized as converts were baptized, if not by force, then under duress.
6. Gibson, *Oklahoma*, 17.
7. Gibson, 43.
8. Gibson, 71.
9. US Government, "Treaty with the Western Cherokee" (1828), https://treaties .okstate.edu/treaties/treaty-with-the-western-cherokee-1828-0288.
10. Tocqueville, *Democracy in America*, 1:353.
11. Gibson, *Oklahoma*, 143.
12. Gibson, 149.

13. The other tract of land was 12 million acres organized as Greer County in the southwest corner of the state but that was in dispute with Texas.

14. Gibson, *Oklahoma*, 175. Steve Newcomb has powerfully demonstrated the link between ideas of a Christian "promised land" in the functioning of the Doctrine of Discovery. See Newcomb, *Pagans in the Promised Land*.

15. Edgar Page Stites, *Beulah Land*, music composition, 1876, https://hymnary .org/text/ive_reached_the_land_of_corn_and_wine.

16. Gibson, *Oklahoma*, 176.

17. Gibson, 179.

18. Henry Dawes, "An Act to Provide for the Allotment of Lands in Severalty to Indians on the Various Reservations," Pub. L. No. Statutes at Large 24, 388– 91, NADP Document A1887 (1887), https://www.archives.gov/milestone -documents/dawes-act.

19. Robert Marshall Utley, *The Indian Frontier, 1846–1890*, rev. ed., Histories of the American Frontier Series (Albuquerque: University of New Mexico Press, 2003), 203.

20. Minnesota Indian Affairs Council, Minnesota Humanities Center, and National Museum of the American Indian, "Basis of Civilization? Dakota and Ojibwe Treaties," Treaties Matter, December 8, 2008, https://treatiesmatter .org/relationships/basis-of-civilization.

21. Minnesota Indian Affairs Council, Minnesota Humanities Center, and National Museum of the American Indian.

22. The history of Amherst College illustrates the intertwining of genocidal intent and Christian mission. The town of Amherst, Massachusetts, from which the college took its name, was named after Lord Jeffrey Amherst, the commander in chief of British forces during the French and Indian War (1754–63). Lord Amherst ordered his men to make a peace offering to the Ottawa nation of blankets infected with smallpox, explaining in a letter to a subordinate, "You will do well to [infect] the Indians by means of blankets as well as to try every other method that can serve to extirpate this [execrable] race." The army carried out his orders, resulting in the deaths of an estimated one hundred thousand Indigenous people, which facilitated the conquest of what was then known as the "Northwest Territory." See Churchill, *A Little Matter of Genocide*, 154.

23. Utley, *The Indian Frontier, 1846–1890*, 205.

24. Wyoming State Historical Society, "Fragmenting Tribal Lands: The Dawes Act of 1887," WyoHistory.org, October 30, 2018, https://www.wyohistory.org /encyclopedia/fragmenting-tribal-lands-dawes-act-1887.

25. The scheme to generate "surplus lands" resulted in staggering losses of

Indigenous lands in a single decade between 1891 and 1901. 1891: 900,000 acres from the Sac and Fox, Potawatomi, Shawnee, and Iowa tribes, generating a land run by 20,000 white settlers; 1892: 3.5 million acres from the Cheyenne-Arapaho tribes, generating a land run by 25,000 white settlers; 1893: 6 million acres from the Cherokee, generating a land run by 100,000 white settlers; 1901: 2 million acres from the Kiowa, Comanche, Wichita, Caddo, and Apache tribes, generating 165,000 entries for a land lottery in lieu of a land run.

26. Gibson, *Oklahoma*, 189.

27. Native Americans were not formally guaranteed the right to vote across all fifty states until the passage of the Snyder Act of 1924. By 1906, whites living on Indian lands in eastern Oklahoma outnumbered Native Americans seven to one. See Gibson, 193.

28. Gibson, 194.

29. Gibson, 195.

30. Richard Mize, "Sequoyah Convention," in *The Encyclopedia of Oklahoma History and Culture* (Oklahoma City: Oklahoma Historical Society, 2009), https://www.okhistory.org/publications/enc/entry.php?entry=SE021.

31. Gibson, *Oklahoma*, 202.

32. David Grann, *Killers of the Flower Moon: The Osage Murders and the Birth of the FBI* (New York: Vintage Books, 2018), 41.

33. John D. May, "Osage County," in *The Encyclopedia of Oklahoma History and Culture* (Oklahoma City: Oklahoma Historical Society, 2012), https://www.okhistory.org/publications/enc/entry.php?entry=OS004.

34. Gibson, *Oklahoma*, 146.

35. Grann, *Killers of the Flower Moon*, 43.

36. Gibson, *Oklahoma*, 146.

37. Grann, *Killers of the Flower Moon*, 44.

38. Grann, 46.

39. Rachel Adams-Heard, "Land Is Power, and the Osage Nation Is Buying Theirs Back," Bloomberg, October 12, 2022, https://www.bloomberg.com/news/features/2022-10-12/osage-nation-fights-to-buy-back-land-after-reign-of-terror.

40. Grann, *Killers of the Flower Moon*, 56–57.

41. Grann, 76–77.

42. Grann, 6.

43. Grann, 8.

44. Grann, 83.

45. Grann, 85.

46. Grann, 85.
47. Grann, 86.
48. Grann, 87.
49. Grann, 87.
50. Grann, 307.
51. Grann, 313.
52. Grann, 306.
53. Grann, 307.
54. Grann, 167.
55. Grann, 277.
56. Randy Krehbiel, "Pride Before the Fall," *Tulsa World*, May 30, 2021.
57. Hannibal B. Johnson, *Black Wall Street: From Riot to Renaissance in Tulsa's Historic Greenwood District* (Austin, TX: Eakin Press, 2007), 7.
58. Johnson, 11.
59. Mary E. Jones Parrish et al., *The Nation Must Awake: My Witness to the Tulsa Race Massacre of 1921* (San Antonio, TX: Trinity University Press, 2021), 7.
60. Johnson, *Black Wall Street*, 10–17.
61. Krehbiel, "Pride Before the Fall."
62. Krehbiel.

CHAPTER EIGHT: THE TULSA RACE MASSACRE

1. Note that in a subsequently printed version of the sermon published a month later, Mouzon gave up any pretense of ignorance about the origins of the violence: "White men did not start the riot. Negroes started it." Ed Mouzon, "Tulsa's Race Riot and the Teachings of Jesus," *Christian Advocate*, July 14, 1921.
2. "Black Agitators Blamed for Riot," *Tulsa Daily World*, June 6, 1921.
3. Mouzon, "Tulsa's Race Riot and the Teachings of Jesus."
4. "Black Agitators Blamed for Riot."
5. One remarkable illustration of Bishop Mouzon's power and popularity is evident in the name of a subsequent pastor of Boston Avenue Methodist Church. Rev. Dr. Mouzon Biggs Jr., who served Boston Avenue Methodist Church from 1980 to 2013, while having no family connection, was named after the beloved bishop Mouzon Biggs. Interview with Rev. Dr. Mouzon Biggs, audio, June 22, 2011, https://www.voicesofoklahoma.com/wp-con tent/uploads/2019/04/Mouzon-Biggs-Transcript.pdf.
6. Mouzon, "Tulsa's Race Riot and the Teachings of Jesus."
7. "Black Agitators Blamed for Riot."

8. Mouzon, "Tulsa's Race Riot and the Teachings of Jesus."

9. Tim Madigan, *The Burning: Massacre, Destruction, and the Tulsa Race Riot of 1921* (New York: Thomas Dunne Books, 2001), 52–53.

10. Madigan, 69; Ellsworth, *The Ground Breaking*, 81; Randy Krehbiel, *Tulsa, 1921: Reporting a Massacre* (Norman: University of Oklahoma Press, 2019), 33.

11. Madigan, *The Burning*, 90, 96.

12. Ellsworth, *The Ground Breaking*, 20; Tom McCloud and Tara Lynn Thompson, *Journey: Tulsa's Century of Christian Faith, Leadership, and Influence* (Tulsa, OK: McCloud Media, 2006), 35.

13. Madigan, *The Burning*, 103.

14. Krehbiel, "Pride Before the Fall."

15. Randy Krehbiel, "Pair of Lynchings Shake Tulsa," *Tulsa World*, May 30, 2021.

16. Krehbiel, *Tulsa, 1921*, 181.

17. Madigan, *The Burning*, 108.

18. Madigan, 121; Ellsworth, *The Ground Breaking*, 37.

19. "5,000 Negro Refugees Guarded in Camp at County Fairgrounds," *Tulsa Daily World*, June 2, 1921.

20. Krehbiel, *Tulsa, 1921*, 81.

21. Madigan, *The Burning*, 222.

22. Madigan, 213.

23. Krehbiel, *Tulsa, 1921*, 86.

24. Krehbiel, 87.

25. Editorial, "Tulsa," *New York Times*, June 3, 1921.

26. Madigan, *The Burning*, 225.

27. Krehbiel, *Tulsa, 1921*, 101.

28. In the aftermath of the violence, Kerr was also a prominent voice encouraging the conspiracy of silence that was the prevailing response among white Tulsans for generations. Ellsworth, *The Ground Breaking*, 43.

29. Krehbiel, *Tulsa, 1921*, 123.

30. Krehbiel, 124.

31. Krehbiel, 121.

32. Ellsworth, *The Ground Breaking*, 86.

33. Krehbiel, *Tulsa, 1921*, 126.

34. Krehbiel, 191.

35. Krehbiel, 105.

36. Krehbiel, 154.

37. Krehbiel, 202.

38. Krehbiel, 162.

39. Johnson, *Black Wall Street*, 241.

40. Madigan, *The Burning*, 227.
41. Krehbiel, *Tulsa, 1921*, 196.
42. Madigan, *The Burning*, 231.
43. Madigan, 231.
44. Krehbiel, *Tulsa, 1921*, 199.

CHAPTER NINE: COMMEMORATION AND REPAIR IN OKLAHOMA

1. Ellsworth, *The Ground Breaking*, 43–44.
2. Krehbiel, *Tulsa, 1921*, 34. There are some reports that the paper also ran an inciting editorial titled "To Lynch Negro Tonight," although no copies of this column are known to exist.
3. Ellsworth, *The Ground Breaking*, 88.
4. Parrish et al., *The Nation Must Awake*.
5. Ellsworth, *The Ground Breaking*, 28–29, 47.
6. Krehbiel, *Tulsa, 1921*, 209.
7. Ellsworth, *The Ground Breaking*, 61.
8. Ellsworth, 6.
9. Madigan, *The Burning*, 252.
10. Madigan, 253.
11. Madigan, 255.
12. Ellsworth, *The Ground Breaking*, 65.
13. Ellsworth, 70, 86.
14. Scott Ellsworth, *Death in a Promised Land: The Tulsa Race Riot of 1921* (Baton Rouge: Louisiana State University Press, 1982).
15. Ellsworth, *The Ground Breaking*, 96.
16. Ellsworth, 109.
17. Krehbiel, *Tulsa, 1921*, 212.
18. Ellsworth, *The Ground Breaking*, 169–71. Later that fall, in September 2000, a group of scholars presented the results of years of work in a 284-page report, *The Tulsa Race Riot: A Scientific, Historical, and Legal Analysis*, which was named by the American Library Association as one of the most significant documents produced in the world that year.
19. *Tulsa Race Riot: A Report by the Oklahoma Commission to Study the 1921 Tulsa Race Riot*, Oklahoma City, OK, February 28, 2001.
20. Ellsworth, *The Ground Breaking*, 176.
21. Krehbiel, *Tulsa, 1921*, 219.
22. "Survivor Medals for Race Riot Victims," Associated Press, March 27, 2001,

https://www.newson6.com/story/5e3683472f69d76f62098171/survivor
-medals-for-race-riot-victims.

23. Ellsworth, *The Ground Breaking*, 276.

24. Yuliya Parshina-Kottas et al., "What the Tulsa Race Massacre Destroyed," *New York Times*, May 24, 2021.

25. "On the 100th Anniversary of the Tulsa Race Massacre, Here Are 3 Docs to Watch," *All Things Considered*, NPR, May 30, 2021, https://www .npr.org/2021/05/30/1000923192/3-documentaries-you-should-watch -about-the-tulsa-race-massacre.

26. "1921 Tulsa Race Massacre Centennial Commission," Tulsa 2021, accessed March 11, 2022, https://www.tulsa2021.org.

27. Jones, *White Too Long*.

28. Bobby Ross, "Tulsa Race Massacre Prayer Room Highlights Churches' 1921 Sins, Seeks Healing," Oklahoma Watch, May 30, 2021, http://okla homawatch.org/2021/05/30/tulsa-race-massacre-prayer-room-highlights -churches-1921-sins-seeks-healing/.

29. Interview with Rev. David Wiggs by Robert P. Jones, Zoom, August 21, 2021.

30. Michael Levenson, "Tulsa Race Massacre Commission Ousts Oklahoma Governor," *New York Times*, May 15, 2021, https://www.nytimes.com/2021/05/14 /us/Oklahoma-critical-race-theory-Tulsa-massacre.html.

31. Campbell Robertson and Audra D. S. Burch, "Anniversary Event for Tulsa Race Massacre Unraveled Over Reparations," *New York Times*, May 29, 2021, https:// www.nytimes.com/2021/05/28/us/tulsa-race-massacre-commission.html.

32. Robertson and Burch.

33. Robertson and Burch.

34. Interview with Chris Moore by Robert P. Jones, February 21, 2022.

35. Krehbiel, *Tulsa, 1921*, 102; Madigan, *The Burning*, 225.

36. Daniel Victor, "At 107, 106 and 100, Remaining Tulsa Massacre Survivors Plead for Justice," *New York Times*, May 20, 2021, https://www.nytimes .com/2021/05/20/us/tulsa-massacre-survivors.html.

37. "Video: Survivors of Tulsa Race Massacre Testify in Congress," *New York Times*, May 19, 2021, https://www.nytimes.com/video/us/100000007771821/tulsa -race-massacre-survivor.html.

38. "Video: Survivors of Tulsa Race Massacre Testify in Congress."

39. Ellsworth, *The Ground Breaking*, 272.

40. Ben Leonard, "Biden Issues Proclamation on Tulsa Race Massacre," *Politico*, May 31, 2021, https://www.politico.com/news/2021/05/31/joe-biden-tulsa -proclamation-491450.

41. Joseph Biden, "A Proclamation on Day of Remembrance: 100 Years After the 1921 Tulsa Race Massacre," The White House, May 31, 2021, https://www .whitehouse.gov/briefing-room/presidential-actions/2021/05/31/a-proclama tion-on-day-of-remembrance-100-years-after-the-1921-tulsa-race-massacre/.

42. Biden.

43. Interview with Rev. David Wiggs.

44. Ellsworth, *The Ground Breaking*, 249.

45. Ellsworth, 195.

46. Ellsworth, 195.

47. Hannibal B. Johnson, *Black Wall Street 100: An American City Grapples with Its Historical Racial Trauma* (Fort Worth, TX: Eakin Press, 2020), 224–25.

48. Jimmie Tramel, "Turning the Page: Former Brady Mansion, Now Owned by Retired NFL Player, to Host 'Born on Black Wall Street' Concert," *Tulsa World*, February 8, 2020, https://tulsaworld.com/entertainment/music /turning-the-page-former-brady-mansion-now-owned-by-retired-nfl-player -to-host-born/article_15663f9f-333b-5f82-b368-4e18d6db54f5.html.

49. Interview with Rev. David Wiggs.

50. Ellsworth, *The Ground Breaking*, 187.

51. Interview with Rev. David Wiggs.

52. Wiggs.

53. Wiggs.

54. Tim Stanley, "Interfaith Leaders Raising $100K for Tulsa Race Massacre Reparations," *Tulsa World*, June 16, 2021, https://tulsaworld.com/news /local/racemassacre/interfaith-leaders-raising-100k-for-tulsa-race-massacre -reparations/article_79c1308a-ae96-11eb-80f3-9b5a7d23b9a8.html.

55. Interview with Richard Wansley and Amanda Chastang, Boston Avenue United Methodist Church, audio, February 22, 2022.

56. Interview with Rev. David Wiggs.

57. Ellsworth, *The Ground Breaking*, 206.

58. Adriana Rezal, "The States Where the Most Native Americans Live," *U.S. News & World Report*, November 26, 2021, https://www.usnews.com/news /best-states/articles/the-states-where-the-most-native-americans-live.

59. Mac Bentley, "39 Tribes Call State Home," *Oklahoman*, February 16, 2003, https://www.oklahoman.com/story/news/2003/02/16/39-tribes-call-state -home/62057840007/.

60. "US Supreme Court Rules Half of Oklahoma Is Native American Land," BBC News, July 10, 2020, https://www.bbc.com/news/world-us-canada -53358330; Laurel Wamsley, "Supreme Court Rules That About Half of Oklahoma Is Native American Land," NPR, July 9, 2020, https://www

.npr.org/2020/07/09/889562040/supreme-court-rules-that-about-half-of
-oklahoma-is-indian-land.

61. Kelsey Vlamis, "Oklahoma Spent Millions on a Legal and PR Campaign to Paint Reservations as 'Lawless Dystopias' and Persuade the Supreme Court to Weaken Tribal Sovereignty, Experts Say," *Business Insider*, July 4, 2022, https://www.businessinsider.com/oklahoma-tribal-land-as-lawless-dystopias -for-scotus-sovereignty-experts-2022-7.

62. Jake Epstein and Oma Seddiq, "Justice Neil Gorsuch Fumes That the Supreme Court 'Failed' to 'Honor This Nation's Promises' as It Rolled Back Tribal Authority in Oklahoma," *Business Insider*, June 29, 2022, https://www.busi nessinsider.com/gorsuch-slams-supreme-court-decision-reducing-tribal -authority-in-oklahoma-2022-6.

63. David Treuer, "Return the National Parks to the Tribes," *The Atlantic*, April 12, 2021, https://www.theatlantic.com/magazine/archive/2021/05/return-the -national-parks-to-the-tribes/618395/.

64. Mark Trahant, "Remembering the Return of Blue Lake," Indian Country Today, July 9, 2022, https://indiancountrytoday.com/news/remembering -the-return-of-blue-lake.

65. B. "Toastie" Oaster, "Questions about the LandBack Movement, Answered," *High Country News*, August 22, 2022, https://www.hcn.org/issues/54.9 /indigenous-affairs-social-justice-questions-about-the-landback-movement -answered.

66. Eve Reyes-Aguirre and Betty Lyons, "It's Time to Give Indigenous Land Back," *The Nation*, November 18, 2022, https://www.thenation.com/article /world/its-time-to-give-indigenous-land-back/.

67. Sid Hill, "Why We Accepted a Thousand Acres of Land Back from New York State," *The Nation*, July 6, 2022, https://www.thenation.com/article/environ ment/onondaga-land-new-york/.

68. Riley Yesno and Xicotencatl Maher Lopez, "Four Case Studies of Land Back in Action," Briarpatch, September 10, 2022, https://briarpatchmagazine.com /articles/view/four-case-studies-land-back-in-action.

69. Duwamish Solidarity Group, "Real Rent Duwamish," December 11, 2022, https://www.realrentduwamish.org/.

70. Treuer, "Return the National Parks to the Tribes."

71. Treuer.

CHAPTER TEN: THE SEARCH FOR HOPE IN HISTORY

1. Seamus Heaney and Sophocles, *The Cure at Troy: A Version of Sophocles's Philoctetes* (New York: Farrar, Straus & Giroux, 1991), 77.

2. Emmett Till & Mamie Till-Mobley Institute, accessed December 9, 2022, https://www.thetillinstitute.org; Jake Sheridan, "67 Years after Emmett Till's Chicago Funeral, His Best Friend Remembers Him," *Chicago Tribune*, September 6, 2022, https://www.chicagotribune.com/news/ct-emmett-till -funeral-chicago-wheeler-parker-20220906-n7e4vysaajbltaochx3f4a54ua -story.html.

3. Fedo, *The Lynchings in Duluth*, 66.

4. Parrish et al., *The Nation Must Awake*, vii.

5. Tell, *Remembering Emmett Till*, 104.

6. Davey, "LETTER FROM DULUTH; It Did Happen Here."

7. Ellsworth, *The Ground Breaking*, 272.

8. Harmeet Kaur, "More than 160 Confederate Symbols Came Down in 2020, SPLC Says," CNN, February 24, 2021, https://www.cnn.com/2021/02/24 /us/confederate-symbols-removed-2020-splc-trnd/index.html.

9. Nicholas Fandos, "House Votes to Purge Confederate Statues from the Capitol," *New York Times*, June 29, 2021, https://www.nytimes.com/2021/06/29 /us/politics/house-confederate-statues-vote.html.

10. Luke Broadwater, "Congress Set to Replace Dred Scott Author's Statue with Thurgood Marshall," *New York Times*, December 22, 2022, https://www.ny times.com/2022/12/14/us/politics/taney-thurgood-marshall-statue-capitol .html.

11. Mike DeBonis, "Congress Votes Overwhelmingly to Make Juneteenth a Federal Holiday. The Day Commemorates the End of Slavery in Texas in 1865," *Washington Post*, June 16, 2021, https://www.washingtonpost.com /politics/juneteenth-federal-holiday/2021/06/16/7be284d8-ceba-11eb-a7f1 -52b8870bef7c_story.html.

12. Zeek Miller and Ellen Knickmeyer, "Biden Is First President to Mark Indigenous Peoples' Day," AP News, October 8, 2021, https://apnews.com/article /joe-biden-lifestyle-holidays-columbus-day-a1ad30d52ad7ff80aa8e7621e2f9a425.

13. Miller and Knickmeyer.

14. The Diocese of Texas did not explicitly describe that initiative as a reparations program, but its stated purpose is to "support the people of our communities who were actually injured by our past actions." David Paulsen, "As Dioceses Pursue Reparations, General Convention Poised for Churchwide Racial Justice Discussion," Episcopal News Service, June 9, 2022, https://www.epis

copalnewsservice.org/2022/06/09/as-dioceses-pursue-reparations-general
-convention-poised-for-churchwide-racial-justice-discussion/.

15. Michelle Boorstein, "Va. Episcopal Diocese to Spend $10 Million for Reparations. But How?," *Washington Post*, August 14, 2022, https://www .washingtonpost.com/religion/2022/08/14/va-episcopal-diocese-spend -10-million-reparations-how/.

16. "Reparations," Episcopal Diocese of Virginia, November 2021, https://www .thediocese.net/resources/ministries/racial-justice-and-healing/reparations/.

17. Rachel L. Swarns, "Catholic Order Pledges $100 Million to Atone for Slave Labor and Sales," *New York Times*, March 15, 2021, https://www.nytimes .com/2021/03/15/us/jesuits-georgetown-reparations-slavery.html.

18. Yonat Shimron, "Southern Baptist Seminary Presidents Nix Critical Race Theory," Religion News Service, December 1, 2020, https://religionnews .com/2020/12/01/southern-baptist-seminary-presidents-nix-critical-race -theory/.

19. George Schroeder, "Seminary Presidents Reaffirm BFM, Declare CRT Incompatible," *Baptist Press*, November 30, 2020, https://www.baptistpress .com/resource-library/news/seminary-presidents-reaffirm-bfm-declare-crt -incompatible/.

20. Deloria and Treat, *For This Land*, 79.

21. Deloria and Treat, 81.

22. Jenna Kunze, "'The United States lags behind' on the Rights of Its Indigenous Peoples, Natives say," Native News Online, May 8, 2022, https://native newsonline.net/currents/the-united-states-lags-behind-on-the-rights-of-its -indigenous-peoples-natives-say.

23. United Nations Declaration on the Rights of Indigenous Peoples, Resolution, New York, September 13, 2007, https://www.un.org/development/desa/indig enouspeoples/wp-content/uploads/sites/19/2018/11/UNDRIP_E_web.pdf.

24. John Chaffee, "Repudiate the Doctrine of Discovery," *Journal of the General Convention of the Episcopal Church* (2009): 371–72.

25. National Congress of American Indians, "President Obama Announces U.S. Support for United Nations Declaration on the Rights of Indigenous Peoples," December 6, 2010, https://www.ncai.org/news/articles/2010/12/16 /president-obama-announces-u-s-support-for-united-nations-declaration -on-the-rights-of-indigenous-peoples.

26. World Council of Churches Executive Committee, "Statement on the Doctrine of Discovery and Its Enduring Impact on Indigenous Peoples," Resolution, Bossey, Switzerland: World Council of Churches, February 17, 2012, https://doctrineofdiscovery.org/assets/pdfs/wcc-document-021712.pdf.

27. Indigenous Values Initiative, "Repudiations of the Doctrine of Discovery by Faith Communities," Doctrine of Discovery Project, July 30, 2018, https://doctrineofdiscovery.org/faith-communities/.

28. Ian Austen, "Canada's Forced Schooling of Aboriginal Children Was 'Cultural Genocide,' Report Finds," *New York Times*, June 2, 2015, https://www.nytimes.com/2015/06/03/world/americas/canadas-forced-schooling-of-aboriginal-children-was-cultural-genocide-report-finds.html; Jason Horowitz, "Francis Begs Forgiveness for 'Evil' Christians Inflicted on Indigenous People," *New York Times*, July 25, 2022, https://www.nytimes.com/live/2022/07/25/world/pope-francis-canada-visit.

29. Pope Francis, "Full Text: Pope Francis' Apology to Indigenous Peoples in Canada," *America Magazine*, July 25, 2022, https://www.americamagazine.org/faith/2022/07/25/pope-francis-apology-canada-243411.

30. Claire Giangravé, "In Canada, Pope Francis Apologizes to Indigenous Peoples, Says It's Only 'First Step,'" Religion News Service, July 25, 2022, https://religionnews.com/2022/07/25/in-canada-pope-francis-apologizes-to-indigenous-peoples-says-its-only-first-step/.

31. Like many Christian apologists, Pope Francis has here engaged in a version of what is sometimes called the "no true Scotsman" fallacy. This term was coined by philosopher Antony Flew to describe a rhetorical strategy that attempts to defend the purity of a group (or in this case an institution) by perpetually changing its defining criteria to exclude any problematic counterexamples. In debate circles, it is also sometimes called "victory by definition." See Antony Flew, *Thinking About Thinking* (New York: HarperCollins, 1975).

32. Thomas Reese, "Pope Francis Not Fully Briefed Prior to Canadian Visit," Religion News Service, August 2, 2022, https://religionnews.com/2022/08/02/pope-not-fully-briefed-prior-to-canadian-visit/.

33. Jelani Cobb, *The Substance of Hope: Barack Obama and the Paradox of Progress* (New York: Bloomsbury, 2020), xii.

34. Cobb, xiii.

35. Ta-Nehisi Coates, "Hope and the Historian," *The Atlantic*, December 10, 2015.

36. Barack Obama, *The Audacity of Hope: Thoughts on Reclaiming the American Dream* (New York: Three Rivers Press, 2006); Nell Irvin Painter, *The History of White People* (New York: Norton, 2011).

37. Coates, "Hope and the Historian."

38. Frederick Douglass, "West India Emancipation," Archive, University of Rochester, Frederick Douglass Project Writings, August 3, 1857, https://rbscp.lib.rochester.edu/4398.

39. Coates, "Hope and the Historian."

CHAPTER ELEVEN: DISCOVERY AND DEMOCRACY IN AMERICA

1. The Big Western Town play set was only one of many western-themed "cowboy and Indian" toys in Sears's Christmas catalog, particularly from the 1940s through the 1970s. The 1972 Wish Book had made the turn toward space toys in the wake of the US landing on the moon three years before, but it still had Johnny West and Fort Apache Heritage Playset in addition to the Big Western Town, all hyped with the promise: "You are there!" Shipped annually to as many as seven million mostly working-class and middle-class households in its heyday, the Sears catalog—where "imaginative ideas become reality," as its 1969 tagline put it—shaped the worldviews of our generation as we reenacted a history with plastic pieces that had been poured in the molds of the old European Christian Doctrine of Discovery. You can see scanned images of the Sears Wish Book here: http://www.wishbookweb.com/FB/1972_Sears_Wishbook /files/assets/basic-html/page-582.html, accessed September 8, 2022.

2. Dana Hedgpeth, "The Week Hundreds of Native Americans Took Over D.C.'s Bureau of Indian Affairs," *Washington Post*, January 24, 2021, https:// www.washingtonpost.com/history/2021/01/24/native-americans-occupied -bureau-indian-afffairs-nixon/.

3. Philip Deloria has provided an insightful, thorough analysis of white Americans' tendency to appropriate Native American dress and customs for our own psychological and cultural purposes. See Philip Joseph Deloria, *Playing Indian*, Yale Historical Publications (New Haven, CT: Yale University Press, 2022).

4. Tocqueville, *Democracy in America*, 1:vii.

5. Tocqueville, 1:xix.

6. Tocqueville, 1:xxi.

7. Robert N. Bellah et al., *Habits of the Heart: Individualism and Commitment in American Life*, updated with a new introduction (Berkeley: University of California Press, 1996). I was introduced to the book in graduate school at Emory University by Steven M. Tipton, a professor who was one of the coauthors.

8. Bellah et al., 37.

9. Bellah et al., 28.

10. Patrick H. Breen, *The Land Shall Be Deluged in Blood: A New History of the Nat Turner Revolt* (New York: Oxford University Press, 2015), 98, 231.

11. "Slavery and the Making of America, Timeline," PBS, Thirteen/WNET, New York, 2004, https://www.thirteen.org/wnet/slavery/timeline/1831.html.

12. Tocqueville, *Democracy in America*, 1:331.

13. Tocqueville, 1:350, 354.

14. Tocqueville, 1:347.

15. Tocqueville, 1:355.

16. Tocqueville, 1:356–57.

17. Tocqueville, 1:378–79.

18. Tocqueville, 1:332.

19. Tocqueville, 1:333.

20. Tocqueville, 1:334.

21. Tocqueville, 1:335.

22. In this section, I follow the insightful work of Joseph J. Heath, who has served as the general legal counsel for the Onondaga Nation since 1982. See Joseph J. Heath, "Statement on the Historical Use of the Doctrine of Christian Discovery by the United States Supreme Court Since 1823," in *Doctrine of Christian Discovery: After Repudiation, What Next?* (Syracuse, NY: Doctrine of Discovery Project, 2014), https://doctrineofdiscovery.org/statement-on-the-historical-use-of-the-doctrine-of-christian-discovery-by-the-united-states-supreme-court-since-1823/; Joseph J. Heath, "The Doctrine of Discovery: Its Fundamental Performance in United States Indian Law and the Need for Its Repudiation and Removal," *Albany Government Law Review* 10 (2017): 112–56.

23. US Supreme Court, Fletcher v. Peck, No. 10 US 87 (1810) (US Supreme Court March 16, 1810).

24. Robertson, *Conquest by Law.*

25. US Supreme Court, Cherokee Nation v. Georgia, No. 30 US (5 Pet.) 1 (US Supreme Court 1831).

26. US Supreme Court, Martin v. Waddell, 41 US 367 (1842), No. 41 US 367 (US Supreme Court 1842).

27. US Supreme Court, Shoshone Indians v. United States, No. 324 US 335 (US Supreme Court March 12, 1945).

28. US Supreme Court, Tee-Hit-Ton Indians v. United States, No. 348 US 272 (US Supreme Court February 7, 1955).

29. US Supreme Court, City of Sherrill v. Oneida Indian Nation of N.Y., No. 544 US 197 (US Supreme Court March 29, 2005).

30. US Supreme Court.

31. US Supreme Court, Johnson & Graham's Lessee v. M'Intosh.

32. Maria Luisa Paul, "Anne Frank Adaptation, 40 More Books Pulled from Texas School District," *Washington Post*, August 21, 2022, https://www.washingtonpost.com/nation/2022/08/18/anne-frank-book-school-texas/; Erika Hayasaki, "How Book Bans Turned a Texas Town Upside Down," *New York Times Magazine*, September 8, 2022, https://www.nytimes.com/2022/09/08/magazine/book-bans-texas.html.

33. "CRT MAP: Critical Race Theory Legislation and Schools," Chalkbeat, February 2, 2022, https://www.chalkbeat.org/22525983/map-critical-race -theory-legislation-teaching-racism.

34. Bryan Avila, "Florida CS/HB 7: An Act Relating to Individual Freedom" (2022), https://www.flsenate.gov/Session/Bill/2022/7/BillText/er/PDF.

35. PRRI, "Challenges in Moving Toward a More Inclusive Democracy: Findings from the 2022 American Values Survey" (Washington, DC: PRRI, October 27, 2022), https://www.prri.org/research/challenges-in-moving-toward-a -more-inclusive-democracy-findings-from-the-2022-american-values-sur vey/.

36. PRRI. There is also solid evidence that these attitudes have been strongly influenced by Fox News and other right-wing media outlets, which have run hundreds of segments denouncing CRT. For example, Americans who most trust far-right news outlets like Newsmax or One America News are especially likely to say that public school teachers and librarians are indoctrinating children (82 percent), as are Americans who most trust Fox News (60 percent). By contrast, Americans who do not trust any TV news or most trust mainstream outlets are much less likely to believe (35 percent and 13 percent, respectively).

37. PRRI, "A Christian Nation? Understanding the Threat of Christian Nationalism to American Democracy and Culture" (Washington, DC: PRRI, February 8, 2023), https://www.prri.org/research/a-christian-nation-under standing-the-threat-of-christian-nationalism-to-american-democracy-and -culture/. For a more in-depth analysis, see Robert P. Jones, "Columbus Day or Indigenous Peoples' Day? The Damaging Christian 'Doctrine of Discovery' at the Heart of the American Identity Crisis," Substack newsletter, *White Too Long by Robert P. Jones* (blog), October 8, 2021, https://robertpjones.sub stack.com/p/columbus-day-or-indigenous-peoples.

38. Anti-Defamation League, "QAnon," May 4, 2020, https://www.adl.org/re sources/backgrounder/qanon.

39. Robert P. Jones, "This Supreme Court's Dangerous Vision of 'History and Tradition,'" Substack newsletter, *White Too Long by Robert P. Jones* (blog), July 1, 2022, https://robertpjones.substack.com/p/this-supreme-courts-dangerous -vision.

40. Debbie Reese, "Renaming the Laura Ingalls Wilder Award Isn't Disturbing, William Shatner—It's Necessary," *The Guardian*, July 10, 2018, https://www .theguardian.com/books/2018/jul/10/renaming-the-laura-ingalls-wilder -award-isnt-disturbing-william-shatner-its-necessary. To her credit, responding to critics in 1952, Laura Ingalls authorized this passage to be changed to

"there were no settlers there." But there were other major problems with references to African Americans as "darkies" and the book's inclusion of a quote, repeated three times, that "[t]he only good Indian is a dead Indian." In 2018, the American Library Association dropped Laura Ingalls Wilder's name from a prestigious children's literature award. Niraj Chokshi, "Prestigious Laura Ingalls Wilder Award Renamed Over Racial Insensitivity," *New York Times*, June 26, 2018, https://www.nytimes.com/2018/06/26/books/laura-ingalls -wilder-book-award.html.

41.   Kelly Brown Douglas, *Resurrection Hope: A Future Where Black Lives Matter* (Maryknoll, NY: Orbis Books, 2021), 157.

INDEX

INDEX

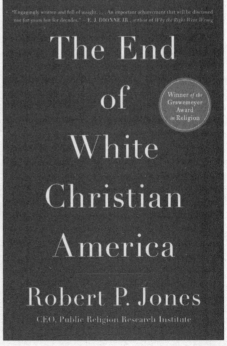